Galician Portraits

IN SEARCH OF JEWISH ROOTS

Galician Portraits

IN SEARCH OF JEWISH ROOTS

ANDREW ZALEWSKI

THELZO PRESS

Galician Portraits

IN SEARCH OF JEWISH ROOTS

THELZO PRESS

93 Old York Rd., Suite 1-421
Jenkintown, PA 19046

www.thelzopress.com
www.galicianportraits.com

ISBN 13: 978-0-9855894-2-4
E-book ISBN: 978-0-9855894-3-1
Library of Congress Control Number: 2014943292

Cover and Interior Design: Peri Gabriel, Knockout Design,
www.knockoutbooks.com

Printed in the United States of America
First Edition

Front cover: *Jews Praying in the Synagogue on Yom Kippur.*
The interior of the Drohobycz Synagogue in Galicia. Painting by Maurycy
Gottlieb (1856–1879). *(Courtesy of Tel Aviv Museum of Art, Israel.)*

For Eli, Zoe, Theo, and Dexter

Contents

Chronology

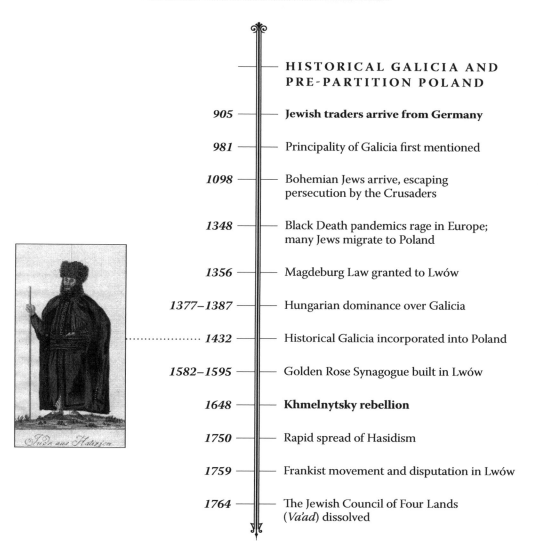

Juda aus Halizien.

HISTORICAL GALICIA AND PRE-PARTITION POLAND

905	**Jewish traders arrive from Germany**
981	Principality of Galicia first mentioned
1098	Bohemian Jews arrive, escaping persecution by the Crusaders
1348	Black Death pandemics rage in Europe; many Jews migrate to Poland
1356	Magdeburg Law granted to Lwów
1377–1387	Hungarian dominance over Galicia
1432	Historical Galicia incorporated into Poland
1582–1595	Golden Rose Synagogue built in Lwów
1648	**Khmelnytsky rebellion**
1750	Rapid spread of Hasidism
1759	Frankist movement and disputation in Lwów
1764	The Jewish Council of Four Lands (*Va'ad*) dissolved

Galician Portraits

1772–1918	**AUSTRIAN GALICIA**
1772	**First Partition of Poland**
	Lwów (renamed Lemberg) becomes capital of the Habsburg Galicia
1773	Jews required to seek permission from civil authorities to marry
	Emperor Joseph II inspects Galicia
1776	Jewish Regulations
1780	Emperor Joseph II travels through Galicia to Russia
	Empress Maria Theresa dies
1784	Josephinian University opened in Lemberg (Lwów)
1785	Jewish Administration abolished
1787–1849	Bukovina incorporated into Galicia
1787	**Jews adopt hereditary surnames**
	German-Jewish schools open
1788	Jewish soldiers recruited for first time
1789	Jewish Toleration Edict for Galicia
1790	Emperor Leopold ascends to the throne
1792	Emperor Francis II ascends to the throne
1795	Third Partition of Poland
	Region of New Galicia (Western Galicia) formed
1804	Austrian Empire established
1806	Holy Roman Empire dissolved
	German-Jewish schools close in Galicia

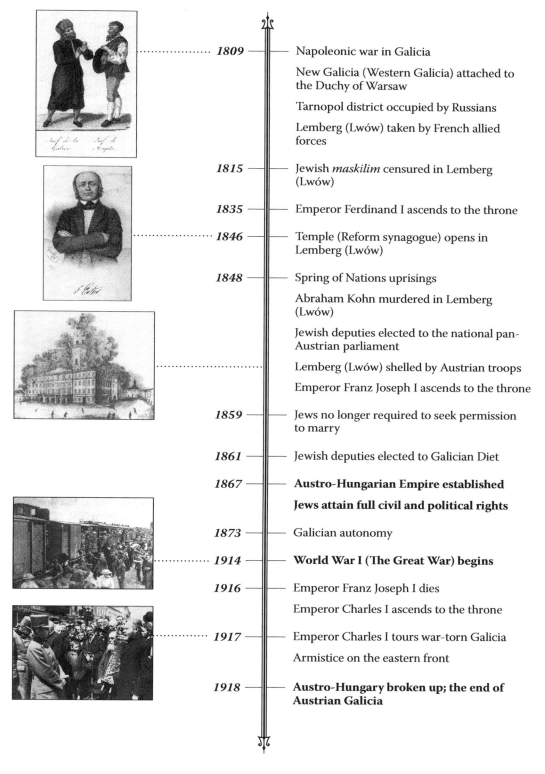

1809	Napoleonic war in Galicia
	New Galicia (Western Galicia) attached to the Duchy of Warsaw
	Tarnopol district occupied by Russians
	Lemberg (Lwów) taken by French allied forces
1815	Jewish *maskilim* censured in Lemberg (Lwów)
1835	Emperor Ferdinand I ascends to the throne
1846	Temple (Reform synagogue) opens in Lemberg (Lwów)
1848	Spring of Nations uprisings
	Abraham Kohn murdered in Lemberg (Lwów)
	Jewish deputies elected to the national pan-Austrian parliament
	Lemberg (Lwów) shelled by Austrian troops
	Emperor Franz Joseph I ascends to the throne
1859	Jews no longer required to seek permission to marry
1861	Jewish deputies elected to Galician Diet
1867	**Austro-Hungarian Empire established**
	Jews attain full civil and political rights
1873	Galician autonomy
1914	**World War I (The Great War) begins**
1916	Emperor Franz Joseph I dies
	Emperor Charles I ascends to the throne
1917	Emperor Charles I tours war-torn Galicia
	Armistice on the eastern front
1918	**Austro-Hungary broken up; the end of Austrian Galicia**

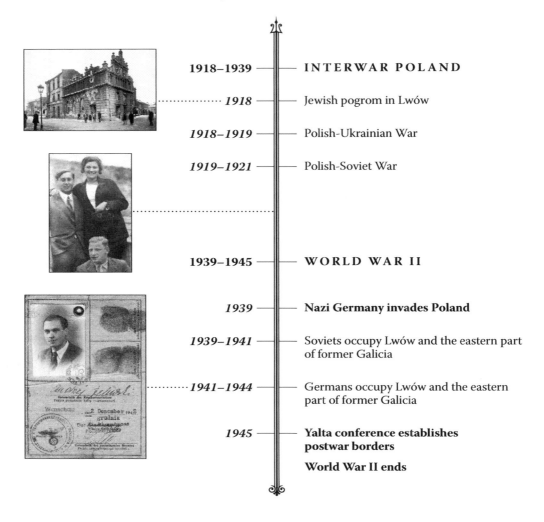

1918–1939	**INTERWAR POLAND**
1918	Jewish pogrom in Lwów
1918–1919	Polish-Ukrainian War
1919–1921	Polish-Soviet War
1939–1945	**WORLD WAR II**
1939	**Nazi Germany invades Poland**
1939–1941	Soviets occupy Lwów and the eastern part of former Galicia
1941–1944	Germans occupy Lwów and the eastern part of former Galicia
1945	**Yalta conference establishes postwar borders**
	World War II ends

Preface

WHEN I FINISHED *GALICIAN TRAILS,* my first book about Galicia, I knew I would soon return to write more on the topic. The place and the stories had turned out to be much too vibrant and seductive not to explore further. Certainly, my decision was partly emotional, since I had been able to unearth more than a few traces of my maternal ancestors, who sometimes had presented themselves with a sharpness that defied the passage of time. There was also the thrill of discoveries that moved far beyond my family.

In this book, I return to Galicia to rediscover its Jewish history. Again, it started as a quest to learn about my own roots. My father was a secular man who in the post–World War II years never talked about his heritage; he was the consummate person of the present who, as far as I remember, never looked back. Other than the names of my paternal grandparents—listed on my parents' civil marriage certificate—he left no hints to connect me to Jewish Galicia; so I had much to discover. But *Galician Portraits* is much more than an attempt to see one family's journey. Its goal has been much broader: to recover the story of all Jewish life there. Contrary to the simplifications that can color our thinking about the past, that community was richer and more diverse than one could ever imagine.

Galicia spanned parts of today's southern Poland and western Ukraine; its history has nothing to do with the Spanish province of the same name. Austrian Galicia, a historical accident that became a reality in 1772 and ceased to exist in 1918, has all the elements of a fascinating story. Its beginning and end were part of major international dramas that profoundly reset the course of history.

The Kingdom of Galicia and Lodomeria (*Königreiche Galizien und Lodomerien*), as it was officially named by the Austrians, became a province under the control of the Habsburg Monarchy in 1772. In its early years, Austrian Galicia was poorly accessible; there were few available roads. To isolate it even more from the imperial seat in Vienna, the natural barrier of the Carpathian mountain range effectively separated the new Habsburg possession from the Hereditary Lands, as the more centrally situated provinces of the Monarchy were called. Galicia's difference, however, was about more than geography. The amazing human mosaic that flourished there often surprised early Austrian visitors.

Over time, the Habsburg Monarchy continued to evolve, first becoming known as the Austrian Empire, and soon tested by the Napoleonic storm that shook Europe to its core. Then, internal conflicts rocked the country, growing from within its restless multiethnic population. Those upheavals were followed by more changes, including a political compromise that led to the birth of the Austro-Hungarian Empire. Yet through all these and other tumultuous events of the nineteenth and early twentieth centuries, the Galician crownland remained under Habsburg rule. At times, its citizens—Jewish and non-Jewish—were only witnesses to tensions evident elsewhere in the empire, but on many other occasions they were active participants in history in the making.

My journey back through time, moving through remote villages and towns, brought to the surface tales about both the nobility and ordinary people. Galicia then was a place where Poles, Ruthenians (later called Ukrainians), smaller pockets of Hungarians and Armenians, as well as newly arriving Austrians, Bohemians, and Moravians (later called Czechs), lived side by side with a large community of Israelites. Regardless of wealth, privilege, or the lack of either, their lives could be remarkable or quite uninspiring. Headlines in the popular press of long-past days sometimes reveal xenophobia, but there were also touching acts of openness and trust that crossed ethnic and religious boundaries.

Unavoidably, in that shared but often contested land, controversies about language, customs, and loyalties surfaced, both in the privacy of homes and in public discourse. In reality, however, the land's diversity was its strength, and is the source of many fascinating tales that can be told today. When researching Galicia one does not have the sense of a pastoral and predictable past; it becomes clear that exhilarating progress was often mixed with painful setbacks there.

The Austrian Monarchy, circa 1787.

The capital city of Galicia provides a backdrop to many stories about Galicia's Jewish past. Frequent changes to its name give hints of the major historical events in the region; at times, it was called Lwów (in Polish), but in other periods it was renamed Lemberg (in German), or L'viv (in Ukrainian). Yet when discovering Jewish Galicia, it is also essential to walk through the smaller towns, with their busy market squares and adjoining streets—typically lined with many

Jewish homes—and to venture into the countryside where some of the characters in this story resided. On occasion, like some Galicians, we find ourselves looking toward Vienna, the heart of the empire, to watch impactful imperial decisions unfold, or to witness other events that would resonate back home.

Unfortunately, probing the past in that part of the world is often more complicated than it might be elsewhere, making the story more challenging to tell. The two world wars that redrew national borders not only permanently erased Galicia from the maps, they also caused memories of it to fade away. Searching for Jewish history is inevitably complicated even more by the shadow of the Holocaust, an event that almost completely wiped out any continuity that might have remained between the past and present, with monstrous brutality.

✒️

GALICIAN PORTRAITS DOES NOT pretend to be written by a historian with a staff of researchers. Whenever possible, however, I have cited original sources in notes. My preference has always been for contemporaneous accounts, which in the digital age are accessible as never before. Even so, with this approach some statements concerning the Jewish community—whether in imperial edicts, expressed by politicians, or noted by casual travelers through Galicia—might seem, from our viewpoint, insensitive or patronizing. Their tone often reminds us that in the early years of Austrian Galicia, Jews and non-Jews only rarely engaged in thoughtful dialogue. Conversations or serious deliberations were more likely *about* each other rather than *with* each other. Yet at the same time, the Jewish community was conflicted within by vibrant differences of opinion on its own participation in the broader society. Listening to all those early voices, even though they might not adhere to today's standards of discourse, presents a unique opportunity to understand life in Galicia.

One of the great bonuses of historical research is coming upon exceptional individuals who were somehow ahead of their time or unique in other ways. Such voices were often to be found in Galicia, and their stories are worth recalling. There were, for instance, the homegrown thinkers and sharp-tongued writers of the Jewish Enlightenment (*Haskalah*), and those who were indignant about prejudice and stood up in defense of their community. There were also other, equally inspiring individuals who never achieved that sort of fame, but their lives are important for me to follow on these pages. Their everyday successes lowered barriers and created better opportunities for generations to come.

Contemporaneous texts and even newspaper accounts, going back to the end of the eighteenth century, all reflect recurring tension in Jewish communities between the old and the new. However, when such sources were not available, I have used information from memoirs or essays written not too long after events, to capture the subtlety of voices often lost with the passage of time. Finally, in the absence of those, I have turned to more recent scholarly or literary works, still trying to capture the spirit of Jewish Galicia with a liberal use of quotes from the main actors of the story.

This book's Appendix provides the full texts of the imperial Patents and Galician regulations that governed the lives of Jews in the early years of Austrian Galicia, giving remarkable insight into the state's approach. That approach ranged from policies to keep Jews separate from the rest of society to "enlightened" pronouncements. Many of them, originally issued in German, Polish, or even in Latin, were translated into English for the first time for this book. These laws offer yet another glimpse behind the curtain at the lives of long-gone Galicians.

ᔥ

AS THOUGH WALKING THROUGH a portrait gallery with paintings in different styles, we encounter, in *Galician Portraits*, Jewish traditionalists and modernists, faces that disappear in the crowd and those that stand out, timid people and fearless individuals. In the background, we can hear a constant debate between those who looked to their community for a sense of fulfillment and comforting order, and others who wanted to open the windows and doors to let fresh breezes, new ideas, come in. There is a richness of spoken and written words—whether in Hebrew, Yiddish, German, or Polish—as Galician Jews debate each other with a flaming passion over which language should be theirs in that polyglot land. Decades pass, and then the entire nineteenth century is suddenly behind them.

At the beginning of the twentieth century, World War I brings an end to Galicia, but stopping my narrative there would seem quite artificial. Thus, I continue to follow the lives of my Jewish ancestors through the interwar period, when a young generation looks at a life full of promise—they seem to be advancing at a pace much faster than their parents did—only to soon face a challenge unlike any before. Thus more "pictures" are added to the gallery of *Galician Portraits*.

While attempting to capture all the features and idiosyncrasies of Galician life, I feel I have barely scratched the surface of the Jewish presence there. Some readers of *Galician Portraits* might passionately feel that this or that aspect was worthy of greater emphasis or is even missing. But let us remind ourselves that in anyone's portrait gallery, the collection of memorable paintings is very individual and can never be complete.

Elkins Park, Pennsylvania
May 2014

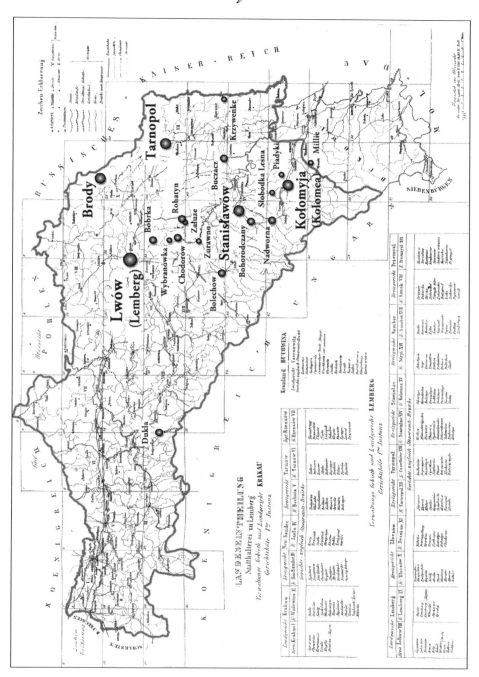

Map of Galicia and Bukovina, showing the towns and villages mentioned in *Galician Portraits*.
(*Based on Administrativ-Karte von den Königreichen Galizien und Lodomerien, BL. 3; 1855.*)

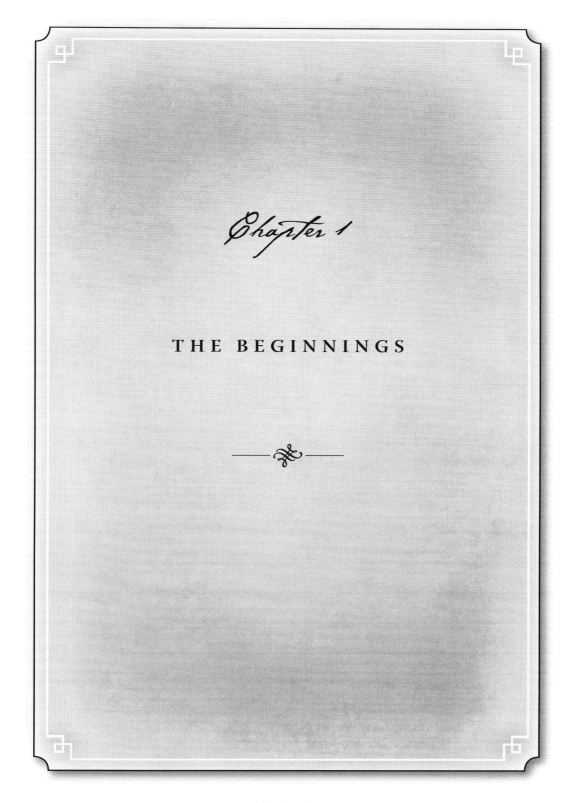

Chapter 1

THE BEGINNINGS

———❦———

*J*EWS TRAVERSED THE LAND THAT would later be called Austrian Galicia from very early times. Stories of the first visitors, such as Jewish traders from the Crimea and the shores of the Black Sea, are shrouded in speculation. What is beyond doubt, however, is that the vast majority of those Jews were Ashkenazim, arriving from communities around the river Rhine. In wave after wave, they would be moving east looking for safety, escaping persecution. The first documented migration happened at the end of the eleventh century. Jews who had settled in neighboring Prague were harassed by the Crusaders with forced conversions to Christianity, and fled to safety again. It was only natural that they would move north and settle in neighboring regions—among other places, in Little Poland (the future western part of Galicia) and in Red Rus' (the future eastern part of Galicia).

Over the next couple of centuries, a steady flow of immigration from the Germanic lands followed. In time, Jews received far-reaching legal protections from Polish princes. As early as the twelfth and thirteenth centuries, they would own land, farm, and administer the mint (with some of the coins bearing Hebrew letters).[1] A particularly large Jewish migration eastward occurred in the fourteenth century. In the wake of the Black Death, the pandemic that ravaged most of Europe (but miraculously bypassed parts of the Kingdom of Poland), a large number of Jews fled German-speaking lands to escape a new wave of brutality. They (and other "undesirable" elements, such as beggars and lepers) were blamed for the death by plague of nearly half of Europe's population. Whether because of isolation behind the walls of ghettos or ritual bathing, Jews were often spared this calamity. But rather than enjoying celebrations of their survival, Jews had their quarters in Franco-German lands ransacked, the inhabitants often killed by vengeful mobs. Many had no choice but to flee to the east.

The Polish king Casimir the Great granted such Jews the right to free passage through the areas he ruled, and those who wished to settle there received permission to rent and take mortgages on the estates of the nobility, as well as to lend money. The king was on a mission to revitalize his country and greatly expand it—the old saying that Casimir "found a Poland of wood and left behind him a Poland of stone" was the truth. The provinces were united, new cities were built, and the indefatigable ruler's kingdom expanded to include historical Galicia in the east. Between 1334 and 1367, not only were Jewish privileges reaffirmed, but several new ones were also added. In 1356 Casimir also granted the "Magdeburg Law" to the city of Lwów, the capital of newly conquered Red Rus' (Galicia), with similar rulings for other, smaller towns of the region. These laws were styled on the provisions granted to cities in Germany, which enjoyed administrative and judicial independence when it came to municipal affairs. For Casimir, the impetus for granting the laws was his desire to stimulate growth. Now, magnates could offer Jews, Poles, Ruthenians, and Armenians the right to settle within the towns' defensive perimeters—along with the privilege, granted to each ethnic group, to be judged according to the laws of their own ethnic or religious community.

In his many laws affecting Jews, the king was generous, and not just in regard to economic freedoms. His edicts spoke of respect for other human beings, challenging many canonical laws of the Catholic Church that fostered separation of Jews from others in society. Instead, Casimir declared that, "if a Jew enters the house of a Christian, no one has a right to cause him any injury or unpleasantness. Every Jew is allowed to visit the municipal baths in safety, in the same way as the Christians."

The story of Casimir the Great would not be complete without mentioning his affair of the heart that transcended ethnic or religious boundaries. The king fell madly in love with the beautiful Jewess Esther (*Esterka*), daughter of a tailor. In a blurred mixture of facts and legend, the tale would later be told about the romance that led Esther to be installed in a royal palace near Kraków. She bore the king two daughters, who were raised in the Jewish faith, and two sons, who were raised as Christians and gave rise to several noble families.[2]

Casimir the Great visiting Esther. Painted by Władysław Łuszczkiewicz circa 1870.
(*The Lviv Gallery of Art.*)

Over the next centuries, Jews became an indispensable part of the area's economy, being heavily involved in the management of vast rural estates, as well as in the trades. The royals and large magnates welcomed them; the coffers of these powerful men were replenished with the revenue brought by Jews. But lesser nobility (country gentry) and burghers (citizens of towns) often viewed them with suspicion as potential competitors. Despite these tensions, the Jews' fate over the next century could not be more different from that of their Sephardic cousins in the other corner of the continent. After Jewish communities of Spain were emptied in 1492 by the Inquisition, their inhabitants fled to the vast lands of the Ottoman Empire in Asia and northern Africa and to a few cities in Europe (such as Amsterdam). At the time when they tried to rebuild their lives in these places, Ashkenazim Jews were thriving in Poland.

At the zenith of Jewish life in that kingdom, no longer did prospective students have to travel to Germany or Bohemia to study religious texts. Famous schools of rabbinic learning were operated first in Lwów and Kraków, and then in many other places. Talmudic scholars from Poland developed their own types of religious studies, attracting students "from one end of the world to another." Their focus was on mastering the interpretation of centuries of rabbinic writings that overlaid the Talmud; a new codification of Jewish laws was also undertaken. Questions were analyzed in excruciating detail. There were frequent interactions with Italian Jewish communities; initially, Hebrew presses in Italy provided books, but soon printing was allowed by royal privilege and Hebrew texts were printed locally. A few fortunate graduates traveled, especially to Padua in Italy, to gain secular knowledge. But in general, there was little engagement by Jews in secular studies. As to the scholarship of the period, what was considered intellectual progress in one century would be labeled hairsplitting and a search for irrelevant detail in the next.[3]

In times of peace, thousands of young Jews attended famous, twice-a-year fairs in a few big towns. There, the men could study with the best teachers, interact with each other, and exchange news with those arriving from afar. No longer were the Jews a downtrodden group of refugees. "Jews, both men and women" it was later recalled with pride, "walked about the fair, dressed in royal garments. For they were held in esteem in the eyes of the rulers and in the eyes of the Gentiles, and the children of Israel were many like the sand of the sea...." For parents, this was also the best time to arrange matches for their daughters or sons. Perhaps with a bit of exaggeration, one author would recall those times when not just hundreds, but sometimes thousands of marriages might be arranged at each fair.[4]

With each passing decade, Jewish fortunes rose and fell with the prosperity of the Polish-Lithuanian Commonwealth, formally established in 1569. Sometimes they were targeted by the bigotry of their neighbors, and on other occasions they suffered (with other groups) at the hands of foreign invaders, particularly along the Commonwealth's eastern frontier. During periods of economic decline in the country, accusations of unfair business practices were common; Christian guilds were hostile to any "outside" competition. But in some cases discriminatory laws that were passed had comic effects. When Jewish merchants in 1643 were ordered to collect less than half the profit granted to Poles on imported goods, it created an instantaneous boom for them; an item was simply cheaper when obtained from Jewish hands.[5]

In good and bad times, Jews governed themselves through autonomous communal institutions called *kahals*, whose authority was in the hands of a few powerful families. Their influence was exerted on the basis of personal wealth, family relations—critical through the matchmaking that could bring powerful families together—and religious scholarship. Even in judicial matters, conflicts among Jews were resolved by the rabbinic courts, without any interference by the state.

The *kahal* leaders assessed taxes, but also provided religious and nonreligious services. They were often in a position to decide who would receive the most lucrative leases from the landowning aristocracy. For better or worse, each community policed itself, so no Jew would undermine another Jew when it came to dealings with a local "lord"; as such, offering a higher payment in return for the same lease was strictly forbidden. In major fiscal and religious doctrinal matters, the communities followed directions from the Council of Four Lands, the Jewish assembly that divided up tax obligations owed to the royal treasury. The council's official emissaries (*shtadlans*) could lobby the crown or the national assembly on behalf of the entire Jewish community. This system offered stability and the sense of a safe, closeted existence for the vast majority of Jews, who did not have to be troubled with affairs of the external world. Yet Jewish autonomy also perpetuated a state of isolation that remained the norm, with a few notable exceptions, until the second half of the eighteenth century.

☞

THE STORY OF MY paternal grandmother's family, as far back as I am able to trace it, begins in Rohatyn. Its history was typical of many places in eastern Galicia where, shortly after the villages grew to become towns, the first Jews would settle. It is also a tale of those ordinary people who moved there and, through better and worse years, lived side by side with Ruthenians and Poles.

Rohatyn was never able to boast that, like the future capital city, Lwów, it had played a grand role in Galicia's development—not even for a brief and fleeting moment. It could not claim to have famous monuments or the charm of nearby Stanisławów. There was nothing to note about any famous scholar or impatient reformer who had challenged the status quo; nor were Rohatyners able to pride themselves on stories that a king, an emperor, or a tsar had slept in their town. The furthest they could go to impress anyone was a story about a short stay by the Grand Master of the Teutonic Knights. In 1497, Grand Master Johann von Tiefen had been ordered to lead a campaign with four hundred knights against the Ottoman Turks, but fell ill of dysentery and never reached the front. The ailing leader had rested in Rohatyn for just one or two nights, which to a casual listener was not likely an exciting tidbit of history.

Nonetheless, Rohatyn's location, at a crossroads that connected important towns of the region, made it possible early on for this inconspicuous place to find its way into historic records. At first, it was a village by the name of Filipowice. A few peasants' huts were scattered there, between the river Gniła Lipa, with its muddy banks, and a brook named Babinka flowing from the east. Then, a small castle was built there. Later, some would speculate that the name of the erected structure, Rohatyn, was passed on to the town. At the end of the fourteenth century, this obscure place briefly became a topic of conversation in faraway Rome. It was there that "the town of Rohagyn (*sic*) in the Halicz diocese" was mentioned in a document issued by Pope Boniface IX, who ordered his local bishop to halt some punitive actions directed against it in 1390.[6]

In subsequent centuries, ownership of the town changed hands more than a few times. In 1460, Rohatyn and all its inhabitants were given as a security deposit to one of the nobles, when the king of the Polish-Lithuanian Commonwealth needed a large cash loan. After more than seventy years in private hands, it reverted to the crown in 1535, but soon other powerful magnates were in possession of the town and the surrounding area.

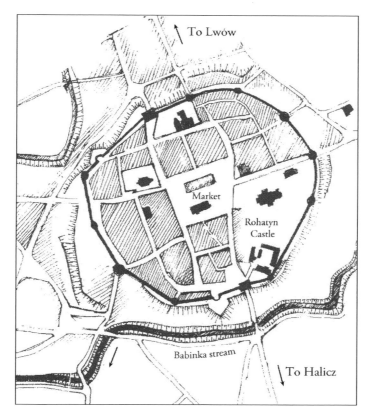

Outline of Rohatyn and its defensive walls from the period between the fifteenth and the mid-seventeenth centuries; rendition based on geological and archeological research. *(Courtesy of Maxym Yasinskyy, Institute of Architecture, L'viv Polytechnic University, Ukraine.)*

As in other places in the region, Jews fleeing persecution elsewhere were welcome to settle in Rohatyn. In 1463, the first Jew from another settlement was mentioned as trading cattle in the town's market; it did not take long for a small number of Jewish households to be established there. What started as the arrival of a few families would have grown into a community of hundreds by the time Austrian Galicia emerged a couple of centuries later.

From the beginning, Rohatyn was a trading post with a defensive fort. Its small castle and the old town were surrounded by wooden walls and an earthen mound. Entry to the town was guarded by the reinforced Halicz and Lwów Gates made of stone; those would stay intact until the end of the eighteenth century. But for most of its history, Rohatyn's reinforcements could slow but not halt frequent raids by the Crimean Tatars, the Ottoman Turks, or the equally feared Cossacks, who swept through the land often, with brutal consequences. More often than not, the townsfolk had to watch, helpless, while their possessions were burned by invaders, and were forced to pay ransoms in money, goods, and sometimes hostages.

Turkish warrior. Illustration from a popular book written by an English emissary to Istanbul, published in the Polish-Lithuanian Commonwealth. (*Paul Rycaut, Monarchia Turecka, Słuck, 1678.*)

Years later, when the memory of that suffering had faded away, Rohatyners entertained themselves with a tale of a local woman who became the power behind the throne in a faraway country. The story was told of Roxolana, a Ruthenian girl who had been kidnapped by Ottoman forces. It was said that, forced into slavery in Istanbul, Roxolana had navigated wisely through rivalry within the harem of the sultan Suleiman the Magnificent, ruler of the Ottoman Empire. Her beauty and intelligence, according to the tale, won the heart of the ruler. The young woman from Rohatyn became a force to be reckoned with, the sultan's favorite wife and the mother of his successor. Over time, the tale of kidnapping morphed into a story of beauty, sexuality, and love. Rohatyners eagerly embellished it, with Roxolana's accomplishments growing more and more legendary over the years.[7]

Among the early Jewish Rohatyners were artisans, merchants, and money-lenders. Other Jews were employed to collect taxes on liquor, and received leases on nearby ponds stocked with fish. If needed, a few Jewish barbers living in town acted as surgeons. The affairs of the Jews of Rohatyn were regulated by decrees passed down by Polish kings, who granted a series of rights to their community. In 1633, they were given royal permission to establish "a synagogue and cemetery, [to engage in] all trades and professions without limitation regardless [if that requires] selling or buying goods." King Władysław IV Vasa announced that the Rohatyn Jews were free to "[own] all types of inns, brew beer, make honey, distill spirits. [Jewish] butchers are free to buy or sell cattle and meat, wholesale and retail, on the market." Importantly, the sovereign ruled that the Jews should have no fewer and no more obligations than their Christian neighbors by proclaiming "they should pay municipal taxes as other burghers, and are absolved from other private tributes." This was a fundamental legal principle, allowing the broader Rohatyn community to be protective of the Jews when they were singled out by the town's greedy owner or his underlings.[8]

Despite royal protection, the growth of the Jewish community in the region was not always free of setbacks. In particular, the Cossack rebellion of 1648, led by Hetman Bohdan Khmelnytsky (Chmielnicki), inflicted horrendous casualties.

Initially, Khmelnytsky's small force revolted against the Poles and became allied with the Crimean Tatars. As they advanced from the steppes of eastern Ruthenia (in today's eastern Ukraine) in a westward direction, carnage was inflicted in the southeastern corner of the Polish-Lithuanian Commonwealth. The Cossacks' brute force was quickly strengthened by a popular uprising of Ruthenian peasants, whose rage was directed at whoever was associated with the Commonwealth's rule in Ruthenia; Polish nobility, and by extension Jews employed to administer their estates, became prime targets.

Stories of betrayal and violence against Jews and Poles, with appalling loss of life, would become deeply ingrained in the minds of many generations to come. A Jewish eyewitness, who managed to escape from a town situated east of Rohatyn, would write in a few years about the horror of bloody massacres in which "the skin was flayed from men who were still alive and their flesh thrown to dogs; the hands and the feet of others were hacked off, and over their still quivering bodies wagons were driven and the horses trampled them with their feet. Grievous wounds were inflicted on men, but they were deliberately not pierced through on the spot; they were cast into the streets so they might struggle with death in horrible agony for a time."[9]

Thus, in the period of the next few years, more Jews were alleged to have lost their lives than during the horrible massacres of the Crusades and in the Black Death. Several hundred communities were left burned and empty in the aftermath of the Cossack wars. Although the estimates would later be questioned by historians, Jewish losses in the region were counted by some in tens, if not hundreds of thousands of lives.

Sadly, Rohatyn did not escape these events, being situated in the path of the Cossack army moving west. The capital of Galicia, Lwów, was also attacked by Khmelnytsky's forces, supported by their allies, the Tatars. When this time the Cossacks could not scale the defensive walls, they entered into negotiations with the city's elders. They would leave, they said, only if the Jews and their possessions were delivered into their hands. Otherwise, the siege was to continue with dire consequences to all defenders. For proof of the attackers' intentions, those

Title page of *Abyss of Despair* (*Yeven Metzulah*). Nathan (Natan) Hannover (?–1683) witnessed the massacres of the Cossack rebellion in 1648. His dramatic account of the atrocities committed against Jews was first published in Venice in 1653. *(Courtesy of the Library of the Jewish Theological Seminary, New York.)*

trapped inside did not have to look too far; the area around the city had already gone up in smoke. And yet, the magistrate of Lwów rose to the occasion, refusing to yield to the blackmail by claiming that their Israelite neighbors were under royal protection and their fate could not be decided by the city. The embattled city dwellers stalled for time, but ultimately, a ransom had to be paid to ensure the Jews' safety—still, not a single person was turned over to the Cossacks.[10]

Over the next decade, fighting in the area was common. As late as 1663, the fields of Rohatyn's suburb, Babińce, lay bare, its houses destroyed and the area eerily empty after another punishing military campaign. But Rohatyners must have been made of tough stock. Even after repeated plundering and burning of their town, the survivors returned to rebuild their lives.

Yet in those tough times, the relationship between local Jews and gentiles could easily spiral out of control. One year, troubles spilled over in Rohatyn's market square; struggles between Jewish merchants and the local guilds were common. This particular time, complaints were raised about Jewish merchants not providing the required pound of wax and certain fees to a guild, for the privilege of selling red-, yellow-, and black-dyed leather shoes, or the favored soft boots made of doeskin. In retaliation, the shoemakers guild ordered its members to seize these and other leather products if found in the stalls or on the tables set up by the Jews in the square; the items were to be kept until the grievances were addressed. Whether the charges were justified or not, we will never know, but one can only imagine the kerfuffle during a busy market day, with shouting and pushing between the parties. In the midst of the commotion, a few lucky Jewish merchants must have rapidly stuffed their wares into sacks and run away as fast as they could.

In 1669, a royal decree by "Michael, the King of Poland by the Grace of God, the Great Duke of Lithuania, Russia, Prussia [with many titles that followed]," responded directly to a plea from Rohatyn's Jews, who requested his permission for unimpeded trading during the weekly market. The new king, in his first year of reign, ruled that, "seeing the need to help [Jews] as soon as possible after they had suffered losses at the hands of an enemy of past times, they can carry on their trades for the benefit of all."[11]

Toward the end of that troubled century, the homes of Jews could again be found in the area around Rohatyn's market square. The most affluent of them would live in "the Lord's House," built of stone, next to the more modest wooden houses of barbers and blacksmiths. Along nearby Lwów Street, which transected the town from north to south, stood the houses of other stall owners and one that belonged to a Jewish musician. Farther away from the market, next to the earthen mound—a remnant of the old fortifications—the rest of the town's Jews

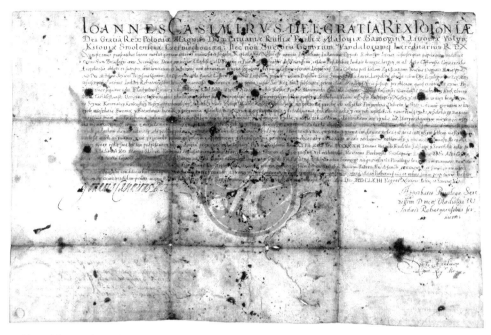

Above: The royal privileges bestowed on the Jews of Rohatyn by Polish king John Casimir (in Polish, *Jan II Kazimierz Waza*) in 1663. The edict was written in Latin and bears the king's signature (in Latin, *Ionnes Casimirus Rex*). (*The Czartoryski Archives, Kraków, Poland.*)

Below: The royal privileges granted to the Jews of Rohatyn by Polish king Michael (in Polish, *Michał Korybut Wiśniowiecki*) in 1669. The edict was written in Latin during the first year of the king's rule, and bears the royal seal. (*The Czartoryski Archives, Kraków, Poland.*)

Above: The cover page of an inventory of the subprefecture of Rohatyn and its landed properties. The document was compiled in 1690. *(The Czartoryski Archives, Kraków, Poland.)*

Left: A list of Rohatyn's population from 1690. The title reads, "Rohatyn Town—The Burghers' Names." The first page begins a list of inhabitants of the town's center. Jewish names were recorded either in a patronymic format [e.g., Jakub Szymszonowicz, meaning Jakub (Jacob), the son of Szymszon (Shimshon)] or were related to the person's profession [e.g., Josio Cerulik probably indicated Josio (Josiah), the barber]. The Jewish names are marked as "*Żyd* (Jew)." *(The Czartoryski Archives, Kraków, Poland.)*

lived in small huts, among them butchers, goldsmiths, tailors, brewers, and cooks employed all over the town. As in our times, where one lived mattered; in spite of short distances that could be covered in a few minutes, rents around the market square and on nearby streets were always higher than those at the town's periphery.

At that time Rohatyn's "Lord," Count Sieniawski, ruled the entire area from a distance; almost everything in and around the town was situated on his land. Each year, one or another Jew received the rights to a lease for this and surrounding towns. In exchange for a fixed amount, to be paid quarterly to the count, the leaseholder would collect money from a long list of town-dwellers' obligations, including rents and the proceeds from breweries, distilleries, taverns, mills, and toll roads. Nobody was excluded, Jews and Christians alike. Living in the "Lord's House," the leaseholder was also responsible for making sure that beer, hard liquor, and honey were available to the townsfolk.

Year after year, someone in Rohatyn would fail to pay their rent; often these were poor Ruthenian serfs who used some of the count's land for their own needs. When unable to pay the fees, they would appeal for the protection of the Greek Catholic Church. On other occasions, some of those who tended apiaries at the edge of town claimed that they had made no honey that year and therefore no rents were due. (Honey-making was a big business for the count's estate, with many half-barrels sent to other towns of the region.)[12]

Left: A lease of Rohatyn issued in the name of "Adam Mikołaj, Lord of Granów, Sieniawski, the Count ... and Voivode of Bełz and Lwów, General Subprefect of Rohatyn." The first page reads, "I gave the lease on my Rohatyn District from the holiday of Saint John of June 24, 1693 until, God willing, the next year of 1694. I leased it for the sum of thirteen thousand Polish *złoty* to honorable burghers of mine, Moszko Juszkowicz and Abramko Szajewicz...."

Right: The contract ends with: "To assure greater attention [to this contract] and its accuracy, I sign in my own hand and confirm it by [my] seal. [The signing] took place in Dźwniogród on the day of 13 April in the year 1693." (*The Czartoryski Archives, Kraków, Poland.*)

However, any suggestion of serene rural life implied by Rohatyn's annual inventories is somewhat deceptive. What developed after the Cossack rebellion and the subsequent conflicts in the area was quite different from the situation that had existed before, even taking into account the previous calamities that had befallen the region. In Rohatyn and other towns, Jewish communities were now laden with a mounting debt. Their traditional self-rule had been weakened, with a subsequent decline in spending on education and communal charity. In many places, an oppressive Jewish oligarchy, responsible for apportionment of taxes on other Jews and aided by increasingly rigid rabbinic leaders, added to the hardship of common people. Signs of a decline were clearly visible.

ᴈ

ENTERING THE EIGHTEENTH CENTURY, the Jewish community of Galicia was exhausted; there was an intense longing not just for physical recovery, but also for spiritual renewal. Since many centers of traditional learning were too rigid in guiding people in those difficult times, the ground was well prepared for dissenters to surface. Many people searched for an explanation of why times were so hard after prior centuries of growth; they sought at least some reassurance that similar calamities would not happen again. Perhaps, they thought, their suffering was a prelude to the imminent arrival of the Jewish Messiah. Others looked in a different direction. They would soon embrace the Hasidic movement, with its new customs of worship and rejection of rabbinic formalism. These pious Jews could express themselves in the religious sphere as never before, with liberating dance and song.

With few exceptions, Jewish scholarship in this period was diverted into a blind alley: painstaking analyses of arguments and counterarguments over details of rabbinic texts. Instead of probing larger questions of morality or engaging, as in the past, in brave literary experiments, scholars' energy was spent on obscure subtleties and the resolution of esoteric contradictions. The endless pursuit of hidden meanings was said to produce an "empty brilliance of mendacious preachers" rather than true scholarship. One contemporaneous Jewish critique noted, "among us have appeared false preachers, little foxes who do great harm.... They concern themselves only with deception and hocus-pocus and spend their time in vain cleverness and dazzlement ... after this confused learning began to dominate our lands, great darkness and confusion came into the world."[13] Another astute observer, a rare example of a Jewish physician educated in Italy, bemoaned, upon his return to Galicia, there was no other land where Kabbalistic superstitions had taken such a strong hold. "Men," he said, "devote themselves so much to demons, amulets, incantations, combinations of names, and all kinds of dreams."[14]

Along with economic decline and this preoccupation with mysticism, a very different crisis was soon to unfold.

In its long history, arguments, even breaches within the Jewish community were not a new phenomenon. But now the internecine struggles, disturbing and confusing many, reached a new level. Jews were split between traditionalists and new religious trends. The latter included on one side messianic sects, and soon the rapidly expanding Hasidism on the other. In the territory that would later become Austrian Galicia, unrest in spiritual affairs divided towns and even families. Physical fights between the proponents and antagonists of various religious sectarian movements, the isolation of one group from another group, and rabbinical excommunications, became common. In fact, Rohatyn was to become the scene of one such conflict.

In the 1750s, clandestine groups in the southeastern corner of the Polish-Lithuanian Commonwealth were eagerly awaiting any scrap of news from the Ottoman Empire. Some of their members even traveled to the cities of today's Turkey and Greece to see firsthand what was going on. This apprehension was not about another possible war with the Ottoman Turks, or the opening of new trading routes. Instead, it centered on a strange movement that had its origins far away in Smyrna (in today's Turkey) and Salonika (in today's Greece). There, someone was promising an end to Jewish misery. To make it even more attractive for the downtrodden left at home, that speaker was not a complete stranger; by birth, he was connected with Galicia.

When in December 1755 Jacob Frank crossed the river Dniestr, which separated the Ottoman Empire and the Polish-Lithuanian Commonwealth, passions were running high. Frank was a leader of the messianic sectarian movement, and rumor was spreading fast that he was the embodiment of the long-gone Sabbatai Zevi, who had ignited powerful debate all over the Jewish world in the previous century. Neither Zevi's eventual conversion to Islam, nor even his death in 1676, had discouraged his covert followers, particularly in the Jewish communities in the east. Their mystical ethos kept alive a belief that, through "transmigration of souls," it was only a matter of time until Zevi, the "Holy King (*Malka Kaddisha*)" would return in a new physical body.[15]

Now, eighty years after Zevi's death, many believed that Jacob Frank was this returning Messiah. After spending several years in the Ottoman Empire, the hotbed of Sabbateans (*Shebsin* in Yiddish) as Zevi's supporters were called, he returned to the Polish-Lithuanian Commonwealth. His local followers were in open conflict with the accepted norms of the day. It was obvious that Frank challenged the authority of the rabbis in religious matters, and their dispute went far beyond minute doctrinal details. But, for traditional Jews, his views in the sphere of morality were equally shocking. Frank preached that the transgression of many boundaries was in fact virtuous. His credo was that, "True happiness is not in the world to come, in the celestial palaces of paradise, but here on earth. Earthly pleasures, the beauty of women, luxury and splendor … everything that the rabbis with their books have stamped with the shameful brand of sin—these are true happiness, the greatest human joy."[16]

Jacob Frank's first stay in Rohatyn lasted only a week, but his teachings fell on fertile ground. Although he would later be painted as an opportunist, abhorrent to Jews and equally mistrusted by gentiles, there must have been something electrifying about him. Many of Frank's utterances in Yiddish or Ladino (the latter learned during years among Sephardic communities in the Ottoman Empire) can sound today like the outpourings of a megalomaniac preaching to the disenchanted: "I have come to destroy everything, and everything that will be built up afterwards will have an everlasting existence." Whether his magnetism was due to his personality, his unashamed lust for pleasure, or his mission against rigid rules, Frank quickly attracted many in the community. For Jews disillusioned with the deprivation and chaos they had suffered in the

Polish-Lithuanian Commonwealth, there was hope when he said, "Do not turn your faces to the past, to what is gone!"

During Frank's visit to Rohatyn, news came that an esteemed preacher from the town, Elisha Shorr, had joined Frank's movement, which caused a sensation in this close-knit community. Soon, other members of the Shorr family and more than a handful of other Jews from Rohatyn had embraced the sectarians. The Shorrs' approval of Frank's teachings had a significant impact far beyond their town; through marriage, the family was connected with several other Jewish communities of the region. Previously closeted sympathies with the messianic movement were now coming into the open.

Not long after Frank left town to tour neighboring communities, he and a group of his fellow sectarians were detained by civil authorities; one of their gatherings was alleged to have been the scene of strange behavior that tested then-prevailing rules of morality. The rumors rapidly spread about sexually explicit rituals that were practiced by the group. If this was not enough to offend traditional Jewish communities, there was also an uproar over the sect's violation of the Sabbath and their often ostentatious transgression of dietary laws. To make the point, adversaries of the sectarians would repeat the story of a certain Samuel, a follower of Frank, who, it was said, had one Saturday dared to ride a horse and smoke tobacco in front of the chief rabbi of Lwów!

Although Frank, as a Turkish subject, was speedily released from custody, the sectarians were doubtless on a collision path with the rabbinic authorities. In recent years, Jewish councils had handed out excommunications for much less-obvious transgressions, trying to stamp out any whiff of dissent. At times, bitter disputes had even arisen about seemingly innocent compilations of a few handwritten Hebrew letters, which could be interpreted as hidden support of the "false messiah," igniting storms of condemnation and support across Europe.[17]

In 1756, however, the accusations were not about obscure meanings of amulets, or of texts published somewhere else. That same year, testimonies at a rabbinic court had unearthed salacious details about the group's supposedly sanctioned rituals. Now, revelations about the sect's recent gatherings became a source of gossip repeated among the Jews of Rohatyn; they all knew firsthand the players in the scandal. The doctrinal debate that was soon to unfold would probably be less understood by the Rohatyners, but the idea that the sectarians were trampling the rules of morality was certain to catch their attention. In the rabbinic court testimony Hayah Shorr, daughter of the respected preacher, was accused of participation in sexual orgies with the permission of her husband. The purported erotic scenes and "sexual hospitality" entangled more than Hayah alone.

When the testimonies and the debate were over, a verdict was announced by the rabbinic council to the sound of rams' horns and with smoke issuing from black candles. Predictably, a severe punishment was meted out to the followers of Jacob Frank. The text of excommunication, under the heading "A Double-Edged Sword" was distributed widely throughout the region. The language was harsh; "the sinners in Israel" suffered expulsion from their communities, with their wives and daughters labeled as whores. One unfortunate Yosef of Rohatyn was sentenced to make a public confession in the synagogue, received thirty-nine lashes, and was banned from town. But the most draconian punishment was the order that he was never to make any contact with other Jews; in effect, he was made a "living corpse." In many towns, Frank's followers were attacked, severely beaten, and in some cases perished. It was rumored that Elisha Shorr was among those who lost their lives.[18]

Despite the harshness of the verdict issued by the rabbinic judges, Frank's movement was not easily quashed. In fact, the situation became even more complicated when debates between the Talmudists, represented by the orthodox rabbis, and the Contra-Talmudists, as Frank's followers wanted to be called, entangled more players. The traditionalists appealed to a local bishop for help in dealing with the sectarians, who in their eyes also dangerously transgressed the beliefs of Christians. Yet their strategy backfired. From then on, the discourse within the Jewish community was to continue under the duplicitous aegis of the Catholic Church. A few Rohatyners traveled to the bishop's seat in Kamieniec Podolski and presented themselves at an ecclesiastical court to vouch for the movement. Frank was perhaps afraid of the outcome or simply wanted to stay above the fray, advancing his views by proxy. He returned to Rohatyn in 1757, while the dispute was underway.[19]

From the beginning this proceeding was a strange affair; the ecclesiastical court was clearly biased in favor of the dissenters. One can only imagine today that when the verdict came, it brought more confusion and pain for all Rohatyners. For one thing, despite earlier admissions of immoral behavior by its members, Frank's followers were suddenly absolved of suspicious dancing and of kissing unclothed priestesses during rituals. In the end, nobody knew who was telling the truth. The court also sided with Frank's followers against the Talmud; what followed was an awful order from the bishop to publically burn the book revered by the Jews. In many towns, house searches were ordered and copies of the Talmud were confiscated. In Lwów, in an act of mockery and desecration, the seized books were tied to horses' tails and dragged through the streets. Later, it was reported that in Kamieniec Podolski, more than a thousand copies of the Talmud had been burned, in an atmosphere reminiscent of the Middle Ages.[20] Rabbis protested that the Church had no right to interfere in internal religious matters, but to no avail. To make matters more dramatic, the ecclesiastical authorities hinted at imminent recognition of the Frankists as the legitimate form of Judaism.

Within a few months, everything had changed again. The unexpected death of the overzealous bishop who had ordered the burning of the Talmud brought a temporary intermission in the escalating conflict. The Contra-Talmudists, however, were left without their biggest supporter. In an unexpected turn of fortune, they found themselves at the mercy of rabbinic orthodoxy, which was incensed by recent happenings. In this rollercoaster of events, several of Frank's followers were forced to escape to safety in the Ottoman Empire, joining their leader who had also fled there. Many believed that, like the "false messiah" of the previous century, Sabbatai Zevi, his living "reincarnation," Jacob Frank, and his followers would be forced to publically profess allegiance to Islam while secretly following their unusual form of Judaism for a long time to come. Yet once again, there was nothing predictable about the situation. In the next year, with a guarantee of safe passage signed by the king of the Polish-Lithuanian Commonwealth, a migration in the other direction started.

The royal guarantee in hand, Salomon Shorr, son of Elisha from Rohatyn, together with other leaders of the sect, soon began negotiations with Church officials for another debate with the rabbis. Despite a papal nuncio's warning that another such proceeding could renew the violence, preparations moved forward for the disputation in Lwów. On orders from the Vatican, the nuncio did prevail over local church officials, in that no verdict was to be announced; instead, written replies from rabbis were requested in response to a seven-point credo by the sectarians. With that agreement in place, the stage was set for the second confrontation. As it turned out, this would be a quite different affair from the previous one.

In the summer of 1759, the most erudite and scholarly individuals from both sides sat at desks across from each other in the central nave of the cathedral in Lwów. They were surrounded by Catholic theologians eager to observe the showdown. The supporters of Jacob Frank included a group of thirteen members, a group who now faced about thirty representatives of the religious establishment. Among the latter, some rabbis had come of their own volition; others had clearly been pressured to attend. (Beforehand, church officials had appealed to the landed aristocracy to use their influence to assure participation of local rabbis, so the entire affair could not later be dismissed.)

The key interlocutors were aided by translators, ready to switch when needed from Hebrew (and Yiddish) to Polish and Latin. Speaking on behalf of the Frankists were Salomon Shorr from Rohatyn and Yehudah Leyb Krysa from Nadwórna. The assembled rabbinic authorities were represented by Chaim Cohen Rapoport of Lwów, Nutka of Bohorodczany, and David of Stanisławów. The first of them, the chief rabbi of Lwów—known to carry on a wide correspondence with the Talmudic authorities of his time—was the unquestionable leader of the rabbinic camp.[21] The presiding church official watched the dispute from a stage, with a group of dignitaries and ladies of the aristocracy seated nearby. Even the public was admitted to the cathedral for a fee, among them a sizeable group of Jewish youth. Nothing had been left to chance; soldiers were positioned outside, ready to deal with any possible unrest.

Yet those who expected a theater-like atmosphere were in for disappointment. The initial exchanges were tedious and difficult to follow for laypeople, especially those without knowledge of Hebrew. It was only when the parties reached the eleventh debate, several weeks after they had begun, that tension among the participants became clearly palpable. Frank's followers put forward an explosive accusation against their brethren: the medieval charge of ritual murder on religious grounds. With that proclamation, an unmarked line was crossed by Frank's sect. The indignant response by Rabbi Rapoport of Lwów would be remembered for more than a century: "You have declared to the world that [we seek Christian blood], not because of hostility or seeking revenge but because of the love of our faith," he calmly intoned, and then continued, "we recognize that your malice toward us and your desire to inflict retribution made you cite past denunciations and certain [criminal] acts, which were caused by the violence or jealousy of individuals, not for fundamental [religious] reasons; as for those, there is no shred of evidence! It is against the laws of nature and reason that we, the descendants of Abraham, could ever demand killing and lust for human blood!"

By now, it was apparent that Frankists had become no longer a separate offshoot of Judaism. Accusing other Jews of perverse blood libel signaled that something more fundamental was about to happen. Some observers even noticed that, upon closer examination, many of the Frankists' doctrinal points bore strange resemblances to dogmas of the Catholic Church. In this atmosphere, Jacob Frank showed up in Lwów to witness the closing of the proceedings. Never shy about making a big impression, he arrived, according to eyewitnesses, like a triumphant eastern prince. Frank sat in a spacious carriage pulled by six horses, surrounded by twelve mounted bodyguards. His retinue was followed by a long column of wagons packed with sectarians, a large contingent of Rohatyners among them. Gentiles rushed to the streets to see the spectacle; nothing like this had ever happened there before. But some disgusted Jews of Lwów hid at home or rushed into alleys to avoid even a fleeting sight of the procession. Many of them were afraid of Frank's "magic" powers. Even meeting his eyes, some believed, could have made them follow the apostate.[22]

Back in Rohatyn, more painful divisions surfaced. Words of condemnation were certainly spoken by many Jewish neighbors when, in the immediate aftermath of the disputation, local followers of Frank gathered with their leader in Lwów in an en masse conversion to Catholicism. Now, it seemed that Frank had delivered on his promise to Church authorities to abandon his faith as the price for the public dispute in Lwów. Other Jews, however, felt the lifting of a heavy burden. For them, the departure of the sectarians from Judaism was the only way to heal the schism rocking the community. As for the Shorrs from Rohatyn, the sons of Elisha were granted, like many among the converts, titles of nobility, and left the town forever. Thus ended one of the strangest episodes Rohatyners—not to mention others in the region—had ever seen.

✒

ONE OF THE TRANSLATORS in the final Frankist debate, Ber from Bolechów, had more than just remarkable linguistic skills. We know a great deal about his life because of his memoir, first discovered only at the beginning of the twentieth century. Covering a few decades before the 1772 First Partition of Poland, it gives a picture of the lives of prosperous Jewish families in a small Galician town near Rohatyn, of the opportunities available to them and the hurdles that could stand in their paths.

The Jews of Galicia, almost without exception, knew Yiddish and some Hebrew. The former was used in daily communications both spoken and written, the latter mainly for religious matters. Their fluency in other local languages, Polish or Ruthenian, varied. Ber, with his worldly knowledge, was certainly an exception. For the vast majority of his brethren, a local Jewish school, *heder,* was the only way to receive some rudimentary education. By the eighteenth century, however, their ossified teaching methods did not encourage the integration of Jews into the wider world. Other Galician schools, not to mention universities, were under the administration of the Catholic Church, making them effectively beyond the reach of Jews.

Despite these obstacles, Jewish leaseholders and traders on magnates' estates had to communicate with their wealthy lords and their subjects; knowing a bit of Polish and Ruthenian was part of their job. Ber was a member of this class, being of a wine merchant family. He and his father were fluent in Polish, German, and Hungarian, although at home they spoke Yiddish. A Christian tutor taught the young man Latin, but when his traditional community viewed this with suspicion, Ber was forced to suspend his studies. There was a certain paradox in his situation; those few Jewish men who were able to break through the barriers around them were not necessarily viewed with pride by their coreligionists. Studying secular subjects or too much interaction with the gentiles' world could always raise uncomfortable questions about straying too far from their faith. Nevertheless, Ber's writings show him frequently moving between Jewish and non-Jewish communities, in both private and business matters.

His worries could easily have fit into today's world: an unhappy first marriage, too much business travel, a few bad deals among more successful ones, and complaints about local politics. He was an observant Jew who was not involved in any new religious trends, but because of his education and contacts with gentiles he was clearly ahead of his time. With amazing ease, Ber covered large distances, doing business with Poles, Hungarians, Armenians, and even Greeks. Back home, nobles and the Catholic Church were his key customers. He commonly brought wine and brandy from Hungary, often more than one hundred casks in one arduous trip. Some of it was sold by Ber at fairs in Lwów and other towns, but most shipments from vintage years went to rich nobles. If a Hungarian Tokay, for instance, was to their liking, the nobles would immediately put their own sealing wax on the chosen barrels, not only to claim their purchase but also to prevent any tampering with the precious wine. The rest was often stored in the cellars of the abbeys. If times were tough locally, good wines were shipped to ports on the Baltic Sea and farther on to Germany.

Although Jews lived in proximity to each other, there were no walled ghettos in Galician towns. In fact, where wholesale Jewish merchants, like Ber's family, had guest rooms in their homes, they accommodated not only their brethren but gentiles as well. From time to time, other barriers had been lowered. For

Monks indulging too much in a new shipment of wine.
(Franz Kratter. Briefe über den itzigen Zustand von Galizien. Leipzig 1786.)

instance, Jews who engaged in trade with monks, like Ber of Bolechów, were allowed to live in apartments on the grounds of certain orders, although they were required to enter their lodgings discreetly through separate entrances. Still, in many other respects Jews remained apart from the rest of society.[23]

But the old order governing the lives of Jews and their non-Jewish neighbors was to come rapidly to an end as the events of the second half of the eighteenth century charted a dramatically different path.

Chapter 2

ENTER THE HABSBURGS

$\mathcal{I}$N THE SUMMER OF 1772, General Andreas Hadik of the Habsburg Army led his troops into the Polish-Lithuanian Commonwealth. A Hungarian nobleman, Hadik had distinguished himself in the eyes of his empress, Maria Theresa, when he had occupied and ransomed Berlin fifteen years before. But this time, there would be no military drama punctuated by spectacular sieges of major cities. The "redcoats"—sometimes referred to as the best-dressed army in Europe—advanced steadily through the strange territory. In the troubled south of the disintegrating Polish-Lithuanian Commonwealth, their smaller units had already been operating with impunity for months. Now, twenty-four-thousand strong, the Austrians encountered no military resistance; the power of the Polish king and his government was almost nonexistent there. As one eyewitness described pre-Austrian times, "There was no law or justice in the country, but might was [superior to] right."[1] Soon General Hadik's proclamation, plastered on walls everywhere by the advancing forces, spoke of imperial protection for the land and its citizens. In reality, the Habsburg Monarchy was answering calls from Russia and Prussia to join them in dividing up the chaotic country.

With troops already advancing from the west and from outposts in the south, Austrian diplomats were in a good position to secure a sizeable share of territory when a detailed agreement among the partitioning powers was signed on August 5, 1772, in Saint Petersburg. The situation on the ground, however, remained complex. There were no reliable maps that would chart roads, forests, or the locations of rivers and cities. Whatever old charts there were, it was soon discovered they contained imprecise or even incorrect information; some villages no longer existed, others had never been marked. Later in the month General Hadik received an explicit order from Vienna: "Collect diligently all information and prepare it for the new government of the province."[2]

The lack of reliable maps was only part of the problem. For the past few years, this area had been a playground of many forces. There were armed confederates who roamed the countryside with impunity and pockets of Russian troops, already there for months on an advance mission. If this was not enough to inflict pain on the local populace, "the boldest and most cunning swindlers ... who in other countries had been able to escape the drawn sword of Themis [justice]" were attracted to the troubled land.[3] Stories of violence abounded; some were surely true and others, which were particularly shocking, might have been made up to justify the change of regime. Regardless who was telling the truth, a false move or an overzealous officer could easily have triggered serious unintended consequences. In the end, however, not a single shot was fired at the Austrians; the local population appeared cautious but not uncooperative.

Among the few large cities of the region, historical Kraków was the first to be overrun by one of the big powers. Predictably, it was the Russians, with their forces positioned not too far away, who took control of the city in August of 1772. When Austrian troops appeared, both sides stared at each other with some degree of uneasiness, separated by the Vistula River flowing nearby. Although this time the two—along with the third aggressor, Prussia—had a common goal, the major powers of central Europe had not always been friends. A couple of weeks later, General Hadik's troops entered Lwów[4] from the west, while the Russian regiment—stationed there for the past several years—was quickly leaving the city in the opposite direction. Again there was awkwardness and no joint celebration, but the Austrian military asserted control of the city without trouble. By the end of September 1772 the operation was nearly completed.[5]

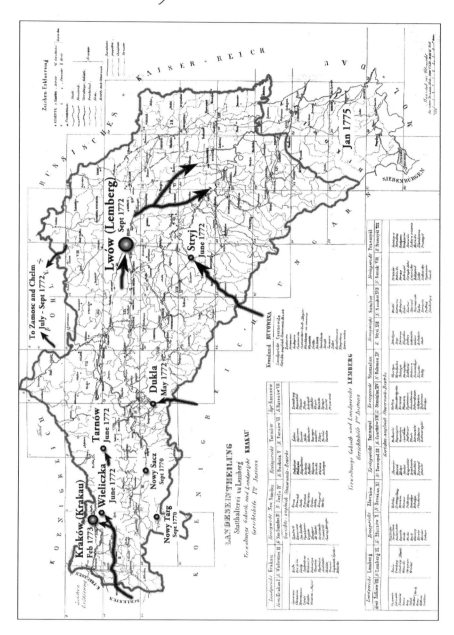

Map of military operations in the southern part of the Polish-Lithuanian Commonwealth that led to the establishment of Austrian Galicia. Between May and September of 1772, Austrian troops marched from Hungary through the Carpathian Mountains and from a small sliver of the territory in southern Poland that had been under Austrian control since 1770, as well as from the west (Austrian Silesia). The future Galician capital, Lwów (Lemberg), was taken by the Austrians on September 15, 1772. Russian troops evacuated Kraków (*Krakau*) on February 15, 1773, when it fell under Austrian sovereignty. The adjoining territory of Bukovina was occupied by the Austrian army in 1774, and formally annexed to the Austrian Monarchy in January 1775. The map shows the borders of the crownland of Galicia (the Kingdom of Galicia and Lodomeria) based on post-1815 status. *(Based on Administrativ-Karte von den Königreichen Galizien und Lodomerien, BL. 49; 1855.)*

In a matter of days, a report was sent from Lwów—now renamed *Lemberg*—to Vienna. "The solemn ceremony to install our new Governor, Count Pergen, will be held tomorrow. The retinue will leave from the Palace of Prince Voivode of Braclaw, where Count Pergen resides, to the cathedral. To this end, the City Council has announced that it will order all guilds [to join] with their flags unfurled; the clergy will also appear with their crosses. Local burghers and the magistrate will accompany the governor from the palace." The walls of the city hall were covered with the edict of Empress Maria Theresa. Its text, printed in German, Latin, and Polish, "to all and everyone watching, reading and listening who ought to know," described Austria's alliance with Russia and Prussia that had redrawn the international borders.

The fait accompli was announced in no uncertain terms. All citizens, without exception, were ordered to accept and obey the new governor, the representative of no less than the royal and imperial Crown. On the designated day, the "Te Deum"—the hymn appropriate for a royal coronation or other similar occasions—was sung in the cathedral, military bands played on the streets, and cannons roared, firing amidst the shouts of, "Long Live Maria Theresa, the Empress, and Joseph II, Our Grace." Indeed, everything seemed to be working out as the new rulers had planned.[6]

Throughout the remaining months of the year, reports from the conquered land trickled slowly to Vienna. Surprisingly, the semiofficial government paper, *Wienerisches Diarium,* put more emphasis on unrelated news from European royal courts; at least, that was what nearly always seemed to populate its front pages. Even when reporting on the unfolding drama of the First Partition of the Polish-Lithuanian Commonwealth, the paper's focus was more on the military and diplomatic activities of Russia and Prussia, while Austrian participation was mentioned in an understated manner. The gloating that had accompanied other conquests was absent. Perhaps Empress Maria Theresa's initial reluctance to take part in this unusual escapade had something to do with the restrained tone. Typically, only a few lines would inform the public about the Austrians taking control of some salt mines and Russian regiments leaving more areas transferred to the Habsburg Monarchy.

Many in Vienna were watching with concern the movements of the Ottoman Turks on the eastern flank of the country. That year more than ever, an attack by Turkish forces could have easily proved disastrous, with the big three powers occupied elsewhere. Luckily for the Habsburgs, nothing happened on the frontier apart from some posturing. By the end of December, a laconic statement had appeared in Vienna that seemed to signal cautious confidence: "Austrians have an accurate record of the people in their share of Poland; as it is customary in other imperial Hereditary Lands [of the Monarchy], everything there is being set up in the right manner."[7]

After some deliberations among court officials about what to do with the new territory, Emperor Joseph II, the son of Maria Theresa and co-regent, prevailed in his demands to incorporate it into the Habsburg Monarchy. To preserve at least some appearance of justice in international affairs, the crown promptly published the fifty-eight-page "Evidence for the Rights of the Hungarian Crown to Red Rus' and Podolia and [the Rights of] the Bohemian Crown to the Principalities of Oświecim and Zator," which was intended to satisfy those who cared about such things. With this formality completed, Empress Maria Theresa, as Queen of Hungary, could claim historical rights to the Kingdom of Galicia and Lodomeria (*Königreiche Galizien und Lodomerien*).

In reality, the official position of the Habsburgs was paper-thin. Historical justification for the so-called "Reclaiming" (*Revindicirung*) had simply been invented. It did not matter that the borders of the new Austrian Galicia were quite different from those of the historical principality of Red Rus' (known by its Latinized name, Galicia), or that any links between the eastern part of that area and the Kingdom of Hungary only dated back to a short-lived Hungarian hegemony of the fourteenth century. Regardless of how dubious those claims were, they seemed only to breed speculation about whether the territory would soon be incorporated into the Habsburgs' Hungary. For the first months, however, the new area of Austrian control would carry no particular name in the Viennese press, being simply referred to as a province; the term "Galicia" was only used in government papers.

Prussia soon followed suit and issued her own tortuous document, spiked with historical details, dates, and genealogical charts, to justify the new military acquisitions. The document was officially named "The Execution of the Rights of His Grace, the Majesty King of Prussia to the Duchy of Pomerania and Other Lands of the Polish Kingdom; with arguments." The document was also reprinted in the official governmental newspaper in Vienna. (Because of its length, it had to be spread through many issues.) Only the regime of Empress Catherine the Great did not bother with such superfluous formalities to legitimize the expansion of her Russian Empire.[8]

Despite apparent calm in Galicia, reports from the governor and the old military commander General Hadik, who had skillfully managed the campaign in the previous summer, did not sit well with thirty-one-year-old Emperor Joseph II. He could not resist the urge to see firsthand his new crownland. In February 1773 the emperor wrote to his closest military advisor about an upcoming trip there. The restless monarch soon expanded plans for a limited visit. In matters of state, Joseph II trusted his own judgment more than that of anyone else, even his most experienced advisors. He believed deeply in his destined right to chart the course of the Habsburg Monarchy and its subjects. In the past, there had been outbursts of discontent, leading to copious correspondence between Joseph and his mother, who could generally temper her son's excesses when it came to his impatient ideas on ways the Monarchy should change direction. She was the one who still had the upper hand in serious matters, while her son was waiting for his turn. But when it came to Galicia, Joseph had a vision, a sense of direction, and would not be dissuaded.

Still, Maria Theresa pleaded with her son to delay his imperial trip for at least a year. In June 1773 she wrote, "How would you manage a crisis if you are there? Neither the [Russian] Tsarina nor the Prussian King have ventured into their new territories yet." But her arguments—that the final treaty had not been signed, nor had the local population sworn an oath of allegiance to the Habsburgs—were ignored. Resigned to her son's decision, Maria Theresa wrote to a family member, "The journey of the emperor has cost me at least ten years

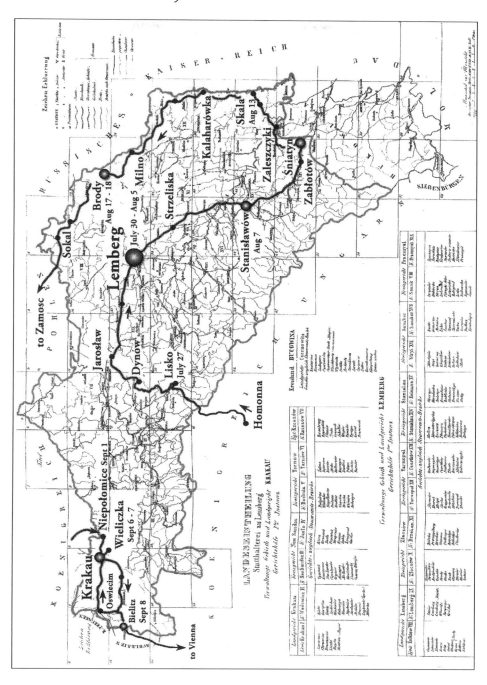

Map of the first imperial tour through Galicia made by Emperor Joseph II between July and September 1773. Joseph II was an early advocate of securing Galician territory as a separate crownland for the Habsburg Monarchy. He took a deep interest in the new province, visiting Galicia in 1773, 1780, 1783, 1786, and 1787. *(Based on Administrativ-Karte von den Königreichen Galizien und Lodomerien, BL. 49; 1855.)*

of my life. He wants to take a route on to [former] Poland and return home by Moravia. He will be tired too much and will feel it in the aftermath; in a few years, he will be an old and broken man."[9]

As for any sensitivity concerning the inhabitants of the newly conquered province, the emperor himself wrote with brutal honesty, "This [visit] is the only assistance I can offer [them] … given their unfortunate situation, there is no other solution [than to accept the new status quo]."

With a typical disdain for pomp, Joseph launched his first fact-finding mission to Galicia with only a small support staff. General Hadik was ordered to await him in Lemberg (Lwów), but was warned not to set in motion any excessive preparations for the emperor's arrival. The traveling party was puny compared to previous court expeditions. The emperor of the Holy Roman Empire and co-regent of the Austrian Monarchy traveled with only six carriages, surrounded by eight mounted soldiers. In July 1773 he left the safety and familiarity of the Hungarian region of the Monarchy, entering a land in which loyalty to him was uncertain at best. But that seems not to have bothered Joseph II at all. At each of the "night stations" where he was to take a rest, he ordered the posting of a single officer with some thirty soldiers. These men were also to provide light patrols in densely forested areas and other potentially dangerous places along the route, more to assure that the tour would proceed on schedule than from any fear of hostilities. Although Galicia's roads were poor and few, Joseph II, with his unbounded energy and hands-on attitude, set a grueling schedule, pushing from one night station to another.

Many years later, a certain Galician eyewitness recalled that there had been no secrecy at all surrounding Joseph II's visit. In that man's town, no one was talking about anything but the emperor, his alleged jokes, and his expected reforms for Galicia. When Joseph was finally within sight, calls erupted in the crowd: "The Emperor! The Emperor!" He was described as being built on "not too large a frame, with a long face not revealing too much, [and] quite energetic body movements. He was dressed in the ordinary red military uniform of a general; his hair was powdered and covered with a triangular hat."[10]

When the emperor reached Lemberg (Lwów), he surprised quite a few in the crowd when, half-jokingly, he reacted to the effusive welcome of the townspeople: "Gentlemen, wait! You don't know yet to whom you belong!" He was much less circumspect when demanding precise information about Galician affairs from his own administration. The emperor's headquarters were modest, in the house of a local pharmacist. From there, he would write his mother about the immense work lying ahead. "The country [of Galicia] seems full of good will; the peasant is the most unfortunate as he owns nothing but his exterior physique. The little nobleman is also poor, but he hopes much for the justice that you will grant him against the big [aristocrats] who suppress him. The aristocrats, however, are dissatisfied [with the new regime], but they put a good face for now."

The six days that Joseph spent in Lemberg (Lwów) were busy. There were many consultations with the governor. It quickly became apparent that public matters were not being taken care of with the urgency needed to remake Galicia. Then, the quality of the administrators—a strange collection of adventurers and unhappy bureaucrats, who pitied themselves for being banished to a strange land—did not instill much confidence in the emperor. To top it off, he seriously doubted whether Count Pergen had the talents to fully implement the government's orders, rather than simply pay lip service to instructions from Vienna. A voluminous handwritten memorandum on Galicia, assiduously prepared by the governor, did not improve matters;

IOH: AN T. ᴅᴇꜱ H.R.R.   GRAF ᴠɴᴅ HERR
ᴠᴏɴ PERGEN, K: K: STAATS. MINISTER.

Johann Anton Pergen (1725–1814), the first governor of Galicia, served from October 1772 to January 1774 in Lemberg (Lwów). Pergen was an experienced diplomat, former deputy foreign minister, and the architect of a system of educational reform for the Austrian Monarchy that placed responsibility for teaching in the hands of the laity.
(Courtesy of the Austrian National Library, Vienna.)

its two hundred forty-four pages, with more than one-hundred-twenty tables, did not seem to quell the impatient mood of the action-hungry emperor.[11]

Joseph was not easy on the governor when writing to Maria Theresa: "You threw Count Pergen here but he does not seem to be hardworking enough.... He's a little idealistic, has large charts, which all, like he, convey one after another wrong [message]; but you get the same slant [from them all]. He wants to do everything alone and takes on a lot, but in the end he does not [finish]. I do not know if his genius and talents are so great, if they cannot be applied to the otherwise conventional regulations, security, and precision [of doing official business]."

Feeling that Pergen would have to be sacked in the not-too-distant future, Joseph, with his usual attention to detail, began looking around for the right candidate for the post. "There must be a man here to see," he wrote, "with the knowledge of our institutions, of the right maturity, disinterested [in personal gains], honest, with a meticulous attitude toward subordinates, and active." He considered General Hadik, who was already in Galicia. Yes, he was a hardened military man, but in the eyes of the emperor he possessed all the needed skills and honesty to serve in the civil government. Yet, it did not evade Joseph while in Lemberg (Lwów) that the wife of the general was a real power in the Hadik household. Would she, he wondered, extend her unwelcomed influences in public affairs through her docile husband? There was also the general's Hungarian pedigree, which, the emperor felt, could send a wrong message about the future of Galicia. In private, Joseph was blunt, wanting to quash any lingering rumors that the new province would be ever absorbed into the Hungarian part of the Monarchy.[12]

After years of neglect, Lemberg (Lwów) was not pretty. Many of its houses were on the verge of collapse. Most ordinary buildings had two, three, or four owners, so little was done about repairs. Some had a few rooms on the ground floor or a single vaulted chamber, while others had only a usable cellar or a stable. In some places, even walking could be a challenge; all kinds of rubbish was freely dumped and piled on the streets, and the pavements had almost more pits than cobblestones. The city boasted a number of old churches and was surrounded by fortress-like monasteries spaced several hundred paces from each other. But the emperor did not likely spend much time touring them, being always wary of the overbearing influence of the Catholic Church. In the old Jewish district, a hidden treasure, the Golden Rose Synagogue, was easy to miss, with its entrance obscured in the surrounding congestion. The city was choking, still surrounded by its medieval walls. Just outside those walls, now-useless moats collected only sewage and dirty water, with a stench that became oppressive from early spring until fall.[13]

The mood of the important traveler could not have been improved when his imperial carriage with six horses became stuck one day on a street covered in mud, after a major downpour. But a big reprieve came when the emperor left the noise and dirt of Lemberg (Lwów) for the surrounding hills. Those tired of the city could not resist being enchanted with the scenery. A few years after the monarch's visit, another traveler retraced the steps of Joseph II to a place in the hills where he had once stood. As he described it, "One side has an overall view of the entire area around the city and the other gives a glimpse of a valley of immense beauty, covered with flowers, in an indescribable harmony of colors.... All the beauty of Eden stands here in its full greatness." Certainly, this visitor was not alone in his impressions about the place. The drawings and etchings sent back to Vienna often featured vistas of the gentle elevations and trails, with the town seen in the background. Even thirty years later, someone else spoke in exalted terms of the same spot: "I cannot hide my feelings … when I look down the hill. Little houses lie dispersed among the green areas, while at the same time, the fields are separated from the hills in the distance. The whole of nature, when one goes there in the morning, seems to quietly celebrate this magnificent scene. This garden is basically nothing but a quiet forest. [Being here, you have] escaped the city noise through a small footpath."[14]

For the restless Joseph II, however, there was little time for leisure; much remained to be done in Galicia to make it a part of the Monarchy. There was one task that the emperor felt obliged to discharge on the spot. According to the original announcement by the three partitioning powers, which had been repeated in Maria Theresa's edict to the people of Galicia, the new province's eastern border was to run along a small river by the name of "the Podhorce." This had seemed to be nothing unusual, and no one had objected to it. There was only one problem; a river or even a stream by that name could not be found anywhere. True to his nature, Joseph took the initiative to resolve this situation. The imperial party traveled south of Lemberg (Lwów), through some areas where carriages could be driven and others that were passable only on horseback. He looked curiously across the river Prut into the wooded territory called Bukovina that was under nominal control

The coat of arms of Galicia, the Austrian crownland (1772–1918).

of the Ottoman Turks. How important, he thought, that land could be for connecting Galicia with the rest of the country! After a few days of inspecting Galicia's eastern frontiers, the emperor reached the river Zbrucz, which cut through a fertile plain. Joseph decreed that this was the place where the Austrian Monarchy would end and the Russian Empire begin. After all the diplomatic wranglings in faraway capitals and subsequent troop movements, it was Joseph who had the final say on the issue of the borders of Galicia, at least for a while.

In mid-September, after six weeks of crisscrossing the province, Joseph returned to Vienna more determined than ever that Galicia was to remain in Habsburg hands.[15] The new map of the farthest corner of the province, the one adjoining Hungary and the Turkish-controlled lands (including Bukovina), seems to have been prepared within days of his return. The reason for this rush would soon be understood. One year later, Austrian troops would fulfill the emperor's wishes, entering Bukovina; the path toward wresting its control from the Ottoman Turks was clear.

After the emperor's return to Vienna, additional surveys of Galicia were promptly ordered and placed in the hands of the military. Imperial instructions to the new crownland, often including handwritten notes from Joseph himself, would now flow voluminously. The Galician governor, Count Pergen, who might have thought that the emperor's departure would signal some reprieve from his job's pressure, was in for some disappointment. Within weeks, the governor was put to work providing answers to one hundred and fifty-four questions stemming from the inspection tour. Any talk of making Galicia part of Hungary was put irrevocably to rest, and in a short time, many other ways of improving oversight of his new possession would be set in motion at Joseph's insistence.[16]

There was one more piece of business, symbolic though it was, that became official a few days after the emperor's return home. On September 18, 1773, almost exactly one year after General Hadik had entered Lwów, this final formality was completed. A treaty between "The Most Gracious Empress Apostolic Queen of Hungary and Bohemia, Queen of Her Hereditary Successions and of all Her Countries" and "The Most Gracious King of Poland and Great Duke of Lithuania" was signed, confirming the reality of Habsburg Galicia on the ground.

🕭

WHAT TRAVELING AUSTRIAN OFFICIALS soon encountered was a land different from any other place in the Monarchy. The difference encompassed more than the landscape, later to be described by some of these visitors as "beautiful, fertile and … expansive" despite the poverty of many of its inhabitants. Arriving from the southwest and proceeding on the few available roads deeper into the province, the officials must have noticed that the farther east they went, the greater were the swaths of territory belonging to Polish land magnates who exercised absolute control over those who lived there. However, the rule of the magnates over their vast domains was not that surprising. In the Austrian Monarchy, the landed aristocracy in the crown lands of Hungary, Bohemia and Bavaria had also tried, albeit less successfully, to push the boundaries of their influence, and they still ruled over their own semi-feudal fiefdoms.

At first, it was not easy for the occupying force of Galicia to communicate with the locals, but the variety of spoken languages there was nothing new either. The Monarchy was already a conglomerate of German, Hungarian, Italian, and Slavic populations; one more conquest of a non-German-speaking people did not seem that extraordinary. As the occupiers progressed through their new land, they observed that a few places in the western part of Galicia showed a conspicuous absence of Israelites, and probably not by chance. Along a major road that linked Moravia and Bohemia with Galicia, there were some towns with a total absence of Jewish names among house owners, craftsmen, and even tavern keepers.[17] But the picture in the eastern part of Galicia could not have been more different. What surprised the imperial army and the new administrators was the size of the local Jewish population; they had simply never seen anything like it. There, virtually no town was without a substantial number of Jews, who had been encouraged to live there for centuries by the land magnates. In the eyes of one attentive Austrian traveler, some places looked almost exclusively Jewish, except for a handful of gentile shoemakers and weavers

A Jew from Galicia. Drawing from a publication by the Austrian physician, Balthazar Hacquet, professor of natural history in the Josephinian University of Lemberg (Lwów) 1787–1805. Hacquet had broad interests in chemistry, botany, and ethnography. *(Courtesy of the Austrian National Library, Vienna.)*

"hardly distinguished by a better shirt" from the poor peasants. When the first census of the new crownland was compiled, Maria Theresa's regime found more than two hundred twenty thousand Jews residing there, more than in the rest of the Monarchy combined. For the staunchly Catholic empress, this was certainly shocking.[18] It was undoubtedly quite a different picture from the central lands of the Monarchy, where Jews, and sometimes the even more distrusted Protestants, were only accepted in some places and forbidden to live elsewhere.

As if this was not enough, the reports by bureaucrats "exiled" to the province fueled government suspicions that many Jews had avoided registering their presence for superstitious reasons (or more likely, fear of taxes). Their repeated communiqués, frequently sent to the Court Chancellery in Vienna, warned that the numbers of Jews in Galicia could be even higher than reported. Yet even this was not the most shocking thing. Maria Theresa—who in the past had exiled a few thousand Jews from Prague (only to reverse her decision four years later, realizing life there had been crippled by her action)—must have been alarmed to hear news of Galicia's synagogues and Jewish schools operating in the open. In fact, the province had more than two hundred synagogues. How different a picture that was when compared with Vienna; there, a small and affluent Jewish community was not allowed to build a synagogue or even open a school. Under the empress, worship by non-Catholics in the imperial capital had to be discreet, and was mainly conducted in homes.[19] However, while touring Galicia the somewhat more tolerant Joseph II had been unable to resist chastising his mother. "Scattered in all countries," he told her, "the Jews here have as many synagogues as they ever want.... Toleration of these people is not harmful to the country...."[20] The Jewish community of Galicia was certainly large, but it was in a sorry state when the first Austrian governor took his seat in Lemberg (Lwów). Their legislative and executive body, the Council of Four Lands (*Va'ad*), had been dissolved by the Polish authorities almost ten years before. During the prior two centuries, that body had negotiated with the royal treasury to determine the overall amount of taxes owed by Jews living there. Who paid what had then been left to the Jewish assemblies to decide. Now, a fixed poll tax was levied on all Jews, regardless of income, and authority for collecting it had been placed outside the Jewish authorities (*kahals*).

Besides purely fiscal considerations, others saw more nefarious reasons for stripping Jews of their autonomy in the years leading to the First Partition. In a theme that was to repeat itself time after time, Jews were blamed for many of the country's ills. Their supposed influence—stories of alleged Jewish bribes of national deputies were repeated through often near incomprehensible rants and rumors amongst the populace—obscured the real cause of legislative paralysis in the Polish-Lithuanian Commonwealth. This had become one more factor that led the region to be seen as ungovernable.

At the time of the First Partition, permanent legislative stalemate had reigned in the Commonwealth. Its laws, which guarded the interests of the conservative nobility, stated that any session of the national assembly (*diet*) could be terminated by any deputy or senator by simply rising and exclaiming, "I disapprove." In the political climate of the time, one of internal strife and foreign meddling, nothing could be agreed on. Yet Jews were still often blamed for behind-the-scenes manipulation of these disorderly noblemen.[21]

To make matters worse, by then the economy of the entire region had been sliding downward for years. Slowly, the Polish-Lithuanian Commonwealth had been seriously weakened by counterfeit coins minted in Prussia. In an insidious scheme of economic warfare instigated from abroad, the fake guldens, which had a lower silver content than the real coins, led to spiraling prices. A confusing state of affairs—with old and new guldens—hampered trade and brought credit into short supply. Many Jewish *kahals*, which had traditionally played the role of local banks, became insolvent. With that ancient vestige of Jewish autonomy gone, Jewish localities were now only loosely connected with each other, and ridden with debt.

In their letters or memoirs, gentiles generally painted, with the same brush, a superficial picture of Galician Jews. Whether it was their dress, their language, or their typical occupations, Jews all seemed to look the same to them. Many Jews of Galicia were poor, but a frequently used stereotype linked all Jews to unjust entrepreneurship. "It is not rare that a peasant, with a sunken melancholy on his face, is seen on foot," one author lamented, "and a Jew in black clothes, a man of lively imagination who goes this way on horseback, brings a serious reflection on the state of the Christian and the Jewish people...." However, in many matters, including those of trade and business, Galicia's different Israelite communities were certainly not the same.

In one small town, Nadwórna, local Jews were recognized by an early Austrian visitor for their commercial operations "over a wide radius" of Galicia. They handled, he noted: "grain, wine, spirits, honey, wax, leather, fur, flax, cloth, fish, and other products." But in another place, the traveler met an even more interesting trader. With obvious envy, the Austrian recorded that one Jewish businessman had returned after a delivery of locally woven products ("two thousand pieces of sack or burlap") to markets as distant as Danzig on the Baltic Coast, more than five hundred miles away. Yet prosperity was not guaranteed in eastern Galicia. In the nearby town of Bohorodczany, for instance, flax weavers bitterly complained about their Jewish neighbors who, they said, "put not enough energy into [market] speculation" and caused their income to drop.[22]

In the countryside, the thinly spread villages and towns could not function without the Jewish leaseholders of the mills, taverns, and fishing ponds, as well as cattle traders, moneylenders, and shopkeepers. The complicated system of leases and an almost endless chain of subleases on various estates kept the local economy functioning. A governor of Galicia once remarked that, in "old times" (that is, before Austrian sovereignty had extended over Galicia), any community became a town or townlet when the first ten or twelve Jewish families moved into modest wooden houses.[23] Putting it simply, without the Jews the landed aristocracy would have been unable to collect any profits, regardless of how fertile the soil.

But standing between the owner or his steward and everyone else had some unintended consequences. Traditional Jewish roles in buying and selling products at profit, the involvement in alcohol distribution—virtually all taverns and inns were under Jewish ownership in eastern Galicia—or extracting rents from Ruthenian serfs and Polish peasants, could easily bring resentment. The Jews' place in village economies created stereotypes with which future generations would have to cope.

⟋

AT THE BEHEST OF the empress, newly arriving Austrian administrators resorted at first to draconian steps to limit the number of Jews in Galicia. Shortly after the edict annexing the territory, a law was passed in the name of Empress Maria Theresa to curtail Jewish marriages. In March 1773 Jews were instructed that marriages were forbidden without prior approval by local civil authorities and payment of a steep marriage tax. She had "learned from the submitted

I.

Iterato Judæis sine Consensu matrimonia inire rigorose prohibetur.

NOS MARIA THERESIA DEI GRATIA, ROMANORUM IMPERATRIX &c.

Notum facimus omnibus, quorum interest.

axima cum offensione Nostra percepimus, quosdam Judæos inscio Rabino, & Nostro consensu destitutos in fraudem Litterarum Nostrarum patentalium die 8va Martii a. c. circa nuptias Judaicas editarum matrimonia inire, perindeque ultro se, uti temerarios mandati Nostri transgressores, rigorosissimorum suppliciorum reos reddere.

Cum autem causa hujus transgressionis mandatorum Nostrorum ex eo oriri possit, quod Judæi hucusque ante Celebrationem nuptiarum apud Dominium Territoriale neque se insinuare solent, neque unquam moris fuisse fertur, Nostra vero plurimum intersit, ut præfatæ Litteræ universales in posterum accuratissimæ executioni mandentur, atque Contraventionibus tam temerariis undique via præcludatur.

Idcirco omnibus Dominiis Territorialibus, Magistratibus & Æconomis Regnorum Galiciæ & Lodomeriæ, ubi Judæi existunt, & tolerantur, severe mandamus, ut omni cum solicitudine exactæ Executioni mandati Nostri sæpius memorati invigilent, Judæos vero omnes, & singulos serio adstringant, ut quilibet desiderium matrimonium ineundi Dominio suo Territoriali indicet, de Testimonio ejusdem sibi prospiciat idque demum una cum attestato Rabini humillimæ instantiæ suæ pro impetrando Consensu Nostro afferat. Datum Leopoli 28. Junii 1773.

S. R. I. COMES à PERGEN.

A   I.

Edict issued in the name of Empress Maria Theresa concerning Jewish marriages in Galicia. Full text in the Appendix. *(Continuatio Edictorum et Mandatorum Universalium in Regnis Galiciæ et Lodomeriæ. A Die 28. Mensis Junii Anno 1773. Emanatorum. Leopoli 1774.)*

documents and other reliable information," the empress said to justify her action, "that early marriages, numerous marriages, and the tremendous growth of families have led to the poor economic state of the Jews." Apparently feeling this was not enough, Maria Theresa issued another edict three months later, which sternly warned rabbis to follow the law or face serious consequences.[24] A few years after that, she declared again: "It shall not be allowed, under threat of the prescribed penalties listed below, for any Jew to marry before he has reliably proven the true amount of his financial assets, according to the previously approved regulations, received permission from the imperial and royal governing body, and paid the appropriate fee.... The punishment of expulsion from the country for Jews who marry without consent, and synagogue leaders who take part ... shall remain unchanged in the future."[25]

Bad laws bred only more bureaucratic obsession with how to deal with the "problem" of Jewish marriages. Behind-the-scene proposals between Lemberg (Lwów) and Vienna continued to be exchanged; they talked about letting only the oldest son from any Jewish family be eligible to marry (similar to the situation in Bohemia), or setting up a threshold of required wealth below which no Jew could marry. Luckily, none of those even more extreme examples of population engineering progressed any further.

As to Maria Theresa, she had been partially right in worrying if the marriage edict was being obeyed, despite its stern language. In reality, most Jewish couples in Galicia could not afford a fee, and continued to marry in religious ceremonies without the required licenses. For countless couples of limited means, this seemed the only practical way to start a new family.

Fortunately, the Jewish marriage law was not always enforced. In fact, some district bureaucrats actually demanded a lowering of that tax, but not based on troubled consciences. Instead, they lamented that the number of marriage applications among Jews was dropping, reducing state income. On other occasions, the issue would resurface with dire consequences. For instance, when a new batch of (gentile) colonists from Germany arrived, an overzealous local official could suddenly dust off the marriage law as a pretext to force "illegally"

Juifs de la Galice.

Jews of Galicia. Drawing of a Jewish couple from the vicinity of Brody, circa 1821. Emperor Joseph II visited that predominantly Jewish town twice during his tours of Galicia in 1773 and 1780. His imperial edict declared Brody a Free Mercantile City, exempt from the commercial tariffs of Galicia. This special status was effective between 1779 and 1879.
(Courtesy of the Centre for Documentation of Borderland Cultures, Sejny, Poland.)

married Jews to vacate their homes for the newcomers.[26]

There were occasional gestures toward the Jewish community. When Joseph II, on his first inspection tour, visited the overwhelmingly Jewish town of Brody, he was famously said to remark: "Now, it is clear why I am chosen to be the king of Jerusalem." But he was only half-joking, since the Habsburgs had, in fact, carried such a title, among many others, since the time of the Crusades.

On a more pragmatic level, the Court Chancellery surely must have noticed that the merchants of Brody had unusually wide-ranging business contacts. The administration was told the reason: thirty years before, when the citizens of the town had received a loan to rebuild their community after a devastating fire, "they immediately dispersed over all the cities and lands of Europe, wherever there were good tradesmen and merchandise. They went to harbors and commercial centers, and for many years engaged in trade with the help of this large fund…. In this way the merchants of Brody became great, multiplied, and were strengthened in all the commerce of the world."[27]

The achievements of Brody were not lost on Joseph II. A few years after his visit, a special imperial privilege was bestowed on that community. Their town, with its nine-thousand-strong Jewish presence, was declared a Free Mercantile City, similar to the tariff-free ports situated on the Adriatic coast. This experiment worked well for the landlocked town. In contrast with the rest of Galicia, which continued to struggle economically, commercial and educational institutions flourished in Brody. Large trading companies, mainly in Jewish hands, received permission for almost unobstructed trade with any city of Europe and beyond. The traders brought silk, cotton, and fine articles of clothing from German towns; pricey coral and dyed fabrics arrived from Italy, tea and sugar from Russia. Despite frequent political and military frictions between the Austrian Monarchy and the Turks, Brody was encouraged to import goods duty-free from the Ottoman Empire and other Asian routes. Unimpeded trade in grain, cattle, and exotic imports from the Turks ultimately made the trading profits of Brody equal to that of all the rest of Galicia. When, a few years after the emperor's visit, a foreign traveler stumbled upon this town, he wrote a glowing report. But clearly his enthusiasm was not about its architecture, which he called "a collection of shapeless wooden buildings." Instead, the visitor exclaimed at the end, "Why could all of Galicia not develop industries as was achieved in the mercantile city of Brody?"[28]

Other official concessions to the Jews of Galicia concerned the appalling practice of baptizing Jewish children. Certainly, that was not a new issue. In 1747, a bulla issued by Pope Benedict XIV had unambiguously declared, "It is unlawful to baptize Hebrew children against the will of their parents." In the eyes of the Catholic Church, such acts were considered "against natural law," but they apparently occurred in more than one region. Particularly egregious were cases of infants being removed from their parents after being baptized.

Now, in a rare nod toward Jews, the Galician governor acknowledged, "Local Jewry that remains under the Monarch's protection brought several justified complaints, asking for solutions in this matter." His manifesto, issued in 1775 in the name of the Empress, forbade such practices under threat of financial penalties and two-year imprisonment. Every citizen of Galicia was warned about the ban, and Catholic bishops were ordered to instruct their clergy about the new law. But even then some loopholes, difficult to understand today, were retained. A midwife or any other layperson witnessing a child's birth was allowed to have the infant baptized if it was deemed to be in imminent risk of dying. Most horrific was the instruction that if the baby ultimately recovered, it was to be taken from the

Reconstructed details from the Chodorów
Synagogue in Galicia, depicting the Zodiac
signs of Leo, Gemini, and Pisces.
*(Courtesy of Beit Hatfutsot, the Museum of
the Jewish People, Tel Aviv, Israel.)*

parents and raised in a Christian home.
To add to the insult, in such a case the
biological parents would be obligated to
provide support for the child's rearing.
In another clause of the manifesto, any
Jewish child reaching the age of seven
could in theory demand baptism against
the will of its parents or guardians. How
often this and other exceptions to the
ban were utilized is unclear today, but
obviously another way to challenge
Jews' rights had sneaked into the law.[29]

There were so many differences
between the Jews of the new crownland and those in other provinces of
the Monarchy, who enjoyed even fewer
rights, that the Bohemian-Austrian
Court Chancellery in Vienna felt compelled to introduce Jewish Regulations
(*Judenordnung*) for Galicia in 1776.[30]
This was a lengthy and dry document;
aspirational goals to incorporate Jews
into civil society were glaringly absent.
The progressive thoughts of Joseph II
were not ready for their unveiling yet.
Instead, the spirit and the letter of the
new law reinforced limitations on Jews
within their own communities. The empress's edict acknowledged that in the
process of "reclaiming" possession of
the Kingdom of Galicia and Lodomeria,
the Jewish population had been found

in a state of extreme disarray. Yet the "solution" imposed was to keep Jews separate in many respects, with their own jurisdiction, education, and special taxation. A chief rabbi and Jewish general administration were put in place to implement directives of the imperial bureaucracy.

In contrast to their brethren from the central lands of the Monarchy, Galician Jews were allowed to hold prayers and to observe their customs openly in the existing synagogues. Yet even there some limitations would apply. No congregation was allowed "under threat of the most serious punishment, to undertake to replace the roof of their synagogue, school, or house of prayer, to repair it, to expand it, or even to build it again from the ground up" without governmental permission. In secular matters, Galician Jews were declared free to practice their professions as they wished, offering their services to all regardless of religion. Yet again, nothing was free of exceptions; where Christian tradesmen or craftsmen were engaged in the same activities, Jews could work only for other Jews. There were limits to Maria Theresa's "protection" even in faraway Galicia.

The poll tax paid by every Jew had already been doubled in 1774, and was now renamed a "toleration" tax; to secure more money an income tax was added.[31] Under the pretext of preventing impoverished Jews from coming to Galicia, Maria Theresa now wielded another tool to deal with the size of Galicia's Jewish population. The provisions of the law made no room for those unable to meet financial obligations, regardless of whether they came from within or outside of the Monarchy. "So that the country, in accordance with the intention of the most high [Empress], may be cleansed of the swarm of *Betteljuden* [poor Jews, literally "begging Jews"], the leaders of each community, under threat of severe physical punishment, must take the greatest care that wandering foreign, lazy, and begging Jews, and in general the disorderly rabble, is not allowed to stay anywhere, but rather that any such foreign *Betteljuden* who let themselves be seen are immediately held, and turned over to the appropriate ... government office for further action. In accordance with this, it is decreed as a law that all Jews who are not able to pay in cash a total of 4 *fl. Rheinisch* in contributions for the *Toleranz* [tolerance contribution] and the levied personal property tax, and for the contribution to the community, shall immediately be considered to be *Betteljuden*, and shall not be tolerated in the country."

Although Galician Jews were theoretically governed by their own leaders, it was far from a true autonomy. The reorganized Jewish communities were ordered to send quarterly, to the governmental offices, lists of those delinquent in taxes. In some places, financially secure members paid taxes for others to prevent reprisals. The fate of those who made it onto the delinquent list could be dire; the law was clear that "such *Betteljuden* which are reported ... must be taken out of the country." Deportations to no-man's-lands between the Monarchy and bordering countries were not unheard of. Even those who under different circumstances were not known for sympathy toward the Jews, were horrified, recalling the sight of horse-drawn wagons full of half-clothed poor being driven in the midst of the winter to the frontier. One eyewitness exclaimed: "What a barbaric treatment! ... The sun rises over them the same way as over the others! How should Jewish people feel in their hearts, if their homeland turns against them?"[32]

No one was happy with the status quo, neither the Jews nor their neighbors. More progressive observers of life in Galicia pointed to the paradox of the Jewish Regulations (*Judenordnung*) of 1776, which had made Jews more separate from the rest of the society, rather than making their integration easier. Soon, opinions were being voiced that with the exception of religion, which ought to be outside of government interference, Jews should have the same privileges as everyone else. A district official from one Galician town made a particularly strong argument in favor of rethinking state policy toward them. His views, now partially obscured by the passage of time, seemed to invoke basic human decency; they were also pragmatic, since such draconian laws were not enforceable in many places.[33]

Over the years, the Court Chancellery and the State Council (*Staatsrath*) in Vienna would return to the topic of Galician Jews several times. It was not long before questions started to arise in the highest echelons of the bureaucracy about whether the order of Maria Theresa to expel poor Jews was still applicable; some councilors openly stated their objections to continuation of these practices. At that time, however, Emperor Joseph II's stand would not support those who advocated leniency. In fact, his orders were explicit: poor Jews must be removed from Galicia, or at the very least, their growth should be contained.[34]

Yet in private, the emperor questioned the practices of his mother in regard to non-Catholics. His arguments about Jews or Protestants were less in terms of human compassion—privately, he did not hesitate to express his prejudices—and more about the state-sanctioned exclusion of potentially productive segments of society. When in 1777 Maria Theresa tried to issue orders that, "in the future no Jews, of whatever reputation, are to be permitted to remain [in Vienna] without my written permission," followed by her highly prejudicial views, Joseph would not remain silent. The same month he wrote to his mother, as though foretelling his intentions: "Half measures don't square with my principles. There must be either complete freedom of worship, or you must expatriate everyone who doesn't believe as you do…. So long as the state is served, the laws of nature and society observed … what ground do you have for interference?"[35]

Despite all the contradictions in the emperor's attitude toward Jews, there were signs that a big wave of change was coming to Galicia.

Chapter 3

NEW RIGHTS FOR JEWS

*A*RRANGEMENTS FOR A SECOND IMPERIAL trip to Galicia unfolded early in 1780. This time it was to be combined with an inspection of Bukovina. As before, there were weeks of planning; Joseph II drew up his own itinerary, calling it, in military style, a "marching route," with, predictably, the same grueling schedule as before. There was, however, an additional twist to the emperor's return to Galicia. When he learned that Catherine the Great was planning her own trip to the adjoining province of her Russian Empire, Joseph II decided to take this opportunity to meet with the empress. Hearing of this, Maria Theresa thought at first he was joking. Sovereigns in that era did not have rendezvous often, and certainly not in places like uncivilized parts of Russia; for such meetings they could use their emissaries. But seeing how serious her son was, Maria Theresa quickly grew concerned. When a positive response from Saint Petersburg arrived, she wrote to one of her trusted ambassadors: "This is new proof of how little able I am to put a stop to the ideas of my son, even though I will be always included in the censure [if things go wrong]." With the departure day approaching, she exclaimed, perhaps more like a typical mother than the powerful ruler of the Austrian Monarchy: "Changes happen every moment; there were already three marching routes.... I confess this journey gives me grief. I feel very depressed."[1]

Galician Portraits

On May 3, 1780, Joseph II's small retinue entered Galicia from Moravia, then progressed rapidly, reaching Lemberg (Lwów) in less than two weeks. He found the new governor of Galicia, Joseph Brigido, well informed, and the emperor praised his work. Brigido was of Italian descent and would ultimately garner qualified respect among the locals, who typically looked with distrust at anyone sent from Vienna. Always a staunch supporter of the emperor's policies, Brigido turned out to be more skillful than his predecessors in balancing official duties with sensitivities in the crownland. As for other civil servants, the emperor's feelings were mixed. "For God's sake," he wrote his mother from Lemberg (Lwów), "don't send any more Germans here." To assuage lingering sensitivities toward Habsburg's rule, his preference was to employ civil servants drawn from other parts of the Monarchy. He also floated the idea of local nobility serving in judicial posts.[2]

After a few days of audiences and preparations for the next leg of the trip, Joseph II left for the predominantly Jewish town of Brody. There, he inspected the citadel and other military installations. Without a doubt, Brigido's personal ties with commercially thriving Trieste on the Adriatic only intensified the emperor's hopes for a similar success with Galician Brody. The town's recently approved, unique status as a Free Mercantile City was surely a topic of their conversations before the emperor crossed into the vast Russian interior.[3]

To make his journey simpler, Joseph traveled to the meeting with Catherine as a private citizen. Under the name Count Falkenstein, he could move more quickly, choosing shorter routes, albeit less comfortable ones. The talks between the sovereigns went well, especially since Joseph offered his tacit support for the Russian ruler's expansion policy. Always ready to learn something new, Joseph accepted the Russian empress's hospitality, extending his travels in Russia for several weeks. Catherine wrote after their encounter: "If I were to begin singing his praises I would never finish; he has the soundest, most profound, most learned mind that I know."[4]

By the time the emperor returned to Galicia, there was no time left for an inspection of Bukovina. After almost six years of Austrian military rule there, the question of what to do next with this territory remained unanswered. But while his carriages were being repaired after the beating they had received during the arduous travel in Russia, he instructed Galicia's governor and military commander to jointly create a plan for Bukovina's future. On the homeward leg of his four months' journey, Joseph dutifully reported to his mother, "This work will be forwarded to me, and I will then have the honor of submitting it to Your Majesty." Then, the imperial party rushed back toward Vienna after his absence of four months. At the Galician border some late mail caught up with the emperor. One delayed letter was from his recent host: "The country that Count Falkenstein has left is filled with the highest respect for his virtues." Catherine the Great wrote, "May you find all your august family in a perfect health!"[5]

Just a few months after Joseph's return to Vienna, he would need to muster all his intellect, experience, and skill. After forty years at the helm of the Monarchy, Maria Theresa died on November 29, 1780. Joseph had often complained in private that time was being wasted until he could govern the country unchecked. Yet he seemed caught by surprise when his longed-for opportunity came. There was no manifesto heralding new directions, such as an impatient son might have prepared in advance. And yet the change was profound. With his mother's passing, thirty-nine-year-old Joseph II became sole ruler, overseeing the possessions of the Monarchy as well as continuing, as Holy Roman Emperor, to exert his influence over several semi-independent countries of Europe. The artificial division of titles and power between mother and son, and their constant arguments about state policies, were over.

There was no doubt among observers that Emperor Joseph II would change his

Emperor Joseph II (1741–1790). After the death of his father, Joseph II received the title, "Emperor of the Holy Roman Empire." As the oldest son of Empress Maria Theresa, he served as co-regent of the Habsburg Monarchy from 1765 to 1780. After the death of Maria Theresa, Joseph II became sole ruler of the Habsburg lands that later formed the Austrian Empire. The painting is attributed to F. H. Fuger, circa 1782.

country in many ways. Some only briefly commented that he would bring "an entirely new order of things." Others went further, foretelling challenges to the long-awaited reforms: "Of his intentions there is no doubt, of his success a great deal." However, those who expected something immediate were to be disappointed. Joseph's decision to retain most of his mother's ministers and other high officials was surprising to those who knew him as impatient.

It was only one day after Maria Theresa's death that a proposal from Count Brigido regarding the fate of Bukovina arrived. His recommendation was to merge that military district with adjacent Galicia. Uncharacteristically, Joseph hesitated. Writing in his own hand, he asked others for advice. Yet in March of 1781 Joseph made it abundantly clear who was in charge: "It is beyond doubt that everything that falls within the purview of central and local government," the emperor wrote to his top bureaucrats, "... depends entirely on my decisions and on the directions I choose to give, based as they are on my convictions and well-grounded judgment."[6]

⫏

ONE OF THE MANY issues that required a new approach was the place of non-Catholics, mainly Jews and Protestants, in the Monarchy. Joseph was ready to address this, and over the next ten years he was, in a very personal way, the engine behind a series of "Jewish laws." From the beginning, the emperor insisted on instruction in the German language to Jews, for all their activities outside of worship. He had always believed in the need to unify his crown lands under a common language and a similar set of laws, yet in the case of Jewish reforms he progressed carefully.

Separate imperial edicts (Patents) were set out for each of the lands of the Monarchy. The intent of these new laws was to reduce both the visible and the more subtle barriers between Jews and Christians. The first declaration, in 1781, was for Bohemia; then within the space of a few months, imperial edicts of Toleration (*Toleranzpatents*) were issued for Austrian Silesia, Lower Austria (including the capital, Vienna) and Moravia. A year later, the Jews of Hungary were notified of their new rights. Each edict was a bit different; some addressed the needs of small urban Jewish communities (for example, in Austrian Silesia and in Vienna), whereas others affected much larger rural populations (for example, in Hungary). All were based, however, on the principles of the Enlightenment, with its emphasis on the value of education and religious toleration.

The preamble of the *Toleranzpatent* for Lower Austria, including the imperial capital of Vienna, poignantly spoke of Joseph II's intent: "From the beginning of our reign, we have shown it to be one of our principal concerns that all our subjects, without distinction of nation and religion, as soon as they have been accepted and tolerated in our states, should take their share of the public prosperity..., [they] should enjoy a legally guaranteed freedom, and encounter no hindrance when seeking in every honorable way to make their living and to contribute by their industry to the general prosperity." And yet, that text had a number of contradictions, as did almost everything that the "enlightened" monarch was undertaking. In contrast to their poor Galician cousins, the more well-off Viennese Jews were still denied a public synagogue—they still had to settle for discreet worship—but they won the freedom to build schools, and to choose their own professions or living places without restrictions.[7] Where they were still in force, state-sanctioned requirements that Jews wear distinctive marks were abolished. At times the reforms actually seemed to go too far for some traditional communities: Hungarian Jews, for instance, had to appeal to the emperor for the right to retain their beards.

In conservative Vienna, Jews were now free to attend public entertainment and wear swords like everybody else. The shadow of Maria Theresa's regulations had been lifted. Anachronistic laws on the books, even if not fully enforced—such as requiring Jews to stay secluded on Sundays—were thrown out. Although the details varied from province to province, the general direction was to reduce special taxes levied on the Israelites. In many areas, Christian schools were compelled to admit Jews and respect their religion and dietary laws. In other places with larger Jewish communities, the opening of secular Jewish schools taught in German was mandated. By 1782, university students were no longer required to take an oath with religious undertones that had precluded Jews and

Protestants from enrolling and earning degrees. With this, another set of doors was opened to the Jews of Joseph's realm.

It was true that the early Patents often required clarifications, changes and supplements (a hallmark of Joseph's reign in other areas as well). Later, critics would point out that the imperial edicts were imperfect. For some, they were seen as not offering Jews full emancipation; for others, the spirit of "enlightened absolutism" included a sometimes patronizing tone. Nonetheless, the Patents represented unparalleled progress.[8]

News of Emperor Joseph II's enlightened policies reverberated through the capitals of Europe. They fell on particularly fertile ground in the Prussian capital of Berlin. There, Jewish writers, Hebraist linguists, and German-Jewish intellectuals (*maskilim*) had been advocating the need for Jews to be educated beyond canonical teachings. These members of the Jewish Enlightenment (*Haskalah*) wrote poetry and satires in Hebrew, translated the Bible into German, and strongly voiced their views through various publications.

Accounts of the early Toleration Patents quickly reached Naphtali Herz Wessely in Berlin. Wessely was a relative newcomer to the city. During his former years in Amsterdam, he had admired the schools of the Sephardic (Spanish-Portuguese) community, which taught its young people more secular subjects than Jewish schools in his native Germany and communities farther east. Born of a well-to-do merchant family, his own luck in business had been spotty at best. Perhaps because of this, his dream was to become a writer.

Wessely composed a short pamphlet, "Words of Peace and Truth (*Divrei shalom veemet*)," published in 1782 in Berlin. In it he gave unqualified support to the policies of Joseph II who, Wessely said, had "unshackled disabling bonds by permitting Jews to engage in all forms of cultivation of the land, to work in all crafts and to trade in all merchandise." This endorsement was not surprising, coming as it did from a Jewish circle of reformers and writers. Much more profound was Wessely's eloquent argument about the value of what he called "human knowledge." The secular education that was opening to Jews was not only to be embraced, he said; in fact, it defined human development. "It is in man's power to study all of these phenomena by means of his senses and reason; he does not need anything divine to comprehend them...." This was an extraordinary view: it held that a Jew could be part of modern society if he lacked knowledge of Judaism but adhered to the principles of western civilization; yet a Jew who commanded religious knowledge could not be entirely defined as a Jew if he lacked secular knowledge.[9]

Wessely and his fellow "enlightened" men insisted that "knowledge of these [secular] subjects can only strengthen the House of Israel and mend the breaches made by the preceding rulers." As an ecstatic, if not even radical, proponent of Joseph II's Toleration Patents, Wessely did not shy away from open criticism of his brethren who were neglecting the study of secular subjects: "There is one people in the world who are not sufficiently

Naphtali Herz Wessely (1725–1805), an early proponent of major reforms in Jewish education. Critical of his brethren who neglected the study of secular sciences, he authored "Words of Peace and Truth" published in 1782. *(Courtesy of the Library of the Jewish Theological Seminary, New York.)*

concerned with "human knowledge"; who have neglected public instruction of their youth in the laws of etiquette, the sciences and the arts. We, the children of Israel, who are dispersed throughout all of Europe and who live in most of its states, have turned our back on those studies. Those of us who dwell in Germany and Poland have been especially negligent in this regard."[10]

"Words of Peace and Truth" was quickly translated from the original Hebrew into French and Italian, and later to German. It was read with great enthusiasm in many parts of Europe. In Italy, Jewish communities—many of them under Habsburg rule at the time—quickly responded to Wessely's appeal and pledged to establish secular schools on their own. But it did not take long for the rabbis of Poland, including her former territories of Galicia and Lithuania, to react with outrage. As Moses Mendelssohn—accomplished author and philosopher, widely respected across the religious divide, and considered the father of *Haskalah*—described it, "From all regions of Poland [and her former territories] the arrows of the ban arrive here, hurtling one on top of the other." There, rabbis reacted with anger to the idea that secular education could be thought superior to teachings of divine laws. From their perspective, the first insult had been the imperial Patents, and now the second—Jewish dissenters were also threatening the influence of rabbis. At most, critics of the pamphlet were willing to concede, "Our children shall study the sciences as adornment; however, the foundation of their education will be in accordance with the command of our ancient sages of the Talmud."

In Galicia, copies of "Words of Peace and Truth" were either burned or symbolically hung on iron chains in the courtyards of synagogues. In neighboring Bohemia, the chief rabbi of Prague—the leader of the community and a subject of the Austrian Monarchy—took pains to argue against the new trend without offending the emperor. Passions were running high, and he walked a tightrope when he loudly professed gratitude to his sovereign for the opening of general education to Jews, but railed against Wessely for encroaching on rabbinic influence: "This man is certainly blind to his own faults. He is worse than an animal carcass, and in the end his corpse will lie like dung upon the field!"[11]

Even at the heart of the Jewish Enlightenment (*Haskalah*), in the open atmosphere of Berlin, there was a talk about whether Wessely would be forced out of the city by his own community. Moses Mendelssohn was privately cautious. Despite his support of secular education for his own children and other Jewish youth in the city, he was wary of state-sponsored tolerance policies, wondering if they were intended as "forced assimilation" and what he called "unification of religion." However, as the leader of Jewish intellectuals in Berlin and a man of reason, he lamented the fury of the debate, confiding to a friend: "What will they [Christians] think when they see that we persecute a writer in this way and prevent him from openly expressing his thoughts?"

Naphtali Herz Wessely continued to feel pressure for months. Berlin's Jewish community leaders received many letters from outraged rabbis from the east, advocating punishments that, at the minimum, would provide a severe warning and silence this proponent of Joseph II's policies. Only when the Prussian minister of education intervened on his behalf (most likely persuaded by more vocal proponents of *Haskalah*) did the Jewish community in Berlin became calmer. In his letter, the official made his preferences known: "I request you to inform me about the status of the matter, so that we shall know how to regard such a man who has set himself the task of spreading culture and proper education among Jews." Then, rabbis from five Italian communities offered approval and support; other Italian scholars even wrote celebratory poems, praising the author of the controversial pamphlet. Clearly, the road toward the modern world was complex on all sides.[12]

ॐ

IN THE FIRST WAVE of new rights given to Jewish communities across the crown lands, there was still one place lacking such an imperial Patent. The conspicuous absence of Galicia was not a matter of indifference by the emperor, or a bureaucratic omission. Joseph II saw, firsthand, the predominantly Jewish towns and neighborhoods during his repeated travels there, albeit mostly from a distance. Despite his rejection of anachronistic courtly etiquette—he was approachable to petitioners both in Vienna and during his travels—there is no record of any personal interactions with Jews during his five trips to the Galician crownland. However, at least some interaction must have taken place, especially since he took up quarters in a Jewish guesthouse while staying in Stanisławów—instead of occupying a castle prepared for his use by a local countess.

The delay in issuing a Jewish Patent for Galicia stemmed more from Joseph's advisors' uncertainty about dealing with the largest Jewish population in the Monarchy. Some freedoms offered elsewhere did not need to be introduced in Galicia; they already existed. Yet given the size and the orthodox nature of that community, other reforms would have to be planned on a much wider scale than anywhere else, making the whole effort a major social experiment. The local Austrian administration (*Gubernium*) in Lemberg (Lwów) pestered the court bureaucracy with memoranda containing their own ideas about how to reform the community there; their harsh views toward Jews were generally moderated in Vienna by the Bohemian-Austrian Court Chancellery or the Council of State (*Staatsrath*).

In 1783, on Joseph's orders, a comprehensive fact-finding mission on Galician affairs was conducted by his trusted councilor Johann Wenzel Margelik of the Bohemian-Austrian Chancellery. After its completion, the impatient emperor personally made several annotations on the report. Among many other issues, the document spoke at length about the role of Jews in Galicia's economy. It captured well the pragmatic view that any talk of limiting the Jewish community's growth through restrictive marriage laws or expulsion of its poorer members would be futile.

In the absence of a major Jewish Patent, the importance of more limited and separate rulings concerning Jewish life in Galicia would not have been apparent to a casual observer. In isolation, those were often confusing and contradictory. Yet changes were coming, at Joseph's insistence. Despite the existence of a separate Jewish jurisdiction, which had been reaffirmed by the harsh *Judenordnung* of 1776, suddenly the courts were reminded that testimonies by Jews (and by women regardless of their religion) were admissible in legal proceedings; religion alone could not be a factor in a court of law. With this settled, a few years later rabbinic courts were forbidden to render verdicts in nonreligious matters, and the Jewish general administration was dismantled. Then, on Joseph's personal initiative, Jews were barred from possessing leases in the countryside, an action bitterly resented by many whose traditional source of income was being threatened or taken away. Instead, Jews were now explicitly encouraged by the government to own land and become farmers themselves, sometimes benefiting from subsidies.[13]

Once, during a trip to the region, Joseph spelled out his thoughts for his ministers in a paternalistic style typical of this sovereign, who felt he knew what was best for his subjects: "[For] Jews to continue in the broader society, they must either engage in good trade and respected crafts or devote themselves to agriculture."[14] When some local bureaucrats seemed to ignore Jewish petitions requesting land parcels, imperial intervention came swiftly in their favor, giving them, in just this one instance, an unprecedented priority over German colonists coming to settle in Galicia.

Emperor Joseph's idea of turning Jews into "productive" peasants would continue to be his pet project. With his thinking now widely known, it did not take long for a visitor to Galicia to extol the idea that "the country would certainly achieve an infinite gain, if the Jews were able to work in field crops. There have already been several attempts [at making it happen] in vain, with some mistakes made, I am afraid not without a cause ..." In the mind of this and many other self-appointed experts, farming was considered a particularly desirable profession. This idea contained some truth, since Galicia was viewed then, and would be considered for years to come, as a breadbasket, supplying agricultural products to the rest of the Monarchy. The idea of a prosperous life as peasants, it was thought, would be happily embraced by the majority of Israelites. Yet, an Austrian traveler through Galicia at least briefly acknowledged that for all such predictions to become reality, "Jews [themselves] have to see the advantages if they are to be attracted into this business undertaking."[15]

Even with the wave of new regulations and the frequent talk by the "enlightened" regime how to render them "harmless (*unschädlich*)" through forcing Jews to engage in certain professions, there were still boundaries that could not be violated in the spirit of the new times. Thus, a proposal from the Galician administration that a certain amount of mandatory farm labor be required of Jews—"so that they get accustomed to field work"—was quickly disapproved by a unanimous vote of the Council of State (*Staatsrath*).[16] Instead, as almost nowhere else in the Monarchy (perhaps with the exception of Hungary), freshly minted Jewish farmers (who had chosen this path of their own volition), suddenly had the right to own land in Galicia, as long as they could afford it.

⟡

OVER THE YEARS, JOSEPH II's attention to the affairs of Galicia and, by extension, the Jewish community there, touched the lives of his subjects in large and small ways. On occasion, imperial decisions in response to reports and proposals from the crownland could affect very local affairs, although they were almost always impactful, if not contradictory at times. Once, for instance, the emperor became appalled by conditions in the Galician capital, a situation he knew firsthand through his travels there. Action was clearly needed; the inner part of Lemberg (Lwów) was in serious decay. Fire hazards that threatened the walled city, and unsanitary conditions in the Jewish section, called for immediate attention. Since the city was Galicia's new provincial seat, Austrian-style urban improvements were being contemplated. The overzealous local government, however, advocated draconian action: all houses in the area were to be seized from their owners and ultimately torn down; even rental tenants would not be allowed to live there.

The emperor's Council of State (*Staatsrath*) delved into this proposal, and most members vehemently opposed it. One of them felt that respect for private property should guide any decision. Another reasoned that if there was indeed "unbearable filth," the city magistrate should take appropriate steps to clean up the area; confiscation of homes would go against the duty and dignity of the ruler of the land, who was more obligated to protect Jewish and Christian subjects on their own property than to infringe upon this right. But the emperor, being an uneven promoter of new freedoms and an impatient believer in his right to better the lives of his subjects, favored razing the "unsafe" area in the Jewish section. In his view, this was more about city planning than directed against any specific group. Facing unanimous protest from his most senior advisors, he modified his stand a bit. The affected individuals were to receive replacement in a newly laid-out section of Lemberg (Lwów), certainly a more humane solution.[17]

At the same time, Joseph II tackled much more profound issues affecting all the Jews of Galicia, not just those living in its capital city. Since 1785, the emperor had repeatedly pressured his generals to open military service to Jews. His War Council, however, would continue to raise objections. The question of whether Jews as soldiers could perform their military duties on their Sabbath—not to mention the challenges the army would face to accommodate their dietary laws—were raised by no one less important than his trusted military man, Field Marshal Hadik. The old veteran of the Galician campaign and former governor was back in Vienna, his prestige bolstered by a new title and the influential position of president of the Council. His repeated objections were not new arguments; in fact, they had been debated outside the hallways of the Habsburg bureaucracy for the past few years.

Even before the emperor had made his preferences known, views on this topic were exchanged far away from Galicia. At first, pamphlets appeared in Vienna and Prague, with the circle of debate soon broadened to governmental officials, experts on Jewish history, and Jewish reformers (*maskilim*). All of them saw military service as part of a grand scheme of Jewish integration into a modern and more open society. Yet their opinions differed on one subject: whether the tenets of Judaism posed unsolvable obstacles for any observant Jews following a call to arms. To assuage doubts, proponents of drafting Jewish recruits reminded the skeptics of biblical tales of brave warriors who had fulfilled their military duties with valor, without conflict with their beliefs. Most men of the Enlightenment, including Moses Mendelssohn, agreed that military service for Jews would ultimately happen.

"If the fatherland is to be defended," Mendelssohn wrote from Berlin, "everybody who is called upon to do so must comply. In such cases, men usually know how to modify their convictions and adjust them to their civic duty." Then, he added wisely, "One merely has to avoid excessively emphasizing the conflict between the two." In spite of his support of the idea in principle, Mendelssohn felt it would be a long time before Jewish soldiers were to become a reality.[18]

Patiently waiting for the right moment to implement changes in his crown lands was certainly not the emperor's strong point. To aid in eventual conscription of Jews and facilitate their interactions in broader civil society, Joseph's next step was a new imperial manifesto, which ordered that every Jew was to adopt a permanent surname. Starting in January 1788, use of the old patronymic names was abandoned. The head of each family was to present the chosen surname for approval to a local civil authority; a requirement that it be German sounding was clearly spelled out by imperial law. However, some exceptions were granted.[19] Later, unconfirmed rumors would swirl about alleged bribes extracted by petty clerks. As one story told, "nice"-sounding names related to flowers and precious metals (for example, *Rosenthal*, *Goldstein*), or alluding to the ownership of land (*Hübner*) required the largest bribes in some places; lower fees were extracted for names of ordinary metals (for example, *Eisen*, *Stahl*).

With Jews now easily identified by their surnames and the military conscription books in Galicia revamped, the Army's transportation and supply units were designated to be the first to admit Jewish recruits. When the army dragged its feet, the emperor cut off the debate. His order for the military stationed in Galicia was clear: start the draft. When, a few months later, alternative proposals to delay implementation of Jewish military service were again brought by the War Council, Joseph was even more explicit: "Without further discussion the Jew, as man and citizen of the state, shall be employed in all tasks that are required of everyone else. His religion will not thereby be injured," the emperor continued, "because he must be left free to eat what he wants to eat, and must not be required to do anything on the Sabbath other than what necessity requires and what a Christian is required to do on Sunday."[20]

ঌৎ

YEARS INTO THE REFORM process, Joseph II personally revised the new comprehensive Jewish Patent for Galicia. Working on a draft submitted by his bureaucrats, he crossed out paragraphs and freely added new principles in his own hand. After his repeated inspections of the crownland, after sending out long questionnaires and fact-finding missions, and after reading the ensuing reports, Joseph II truly felt he knew what was best. It was an example of pure enlightened absolutism. In those times, no one would have even thought to consult with a few Galician Jews on their fate. Neither did officialdom formally ask the reform-minded *maskilim* of Berlin for their opinions (they would, however, play a part in the execution of Joseph's vision). The closest that the Monarchy came to receiving a Jewish view on the imperial edict—albeit indirectly—was some improvements suggested on a draft by one of the Court Councilors, who had close relations with the Jewish community.[21]

Somewhere in Galicia in the 1780s. Illustration from a popular book written by
the Austrian visitor, Franz Kratter. *(Franz Kratter. Dreyßig Briefe über Galizien oder
Beobachtungen eines unpartheyischen Mannen. Wien 1787.)*

The Jewish Patent for Galicia was finally issued in the emperor's name on May 7, 1789. Its preamble read, "After rendering prior decrees concerning Jewry, it was judged based on and according to the undertaken laws of Toleration ... that all existing differences between Christian and Jewish subjects that have been sanctioned by the law until now be abolished." The stated intent of the Patent was "to provide safeguards for the Jews living in *Galicia* [so they may] benefit from all rights and freedoms enjoyed by our other subjects. In general, from now on, Galician Jewry has the same rights and duties as other subjects."

What followed was a declaration that the Jews were free to practice their religion and build synagogues. Their elected rabbis were to oversee religious instruction only, and maintain community registers of births, marriages, and deaths in the German language. In other matters, a Jew was under the jurisdiction of civil institutions in the same way as everyone else, with the right to petition the government (in German). A system of secular schools was introduced; attendance of Jewish children was mandatory so they could learn writing and the German language. Prior restrictions on Jews regarding the size of families or place of residence were eliminated.

Undoubtedly, the removal of the despised marriage tax was met with approval even among the most ardent traditionalists. The Jews of Galicia were now free to engage in any craft, trade, and profession available to other citizens; they were also free to carry merchandise from house to house in towns and villages. The only legal restriction retained from recent regulations was a temporary ban imposed on Jews that prohibited them from taking on many traditional leases in the countryside. However, the right of Jews to own land was preserved, and Jewish communities were encouraged to finance the settlement of their poorer members in agricultural communities.

Although it would be years before Jews could fully participate in the affairs of the crownland, an important legal framework was beginning to take shape. The emperor's edict laid out the modern principle that with privileges came duties to the state. The new law of the land had other provisions that diverged from centuries-old customs that had kept Jews separate. For the first time, Galician

Jews had the right as citizens to participate in municipal elections. The military conscription of Jews was reaffirmed, with the provision that their religious customs be observed, similarly to those of Christian soldiers. Lowering the barriers between Jews and non-Jews even further than the year before, the edict stipulated that those Jews who wished to serve in military formations, beyond those dealing with the troop supplies and transportation, be accommodated.[22]

Despite the title running across the first page of the edict that "Jews are accorded equal rights and freedoms to those of Christians," the law was by no means perfect in today's sense. Some provisions retained contradictions or contained language that would sound offensive to the twenty-first-century reader. The freedoms offered by the enlightened ruler had their limits; for instance, Jews "caught in the villages while making a living in any other way than two circumstances [farmers or craftsmen]" were to be "severely punished" along with any manor owners who had been looking the other way. The emperor's grandiose plan to move masses of Galician Jews toward more "appropriate" professions was only partly successful. Newly opened Jewish agricultural colonies were criticized by both Jews and gentiles as failing enterprises, and many of them would not survive for long. Yet with a stroke of Joseph's pen, some Jews who could afford purchase had become legal owners of land that would still be in their families a generation later.

However, in some ways the new edict did not live up to its billing. Harking back to old times, the law preserved remnants of special taxation, including the Toleration Tax (with Jewish farmers being exempted) and a special tax on kosher meat. Thus contradicting the edict's uplifting preamble, Jews were to pay the state for "protection" and the observance of their customs. Still, the new law offered the emperor a platform for additional revisions to more timid Jewish Patents for other crown lands. In Galicia, many provisions of the new law were embraced at once, but others were bitterly fought over by its Jewish recipients. Joseph's successors continually tinkered with it, often reversing some freedoms, but the Patent remained the most progressive law in the Habsburg realm for the next seventy-eight years, until the emancipation of Jews was finally reaffirmed in the constitution.

By the end of 1789, a year that had been marked by other sweeping edicts but also by erupting troubles within the Monarchy, Joseph II was visibly ill. His mood was not helped by news from the Austrian Netherlands (today's Belgium) that it was slipping away from the Habsburgs' influence. Similar troubles were palpable in Hungary, which was on the verge of revolt. Some consolation, however, came with victories in a nearby corner of the Monarchy; a military campaign against Turkish forces in the territories of today's Romania and Serbia was, for a change, wildly successful. Celebrations rarely seen before erupted in Vienna, and they would be remembered as a remarkable break from mostly bleak news for years to come.

Keeping in mind Joseph's attention to detail, it seems he must have been aware that his Galician reforms were bearing some fruit. More than a thousand Jewish recruits from Galicia would ultimately serve in the conflict with the Ottoman Empire. One can wonder today if, a few weeks after victories in the Balkans, the ailing emperor might have been shown the news from Paris. There, at the National Assembly, a liberal deputy was referring to the spirit of the Galician Patent when he said, "Everything must be refused to the Jews as a nation; everything must be granted to them as individuals.... The Jews in the state of *the emperor* enjoy not only the rights of citizens, but also the possibility of attaining those honorific distinctions that we have destroyed and which still survive there in all their force."[23]

Joseph II died on February 20, 1790. When the news of his passing reached the State Chancellor, a holdover from Maria Theresa's time, the old prince coldly remarked: "That was very good of him." The reaction from a group of Jewish literati in the Prussian cities of Berlin and Königsberg was much more animated. The contradictions within the "enlightened" Jewish policies of this impatient man were not remarked upon by those enthusiastic members of the *Haskalah*. In the flowery and exaggerated style typical of their times they wrote, shortly after the emperor's death, "He raised the beauty of Israel from the dustheap and brought it into the chambers of knowledge.... He set his pure heart towards the children of Israel and gave orders to lead them to school...." Even a few years later, poetry about the "gracious king" continued to appear in the pages of a Jewish literary periodical published in Berlin.

However, many argued that the late emperor had tried to do too many things in too short a time. In the minds of others, despite the unquestionable impact made on the lives of his subjects, history would not be kind to him. Among other enlightened monarchs similar to Joseph II—Catherine of Russia and Frederick of Prussia—he was the only one denied by the historians the title "the Great."

A year after Joseph's death, someone from the late emperor's inner circle jotted down a private note, telling more than future volumes of historical analysis would about Joseph II's strengths and faults: "The government's influence is now stronger that I ever imagined it could be in the time of the poor dead emperor. He used to infuriate us. But what activity, what fire, what wealth of ideas he conveyed to us all! You could not speak or write enough, topics were never exhausted, and a thousand things were left over for the next time. Now there is none of this. It is as if everyone has been struck dumb."[24]

Chapter 4

HERZ HOMBERG'S

BATTLEGROUND

*G*ALICIANS ALWAYS SEEMED TO HAVE plenty to complain about in any new law. However, when in May 1789 the Galician Patent for Jews was announced in synagogues and on government circulars, the reaction was anticlimactic. There were no street celebrations or passionate speeches about the dawn of a new era. Nor were there any protests worth recording by the guilds, which had previously been fearful of competition from Jewish craftsmen. Instead, Galicians of all backgrounds—Poles, Ruthenians, and Jews—tried to absorb the impact of a new land and taxation law (*Urbarium*) issued in the same year. Although fiscal obligations levied on small and big land owners in the impoverished crownland were actually lower than those imposed in the central, mostly German-speaking, lands of the Monarchy (including Bohemia), nobody wanted to believe it. In particular, the Polish landowning class preferred to portray itself as the victim of an overreaching bureaucracy, and still saw as "foreign" the rule of the Habsburgs.[1]

Jews in turn grumbled, regardless of their wealth, at the prospect of military conscription. Many of them worried about pragmatic issues, mainly the impact of men being away from their families. Frequently, they would have fathered many children by the draft age, which was not surprising given that Jewish boys married as early as the age of thirteen. For the traditional community in Galicia, the dilemma was not only responding to military duties without violating the Sabbath;

there were other objections as well. Wearing the military uniform was criticized as a violation of religious customs. Even when the army issued clothing free of the mixture of wool and linen (*shatnez*) prohibited by Jewish law, it did not lessen objections. On the draft issue, in fact, some Galician Jews seemed in terrible distress. "There was great mourning," read one letter sent to brethren in the Austrian part of Italy, "...public fasting, weeping and wailing.... Many of our people fled to the uninhabited wilderness." In some places (like Brody), Jews armed with clubs resisted the draft, whereas in others (like the Stanisławów district) they ran away in large numbers. Somehow, Joseph II's intent to use military service as a tool toward toleration was not working.[2]

Amazingly, though, these reactions in Galicia became the subject of a broader conversation. Open letters from Jews living elsewhere addressed their Galician brethren on this topic; how widely such missives were read remains unclear today. A letter bearing the name of a rabbi from the cosmopolitan city of Trieste, on the Adriatic coast (a free port within the Habsburg Monarchy), called on Galician Jews not to look ungrateful in the eyes of the emperor in opposing the draft. Others tried to diffuse a presumed conflict between religious and newly acquired civic duties with an anonymous appeal to Galician Jews: "Worship God through His commandments in your leisure time, and [serve] the emperor through his orders in wartime and in battle." This was only a prelude to a powerful struggle between old and new that was about to erupt in Galicia.[3]

The opening of secular education to the Jews of Galicia (and to those in other lands of the Monarchy) was an essential part of Joseph II's bold plan of enlightened policies. But in Galicia it brought unexpected consequences. Given the size of the Jewish community, it was widely expected among the echelons of Habsburg's bureaucracy that German-Jewish schools would be the cornerstone of the emperor's policy of remaking the crownland; as such, their success was even more important than in other provinces of the Monarchy.

Herz Homberg, the newly appointed superintendent of Galicia's German-Jewish schools, arrived in Lemberg (Lwów) in 1787, ahead of the Galician Jewish Patent. Knowing the task there would be a large one, Homberg did not come alone.

Twenty-eight handpicked Jewish teachers from Bohemia, early supporters of the Jewish Enlightenment, accompanied him, all emboldened by the early successes of the new educational system elsewhere.

At first glance, Herz Homberg seemed an ideal person to serve as the superintendent. He was Jewish, born in Bohemia. It was generally assumed, by the government ministers in Vienna who had appointed him, that his life experiences would be ideally suited to helping him bridge the gap between orthodoxy and the winds of change. In his youth, Homberg received a traditional religious education; he had learned German starting only at the age of eighteen. Then, to pursue secular studies in a more permissive environment than that of Bohemia, he relocated to

Herz Homberg (1749–1841), a radical supporter of the Jewish Enlightenment and the first Jew to receive an advanced degree from the University of Vienna. His tenure as the superintendent of German-Jewish schools in Galicia was highly controversial. *(Courtesy of the Austrian National Library, Vienna.)*

Berlin. In due course, Homberg had found himself in the center of the Jewish Enlightenment (*Haskalah*). Highly respected by the leader of the movement, Moses Mendelssohn, Homberg became a tutor to his children, and an increasingly trusted protégé.

By the 1780s Homberg, then in his thirties, was working with other writers, Hebraic scholars, and philosophers, contributing to elegant German translation of biblical texts and providing their commentaries in Hebrew (informally known as *Bi'ur*). Feeling the excitement surrounding Joseph II's early Edicts of Toleration, he decided to return to the central lands of the Monarchy and enroll in the service of the emperor. He became the first of the Jews who took advantage of the imperial policy that opened university education to them. His academic talents were on display when, besides being the first Jewish graduate, Homberg received an advanced degree in philosophy from the University of Vienna, with distinction.

Nothing was controversial about Homberg's subsequent teaching appointments in German-Jewish schools: first, in Gorizia (in today's northeastern Italy) and then in neighboring Trieste. In the open environment of these Italian provinces of the Monarchy, Homberg's efforts to combine a secular curriculum in German with religious studies were successful. The arrangement satisfied both the Jewish reformers and the traditionalists. The Jews there had spoken Italian for a long time and attended public schools, and had the right to practice medicine.

During Homberg's stay in Trieste, German-Jewish schools opened in Bohemia and Moravia. To appease orthodox Jewish circles in these provinces, their curriculum was limited to secular subjects, leaving religious studies to the traditional Jewish schools. In a clear win for modernity, Bohemian German-Jewish schools soon started to admit girls along with the boys. Joseph II's social experiment seemed to be working along Enlightenment principles that satisfied both the state and the Jewish reformers.

In the meantime, Galicia also seemed to be poised to embrace change. In the mid-1780s, several public schools (*Normalschulen*) opened there. Inconspicuous among them were seven schools for Jewish youth, with their secular curriculum taught in German. At first, the administration of these Jewish schools was punctuated by typical worries, such as ensuring that there was enough firewood for classrooms in the winter—nothing unusual for any school in the crownland. In Lemberg's *Krakauer* suburb, the same place where Jews had been told a few years before to build homes to reduce congestion of the inner city, a new school building was erected. Its one hundred and ten boys did not lack enthusiasm; as a visitor good-naturedly remarked, the students "with the loudest sign of satisfaction, applaud those present who were tested [in the classroom]." Certainly these events were a drop in the bucket but, for now, nothing seemed out of the ordinary.[4]

As the new superintendent, Herz Homberg would be given significant powers. Naturally, he was put in charge of appointing the teachers needed for a growing network of public schools for Jews. But he was also expected to distribute the funds for Jewish education; he was tasked with censoring Jewish books printed in Galicia and could call on the police, if necessary, to enforce his regulations. When Homberg arrived in Lemberg (Lwów), he could not have looked more alien to Galician Jews, almost all of whom followed rabbinic orthodoxy or charismatic *tsadikim* (spiritual leaders of Hasidic communities). This man of the Enlightenment in his powdered wig (with pigtail), dressed in the so-called "German" style (wearing culottes), spoke in perfect German. Upon hearing Galician Jews responding in Yiddish, Homberg could be visibly upset—all reformers at that time derided the Judeo-German dialect as mutilated German, or even worse, called it a "stammer"—which would not sit well with traditional Jews for whom it was their mother tongue.[5]

It did not take long for Homberg to broadcast his intentions. He wrote, in Hebrew, an open letter to the leaders of Galician Jewry. If "A letter to the Shepherds of the Scattered Sheep of Israel" would have merely been printed in a foreign literary publication and read by Jewish reformers (of whom there were likely only a few in Galicia), its reception would have been far less hostile. In 1788, however, Herz Homberg's message was printed for all to see, under sovereign decree in Lemberg (Lwów). Its content started on a positive note, highlighting the great benefits of Joseph II's reforms to the Jews, as well as the fact that there was no conflict between the new laws and the traditional faith. Homberg portrayed himself, with some accuracy, as an expert in education, having only the interests of Jewish youth in mind. He even suggested that the advice of rabbis could be of value, particularly regarding the content of secular education and the training of new Jewish teachers. But once the niceties were stated, the rest of Herz Homberg's appeal was anything but reconciliatory. Its tone was patronizing, with the superintendent emphasizing that the ultimate decision would be his: "And if your ideas are not satisfactory, I will compose some of my own … and will send them to their Excellencies, the government ministers, and whatever they decree is that which will guide us." Galician Jews were further warned that if they dared to not follow his advice, he would notify officials close to the throne.[6]

The open letter did not change the attitudes of Galician rabbis. If anything, the heavy-handed message cleared a path toward open conflict. Soon, Herz Homberg could not find a safe house in which to stay in the Jewish neighborhoods of Lemberg (Lwów); he had to live, reportedly under police protection, in a predominantly Christian part of town. In the counteroffensive launched by traditionalists, much slanderous gossip about him was repeated with outrage across Galicia. Each of these stories was more ridiculous than the last; nonetheless, they slowly became ingrained in the minds of local Jews, where they would remain for generations to come. How could any parent entrust the education of his children to this evil man, who was said to sit, surrounded by police, in front of a synagogue in Lemberg (Lwów), eating non-kosher meat purposely to offend his brethren?

Traditionalists were further incensed when the Galician Patent declared that "Where a German school is established, no youngster will be admitted to receive lessons from the Talmud without a certificate from a teacher of the German school [saying] that he appropriately attended the German school and succeeded in learning." It was not just Herz Homberg, but his cadre of secular teachers who were viewed with suspicion, if not open hostility, by local communities. These foreign-looking and often strange-sounding men had been ordered to report any violations to the authorities. The consequences could be real as stipulated by the law; for instance, "the head of the family whose children receive [religious] education without the certificate from the teacher of the German school will be punished with three days in jail for each child." When, in a few years, a couple of female teachers arrived to work in the newly opened schools for girls in Lemberg (Lwów) and Brody, the sensitivities of those communities were offended even further. As if teaching girls was not bad enough, Herz Homberg was also accused of nepotism when his brother, Simon, and sister-in-law, "Mrs. Ch. Homberg," took coveted positions in Lemberg (Lwów).

Despite later criticism of Herz Homberg's efforts, one hundred and seven German-Jewish schools with approximately one hundred and fifty teachers operated in Galicia at the peak of his activities there. The methods of teaching were modern,

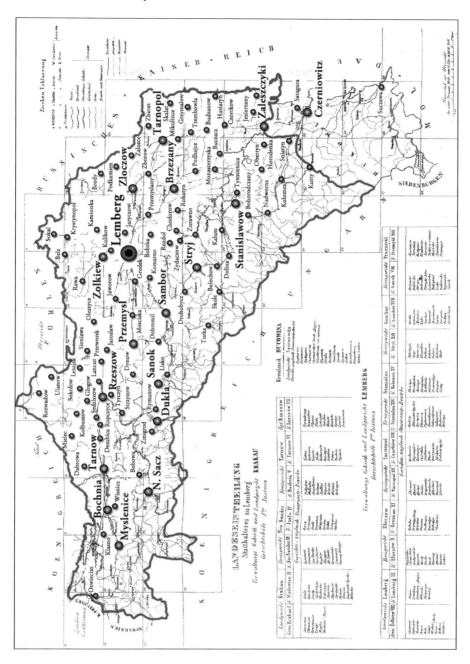

The network of German-Jewish schools in Galicia and Bukovina. Four schools were situated in the capital, Lemberg (Lwów); others were in district cities (*Kreis*) (e.g., Stanisławów) and in several smaller communities (such as Bohorodczany, Nadwórna, and Tysmienica). They operated between 1787 and 1806. Seven additional schools from the district of Zamość, which was part of Galicia during these years, are not shown. *(Based on Schematismus für die Königreiche Galizien und Lodomerien. Lemberg 1792 and 1796.)*

based on understanding of the subjects rather than mechanical repetition. Their novelty also included the introduction of grades based on the performance of students. Nevertheless, most of these establishments were simple "trivial" schools (*Trivialschulen*) providing instruction in German and teaching Hebrew grammar and civic duties. In Lemberg (Lwów), the main school (*Hauptschule*) offered four years of education and doubled as a school for teachers. Graduates of the schools could establish careers in the crafts or business. At least in theory, those finishing the main school could go on to higher education and then enroll in the University of Lemberg (the Josephinian University) opened on the initiative of Emperor Joseph II in 1784.

However, with animosity growing between the autocratic school superintendent on one side and Galician parents and orthodox rabbis on the other, there would be no fond memories of the educational network. Nobody recalled later, with well-deserved pride, that in some places, like the small town of Bohorodczany, the school for Jewish boys predated the establishment of a public school for Ruthenian or Polish youth. Despite good intentions, the awkward implementation of progressive thinking undermined the reforms; the battle with the traditionalists only intensified over the years.

Homberg saw his mission as one extending far beyond what had been espoused by his less radical colleagues during the heyday of the Jewish Enlightenment in Berlin. With unyielding constancy, he continually hurled accusations against rabbinic Judaism. Not surprisingly, even in Lemberg (Lwów), the capital of the crownland—which might have been more receptive to new trends than the small Jewish towns (*shtetls*)—the German-Jewish school had fewer attendees than the traditional Jewish religious schools (*heders*) scattered around the town. Through memoranda sent to Vienna, Homberg expressed the view that to end Jewish isolation in the enlightened society, the powers of rabbis must be limited. Homberg wanted the state to appoint spiritual leaders of the Jewish community who were trained far away from the "bad" influence of Galicia, in the only state-sponsored rabbinical school, located in Prague. There, the scope of Talmudic studies was to be limited. Predictably, even the casual use of Yiddish was to be prohibited in all schools.

Not surprisingly, these proposals did not bring the superintendent many supporters from the Jewish population. Furthermore, modern ideas regarding, at least, some measures towards the equality of women—who would have had an access to education possible only in secular German-Jewish schools—were met with a frosty reception. A replay of Berlin salons, in which young Jewish women conversed in French and charmed visitors with their knowledge of literature, never happened in Galicia, which must have seemed like a different universe. When the school superintendent, turned censor of Jewish books, proposed to start burning "bad" volumes, that step was too radical even for the High Court Chancellery in Vienna. The proposal was wisely rejected without much debate; tensions were already too high in the crownland.[7]

ᴈ

ALTHOUGH HERZ HOMBERG CONTINUED to be in charge of Galician German-Jewish schools, starting in the 1790s he would spend long periods of time in Vienna. The official purpose of these visits was to shape governmental policies toward the Jews of his native Bohemia. But back in Lemberg (Lwów), the extended absences of the superintendent only fueled rumors that he was avoiding alleged judicial proceedings for poorly defined transgressions. Then, Homberg's reputation in Galicia shifted from bad to worse.

It all started with a confidential proposal in 1795, by a Lemberg company operated by Messrs. Salomon Kofler and Ignaz Kratter, to collect new tax revenues from the Jews of Galicia. This in itself was not surprising, although it should have raised suspicion of unscrupulous practices on the part of the tax collectors: they proposed to keep a profit from the collections for themselves, in return for a flat annual fee paid on behalf of the entire crownland to the government. The most controversial aspect, however, was a new tax they proposed to levy on Galician Jews: a tax on the lighting of candles during Jewish holidays and celebrations.

Apparently Emperor Francis, who was now at the helm of the Habsburg lands, hesitated on first hearing the proposal. At its core, it was coming dangerously close to taxing individual religious practice, which could be one step too far for the enlightened Monarchy.[8] Francis inquired of Homberg, his school superintendent and expert on Jewish affairs, whether the idea could be considered a violation of religious freedoms. What sealed the imperial decision was Homberg's reply: "If Jews are free to light as many candles as they wish, this likely means that religion is not violated; neither the freedom of religion nor tradition suffers whether a candle costs one or three coins."[9]

One morning in the summer of 1797, the Jews of Galicia woke up to learn that Emperor Francis had altered the provisions of the Galician Patent, issued less than ten years before by his late uncle, Emperor Joseph II. This time, no lofty words were evoked in the preamble to the new imperial edict. Instead, the emperor declared in dry and matter-of-fact language that the taxes paid by Galician Jews were simply too low. To "rectify" the situation, the old Jewish taxes had been replaced by one more beneficial for the imperial treasury: a tax on the lighting of candles during the observance of Jewish traditions. From now on, these payments were required from each Jewish family when lighting a candle or an oil lamp on the Sabbath, on Hanukkah, or even when observing a parent's death; the tax was also extracted on candles brought to schools or synagogues. Nothing was to escape the tax collectors; neither torches nor candles used during weddings were exempted.

The feared agents of Messrs. Salomon Kofler and Ignaz Kratter would now be allowed to enter Jewish homes on the Sabbath to carry out domestic inspections; finding burning candles brought financial penalties on those unable to provide receipts for payment of the tax. There was also a sudden reversal of previous laws that had prevented

Galician coin with the Habsburg double-headed eagle.

rabbis from issuing curses on their congregants. To the contrary, they were now ordered to "seriously condemn forever" violators of the new law, and the names of the offenders were to be posted on blackboards in synagogues.[10]

Almost immediately, Herz Homberg was accused by Galician Jews of benefiting financially from the new law. Any remaining shreds of goodwill toward him vanished, amidst suspicion that he was receiving commissions from the tax-collecting agency in Lemberg. Such unconfirmed innuendoes, as well as the repeated rumors about investigations into Homberg's supposed illicit activities, would continue to swirl around the superintendent. Coincidentally, Homberg suddenly seemed to become quite wealthy, but nothing was ever proven.

Homberg continued to oversee the German-Jewish schools, but from 1799 he exerted his influence solely from a distance. His supporters interpreted this as the rise of the superintendent in the imperial bureaucracy in Vienna, but his many enemies reveled in stories that Homberg was fearful of returning to Lemberg, where he might have to face legal consequences for his purported mismanagement of the schools, or the wrath of his coreligionists.

In 1806, Emperor Francis dissolved the secular Jewish schools in Galicia, and their students were accepted into the general public schools. Traditionalists viewed this as a victory and a celebrated failure of the overzealous Herz Homberg. The closure was in a clear difference with other parts of the Austrian Empire. (In neighboring Bohemia and Moravia, German-Jewish schools successfully continued until the end of the century.)

Even Galician Jews who supported reforms and education, although at a slower pace, ridiculed the results of the German-Jewish schools, particularly in Hasidic communities. One example of this was a humorous essay in which students were able to read German letters without understanding their meanings. This was more than a subtle jab at Homberg's methods; the imperial educator was being lumped with the traditional teaching methods of Jewish religious schools (*heders*), where mechanical repetitions by young students were the norm.

The truth about the success or failure of educational reforms in Galicia was most likely more nuanced. Undeniably, the early nineteenth century had produced an increasing number of university-educated Jewish professionals there. In the first few decades, a gradual entry of Jews into the provincial bureaucracy was also taking place. Their numbers were still appallingly small, given the size of the Galician Jewish population; but nonetheless, so many would have been unthinkable just two or three generations before.

With the German-Jewish schools closed and Herz Homberg living elsewhere, it might have seemed that his influence on Galicia would quickly fade away. In the end, however, he was to have the last word. While living in Vienna, Homberg authored school textbooks: some of them in Hebrew, others in German. He also published a "Jewish catechism," which combined moral laws stemming from the Ten Commandments with civic duties, and shared universal principles of Judaism and Christianity. (On its front page, he reminded readers that he was a disciple of the revered Moses Mendelssohn).

Even some of his critics would later admit that Homberg's books were well written. They would probably have been quickly forgotten, were it not for an 1811 Court Chancellery decree attempting to improve the "moral" standing of Jews in the Kingdom of Bohemia (containing Bohemia and Moravia) and the Kingdom of Galicia and Lodomeria. As a result, all Jewish couples wishing to marry were mandated to purchase the soon-published Homberg's catechism in German, and to demonstrate their knowledge of it in front of magistrate clerks, a lay representative of the local Jewish community, and a registered rabbi or teacher of religion. This law remained on the books until 1857.[11]

In response to these requirements, acculturated Jews would repeat, with a laugh, stories about young men hastily memorizing whole sections of the book in a language they did not understand. On occasion, this could lead to comical situations; it was said that when a hopeful groom was asked by a clerk some innocent nonreligious question, he might respond by reciting pages of Homberg's catechism. But there were more serious consequences as well. In the eyes of many, the "morality test" was blamed for the fact that the vast majority of observant Jews in Galicia no longer married legally. (That would include many of my ancestors.) The need for a couple to solicit additional permission from local civil authorities, even before they could present themselves to a state-accredited rabbi, did not help either. In one year, a mere 137 couples had registered for legal marriage in the entirety of Galicia and Bukovina. With a total Jewish population of about two hundred and fifty thousand, the situation was not lost on the authorities! An internal circular, "Illegal Jewish Marriages Should Not Be Allowed," made its way through the towns of the region, but it would not have much impact for several decades to come.[12] For the majority not married in a state-sanctioned ceremony, their children were designated as illegitimate in communal birth registers.

The patchwork of marriage laws had some unintended consequences. Young Jewish men of an age to be drafted into the military—often already married and with their own children—quickly discovered that they qualified for an exemption: they would claim that their "unmarried" mothers depended on them for support. More official clarifications followed, supposedly to correct the confusion: although many thousands of Jewish marriages were still legally invalid, for the army the mere cohabitation of the father and mother of a prospective draftee was good enough. Where there was legitimate financial hardship, military commissions could not hear a case; other cumbersome measures had to be put in place to address any well-founded exemptions. Thus in many strange ways, Herz Homberg's efforts to reform his brethren cast a long shadow on Galician Jews for years after he died (in Prague in 1841 at the age of ninety-two). Instead of celebrating the old man's pioneering work in Berlin, his literary accomplishments, and the unquestionable educational talents he'd displayed when young in the Italian provinces, memories of him were never kind in Galicia.

℘

AT LATER TIMES OPINIONS would surface that Herz Homberg had set back Galician Jews' opening to a broader world for some fifty years. The "villainous" school superintendent was blamed for more than unleashing hostile reaction to educational reforms during his short stay in the crownland. After his departure, it was reasoned, the traditional communities guarded "their" affairs with vigor, viewing with suspicion any modernizing trends. In reality, the situation in the first half of the nineteenth century was much more complex.

The three consecutive successors of Joseph II either did not have enough time on the throne, or lacked the will to pursue the spirit of his reforms. Although he had been groomed to rule by his Uncle Joseph, the emperor Francis had much less inclination toward social experimentation. Under him, many earlier laws were rolled back; for instance, newly gained Jewish rights to own land were curtailed. In an age when having land could be the ticket to prosperity and stability for generations to come, new purchases were suddenly discouraged by a legal twist: Jews would be allowed to buy land, but without the right to pass it to their heirs. Those Jews who had benefited from unconditional land ownership under the Patent of Joseph II had to await further regulations. A clarification in their favor finally came after twenty-six years of uncertainty.

Yet the gains of past reforms were not entirely erased; a land survey ordered by Francis in 1820 showed a surprising number of small Jewish landowners. Confusing instructions to local administrators would become the norm over the next several years. Some types of land, but not others, became legally accessible to "qualified" Jews. Just who was the right sort of buyer turned out to be less obvious; in the end, the law was probably not strictly adhered to.[13]

Despite all the odds, a small group of Galician Jews persevered in their calls for secular education. They focused on the studies of science and languages, stubbornly insisting on Jews' rights to lives different from those of the past. Many of this group argued for the loosening of some traditional customs, so as to fully embrace Enlightenment values. In modern terms, these Jews represented the "counterculture" of the day. At times, more vocal members of this informal circle were seen by traditionalists as backstabbers who were scheming with authorities to alter traditional ways of life. In reality, their challenges to prevailing norms within the Jewish community varied. For the most part they were not radicals on the scale of Herz Homberg, although some of them did not shy away from sharp literary exchanges with opponents.

These modernizing Galician Jews were often called "Germans," not primarily from their use of that language, but mainly because of their rejection of traditional Jewish garb or old-fashioned Polish long coats. Instead, they wore western

European dress. In the first decades of the nineteenth century, they explored "the other world" as never before, some venturing into the theater, others studying languages, and almost all writing books. In the tradition of past revivals of Hebrew literature, the so-called Spanish or the Italian School, these Jewish Galicians who expressed themselves in verse or prose would come to be called the founders of the Galician School. Their biting satires went after fundamentalist rabbis and *Hasidim*, two groups that were at odds with each other, but united in the common goal of opposing all modern trends. For the reformers, the world of *Hasidim* was a place where "one could touch the pitch blackness all around with one's hand."[14]

Their inspiration came from an unlikely source. Nachman Krochmal lived his entire life in Galicia. His orthodox mother paid a fine rather than send her young son to a secular "*Normalschule*," in fear of bad influences; this would become one of many contradictions present in his life. Krochmal's capacity for learning became evident later, when over a period of ten years he mastered an astonishing number of languages, becoming fluent not only in Hebrew, Aramaic, Arabic, and Syriac, but also Latin, Greek, German, and French. With unmatched intellectual curiosity, he probed the past, but he also became an avid reader of contemporary German literature. Amazingly, all these studies were undertaken in a small town, without a single day spent in university! At roughly the age of twenty, Krochmal became ill from overwork and exhaustion, and was sent to Lemberg (Lwów) for treatment. His emaciated look brought an incidental comment from a passerby, who was ironically not far from the truth; he surmised that Krochmal's haggard appearance was "because he carried around heretical books."

A deliberate philosopher who would not rush to publish his own texts, Krochmal saw his religion as one that could evolve over time without losing its basic tenets. To many this idea came as a welcome revelation, an indication that the ideas of the *Haskalah* could be accommodated without conflict. To fundamentalists, this bordered on heresy. Krochmal's erudition, combined with his knowledge of history and philosophy, attracted a small group of Galician Jews, whose studies and debates with him were conducted in person or correspondence. Many of his students came from Hasidic families. Those brave enough to visit Krochmal recalled, even years later, walks in the forest or through fields when, "One was not to be sated with his wise conversation. Every word of his was filled with knowledge."

Yet Krochmal was not an oracle, making pronouncements in isolation from reality. Despite a mild nature, he was able to voice his strong views in unambiguous terms. When a young man—one of many—wavered under the pressure of the Hasidic community and surrendered his "heretical" books, Krochmal wrote an open letter, a passionate appeal to those weak at heart. "Hearing this [news], my heart boiled up, but I was even more bewildered to hear that they frightened you and that your terror was so great that you meekly agreed to hand over your good and proper books for burning, and that you begged the foolish wretch who is their leader, like a boy who cries under the rod. My dear friend, you have behaved foolishly and acted very unjustly.... At the age of twenty you ought to be a fighter and not tremble and be afraid before a petty little man."[15]

Much later, another of Krochmal's followers remembered being married at age thirteen, becoming a widower only a year later and quickly remarrying on the orders of his father. Living surrounded by the Hasidic community, he recalled that his "understanding did not light up in this darkness" until he came under the infectious influence of the enlightened *maskilim.*

Over time, the life pursuits of these and other likeminded young men led them in different directions. Some became tutors to the affluent in the Jewish community, teaching a wide range of secular subjects, or engaged in traditional professions, such as alcohol distribution or tax collection. Others ventured into "new" occupations. Only two years after its 1784 opening, the Josephinian University in Lemberg (Lwów) awarded the first doctorate in medicine ever given to a Galician Jew; that accomplishment was not lost on a foreign observer who ventured to Galicia.[16] A decade later, another door was opened when the university professors discussed an idea from a doctor of the Jewish community in Lemberg (Lwów) who wanted to give free lectures on eye diseases. The project never got off the ground, but the debate about it was progress in itself.[17]

Among the early pioneers, Jakob Rappaport was not far behind. He came from a distinguished family; his father was an accomplished person who had published medicinal texts in Latin, years before the trends of *Haskalah* reached Galicia.[18] Young Jakob started to study German, Latin, and Polish at the age of fifteen. Apparently he was a quick learner; he would master the three languages within two years. Rappaport first studied philosophy, then turned to medicine. He graduated from the university in 1804 and opened a medical practice four years later in Lemberg (Lwów); he would become a corresponding member of the Viennese Medical Society.

Zu Lemberg praktizirende Aerzte.

Herr Lorenz Edler v. Preſſen, k. k. Gubernial-
rath u. Protomedicus emeritus, geweſener Direk-
tor der mediziniſchen Fakultát.

Hr. Joſeph Hibl, k. k. Vize-Protomedikus.
— Jonas Reſſig. ▪
— Anton Marherr, Profeſſor emeritus.
— Thomas Sedey, Profeſſor emeritus.
— Franz Maſſoch, Profeſſor emeritus.
— Peter Krausnecker, Profeſſor emeritus.
— Paul Berezowski.
— Andreas Markowski.
— Dominik Predozer.
— Friedrich Oloff, k. k. Kreisphyſikus.
— Simon Sliżewski.
— Karl Ferrary.
— Johann Kaſpary, erſter Stadtphyſikus.
— Ritter von Spaventy.
— Gayo.
— Jakob Rappaport.
— Towarnicki, Aſſiſtent im allgemeinen Kran-
kenhauſe.

Hr. Moiſes Mahl.
— Anton Noel.
— Friedrich Pleſſel.
— Emanuel Rohrer.
— Johann Franz Kowalſki.
— Chladek, Doktor der Wundarzneykunde.

Jakob Rappaport was listed among physicians in Lemberg (Lwów) in 1808. He was one of the first Jewish doctors who graduated from the university there in 1804. Within the next few years, there was a steady increase in university-trained Jewish physicians in Lemberg (Lwów). (*Schematismus des Königreiches Galizien und Lodomerien für das Jahr 1808. Lemberg 1808.*)

Highly regarded in his professional circles, Dr. Rappaport engaged in lively exchanges with the best physicians from German-speaking lands and the former Poland, as well as those from Russia. He became recognized for providing free medical care for the poor, as well as for a commonsense approach to treating cholera, earning respect from all corners of Lemberg (Lwów). Rappaport went far beyond serving just the Jewish community; his reputation grew well beyond the city and transcended religious or ethnic boundaries. Another invisible barrier to Jews had fallen.

Jakob Rappaport (1775–1855), eminent Jewish physician and an early supporter of the movement to build the new Temple (the German-Israelite Prayer House) in Lemberg (Lwów). He came from a distinguished rabbinical family; his father was a fully accredited physician in Galicia in the eighteenth century. *(Courtesy of the Austrian National Library, Vienna.)*

Another notable member of the early movement was Joseph Perl, who came from an affluent merchant family in Tarnopol, which became another center of Galician *Haskalah*. Early in his life, like many of his generation, he became attracted to Hasidic rituals. On subsequent business trips, however, Perl encountered Jewish men of the Enlightenment and quickly embraced new trends. He became an educator, opening a Jewish school in Tarnopol in 1813. Next to it, Perl established a "Temple for Regulated Worship," an early precursor of the Reform movement in Galicia where the sermons were given in German on the holy days. In many respects, he was lucky; whether it was his financial independence or support of local governmental administrators, Perl seemed less susceptible to attacks by traditionalists and continued his activities largely unhindered. On a number of occasions, he was able to offer financial help to many struggling *maskilim*.[19]

The Jewish faction of "Germans" from Lemberg (Lwów), Tarnopol, and Brody did not spare their own communal establishment—"band of town fathers and

A view of Lemberg (Lwów) from the early nineteenth century.
The town was the seat of Galicia's provincial government and the university, and had a large Jewish community. (*Courtesy of the Austrian National Library, Vienna.*)

householders"—from the literary criticism. There, they pointed to the insincerity of scholarly rabbis and Jewish families of privilege, whom they accused of maintaining the status quo as a way of controlling their brethren. For years, some of them continued to wonder, with biting wit, how it was that the most despised taxes were collected by their own. While the biblical King Salomon had spoken about nature and written poems, they said with irony, the present day Salomon—the one who had proposed the tax for and harvested the payments on candles—was concerned only about profit.[20]

Regardless of their professions, the reformers gravitated to each other with the same quest for intellectual stimulation and the same cultural inspiration, all inspired by the *Haskalah* movement. Neither contemporaneous nor later critics of Joseph II would ever admit that the access to professional careers made available to the Jews of Galicia, regardless of how small their numbers, was to some degree a consequence of the late emperor's policies.

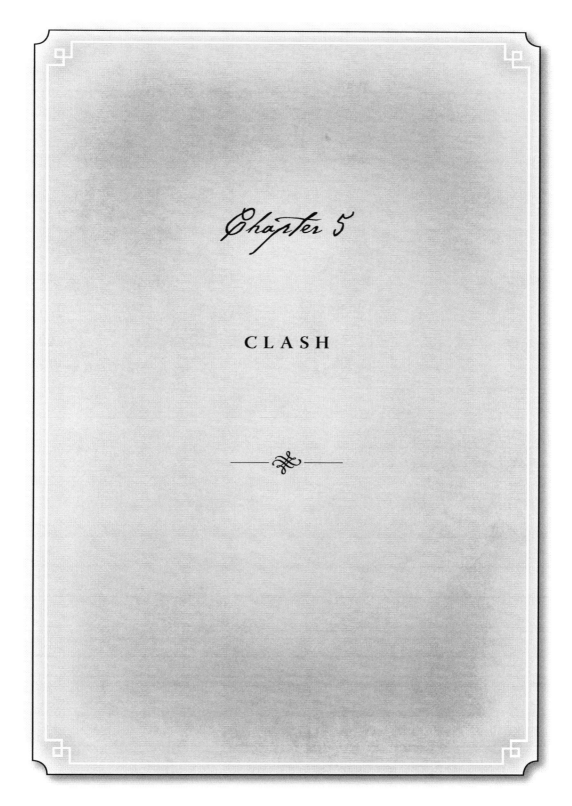

Chapter 5

CLASH

———✦———

A BIG BATTLE BETWEEN MODERNITY AND tradition took place in Lemberg (Lwów), home to more than twenty thousand Jews. The city expanded greatly under Austrian rule; it was always full of officials from different corners of the Empire and visiting troops who frequently held maneuvers there.[1] In the waning years of the eighteenth century and at the beginning of the next century, the city's social scene was particularly lively during its famous fair, called for as long as anyone could remember the "Lemberg (Lwów) Contracts." In the tradition dating to pre-Austrian times, the sitting governor would publically declare months in advance: "to all who ought to know," his official permission to hold this fair. The announcement, which was sent all over Galicia, carried a pledge to maintain the safety of the roads, and guarantees of unimpeded passage to domestic and foreign visitors, regardless of from where they were coming. No doubt, those who still hesitated about whether to make the trip must have felt reassured by the governor's promise that the city would be well stocked with food. And as if this was not enough, the annual ritual of holding negotiations and making transactions, both small and large, was declared free of any hidden taxes.

When the time finally came and visitors descended on Lemberg (Lwów), the crowd—estimated by eyewitnesses to be in the thousands—could not have been more interesting to watch. The nobility, in their old-fashioned attire of caps, long tunics, and furs, mixed with Jewish merchants and their agents. Bureaucrats, military officers from far reaches of the Austrian Empire, and all sorts of craftsmen were also there. If the small army of local lawyers swarming around the gatherings suggested this was a disagreeable crowd, nothing was further from the truth. Jewish and non-Jewish *advokaten* were simply there to be ready to put any contract in writing, whether for the sale of a manorial estate or for numerous leases; they would then promptly file the papers at the right office in the capital.[2] Not far from them, Jewish traders stood by to guarantee deliveries of fresh or salted fish to anyone wanting to stock up before Lent; and for those with deeper pockets, caviar from the Caspian and Black Seas was also available.

All this Lemberg (Lwów) business was mixed with the carnival season. Among the local merchants, if not enough money passed into their hands at this time, it was bitterly complained about for the rest of the year. But the serious trading in grains, furs, wool, and whatever other commodities were available was accompanied by lighter affairs. For the visiting nobility, it was the prime time for shopping in eight trading houses, both domestic—three of them owned by Jewish proprietors Zudig, Balaban, and Gößl—and foreign, which provided luxury items for all of eastern Galicia. Almost without exception, every noble lady bought elegant clothing, fine lace, and pins for her carefully arranged hair that were said to shine like "teeth of gold, steel, and precious stones." The typical husband, as one Austrian visitor remarked tongue-in-cheek, even if he did not "put on a pair of white silk stockings and shoes throughout the entire year, would rush during the harshest winter in this costume to the balls.... [It was there that] all the latest Viennese fashions, brilliant and bizarre, were on display, with a joy visible in peering eyes that mixed with craving." For more serious pursuits, wooden stands around the city, managed by booksellers wrapped in furs with their fingers frozen, offered old books at discounted prices.

Housing for this entire crowd was a big problem during "the Contracts"; rents during this period were hardly lower than those in Vienna. The wealthiest, who traveled with their entire families, rented decent accommodations at ridiculously steep prices; other, less titled nobles took the best rooms in apartments of the city bureaucrats, while officials' families managed during these busy weeks by being squeezed into offices. But the largest group of eager visitors, the simple country gentry, usually traveling without their wives or daughters, rented rooms in the poor district. A remarkable sight was described in a report to Vienna; row after row of houses where "at the ground level, Jews inhabit one wing and Polish noblemen another. A Polish noble could seek in vain even one room that has decent furnishings, similar to that of the nastiest laundress in Vienna. He finds nothing but an old table and a still more ancient candlestick without a candle, and then some planks stapled together, which have four wooden legs and are raised a half-foot above the floor."[3]

All in all, the attractions of doing business and enjoying the atmosphere of the Lemberg Contracts were usually too great to make a fuss about lodgings. After a few weeks everyone would rush back to the country, with promises to come again next year. No one would leave empty-handed; some departed with new clothing and household items, others with trunks full of books or musical sheets, or even riding a new carriage, hoping this time to travel the pothole-filled roads in a bit more comfort than before.

In an odd way, the situation in Lemberg (Lwów) was somewhat of a paradox. There open commerce flourished, well beyond those electrifying months of each year. And yet most Jews were poor—manual laborers and porters; only a few were able to show success. With unmasked envy, a traveler passing through the provincial capital in 1803 could not help noticing several new two- and three-story houses built of stone, rather than cheap wood, with all but one belonging to Jewish merchants. At the same time, Lemberg's (Lwów's) Israelite community, although not monolithic by any measure, remained overwhelmingly under the influence of the rabbinic fundamentalist hierarchy. None of the Hebrew printing presses in the capital city—which published books not just for Galicia, but also for export to South Prussia (*Südpreußen*), Russia and Hungary—would have dared to spread the rebellious message of foreign or domestic *maskilim*.

When it came to Friday nights, the rules of the Sabbath were strictly observed, with Jewish neighborhoods coming to a virtual standstill. The sight of ropes suspended between houses and roofs, as if snaring the alleys in a large web, was common; these were the arteries of communication that could offer observant Jews, who were not allowed to carry any item outside their dwellings, a way to pass along a message or a parcel between buildings. No matter how much money was offered or how urgent the business of a gentile, the Jewish coachmen—who, on other days, were valued for their speedy services—would not move their carriages or wagons. Only little girls could be seen scurrying around with prayer books that their fathers or uncles needed in synagogues. Even carrying a live chicken to a sick relative would have been frowned upon by the orthodox rabbis.

At times, strict observance of such religious customs brought curiosity from gentiles. They were told that some rules could be waived only when facing mortal danger, for instance when traveling to the semi-barbaric lands of Moldavia and beyond.[4] Otherwise, the elders of the Jewish community in Lemberg (Lwów) had no appetite for any deviation from centuries-old practices and beliefs. Their past battles against Herz Homberg were now legendary, but a different struggle was about to break out.

The clash between the fundamentalists and the modernists became apparent in 1815, when an old-fashioned ban of excommunication was suddenly nailed to the door of a synagogue. Its message was there for everyone to see: "Dear brethren of the household of Israel. It is known that for a certain time now culture and education, and also the study of the German language," the condemnation read in Hebrew letters, "have begun to spread among us. Those chiefly responsible are … well-known young people…. They publicly recite Scripture in German translation, with commentary of the philosopher Moses Mendelssohn. They also agitate among all their friends and acquaintances, urging them to study languages and sciences. Therefore, with the authority of the Torah and of holy rabbis, we decree against them and against their colleagues and against all who hold with them, the great excommunication …"[5]

Although the condemnation was anonymous, since such acts were already forbidden, everyone knew the force behind it. Jacob Ornstein, the chief rabbi of Lemberg (Lwów), was a staunch defender of traditional ways of life. Facing the challenge on a very different scale than before, the group of young reformers did not waste time. They promptly translated the text of the ban from Hebrew to German, most likely with some purposeful exaggeration, and presented it to the town authorities. Under mounting pressure from the local government, the rabbi was obliged to address the issue publically in the Great City Synagogue of Lemberg (Lwów). The old man spoke to the gathered crowd: "In regard to the ban of excommunication issued this summer against the study of foreign languages and especially the four individuals named…, let it be known that these bans of excommunication broke the laws of His Majesty, the Emperor, and the laws of the state." Then, he continued in a wavering voice: "Therefore, these bans are rescinded and anyone who issues such again will be punished." He would declare no objections to the use of German, or to secular studies. As if this was not enough, a young member of the *maskilim* sitting in the back row of the synagogue would exclaim with unhidden joy, "Louder, Rabbi, louder; we cannot hear you!"[6]

But this turned out to be a Pyrrhic victory; those named continued to be ostracized by the orthodox majority. No longer able to secure a steady income, a few of the early reformers had to move from one town to another and even leave for other lands of the Austrian Empire. Yet many others weathered the storm and remained in Galicia. With perseverance and the passage of time, they had their share of bittersweet victories. This would have been evident in an elegant satire written by Isaac Erter, one of the four men who had been targeted by the angry Rabbi Ornstein. The rabbi was a recognized scholar, but a few years after the confrontation in Lemberg (Lwów), the rebels brought into question the veracity of his writings. In the

Isaac Erter (1792–1851) was raised as a Hasid, but became one of the most vocal proponents of the Galician Enlightenment. After fleeing from Lemberg (Lwów) to Brody, Erter went to Budapest to study medicine. He became admired for his satirical writings, seen today as early examples of the modern Hebrew literature. *(Courtesy of the Library of the Jewish Theological Seminary, New York.*

story woven by Erter for his readers, when an enormous book bearing the rabbi's distinguished name was placed on a magic scale—one that could distinguish originality from plagiarism—this magnum opus suddenly shrank; apparently the pages of "stolen" text had magically disappeared! Now, the tables had turned. In his satire, Erter claimed that the rabbi had actually written only the title page of his famous scholarly work.[7]

Solomon Judah Löb Rapoport (1790–1867) authored six highly acclaimed monographs on medieval Jewish scholars. During his youth in Lemberg (Lwów), he engaged in several activities forbidden to Orthodox Jews. He would often sneak away to attend the theater; he also studied French. Rapoport was among the *maskilim* who were excommunicated in 1815 by the "great inquisitor of Galicia," Jacob Ornstein. In 1840, he moved to Prague, Bohemia, where he would become the chief rabbi. *(Courtesy of the Library of the Jewish Theological Seminary, New York.)*

In due time, another intellectual among the "heretics," Solomon Judah Löb Rapoport, would secure his place among the most accomplished European Jews of the period. He would write biographical essays based on Talmudic texts, with an attention to historical facts unheard of until then. The scholarly content, published over a period of three years in Vienna, earned praises from as far away as Italy. Yet even that serious work sparked the ire of Orthodox religious leaders. Then, in a further reversal of fortune, this rebel turned scholar would have the last word, becoming chief rabbi in the more permissive Prague. Not bad for someone at risk of excommunication from the Jewish faith some years before![8]

Meanwhile, there was slow progress to be seen in Galicia. The next wave of modern German-Jewish schools was established, first in Tarnopol and then in Brody. In particular, Brody's special status as a commercial center that linked German hubs of commerce with Russia and the

Middle East fostered contacts across many cultures; that extended its citizens' acceptance of secular education. This was not lost on one of the *maskilim* who, bruised after battles elsewhere, would exclaim with a dose of exaggeration: "The city of Brody is superior to all the cities of Israel in this country. The ways and thoughts of its people are higher than the ways and thoughts of people in the other cities of the country, just as the reason of a man of virtue is higher than the reason of a young child limited in the quality of understanding."[9]

Certainly, he was not alone in his praises of this unique place; a Jewish writer from the Italian province, once frustrated with his own Orthodox community (which was generally more moderate than its brethren from Galicia), would comment to his *maskil* acquaintance from faraway Brody: "You have friends such as your heart desires, and can converse with them." Perhaps unaware of that place's local

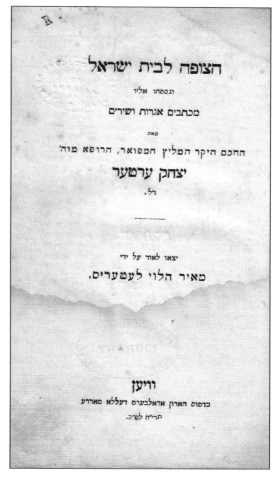

הצופה לבית ישראל

ונספחו אליו

מכתבים אגרות ושירים

מאת

החכם היקר המליץ המפואר, הרופא מוה׳

יצחק ערטער

ז״ל.

יצאו לאור על ידי

מאיר הלוי לעטעריס.

ווינען

בדפוס האדון אדאלבערט דעללא מאררע

תרי״ח לפ״ק.

The Scale: A Vision of the Night (*Moznei Mishkal*) by Isaac Erter. First published in the Hebrew literary-scientific journal *Bikkurei Ha-ittim* (*First Fruits of the Times*) in Vienna, 1823. With memories of the excommunication still fresh, *The Scale* took a satirical swipe at Jacob Ornstein (the rabbi of Lemberg), accusing him of plagiarism. This cover page is from the edition published in 1858, in Vienna. (*Courtesy of the Library of the Jewish Theological Seminary, New York.*)

struggles, the Italian lamented his own "zealots who trample everything precious with their feet and declare every seeker after truth a thoroughgoing heretic."[10]

The slow, stubborn progress in Galicia was in more than social or literary contexts. In 1832, a pharmacy owned by a university-educated pharmacist opened in Tarnopol. For a cursory observer of Galician life, this might have been nothing extraordinary—if not for the fact that this was the first license given to a Jew in the entire Austrian Empire; so another small nod toward a new way of life was made.[11]

The circle of modernists who remained in Lemberg (Lwów) was slight in number, but diverse. It included *maskilim* not much concerned with religion; others who, in worship, continued to adhere to traditional Judaism; and a growing number of Jews interested in the Reform movement emanating from Germany. One of those was Moritz Rappaport (unrelated to the Jakob Rappaport mentioned before), who came from a family where new trends were tested daily at home. His father was an early proponent of change, but his mother remained firmly Orthodox. The young man was sent to Vienna to be educated in a Catholic *gymnasium*, followed by medical studies at the university. When he returned home, Dr. Rappaport established a successful practice; after busy days with patients, he also found time to write poetry for which he would later be acclaimed.[12] Another member of the group was Marcus Dubs, an aspiring entrepreneur, who in his youth had spoken only Yiddish but taught himself Polish and German. Among them were also two lawyers, the first Jewish members of the local bar.[13]

An opportunity for the reformers to make an impact on the local scene came when the unyielding chief rabbi of the Lemberg (Lwów) district died in 1839. The next year, the reformers finally convinced local authorities to appoint some of their number as representatives to the board that oversaw Jewish affairs in the city. Suddenly, the professionals and the intellectuals were in a position to invite a progressive preacher to modernize Jewish education and worship in the capital of Galicia.

⁓

ABRAHAM KOHN HAD A gift for public oratory and a lot of energy. Born in Bohemia, he was the son of a peddler, yet was able to acquire education without much assistance. He completed philosophy studies at the Charles University of Prague. For the next ten years, Kohn served as a rabbi in Hohenems, a small Austrian town in the Rhine valley. Despite his youthful appearance, he managed well the spiritual and educational needs of some ninety Jewish families residing there.

Kohn slowly became recognized beyond his local community through his writings. First, a small collection of his sermons was published in Prague. Then, the textbook of a Hebrew grammar for Jewish schools appeared, which Kohn had financed himself. His other writings, more scholarly in nature, challenged some of the prevailing dogma, methodically separating customs from true religious laws. For example, not playing music on Sabbaths or holidays was one of those restrictions Kohn thought should be discontinued. In another piece, he argued that rules on head coverings or even the shaving of hair by married women lacked religious justification and were more likely "old-German rather than old-Jewish customs."

Reincarnation (Gilgul Nefesh) by Isaac Erter. Probably the most popular of Erter's writings, it was first published in 1845 in Hebrew, and later translated into Yiddish. With satirical imagination it described the journey of the soul, which moved through human and animal characters.
(Courtesy of the Library of the Jewish Theological Seminary, New York.)

He preached by example; his wife, Magdalena Kohn, whom he married while in Hohenems, wore her hair uncovered.[14]

By the summer of 1843, Abraham Kohn had received three offers, two from Germany and one from Galicia, to become preacher to larger Jewish congregations. For the thirty-six-year-old rabbi, the invitation from Lemberg (Lwów) was probably the most difficult to decline. He was informed that he was a candidate for "religious instructor and preacher" there. It was true that Lemberg (Lwów) was far away, and associated with memories of Jewish resistance to Herz Homberg's ideas, which were well known beyond Galicia. But the opportunity to make a difference there was also tempting. Kohn agreed to take the long trip in August to be interviewed by the progressive board members; this was also an opportunity

Abraham Kohn (1807–1848) during his service in the Alpine town of Hohenems. His writings in the *Scientific Journal of Jewish Theology* (*Wissenschaftliche Zeitschrift für jüdische Theologie*) attracted the attention of reformers in Lemberg (Lwów) after they were first published in 1839. *(Courtesy of the Austrian National Library, Vienna.)*

for Kohn to gauge whether the city was the right place to settle with his family.

Given the frictions between the modernists and traditionalists, there was naturally some apprehension in town before Kohn's visit. A few weeks before the appointed date, an announcement was issued about a sermon to be given in Lemberg's Great City Synagogue by the chief rabbi of Hohenems. Nothing was left to chance: the congregants, many of whom had never encountered a preacher like Kohn, were "instructed and required to behave quietly, to sit in their seats during the sermon, and [neither] speak nor walk about." On August 19, 1843, the synagogue was most likely well attended and the preacher probably veered away from anything too controversial when he addressed the gathered crowd. Despite some initial nervousness, Kohn must have made an excellent impression. Apparently everything went well, and the next day a contract drafted by the reform-minded board was signed.

The language of the agreement was clear about the responsibilities awaiting Kohn. He was to serve initially as a teacher of religion and overseer of the orphanage in Lemberg (Lwów); there was also the exciting prospect of a Reform synagogue under construction, where Kohn would eventually serve as spiritual leader. The offer of a better salary than he was receiving in Hohenems must also have been a factor in Kohn's final decision.

After he returned to their small town tucked in the mountains, Kohn and his family wrapped up their affairs and prepared for a new life in Galicia. They would not start the trip for several months, however; quite possibly they did not want to travel during the winter, and most likely, Magdalena Kohn was not able to travel yet because she was pregnant. When they did make the trip with their newborn son and three other children, they took a circuitous route, first going to Switzerland and Bavaria to see the wife's relatives. They stopped in Vienna and from there took a train to Galicia. Railroad tracks had not reached Lemberg (Lwów) yet; the last leg of the journey was made in a horse-drawn wagon. On an evening early in May 1844 the Kohns finally arrived at the city gates; they were greeted by a group of horseback riders, all young Jewish reformers. Certainly, this was a hopeful sign of welcome.[15]

On the following Saturday, the new preacher gave his first sermon in a different synagogue in front of a mainly Hasidic audience. The Great Suburban Synagogue of Lemberg (Lwów) was packed; it was obvious that high hopes were vested in Abraham Kohn, and not just by a group of Jewish reformers. In the first row sat the governor of Galicia; the military head of the district and the city president were also prominently seated. When Kohn appeared after a few prayers, the shock to the traditional Jewish audience could not easily be overstated. Dressed like the progressive preachers of Vienna or Prague, Kohn must have looked, to the local congregation, more like a Catholic priest or a Protestant pastor than a rabbi.

Kohn introduced himself as a messenger of peace (*Friedensbote*). When he spoke (in High German), his message was one of moderation; he acknowledged that the pace of reform he envisioned might strike some as slow. Kohn stressed this was not out of any fear on his part, but because consideration had to be given to local sensitivities. Yet in spite of these reassuring words, many heads were turning, and irritated voices could be heard: "What is he saying?" Most of the Yiddish-speaking audience could not understand their new preacher! Later, unconfirmed reports would surface that a few incensed Jews had torn their clothes, as if at a funeral, responding to the new rabbi's act of "desecration"— daring to preach in German in their synagogue!

The front cover of the printed inaugural sermon by Abraham Kohn. The event took place on May 11, 1844 in the Great Suburban Synagogue of Lemberg (Lwów), and reportedly evoked mixed reactions from the Orthodox congregants.

Luckily, a large number of the ushers—wisely recruited from among Jewish youth attending local schools—came in quite handy, maintaining order that Saturday. Once again, what was liberating progress for some had been seen by others as provocative and a violation of their spiritual needs. Soon, outrageous fantasies would be spun about the presumed transgressions of the newcomer, and would even find their way to a pamphlet designed to inflame the community. In it, Abraham Kohn was compared to the Roman emperor Titus, whose legions had destroyed the Second Temple in Jerusalem in 70 CE. Clearly, the battle for minds and souls was being waged from both sides.[16]

Although Kohn had been certified to teach in Jewish schools by the same Herz Homberg who had made so many enemies in Galicia, his style was very different. In his soon-published articles "Letters from Galicia," Kohn certainly sounded less militant than Homberg. In fact, he scolded many of the *maskilim* for speaking with such contempt about Hasidic practices. For him that sort of worship, which was definitely foreign to his taste, earned some respect nonetheless because of its "heart and soul."

ა

KOHN HAD THE INSIGHT to see an emerging opportunity, a way to introduce more changes to Galician Jews than might have been realized through secular education and encouragement toward more open ways of life. In his own words, he said that Hasidism itself "was a popular reform that paved the way for more rational reform. In particular, it has brought more freedom into synagogue ritual and in the course of time has permitted itself significant changes."

"Rational reform" was what Kohn now started to implement in Lemberg (Lwów). Moving beyond scholarly writings, he began giving the sort of sermons that had never before been heard in the town—advocating, at first in small ways, different lifestyles, such as the idea that women wear their hair unshorn. Yet, Kohn was also a modest man who understood well the challenge in front him, as a European-educated young rabbi vying to earn the trust of a large Orthodox community.[17]

Not long after settling in the city, Kohn was given the coveted position of district rabbi, which had remained vacant for several years. Predictably, this enraged many in the community. Especially deep resentment was felt among ultraconservative descendants of the late Rabbi Jacob Ornstein's family; for them, being bypassed for that appointment was more than a personal setback. As they saw it, this signified the threat of losing privileges that extended for that family beyond the basic sphere of spirituality.

When that agitation against Kohn in Lemberg (Lwów) did not amount to anything, his opponents raised their game. In a petition to the Court Chancellery, they demanded removal of the apostate whom, they said, "Leads an immoral life and has not the slightest scholarly qualification to serve as a rabbi." In the tradition of the Viennese bureaucracy, memoranda were written, with inquiries sent to the places where Abraham Kohn had lived before coming to Galicia. When nothing but glowing opinions were sent back, the Court Chancellery rejected all protests and confirmed the legality of prior elections of the Jewish communal board and the new rabbi.

Abraham Kohn (1807–1848). The image is probably from the time when he lived in Lemberg (Lwów).

To add another insult to the Orthodox, a new Jewish school opened in 1845. It was an immediate success; five hundred and eighty children enrolled in its first year, with many others turned away for lack of space. In two years, the number of students—boys and girls divided into six grades—rose to more than seven hundred; without doubt this was the best evidence that despite obstacles, many Jewish families were choosing a new future. Like the former Homberg schools, this modern public institution taught its pupils mainly in German but, reflecting a new flexibility, it also offered some lessons in Polish. In short time, visitors had only words of praise: "Languages and arithmetic are not taught better or more thoroughly anywhere else [in Galicia]." Perhaps in an effort to avoid mistakes of the past, secular subjects were complemented by classes in biblical history and by religious education in Hebrew, based on texts prepared by Rabbi Kohn himself. If children seemed to be somewhat overloaded when it came to studies of Hebrew language, a Jewish observer quickly added that "this is necessary if the demands from the various sides are to be taken seriously." Despite initial worries how the school would be received, the high attendance seemed like a hopeful sign; some wanted to see that as a vote of confidence by the broader Jewish community, "especially since the students came from homes of the most diverse religious views."[18] Plans for a school to train new teachers, molded in the spirit of the mild reforms, were drafted to replicate the success of Lemberg (Lwów) across Galicia.

In September 1846, Kohn officiated during the opening of the new Reform Temple, which was officially known as The German-Israelite Prayer House (*Deutsch-israelitisches Bethaus*). This was the culmination of a six-year effort by the local circle of reform-minded Jews, and financial contributions from both Jewish and non-Jewish sources. The approach of those founders was not as monolithic as one might suspect today. Knowing that that they were charting new directions, there had been early hesitation among some about how far they could go.

The respected Dr. Jakob Rappaport had addressed his colleagues when the new synagogue's planning was just taking shape. Speaking at their first meeting, he had used words of caution: "Today we are [planning] a sanctuary with a regulated liturgy, and hence we should take care that the majority of our brethren, who still cannot or do not want to use this sanctuary, should not turn against us. And this would definitely happen if the prayers were not in our ancient Hebrew language but in German, or if we were to drop some parts of the prayers, thus provoking our Orthodoxy." Then, he continued, "We should not be shy about our nationality [Jewish identity]; I meet all sorts of people and I must confess that people do not hate us so [much], as some suggest. Likewise, we should not be shy about our liturgy, either about its language or its ritual...."

But finding a middle ground, one that was satisfying to everyone, turned out to be difficult. This group of physicians, lawyers, and a few merchants was seeking to establish a synagogue that would offer a different liturgy than that practiced in the old synagogues of Lemberg (Lwów). They did not hesitate to send letters to reform-oriented rabbis in Vienna and Prague, asking for advice. Their petitions to the government spelled out their desire for services led by a progressive preacher, with a modern cantor and choir, and ethical instruction.[19]

The new synagogue stood in the center of the Fish Market (the Old Market). It was built in the neoclassical style, following the example of a progressive synagogue in Vienna. But in contrast to the Viennese temple (*Stadttemple*), which was hidden from view, Lemberg's (Lwów's) new addition was an elegant building boldly visible to everyone. It stood in direct proximity to Christian places of worship, a clear sign of a more permissive environment, and was only a few streets away from the cultural centers and governmental institutions of the Galician capital city. Its opening was an event to watch; the military provided ceremonial grenadiers and a cavalry unit, which stood in attention in the square. Later, some would speculate that this was merely for the protection of the crowd, but regardless of motive the military presence added to the splendor of the day.

Upon entering through the west entrance, the invited guests found themselves in a round prayer hall, with arranged pews in the center. The graceful interior was domed by a large cupola and encircled by two tiers of columns supporting slightly bowing galleries.[20] The Progressive Synagogue, as it would be known in later years, was filled with Jews and non-Jews that day, including civilian and military officials. By no coincidence, Dr. Moritz Rappaport—not to be confused with the aforementioned Dr. Jakob Rappaport—one of the founding members of the committee, was among the celebrants. For older participants, there was an inescapable sense of irony: Jakob Rappaport was a cousin of Solomon Judah Löb Rapoport, who had once been excommunicated by Jacob Ornstein, the chief rabbi of Lemberg, for his "dangerous" studies. Now, with that rabbi, known as "the great inquisitor of Galicia," gone, many in the crowd hoped that the opening of the Temple was another sign that progress was unstoppable. Even one of the non-Jewish donors was given an honorary seat in the synagogue for life.

After speeches given in German by Rabbi Abraham Kohn and others, the Jewish men's choir sang, with a baritone singer said to be particularly impressive. A newspaper reporter who was present, glancing at the upper galleries, gallantly noted that they were "filled by the beautiful faces of the daughters of Israel" wearing modern dress. The correspondent did not fail to mention that across the street from the Temple, a new Jewish restaurant was attracting patrons with a long menu written in German (and a few copies in Hebrew), female waiters, and surprisingly diverse dishes. In a good-natured swipe at traditional Jewish cuisine, which the writer perhaps viewed as not always attractive, he declared that this culinary establishment could "lure" many from across Lemberg, despite its steep prices.[21]

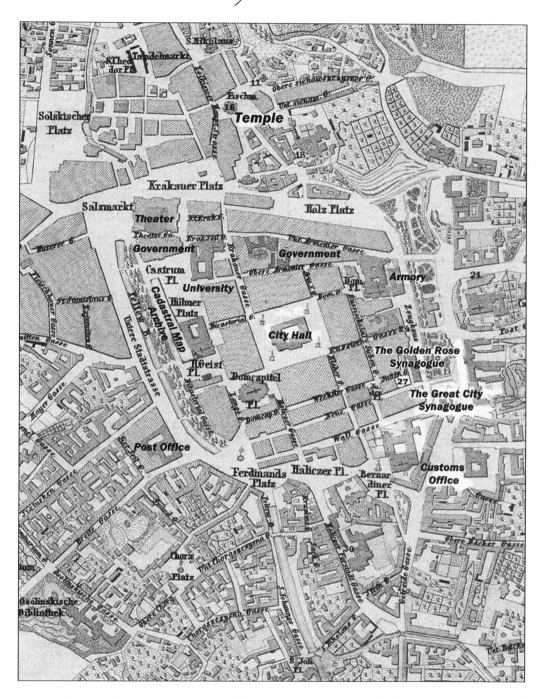

City map of Lemberg (Lwów), showing location of the new Temple (German-Israelite Prayer House), later renamed the Progressive Synagogue (marked as 16), which was erected in the "Fish Market" (also known as The Old Market), north of the city center. The Great City Synagogue (marked as 27) and the Golden Rose Synagogue were situated in the old Jewish district. *(Based on Administrativ-Karte von den Königreichen Galizien und Lodomerien, BL. 24; 1855.)*

The Progressive Synagogue of Lemberg (Lwów). An undated photograph
from the period before World War II.

Other reports, filed by Jews themselves, spoke about their new Temple as a symbol that a deeper cultural shift was in the making. One local correspondent enthusiastically exclaimed, "Our future is in the hands of Austria, our spiritual-political rebirth can only be a German one ... our language is a German dialect." Despite earlier concerns about how the new German-Israelite Prayer House would be received, the signs reported a few months later were encouraging: "choral singing is finding more approval and the sermon is winning over more hearts all the time.... Most of the members of the congregation who dress in the German style cannot take part in the [Orthodox] worship services, attend services at the new Prayer House on Friday evening, and on the Sabbath with their wives." A few Orthodox men and women—"dressed like Polish Jews"—were also spotted there. Perhaps, as someone mused, they found that "here too, one can pray with concentration."[22]

Yet these hopeful signs were more the exception than the rule; battles between the modernists and the traditionalists soon affected many aspects of life.

In Lemberg (Lwów) in 1847, the Jewish community board opined to the authorities that traditional garb ("fur hats and caftans") should be eliminated in the conduct of official business by the administration's officers and hospital workers, as well as by couples applying for marriage licenses. With some degree of truth, they remarked on the intergenerational tensions that existed in fundamentalist and Hasidic families, which prevented more people from wearing "German" clothing. By convenient "coincidence," petitions by young people from Lemberg, Brody, and Tarnopol suddenly flooded civil administration offices, requesting governmental action to abolish the traditional dress code. To top off their campaign, one Saturday throngs of young Jewish men in smart modern suits paraded through the streets of Lemberg, to the disgust of the traditionalists.

But the Orthodox had their ways to punch back. They launched a campaign, with the help of like-minded communities in other towns, which wrote repeatedly to the Galician governor's office, with dire warnings against changing traditional Jewish garb. Their argument was not religious or cultural; that would have been too simple for the bureaucrats to dismiss. Instead, they sounded the alarm about allegedly massive supplies of fabric used for the production of such clothing, and the hardship that any changes to the law would bring to the lives of clothing merchants and numerous tailors. Not surprisingly, their nemesis, young Rabbi Kohn, promptly dismissed these false arguments, only further accentuating the schism.

Kohn's practices of quoting the Bible in German and removing elements of traditional services that he considered "medieval," were bold, bringing on the scorn of the Orthodox. That storm would likely have passed, since those changes, albeit outrageous to the other side, were still within the boundaries of his contract as "religious instructor and preacher." But once the Reform synagogue opened, Kohn increasingly targeted from the pulpit leaders of the Orthodox camp who benefited financially from the status quo. In particular, his public condemnation was directed at those Jews who were in charge of collecting, at hefty profits, the despised candle tax and taxes on kosher meat. When a famine struck Galicia in 1847, he cautioned them and others not to be ostentatious with displays of wealth.

A view of the interior of the German-Israelite Prayer House (the Progressive Synagogue) in Lemberg (Lwów). *(Lithograph by Piller Publishers, Lemberg; 1846.)*

In the fall of the same year, Kohn journeyed to Vienna with a petition urging abolition of the anachronistic taxes, based on the dire economic situation at home. When this failed to convince the authorities, at his next opportunity—the following year—Kohn signed another petition to the emperor. This time it was a much broader demand for the removal of any remaining signs of inequality based on religious affiliation, including the infamous taxes. In the midst of the revolution then spreading across the Austrian Empire, that appeal included a broad-based call for reforms, signed by Galicians of all stripes, including Polish aristocrats, professionals and politicians, as well as clergy (a bishop of the Catholic Church, Greek-Catholic Orthodox priests, and Rabbi Kohn).

The same month, "The Call to Israelites!" was issued in Lemberg (Lwów). There, most likely for the first time, they were addressed as, "My Dear Brothers." In a mix of German and Polish, the pamphlet called for support of the cause; the promise of inclusive society seemed within reach. On the surface, however, the German-speaking rabbi was in an awkward situation; some demands from within Galicia at that time were fueled by nationalistic aspirations, aiming to weaken political and cultural bonds between the crownland and Vienna. Yet, Kohn had no difficulty siding with the spirit of reform. With unbounded energy, he traveled with a large delegation to Vienna, where he helped to translate the group's document into German while they waited for an audience with the emperor.[23]

Back at home, the agitation against Kohn did not lessen; in fact, it was being rolled out on more fronts. A few weeks after his return from Vienna, a mob attacked Kohn's house, breaking windows; only the arrival of the armed national guard averted a more violent confrontation. His enemies spread fears among the Orthodox population that ending payment of religious taxes would bring a loss of government protection. Kohn's qualifications as a leader of the religious community were questioned among fundamentalists, some arguing that carrying a handkerchief in his pocket and an umbrella in his hand on Saturday was unseemly for a rabbi! Even the nationalistic fever among Poles during the revolutionary period in 1848 was exploited, with the traditionalists demanding, to no avail, removal of the "foreign" rabbi.

On another occasion, when returning from the school, Kohn was physically assaulted on the street. The situation was becoming increasing intolerable, and in the summer of that year he submitted a proposal to resign. However, the reformers—the rabbi's unwavering supporters—knew that would be viewed as a retreat, in which case whatever gains had been made could be at risk. They were able to convince Kohn to resign from the office of district rabbi, but retain his leadership position in the Temple and the school. For the moment, it looked as though a catastrophe had been averted.

On the morning of September 6, 1848, rumors started to circulate through the streets of Lemberg (Lwów) that cholera had broken out in the Kohn household; only later did it became clear that a conspiracy was already in the works and that this was an attempt to cover the plotters' tracks. In reality, Abraham Kohn had taken his children for a morning walk, while his wife, also in excellent health, was running a few household errands at the local market. In the afternoon, there were a few visitors at their house. Excitement was building about the upcoming first issue of a newspaper prepared for the Jewish community of Lemberg (Lwów), the brainchild of Abraham Kohn.

After dinner in the evening, the family became violently ill, but not due to a sudden spread of cholera. It turned out that earlier in the day, an unsuspecting cook had let a stranger into the Kohns' kitchen. The man had innocently claimed that he wanted to light his cigar from the stove, but apparently he managed to drop arsenic into a pot of soup being prepared for the evening meal. Abraham Kohn and his youngest daughter died a few hours after midnight. The rabbi's wife, Magdalena Kohn, and four other children were all taken ill but ultimately survived.

News of the assassination spread with the speed of light through Lemberg (Lwów). Luckily for the leaders of the Orthodox agitators, they were promptly arrested, sparing them from the revenge of the slain rabbi's emotionally charged followers. The funeral that followed included a citizens' guard that carried Kohn's casket to the Reform synagogue. Additional solemn ceremonies were conducted in the second synagogue, where two Orthodox deputy rabbis spoke, trying to heal the rift, albeit too late. Rabbi Kohn was laid to rest next to the grave of his predecessor Jacob Ornstein.

On the day of the funeral, an alleged assassin came to the attention of the authorities. A poor-looking man asked a barber to shave his beard and cut short his side curls, an unusual demand for an Orthodox Jew. After the man, Lieber Pilpel, was arrested, he was recognized by one of Kohn's children and a few servants, who remembered him asking whether he was indeed in the rabbi's kitchen. Gruesome rumors that the body of Kohn had been dug up and reburied elsewhere in the cemetery by his opponents were repeated throughout the city. To prevent any acts of desecration or vandalism, Jewish members of the national guard were posted by the fresh grave for days.[24]

⟩⟩

PARADOXICALLY, THERE WERE SOME reasons to celebrate, and in a broader sense Kohn's philosophy ultimately prevailed. For the first time, Jews were elected that year to municipal councils in Galicia. In Lemberg (Lwów), those were almost exclusively from the progressive camp. One month after Kohn's death, the first elected national parliament in the Austrian Empire debated the issue of Jewish civil rights, and the issue of taxes on meat and candles unavoidably surfaced again. Perhaps as the result of earlier petitions by the late rabbi, this time the Minister of the Treasury voiced no objection to their abolition. When a deputy tried to argue that these taxes were not religious—but purely income-based—the Jewish parliamentarian representing the city of Brody responded in High German. His logic was simple: how was it possible for a poor religious Jew paying tax on a kosher-slaughtered chicken to be wealthier than a rich secular Jew who, for a similar chicken slaughtered in his kitchen, owed no tax? When others suggested deferring a decision on these matters, he rose again, stating that over thousands of years Jews had survived worse things than these taxes, but that it was the matter of honor for the first elected parliament of Austria to decide whether to sanction relics of such a barbaric past. The vote, 243 for and 20 against abolishing the tax, moved the issue to the dustbin of history.[25]

Chapter 6

ROHATYN REVISITED: FROM JUKIEL TO REGINA DUB

$\mathcal{T}$HE LIVES OF ALL ROHATYNERS, including my ancestors, were altered in large and small ways with the arrival of Austrian rule in 1772. As the map of a new Galicia was drawn by the Habsburgs, entire villages and towns changed hands. In some cases, absentee land magnates never returned to far-flung territory to reclaim their estates. Now, their possessions were often scattered and separated not by distance alone, but also by the newly established international borders. At times, the affairs of semi-abandoned dominions badly needed attention until the new administration could slowly take control of the land in more than a military sense. Within a few years after Austrians established themselves in the new crownland, members of the absentee landed aristocracy were told they would have to pay double their taxes on their Galician properties unless they could prove they had lived somewhere under Habsburg rule for at least six months of each year.[1]

In the case of Rohatyn, the town had already suffered neglect for some time, even before the First Partition. When Count Sieniawski had died years before, its ownership had passed first to his powerful wife and then to their daughter, but it's unlikely that any of them viewed the town as more than just a source of revenue. There would be a short period when the Rohatyn district was administered by the Greek-Catholic Archbishop of Lwów, Athanasiy Sheptytskyi

(Szeptycki), who was a member of the Ruthenian nobility, before passing again to other hands.[2]

Between 1775 and 1780, representatives of Maria Theresa and Joseph II transferred ownership of the town and surrounding villages to one Countess Lubomirska. This was certainly not an act of generosity, but an exchange of properties between the countess and the Habsburg government. It didn't hurt that Countess Lubomirska had been supportive of Austrian interests in Galicia even before partition. Following the tradition of prior absentee owners, the countess lived elsewhere, governing her new dominion from a distance.[3]

Rohatyners must have been watching this change with some apprehension. In past decades, such shifts had often meant new and unwelcome obligations for everyone. These were generally imposed as required purchases of unwanted items, usually those produced by the manorial estate of the new land magnate. However, this time the transition seems to have been uneventful. No complaints were lodged, as far as we can gather today. Some could argue that this was due to the virtues of the countess, who was considered an unusual woman for her times. She was keenly interested in politics, a thoughtful individual whose curiosity went beyond the superficial gossip of the day; there has been recent speculation that she was the author of two serious treatises devoted to the behavior of her own class, which were found in her papers after she passed away. One of the manuscripts was critical of the nobility's treatment of the burghers, who were mostly excluded from making laws that governed their lives. But less idealistic Rohatyn observers could dryly reason that the countess's peaceful tenure was due more to Austrian rule, which to some degree curbed the excesses of the nobility.[4]

From the early years of Austrian Galicia, a picture of Rohatyn has emerged as "spread, in part, over the hills and, in part, over the valleys … its soil is mostly clay-like but in some places black soil is visible…. Besides houses and [vegetable] gardens, the town contains arable fields, pastures, meadows, ponds, and a small forest within its boundaries."[5] Countess Lubomirska owned the manorial estate *Jurydyka* in Rohatyn, which was within walking distance of the focal point of town, the market square. Her property extended eastward toward the suburb of Babińce.

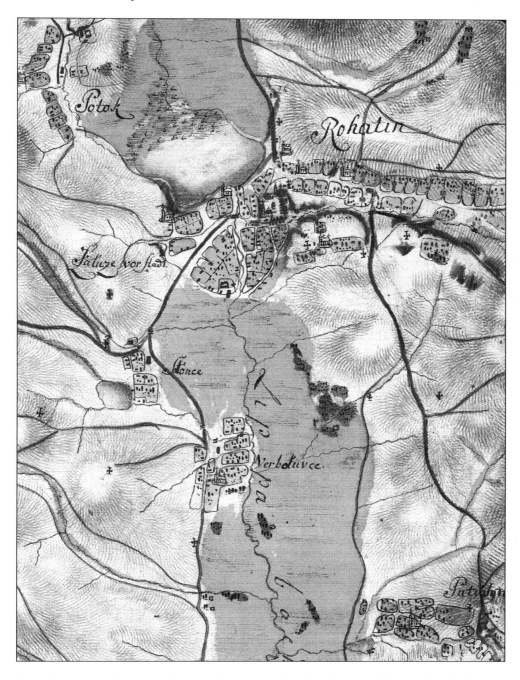

Map of Rohatyn and the surrounding area. It was commissioned on the order of Emperor Joseph II, as part of a complete cartographic survey of Galicia between 1779 and 1883. The work was overseen by Friedrich von Mieg. Given the attention to topographic details and potential military use, these maps remained classified for several years. *(Courtesy of Kriegsarchiv, the Austrian State Archives, Vienna.)*

Its name, still in use in 1787, referred to the legal authority (in Latin, *jurisdictio*) of the owner. As with most properties in the hands of aristocrats, the land and the people living there were governed by rules separate from municipal regulations.

By the end of the eighteenth century, however, the influence of the old power was beginning to wane. In Rohatyn, changing owners who had sold some of their possessions must have contributed to this; at that point, neither the castle, already falling into disrepair, nor most of the land within the town's boundaries, still belonged to the countess. In her place, the Church, with its six local parishes that included both Roman Catholic and Greek-Catholic Orthodox churches, owned more property than anyone else. Most of the land was leased to local peasants, but some fields were kept by the parishes. In line with the legal and moral standards of the time, clerical property was often tilled by Ruthenian serfs. One of the two breweries in town was also owned by a local church, competing with a similar enterprise of the countess's. It would be a few years before Emperor Joseph II would curtail the right of the Church and individual priests to be involved in "unholy" commercial activities.

The Rohatyn of 1787 was a town of two worlds; they were not entirely separated, but not fully integrated either. According to the Josephian land survey of that year, Jews, for the most part, lived close to each other. There were more than one hundred Jewish-owned houses in town. In the midst of their neighborhood, there were non-Jewish households and military stables. Some things had not changed; Jewish homes continued to concentrate around the market square. This time, however, names such as "Leyb, the son of Meyir," and "Szajer, the son of Wolf," identified a new generation there. Increasingly, however, other Rohatyners with Yiddish-sounding names spread out southward and northward along the main thoroughfare, Halicz Road, and farther south along Bursztyn Road.

Other Jewish homes sprang up in a westward direction, dotting the streets that led toward the river of Gniła Lipa. Theirs was a neighborhood with plenty of foot traffic. On the market days that Rohatyn was well known for, peddlers and farmers carried in their goods, livestock was brought to the yards, and everyone wanted to sell or buy something. The noise of the traders and the wagons passing over the few cobblestoned streets, as well as the smells of horses and other animals, must have filled the air on those busy days. On the Sabbath and Jewish holidays, the Israelites of Rohatyn streamed to the three places of worship, two of which were only a short walking distance north of the market square; other synagogues were to be built in years to come. The ritual bathhouse, another building that belonged to the *kahal,* was situated closer to the river. The sick of Rohatyn were well cared-for; one of the four hospitals in town was the Jewish hospital, supported by its community. The Jewish cemetery was situated at the eastern outskirts of town in the area that was called *Jerusalim* by the locals.

Polish Jews. Etching from a monograph entitled "National Costumes in Imperial & Royal [Austrian] Lands," published in Vienna at the beginning of the nineteenth century (1803–1821). *(Courtesy of the Austrian National Library, Vienna.)*

To curious visitors, Rohatyners could point out nine manor houses, now mainly parish rectories or clergies' residences. Those were one-story structures, larger than other dwellings, often with a few steps leading to a porch in front— but nothing fancy by today's standards. Close to the remnants of the old defense fortifications were other structures that locals called "wineries." In reality, those were wine cellars or warehouses on the manorial estate of the countess that were leased to local Jewish merchants Leyb, Srul (Yisrael), and Zus (Zuskind). Almost every year, wine and other fine spirits were brought by them from winegrowing regions of Hungary. These were luxury goods, always in great demand by the nobility and the Catholic Church.

The town had two schools in its center; one, Jewish, stood near the synagogues. The other, Christian, was by the main church, called Fara (later Saint Nicholas Church), on the eastern side of the market square. This was the environment in which Jukiel, son of David and possibly my earliest known ancestor, lived at the time in which he was recorded in the survey of 1787. With some hesitation, I looked at his name on a fraying page in the survey ledger. It was written in the patronymic manner, which makes drawing a straight line between him and those who followed quite challenging. But there was one additional detail, which connected Jukiel and all the other members of my family who lived after him in Rohatyn: they appeared to have shared the same residence from 1787 (and perhaps earlier), over the next hundred years. *Is that*, I asked myself, *a coincidence?* Or had I stumbled on the precious sort of link that eludes so many trying to untangle the web of Jewish genealogy? The skeptic in me said that we would never know with absolute certainty, but my hopeful side gave me a bit of room for speculation, once more details came to light.

Jukiel lived in a house on an unpaved road later called Orthodox Church Street, which ran from the market square westward toward the river. In this diverse neighborhood, Jewish and Polish homeowners lived next to each other; across from them was a Greek-Catholic church serving the Ruthenian population, called locally the Brick Orthodox Church to distinguish it from the more typical wooden Orthodox churches in other parts of town. In the fall of 1787, groups of survey-takers were going door to door, asking for the name of the head of each household. When they got to Jukiel's house, everything seemed to be in order. They dutifully recorded his name in a polonized manner: Jukiel Dawidowicz. Unfortunately for us today, they were not interested in finding out who else lived there, simply noting in their ledger that Jukiel did not own any land. Then they moved on down the street, repeating their task at each house and painstakingly taking measurements of any vegetable bed, field, or pasture they could find, regardless of how small it was.

This was a massive undertaking, and not just in Rohatyn. It was being conducted in anticipation of a major land and tax reform (*Urbarium*). Each community in Galicia—along with several other crown lands of the Monarchy—was carefully surveyed, with each house and plot of land recorded in specially prepared registers. In the spirit of Joseph II's activism and belief in data, nothing was to escape the surveyors. The imperial decree that spelled out all the procedures for selection of trusted overseers in each village or town was already two years old. There was some anxiety about whether the project could ever be completed in Galicia, but the emperor was not known to take no for an answer from his administration.[6]

As in most Galician towns, the surveyors found that the land belonged exclusively to non-Jewish residents. In many instances, this was by choice; in other cases the difference stemmed from restrictive laws that still cast a shadow on the lives of small communities. But big changes were looming on the horizon. Emperor Joseph's temporary laws announced just two years before and the upcoming edict would open, albeit for a short time, an opportunity for Jews to legally own land.[7]

Besides providing answers to the survey questions—that fall, Jukiel the son of David and his coreligionists had other official business to attend. In a sudden departure from tradition, Jews were told they must adopt fixed and hereditary surnames. One can only imagine today the puzzled looks on the faces of many, followed by probing conversations in various homes when the question of a new surname was discussed. Within the next few months, the Jews of Rohatyn took names that had never been heard before in their town. As demanded by the emperor's edict, German-sounding names were preferred, if not explicitly

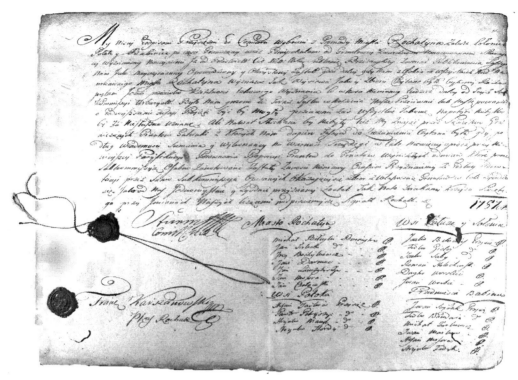

The land survey of 1787. The representatives from Rohatyn and the neighboring communities certify to the accuracy of the data. Several Jewish house owners, still carrying patronymic names, are found in Rohatyn in November that year. The document also provides information about Jewish communal buildings in town.

The document starts, "We undersigned under oath, chosen for the land survey from the town of Rohatyn, and from the bordering, in part, Załuże, Soloniec, Potok and Babińce, as well as the plenipotentiaries of the Land Authority, hereby declare to the Imperial and Royal Sub-commission from Brzezany...."

required. They had to be agreed on, not just by the applicants, but also by a local magistrate. In a short time, Fausts, Horns, Glasbergs, Uiberals, Nagelbergs, Blausteins, and Ziglers, to mention just a few, appeared among the citizens of Rohatyn, and from that moment on these names were proudly passed from one generation to another. But Jukiel, the son of David, seems to have adopted a different sort of name; those living in his house were to carry the surname *Dub*. Clearly, it was not German sounding; the word *dub* meant "oak tree" in Ruthenian. Was it a nickname given to Jukiel or someone else in his household, a reference to physical strength? That is not implausible; a popular local saying often referred to able-bodied men as "strong like an oak tree."[8]

Decades would pass; but only rarely, if at all, did news from Rohatyn make it onto the national scene. Yet in July of 1817, the town suddenly found itself in the spotlight, sharing it with no less an important person than Emperor Francis, who happened to be touring Galicia at the time. The emperor of Austria did not pass through the streets of Rohatyn; his itinerary took him to Lemberg (Lwów) and other neighboring towns before he journeyed to Bukovina. The front page of the only newspaper published in the crownland featured a dry report about the imperial visit, competing for attention with shocking news from Rohatyn.

An eyewitness account had been delivered on horseback to Lemberg (Lwów) days after a frightening event there. The vivid story about the Dubs' neighborhood described a true disaster. It read, "The weather was beautiful with clear visibility; only the heat of the sun was bothersome. At noon, a cloud appeared in the southwest, rapidly increasing in size. It descended low and darkened the horizon, transforming the day into darkest night. At the same time, such a violent and powerful storm struck that it is difficult to describe…; hail and massive rain overturned huts, barns, and sheds, while lifting up and blowing away stacks of hay, houses' roofs, huge trees in the forests and fruit trees in the orchards; [all this happening] in the blink of an eye." Then, the eyewitness described what happened next: "The heavy downpour of hail—the size of hazelnuts and in a few places larger—covered the ground a couple of feet deep, and stayed there from that afternoon until the next day. [The hail] mangled rows of growing grain and vegetables, and killed geese and other birds, as well as young calves in the pastures. People running for cover were injured and bloodied. The streams overfilled with water that damaged the mills, big and small, and this entire disaster, which will be remembered for a long time, occurred in the course of half an hour." The report was reprinted a few weeks later in faraway Kraków, testifying to the ferocity of the event.[9]

Just three years after this rare mention of Rohatyn, another land survey, this time taken on the orders of Emperor Francis, collected more invaluable information in Galicia. By that time, the town seemed to have fully recovered from that natural disaster. By 1820, Samuel Dub was head of the family who lived in the old house of Jukiel. In time, there would be other names in the family tree, but this

Samuel was like the root that anchored it in unsteady soil: invisible to us due to the passage of time, but still important, allowing new branches of the family to sprout.

As before, the Dub family dwelling stood on an unpaved road in a busy part of town. The old city gates were already a memory; in their place, new Jewish houses had been erected. But the differences were more than a few new buildings. Full Jewish emancipation in the Austrian Empire was still many years away, but the reality was that society was changing. The reforms put in place by the late Emperor Joseph had borne some fruit, despite being hampered by the zigzag of reversals instituted by his successors. The Church had been forced to yield some of its former influence. On the local scene, the parishes owned less land and no longer had the same commercial presence. The old Dominican cloister, which had been situated not far from the town's main synagogues, had already been closed for years; its main building and surrounding garden had been converted into a hospital.

The Krasiński family, after inheriting the possessions of Countess Lubomirska, had acquired additional church properties in town with the government's permission. More than a few Jews of Rohatyn had benefited from the non-discriminatory laws passed by Emperor Joseph; some now owned small plots of land near their family dwellings, and others had been able to purchase houses that had belonged to the departed friars.[10] There were also other subtle changes affecting Rohatyn's economy. Perhaps the taste for fine wines had considerably waned, or affordability had become an issue. Fewer aristocratic families and the reduced number of monks living in the area were likely having an impact as well; in any case, the buildings for storing imported wine were gone. In their place, stables and tanneries had been built on the grounds of the Krasiński manorial estate.

❧

DESPITE SPOTTY RECORDS, PAPERS carrying the name Dub can be found, mainly for Rohatyn and its environs, covering the next sixty years. My great-great grandfather, Sender, was most likely the oldest son of Samuel Dub. In due course, he would become an influential member of the community, charting a new path, and not only for himself. Sender was clearly the towering figure among his brothers, but not necessarily in a physical sense; there's no way to know that since no early photos of him and his siblings, Wolf and Leiser, have survived. We do know that Sender's presence was felt by others throughout his life because of his entrepreneurial drive; he left many traces of that behind. He was able to break through a number of barriers in Galician society.

Given what Sender Dub accomplished, he was almost certainly literate. Yiddish would have been the language that he learned at home and used in his youth, but his later professional endeavors also required him to speak Polish, Ruthenian, and German. How and where he received his education remains a mystery. Growing up in Galicia in the 1820s, a Jewish boy from Rohatyn had only a few options. It is safe to assume that Sender spent a few years in a traditional *heder*, where he learned to read Hebrew and received a religious education. With the network of German-Jewish schools already closed, he could have learned German, reading, and math in the elementary school (*Trivialschule*), located next to the Fara church in the center of Rohatyn.[11]

Jewish school (*heder*) in Galicia. Lithograph by K. Pomian 1880. *(Courtesy of the Centre for Documentation of Borderland Cultures, Sejny, Poland.)*

For those whose families could afford it, the two Jewish secular schools, located in different towns of eastern Galicia, were other possibilities for formal education during Sender's youth. One choice was the *Israelitische Realschule* in Brody, which taught a blend of bookkeeping, trade skills, and geography for those preparing for professions in business. The other choice was the *Deutsch-israelitische Hauptschule* in Tarnopol, operated by the respected Jewish reformer and educator Joseph Perl. There, the focus was more on learning German, Polish, and Hebrew, with a course of instruction that continued for four years. Perl was a vocal opponent of *Hasidim,* whom he battled and even ridiculed in his writings. His school was well recognized for its educational successes, and its founder received a number of accolades from the imperial bureaucracy.

In reality, however, these opportunities were available to only a very few. In the 1820s, Perl's school had one hundred twenty pupils, a staggering number compared to the mere three hundred Jewish kids enrolled in all other "folk" schools in the rest of Galicia. For the Jewish population, which in Sender's early years exceeded two hundred thousand people in eastern Galicia, this was still a tiny drop in the bucket.[12]

Sender was introduced to the broader world at quite a young age. When still in his early twenties, he worked as a Galician cowboy, delivering herds of oxen to Moravia (in today's Czech Republic). Traders from Galicia and, on occasion, even from the fertile steppes of Bessarabia (in today's eastern Ukraine and Republic of Moldova), descended with their livestock to a famous fair there. For Sender, the trip would have started in the town of Żurawno, where he and others gathered their fattened cattle. Over the next four weeks, he would run his herd across the Galician crownland into Austrian Silesia, and then proceed south to Moravia, where he would finally reach the fair in Olmütz (*Ołomuniec* in Polish or *Olomouc* in Czech). Covering the distance of over four hundred miles a few times a year, with more than one hundred animals each time, was tricky. Galician traders always worried about the poor state of the roads along the way, which could easily ruin their plans for a speedy passage. There were also frequent concerns about herds contracting diseases at the feeding stations positioned along the trails.

During these treks, news from Hungary was eagerly awaited in Galicia and along the way; a poor year there with lower-weight animals spelled a good year for Sender and other Galician traders. In some years, however, the Hungarians, who had the advantage of a shorter distance to travel, would have heavy oxen; that could easily dim the prospect of Galician profits. For the Galicians, going all the way back with the livestock was never an option; they had to be sold, and at the best price possible.

From Galicia alone, approximately eighty-five thousand head of cattle were sent to the fair every year. The big event in Olmütz supplied meat for the markets of Vienna, Prague, Brünn (*Brno*) and several other cities of the Austrian Empire. Every Wednesday, with the exception of Jewish holidays, information from the trading day was dutifully relayed on the coach back to Lemberg (Lwów). How many oxen were delivered and sold, whose herd was sold and at what prices, were reported in the government newspaper six days later; this was the mercantile stock exchange ticker of the day.

In early September 1837 the trading was clearly brisk. Galicians knew well that their competitors from Hungary could not undercut them this time. Sender felt confident; he brought to the fair one hundred forty oxen in excellent condition, all heavy and healthy. He set his price high and bargained hard. Even when by noon all but his herd had been sold, Sender did not back off from his position. We will never know whether those were his own instincts, or whether the young man was operating under the orders of someone else. But his patience seemed to work; as reported the next Wednesday in the dispatch to Lwów, Sender Dub had been able to sell his precious cargo without a problem. But there was little time for him to celebrate; he rushed back to Galicia for another run. By the end of October, Sender was back in Moravia selling a new herd of one hundred twelve animals. The report of his last trade shared the pages of *Gazeta Lwowska* with uncommon news from the United States, where seventy women delegates were gathered in New York City to sign a declaration against slavery.[13]

Another decade passed. In 1848, the waves of unrest that shook one province of the Austrian Empire after another were also spreading through the streets of

Vienna. The Galician capital city of Lemberg (Lwów) was in a state of fervor for many months. Proclamations of brotherhood brought Galicians together in their quest for a greater voice in national affairs. An appeal "to our brothers" spoke about the Jews being accepted with open arms, with the demand that unity be achieved through universal acceptance of the Polish language. Not to be outdone, the progressive governor of Galicia, Franz Stadion, tried to defuse the situation by appointing an advisory council with the inclusion of Poles, Jews, and the previously mostly silent Ruthenians (later called Ukrainians). Later, some would argue that the governor's actions had helped the latter chart their long, and not always easy, path toward cultural, linguistic, and ultimately political independence. The Jewish community was represented on the council by Rabbi Abraham Kohn (soon to be assassinated), Rachmil Mieses, and Florian Singer.

In the debate about language and culture in multicultural Galicia, early discussions focused on education. The council decided that Jewish schools should be left without major changes for the time being; perhaps there were too few of them to experiment with in those uncertain times, and new Jewish legislation was being called for. In the discussion, Poles appeared to yield to the demands of Ruthenian representatives, agreeing to the teaching of the Ruthenian language in some rural schools. Nonetheless, one patronizing voice, which foretold future struggles, claimed arrogantly that Ruthenian was mostly a spoken language and did not seem suitable as a language of scientific instruction in schools. Interestingly, German was considered by another member of the council to be the most appropriate language for high schools, even at the expense of classical languages (Latin and Greek).[14] Probably these arguments seemed very remote to most Rohatyners. Even when Austrian troops shelled Lemberg (Lwów) and brought it again under Habsburg control in November 1848, those events largely bypassed the small town. At home, there was more concern about a cholera epidemic that had struck that autumn in eastern Galicia.

The Jews of Rohatyn had to wait before they would learn whether the proposed changes in the Austrian Empire would finally yield them full emancipation. Although a progressive constitution drafted that year was never implemented,

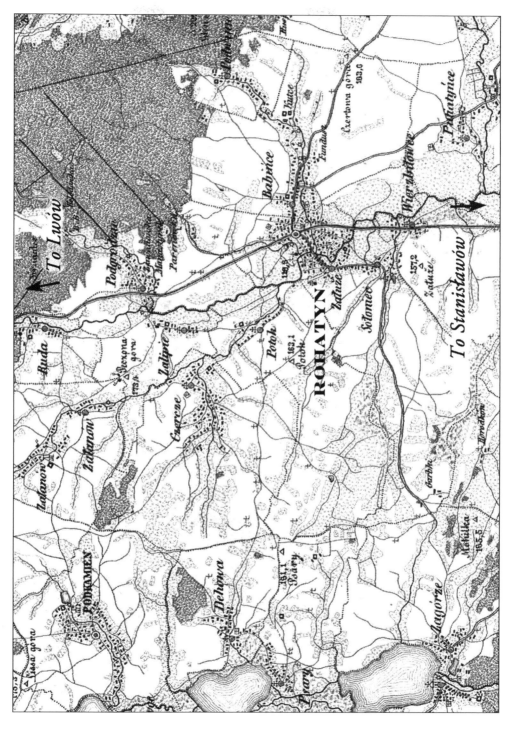

Map of Rohatyn and the surrounding area. *(Based on Administrativ-Karte von den Königreichen Galizien und Lodomerien, BL. 32; 1855.)*

its explicit promise of the opening of all professions, and unrestricted ownership of land, to Galician Jews, did produce some results. The law remained confusing with its loopholes and exceptions, but land registers started recording more Jewish names as legitimate owners.

Despite all those turbulent times, Sender Dub, now reaching his forties, was apparently doing quite well. No longer was he running herds of oxen to Moravia; now, this was the job of someone else working on his behalf. He owned the house that had been his father's, the same one that had belonged to Jukiel. Clearly, the torch had once more been passed to the next generation.

Around that time, there were also many changes in his family's life. Sender married Rifke Seinfeld, and their household grew rapidly; new babies arrived almost every other year. There were Rachel, Samuel, Mindel, Rikel, Israel, and Chaje, all born in the same ancestral house in the center of Rohatyn. Luck seemed to be on Sender and Rifke's side; their six infants would all survive to adulthood, somewhat unusual for their times. The Dubs' house, number 86, continued to be a busy place. Over the years, Sender's two brothers would bring their new wives to the family dwelling, and there would be the subsequent arrival of more children.

Not far away from 86, just a few steps across the unpaved street, lived the Faust family. Over several generations, many of them became well-known musicians (*klezmorim*). With a bit of imagination, one can hear the sounds of violins, cimbalom (*tsimbl*), and wooden flutes at major holidays, weddings, or family celebrations in the Dub house, made more festive by the talents of their neighbors.

In the 1850s, Sender's brother Leiser Dub married Etel (*sic*) whose maiden name is not found in the few surviving records. This and other entries on Etel and many other Dub women are disappointingly scant; one can only imagine their life stories, which of course were much more eventful than might be assumed by their fleeting mentions in the town's registers on the occasions of marriages, births, or deaths. For Leiser and Etel, their first child would be born in the ancestral home, but soon they would move, although not far away. For the next several years, Leiser, who was a merchant, stayed in Rohatyn; only later in life would he settle in a small village south of town. He remained friends for many years with Juda Rothen and his wife Blime. Juda came from the nearby small town of Stratyn, which was the seat of a Hasidic dynasty that had originated there at the beginning of the nineteenth century. From time to time, there were tensions regarding the line of succession in that Orthodox community, which led to more than a few families relocating to Rohatyn; but a more prosaic search for jobs was also a frequent cause.

After moving to Rohatyn, Leiser's friend Juda became one of several teachers in a traditional Jewish school (*heder*). Apparently, they knew each other well; when Juda and Blime's son was born, his parents trusted Leiser Dub to confirm to the authorities in Rohatyn that they were indeed a married couple. From what we know about him, it seems likely that Leiser had a very traditional lifestyle. Perhaps in recognition of their shared values, on another occasion he was honored by the Orthodox couple from Stratyn by serving as *sandek* (godfather) during the circumcision ceremony of their newborn son.[15]

Another brother of Sender's, Wolf Dub, married Chane Rosenzweig and would remain in the family house a bit longer. When it was time for them to establish their own home, they would move to the nearby suburb of Babińce; Wolf took a lease on a farm there. The land in that neighborhood was divided by the road that carried travelers to and from Rohatyn. Defying the rules of geography, the southern part was called Upper Babińce, while the area above the road was Lower Babińce. Like many places around Rohatyn, the largest swath of land there was owned by the Krasiński family; it seems quite possible that Wolf managed one of their properties. There, he and Chane would have nine children.

Sender continued to be fortunate in his professional endeavors, becoming reasonably well off. What his business focus was, through the registered "*Sender Dub et comp*," is not entirely clear. We can only surmise that it was wholesale trade in livestock and agricultural products. Later, he would be involved in yet another business in town, under the name of "*Sender Dub & Alter Weidmann*," linked to liquor distribution.[16] Based on the amount of income tax he paid, Sender ended up among the top-twenty citizens of Rohatyn. Although tax payments are not exactly a welcome distinction (for anyone at any time), that fact sheds some light on his entrepreneurial success. But for Sender, owning two houses in town and running successful businesses were not reasons to become complacent.

Owing to special skills and/or some luck, Sender's life story seems to be even bolder than that of the next generation of Dubs. Yet there is little information left that could describe him as a man. What can be reconstructed, from a few dry entries in official registers, points to a person with a very active life that extended well beyond the *shtetl* (small town) of Rohatyn—one who engaged in professional interactions with both Jews and gentiles.

The administrative seal of the Jewish community of Rohatyn, circa 1859.

After the laws of Austro-Hungary finally made Jewish emancipation possible in 1867, Sender must have witnessed debates between friends and family members who were for and against assimilation into secular ways of life. Yet their choices were not always straightforward. In 1868 six Jews, who had been elected to the city council for the first time in the history of Rohatyn, made a proposal to phase out many traditional institutions of their community. The proposal would simply have assured that the affairs of Jews, like those of all other inhabitants of Rohatyn, would be handled by the civil administration; yet many in the Jewish community vehemently opposed this idea.[17]

The decisions Sender Dub and other Jews were making in those days could be quite impactful on their personal lives. Whether they concerned different forms of Jewish worship, a choice of the language spoken at home, or the dress code, the norms of acceptable social behavior were broadening for many Jewish families. Others continued to see deep value in unaltered adherence to tradition. Within Sender's generation, old values and norms were being challenged, and mixed with new ones, to a larger degree than ever before.

ல்

JUST WHEN EVERYTHING SEEMED to be going well for the Dub family, their happiness was interrupted by the premature death of Sender's wife, Rifke, in June of 1862; she had only been approaching the age of forty. Although no details have been preserved, her disappearance soon after their youngest daughter Chaje was born suggests some complication of childbirth. But there was little time for mourning in the household, which was otherwise teeming with life. Sender's children were surrounded by several new additions to the extended Dub family, all living under the same roof. Luckily, there would be no shortage of nursing mothers and other helping hands to take care of the orphaned children. When, two years later, another baby girl was born in house number 86, she was appropriately named Rifke, doubtless in reverence to her late aunt.[18]

Still in his fifties, Sender Dub remarried in the mid-1860s. Soon, his new young wife bore him a son. There were clear signs of renewed optimism and confidence in Sender's life. Regardless of whether those were brought by the new marriage or by good fortune in business, Sender started to think big, and his new ideas were not just about local opportunities. In 1869, he bought three estates near the Russian border, about one hundred miles east of Rohatyn. Eight years later, he plunged more money into the area, increasing his possessions to more than two thousand hectares of land (an area almost six times bigger than today's Central Park in New York City).

Right: Sender Dub (1806?–1906) was recorded in a Galician land register as the owner of the estates Krzyweńkie, Oparszczyzna, and Wasylków in the district of Tarnopol, Galicia. The entry of 1871 followed district court approval on April 27, 1870.

The largest of these three estates was in the village of Krzyweńkie. It included farmland, a mill with a distillery, and a tavern. In the neighboring village of Wasylków, additional hectares also now belonged to Sender. The smallest of the three villages was called Oparszczyzna; it was so little it was often omitted from maps. For Sender, these were investment properties; how much time he spent in the place is unknown, but more than one hundred twenty people lived and worked there. The records left behind reveal busy financial activities, with Sender leasing part of the property to others. Typically, such contracts were drawn up for extended periods of time, such as one between Sender Dub and Leib Bartfeld for the period from June 1876 through the end of May 1882.

There were also a few charitable deeds for Sender to take care of. These were specified in his land contracts, down to the smallest detail. Following an old tradition passed from one owner to another, the Krzyweńkie estate supplied a long list of items to the nearby hospital for the poor. This practice dated from 1822 and would not be changed with the arrival of Sender Dub. Every year several bushels of rye, wheat, buckwheat, barley, and millet, not to mention peas, were included among the donations. Then there were deliveries of six big slabs of bacon, two large buckets of butter, and another two buckets filled with cheese. In the winter months, two to four horse-drawn wagons filled with firewood left the estate every week for the hospital. As if this was not enough, the estate owner was expected to donate a wooden bed every ten years.[19]

After paying off some lingering debts left on the books by previous owners, Sender began to leverage the newly purchased estates as potential investments for others from Rohatyn. Among those who wrote sizeable checks were Moses Nagelberg and Count Ludwik Krasiński, both well-regarded and influential citizens of the town. The members of the Nagelberg family were descendants of the learned rabbi, David Moshe Avraham (also known as Rabbi Adam), of the eighteenth century; in later years, they were the town's grocers, joining a growing Jewish middle class. Count Ludwik Krasiński was also familiar to many; even without all the privileges his ancestors had enjoyed, Ludwik still owned much land and several buildings in Rohatyn.

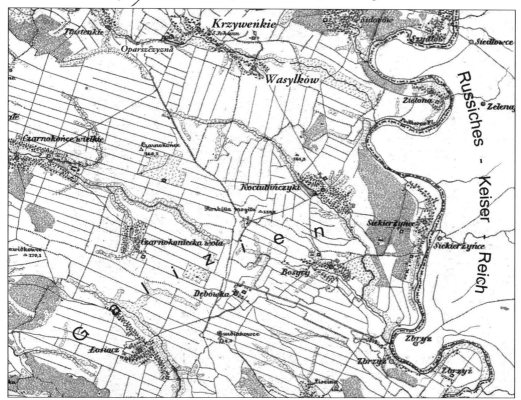

Map of the border region of Galicia. The villages of Krzyweńkie, Oparszczyzna, and Wasylków were close to the border between the Austro-Hungarian and Russian Empires. *(Based on Administrativ-Karte von den Königreichen Galizien und Lodomerien, BL. 46; 1855.)*

The Krasiński family was involved in philanthropic activities in town and seemed to understand the need to adapt to changing times. Some of them would become involved in local banking. Yet for Sender Dub, making a profit on loans or other forms of investment could be a double-edged sword. Time after time throughout history, Jews were heralded as financial wizards, only to soon be accused of immoral moneylending practices. Perhaps to avoid dangerous shifts in public sentiment, or just to pursue the spirit of financial self-reliance that was gaining popularity in Galicia, he decided to try something different. In 1882, Sender Dub and other citizens of Rohatyn established a local Credit Association. In essence, it was a modern financial company with shareholders; its members were required to contribute relatively modest monthly investments that provided capital for lending purposes. Sender became the head of the nine-member board, serving until at least 1888.[20]

Despite the focus on business and his second wife, Sender also made sure that the children from his first marriage were taken care of. Sending them to work for extended periods on his large estates, close to the border with the Russian Empire, was not a good option. Instead, he chose something closer to Rohatyn. In the early 1870s, Sender took a lease on a modest estate southwest of town, in a place called Załuże. It was situated close to Rohatyn, effectively adjoining the town, and barely separated from it by the river. Before the Dub family moved there, it had been a sleepy farm with one manor house and only six people on its premises.

Things changed quite a lot there with the arrival of the new residents. In just a few years, the formerly sedate place became home to thirty-eight people, including fifteen Jewish occupants, the majority of them Dubs. Except for three of Sender's daughters who had married local merchants, the rest of the children from his first marriage moved there. But even Rachel, who remained in Rohatyn to live with her family in her parents' old house, and her sister Mindel, who was married to Hersch Goldschlag from Rohatyn, were not far away from the rest of the Dubs. The same was true for Rikel, who after her marriage to Markus Kontes moved to Stanisławów but would visit the family often, spending extended periods in Załuże. The rest of Sender's children would marry and have their children grow up on the estate.

The Dub family employed mostly Ruthenian farm workers, as well as a few Jewish helping hands from the neighboring village. Among them was Moses Klarnet, the Jewish caretaker, who lived on the premises. The Dubs were probably more respected than feared by the workers. From time to time, Sender and one of his sons were invited to offer blessings when Jewish children were born in the village. If new clothes were needed for these or other special occasions, Sender or his son Samuel could easily seek the skills of a tailor by the name of Hersch Turner from Rohatyn. At first glance, his surname was unusual among Galician Jews—many generations later, there would be much speculation about the meaning of the name Turner when written in Yiddish. Had we been able to listen in on private conversations of Dubs and their neighbors—Turners, Fausts, Horns, and many others—we could have heard men and women talking about a wide variety of daily affairs. Most likely these would have ranged from the health of livestock and crop yields to the intricacies of land prices and other investments. And of course in most years, news would be exchanged about which of the women in the family were pregnant or had recently given birth. When the time came, some of those families relied on the same midwife, Etel Wandmejer, who in due course delivered many Dub and Turner children. In yet another way, Galicia, even in its small towns and villages, does not cease to disappoint anyone interested in tidbits of family history![21]

These stories notwithstanding, the extended Dub family maintained their contacts well beyond the Jewish community. If nothing else, successfully administering the estate required it. In contrast to more conservative Jews who spoke only Yiddish (which was often mistakenly classified as German during censuses), the Dub family on the Załuże estate identified Polish as the language of their daily communication at home.[22]

Perhaps the only area that was left untouched by the many social changes taking place was marriage, which was still expected to occur within one's religion. But even in this area exceptions were beginning to appear. One year, readers of the Galician national newspaper learned about a Christian woman wishing to convert to Judaism, in order to marry the man of her choice. To assuage sensitivities on both sides, the correspondent quickly added that under the new civil laws, anyone over the age of fourteen was allowed to freely choose a religion.[23]

Sender's oldest son, Samuel, followed a more traditional approach and married Cypre Rosa Horn. As the majority of Jewish marriages were still being arranged between the families of the groom and bride, we can only imagine today what could have led the parents of Samuel and Cypre Rosa to cross paths and to make this important decision about their children. To start with, the bride shared a last name with a long-established family of merchants from Rohatyn, who undoubtedly had known Dubs for generations. The Horns were well-established local flour dealers, bakers and grocers. In those times, they were involved in professions dealing in products that could easily have come from the Dub family's agricultural enterprise. But to add a bit of mystery—Cypre Rosa was not a local girl. Instead, she came from Buczacz, a Galician town situated further east, closer to Samuel's father's big estates. Was she a relative of the Horns from Rohatyn, or was the identical maiden name just a coincidence? Probably we will never know.[24] But little can be said about the groom, as well.

In a somewhat paradoxical way, Samuel Dub would leave fewer clues about his personality than Sender did. The tidbits of records available paint a picture of a man growing up in the shadow of his more successful father. At the time when Samuel and Cypre Rosa were already living together on the Załuże estate, he seemed to repeat at least an early part of Sender's career. His profession was recorded in one document as a cattle dealer who worked into his forties on the estate, which was still leased in the name of Sender Dub. Perhaps history would be unjust to Samuel, but no records survived to attest to his travels to distant markets, or brilliant transactions that could be recalled with satisfaction around a family dinner table.

Samuel and Cypre Rosa had three girls, Freide (meaning "joy"), Taube (meaning "dove") and Rifke, who was always known as Regina; all were born a few years apart in the 1870s. Regina, the youngest, was born on July 1, 1879. Four days later, the little girl was brought in a carriage from the home in Załuże to the synagogue in town. As required by law, her birth and the ceremony were recorded in the civil register for the Jewish community. The names of the baby and parents were followed by that of a friend from Rohatyn who gave the blessing, and even the name of

The signature of Samuel Dub, attesting that Cypre Rosa Horn was his lawful wife. The note was cosigned by the witness Adler Weidman from Rohatyn. The statement, typical for the majority of Jewish couples lacking state-recognized marriages was made on the occasion of the birth of my paternal grandmother, Regina (Rifke) Dub, on July 1, 1879.

Rohatyn. General view. *(Postcard from the early twentieth century.)*

Rohatyn. A scene from the market square. *(Postcard from the early twentieth century.)*

the midwife who had assisted with the delivery was dutifully written down. Yet there was still one more small detail for Samuel to complete before they could go back home. Like the vast majority of their Jewish friends, Samuel and Cypre Rosa had been married only in a religious (ritual) ceremony; they had no state-sanctioned marriage certificate. Hence, on the edge of the page, Samuel provided a signed statement that Cypre Rosa was his lawful wife, with a witness attesting to it. Regina, my future paternal grandmother, was now officially entered into the records of Rohatyn, and another chapter of the story began. Of her life we shall speak later on these pages.

Chapter 7

KOŁOMYJA:

FRÄNKELS AND HÜBNERS

*T*HE TWO FAMILIES, THE FRÄNKELS and Hübners, were connected not only by the proximity of the places where their members had lived for generations. Their life stories came even closer together when they were joined with each other through the marriage that ultimately produced my paternal grandfather; but of this a bit later. The place that both families called home was clearly distinct from the western part of Galicia. The difference was even felt when comparing it with the closer Lemberg (Lwów) or Rohatyn. As late as the mid-nineteenth century, this most southeastern corner of Galicia— natives called it *Pokucie*—still retained some of the feeling of a frontier. In places, the land there was dotted by villages, where forests were stubbornly giving way to fields. It would never be too long there before one would come across, or at least hear the sound of another mountain stream rushing down from above. But in other places, one could encounter fertile plateaus.

From the nearby thickly wooded mountains the highlanders, a group called Hutsuls, often descended into the towns with their wares. They were a tall people, with so-called "falcon faces"; many wondered over the years about their origin and customs. Were they Ruthenians living in isolated communities, or a tribe that might have migrated from as far away as the Caucasus Mountains centuries ago? The men typically dressed in sheepskins, with their furry wool worn inside; they often carried curved pipes in their mouths. The women, known as excellent horseback riders, were also easily spotted; young Hutsul girls wore their characteristic attire adorned by charming pompoms. The days when the Hutsuls had been feared as brazen robbers, ready to pounce on unsuspected travelers in the wooded areas, or even to wreak havoc in the marketplace, were long gone. And yet their looks often invited speculation about the highlanders' fearless past. Despite the passage of time, the legends about Hutsuls continued to interest both other natives of the area as well as visitors. As if that area was not exotic enough, traders from the Ottoman and Russian Empires were frequently seen in many towns and villages frequented by Fränkels and Hübners.[1]

The Fränkels were accustomed to moving back and forth across the border between Galicia and Bukovina. Like the vast majority of Jews who settled in Bukovina, their parents or grandparents had most likely come there from Galicia. After the Austrians annexed Bukovina from the Ottoman Turks, many impoverished Jews (*Bettlejuden*), unable to pay taxes there, were promptly expelled by the new administration, only to be replaced by marginally better-off brethren arriving from Galicia.

Jews of Galicia and Subcarpathia (Carpathian Rus'). Drawing of Jewish men circa 1821. *(Courtesy of the Centre for Documentation of Borderland Cultures, Sejny, Poland.)*

Mordko Fränkel, my earliest ancestor that I could track down in that family line, was born on the southern side of the river Czeremosz, which separated Bukovina—then an administrative district of Galicia— from the rest of the Kingdom of Galicia and Lodomeria. When he was born in 1824, the place of his birth, the small settlement of Millie (Мілієвє in Ruthenian), was nominally in the district of Bukovina, but in reality nobody paid much attention to the border. Even after 1846 when the two separated from each other, with Bukovina acquiring the status of Duchy in the Austrian Empire,

Galicia and Bukovina stayed connected by many family ties and established administrative links.

In some respects, Jews fared better in sparsely populated Bukovina than did their cousins in Galicia. For years, Bukovina was still a frontier province, on the outer edge of the vast Austrian Empire, where fewer rules restricted Jews' rights. When Mordko was fifteen years old, Scottish travelers passing through the region encountered affluent Jews in the grain trade there. Less prominent Israelites told the curious visitors, with obvious relief, that they were not subject to the punitive tax on "lights," or Sabbath candles, which was demanded in Galicia.

Outside the towns in Bukovina, it was not uncommon to find a Jewish toll collector on a country road, sitting by an ominous-looking giant log suspended a few feet above the ground. Doubtless this was an effective way to make sure tolls were paid; the log was ready to be dropped on any cart whose driver tried to get past for free. Perhaps the deterrent worked well; no stories of injuries inflicted on naughty drivers have been passed down. In other places, as the traveling Scotts observed, tolls were collected without contraptions at wooden bridges, "covered over like a 'penthouse' [a shelter with a sloping roof] from end to end." In times of harvest, the country folk cutting down a field of oats with a scythe or picking potatoes were a common sight around.[2]

Many Jews by the name of Fränkel lived in Millie, some engaging in farming and others making ends meet as shopkeepers. But Mordko would not stay there for long. When he married Sura Rath, the couple temporarily settled in the village called Piadyki, a bare three miles from Kołomyja, on the Galician side of the border. It was there that their only daughter, Rachel (Ruchel), was born in 1851. Soon the Fränkels, with Rachel and her young brother in tow, would move on.

We can only speculate about why, in 1858, Mordko Fränkel set his sights on the Galician village of Słobódka Leśna. A large estate there, with its buildings, some fields, and a forest, was changing hands. For the former owners, the cold realities of needing hard cash must have overtaken any lingering sentiments about tradition, when single-family ownership was still common elsewhere in Galicia. Now, the owners of Słobódka Leśna's estates were changing every few years; the land was being divided and leased out. In the midst of these changes, Mordko Fränkel arrived to take a lease on one of many agricultural properties there.

The Jewish homes in that area were all wood, modest at best. Thatched with straw roofs, they could sometimes be distinguished from peasants' dwellings by plastered walls washed with a light blue visible from the road. Soon, other members of the Fränkel and Rath families joined Mordko and his family at their new home. At the beginning, it seems, members of the family were trying to outdo each other to succeed there. Itzig Fränkel and Munisch, Jacob, and Mashla Rath, Sura's relatives, all arrived to try their luck. Among their neighbors were other Jewish farmers, as well as some descendants of the German settlers brought long ago to Galicia by Joseph II—mostly small entrepreneurs, who were moving to the area as well.

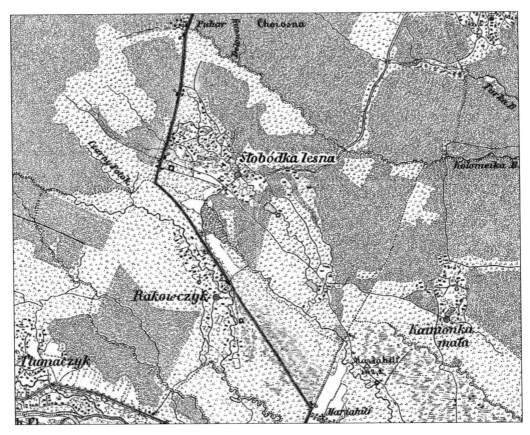

Map of Słobódka Leśna and surroundings, located north of Kołomyja (*Kolomea*) circa 1855. The Fränkel family arrived there in 1858. (*Administrativ-Karte von den Königreichen Galizien und Lodomerien, BL. 49; 1855.*)

Within a few years, Mordko seemed to be getting the upper hand over his neighbors. Without a doubt, the Fränkel family would have celebrated one year when a court ruled in Mordko's favor, adding to his land some contested forest containing an estimated five thousand pricey oak trees! When looking at a few preserved pages of the land register, as with many official documents, our wish to know more about this event is only partly fulfilled. Information about the other parties involved, not to mention the emotions behind this particular dispute, are lost in the mist of history. And yet it is obvious today that, over time, Mordko's profits became more predictable and bank loans started to flow more easily. One small success seemed to breed another. His entrepreneurial skills already tested, Mordko secured the rights to oversee all the land leases on behalf of the estate's current owner, which could not have been a minor feat amongst so many new-comers, all driven to succeed in Słobódka Leśna. And this success did not stop Mordko from pushing his luck even further.

By 1874, fifty-year-old Mordko Fränkel had become the owner of the farming estate, buying out land parcels that he or his relatives had merely leased before. This was a "friendly takeover"; the other Fränkels and Raths would remain there, working in what looks like a family enterprise, for the next twenty years. At the risk of oversimplification, one could say that Mordko and others like him were unknowingly fulfilling the almost one-hundred-year-old call of Emperor Joseph II and several Jewish reformers. Jewish land ownership was becoming a reality, at least for some. Certainly, conditions in Galicia were far from ideal; many of its inhabitants were poor and countless Jews would choose to emigrate in the years to come to build better futures for themselves elsewhere. For others, none-theless the opportunities at home were slowly within their reach as the society around them, with all its imperfections, was becoming more open.

Mordko's part of Słobódka Leśna covered an area of more than three hundred and fifty hectares (slightly larger than Central Park in New York City). Within its boundaries, there were a manorial farm, one tavern, and more than thirty buildings, including houses and many stables. Since the estate was a cattle and horse farm, the open space was largely grazing lands and meadows, with a small portion used for the cultivation of crops. To assure its smooth operation, several workers lived there. In line with changing times, the Jewish owner was an equal opportunity employer, with Greek Catholic and Roman Catholic laborers working alongside Jewish farmhands.[3]

But life in Słobódka Leśna was about more than leasing and buying land. Mordko and Sura's household would have been considered rather small for the times—only one girl and two younger boys. When their daughter Rachel was about twenty years old, she married Salomon Leib Hübner, two years her senior. How their families met and arranged the marriage will probably never be known. Was there a connection between other relatives, who played the role of matchmakers? Certainly that is possible. Even more likely, business links between Mordko Fränkel and the Hübner family led to the union.

As was the case with many Jewish families of the time, neither the young couple nor their parents bothered to travel to the neighboring town to gather needed approvals from the civil authorities and pay for an expensive marriage license. Instead, the signing of the *ketubah* (marriage contract) by the witnesses, reading it aloud under a *chuppah* (wedding canopy) and the *Sheva Brachot* (the seven blessings) bestowed on Rachel and Salomon by a rabbi, were considered sufficient for a marriage, following age-honored tradition. It would be another twenty years, with several children born of this union, before the marriage was finally made valid in the eyes of the state.

‍

The groom, Salomon Hübner, and his family were from Kołomyja (*Kolomea* in German, *Kolomey* in Yiddish, *Коломия* in Ruthenian), no more than ten miles away. Most likely, the town had been named after the thirteenth-century Hungarian Prince Koloman, who had ruled historical Galicia. (On the other hand, some with an appetite for phonetics surmised that it had been named *Colonia,* meaning an outpost, in the time of the Roman Empire.) Except in German agricultural settlements in the suburbs north of town, Baginsberg and Mariahilf, Jews made up roughly half of Kołomyja's population; the rest were Ruthenians and a small community of Poles. In the center of town (called by the

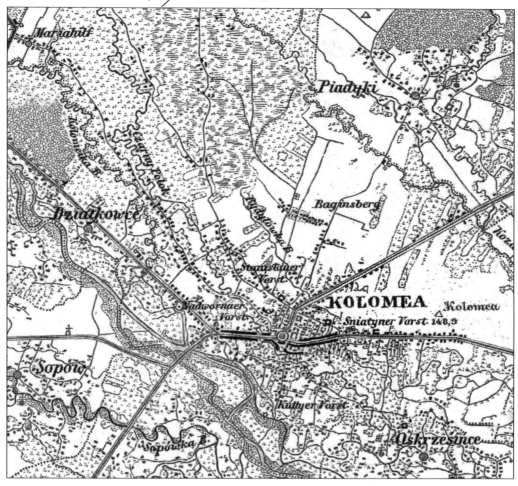

Map of Kołomyja (*Kolomea*) and surroundings circa 1855. Four suburbs named after neighboring larger
towns, Śniatyn (*Sniatyner*), Stanisławów (*Stanislauer*), Nadwórna (*Nadwornaer*), and Kutty (*Kuttyer*),
are marked. North of the town, two German agricultural colonies, Mariahilf and Baginsberg, are visible.
(Administrativ-Karte von den Königreichen Galizien und Lodomerien, BL. 49; 1855.)

locals *Ringstadt* or *Stadt),* Yiddish and German were almost exclusively heard;
that area was more than eighty percent Jewish.[4]

Locally raised cattle were a big business in Kołomyja. The town's predominantly Jewish merchants supplied not only meat, but eggs, feathers, and bristles to
customers all over Galicia and even as far as Vienna.[5] A visitor toward the end of
the nineteenth century described the wide market square with its base of large and
uneven cobblestones. Ruthenian peasant women arrived in the morning with eggs

or young cucumbers for sale, while bearded Jewish men "in long black gabardines" mingled with the crowd. Jewish water carriers passed by with barrels from "good" wells (ordinary wells frequently yielded a somewhat salty liquid). Here and there, groups of brokers stood ready to make deals in grain, cattle, or some other commodity. Mostly Jewish flour shops and trading outposts packed the market square. This central part of town was quite plain looking; only the eastern part of the square aspired to be a bit more upscale. That was the place to stroll alongside brick buildings housing more prominent businesses, with young army officers, high school students, and society ladies all exchanging glances. A few carriages for hire (*fiacres*) stood nearby, always ready for a short trip. In those days, one might still have spotted an old Turk wearing a distinct headdress. Half Turkish Muslim, half Sephardic Jew, he had married a local Jewish woman, and was a reminder of the days when Ottomans had governed the area.[6]

As best one can estimate from spotty records, Hübners lived in Kołomyja at least as far back as the 1820s. Samson and his son, Salomon, were both born there. The older Hübner was often called "Szymszon" by his Yiddish-speaking contemporaries; the name Samson was only used in official documents. He was certainly well off; owning a house in the eastern suburb of *Sniatyner Vorstadt,* as he did, suggested relatively prosperous status. Shortly before 1849, Samson Hübner married Sossie Hilsenrath. In their case, there is no mystery about how they met. They had grown up in the same neighborhood; several families with the name Hilsenrath lived up and down the street from Samson's house in *Sniatyner Vorstadt.*[7]

A few years after they started a family together, the Hübners narrowly escaped a tragedy that affected many in their neighborhood. As was the case every year, crowds packed the Great Synagogue on Yom Kippur in 1853. Men gathered in their best caftans and velvet- or fur-brimmed hats. Women with small children filled a separate section of the temple, as was the custom. Then, suddenly, someone shouted "Fire!" Only later did it become clear that a few thieves had wanted to create confusion to steal the women's jewelry. Panic and a stampede toward the narrow exit, accompanied by loud screams, rapidly turned the synagogue into a deathtrap. In a few minutes, thirty-three women and two children lost their lives.

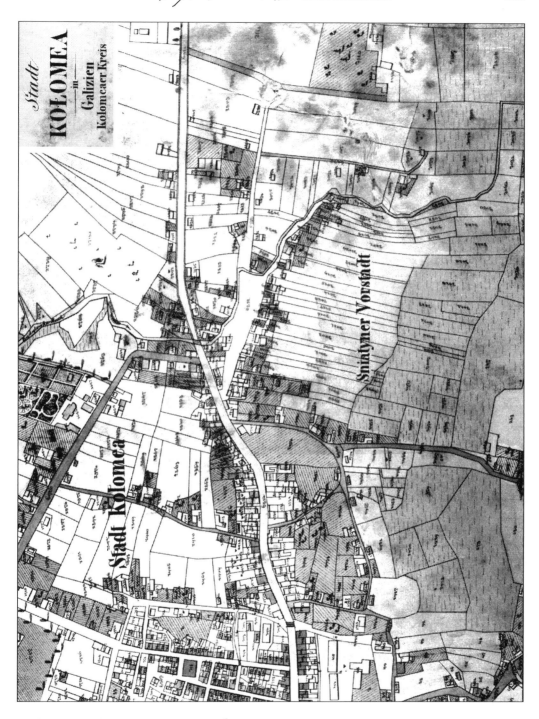

Cadastral map of Kołomyja (*Kolomea*). The Śniatyn suburb (*Sniatyner Vorstadt*) located on the western edge of the town, had been home to the Hübner family since at least 1827. *(Section of the cadastral map from 1859.)*

Luckily, Sossie Hübner and her young child came out unscathed, although the event would not be easily forgotten. In the aftermath, someone expressed the mood of the community: "Sun and moon darken, and the stars of the heavens do not shed light either. Oh, one must cry out in witness to the tremendous distress. The stern decree of utter destruction came down upon tranquil women, faithful daughters tender and delightful, and also ... playful children...." When the pain was somewhat diminished, a community rule was put in place that forbade Jewish women of the town to wear jewelry on Yom Kippur. This rule continued to be adhered to for many years. One wonders today if its observance was just to prevent copycat crimes, or perhaps it was another way to remember those lost on that day.[8]

Not much is known about Samson Hübner's profession. Most likely, he was a merchant who made his living in grain or cattle, or selling spirits; all were quite common professions in his community. It is not difficult to envision him among almost seventy Jewish wholesalers and several hundred retail traders and small shop owners, who were the main dealers in commerce there. Over the years, other business-oriented Hübners from Kołomyja dealt in hides and leather, bristle and horsehair products, and beer distribution.[9] In any case, in his later years, Samson Hübner was simply referred to in records as the owner of the house in Kołomyja.

Salomon Hübner was the oldest of Samson and Sossie's children. When he was growing up, the Jewish community was overwhelmingly Orthodox but by no means monolithic. Past bitter and protracted struggles between the *Hasidim* and their rabbinic opponents (*mitnagdim*) had largely been set aside. However, once doctrinal differences and competition for influence had touched the town, they did not entirely disappear. On occasion, conflicts—more likely strong arguments or a few scuffles—would still erupt in the synagogue courtyard. But a fundamental fear of the *mitnagdim,* that the spread of the Hasidic movement would ultimately mean an end to Judaism, had been allayed. Instead, the former adversaries became united in the common goal of resisting the Jewish Enlightenment.

When *Haskalah* voices from Berlin and homegrown rebels had tried to discredit the *Hasidim* and move the community toward modern ideas, they did not seem to get too far in Kołomyja. The town seemed worlds away from Lemberg (Lwów), Brody, or Tarnopol, where the reformers were making their choices seen and heard. In contrast, tradition did not easily give in to these new trends in Kołomyja.

In later years, stories were told of a fiery Rabbi Hillel Lichtenstein "whose mouth was like a torch," who held sway over the town's religious Jews for more than twenty years.[10] Born in the Hungarian part of the empire (today's Slovakia), he became the leader of Kołomyja's Jewish community in 1867. He was a charismatic speaker who reminded many of the old defenders of the faith who had opposed any flexibility in doctrinal affairs. Prior to his arrival in town, Rabbi Lichtenstein had earned some notoriety in his native Hungary for orchestrating an ultra-Orthodox manifesto and vigorously campaigning for it. His nine-point credo castigated traditional communities where any deviation might be considered, regardless how small, from the strict interpretation of Jewish laws. Lichtenstein argued strenuously in his oratory and writings against any forms of assimilation, including linguistic ones.

The choice of a spoken language had been a matter of heated debate among Galician Jews since the end of the previous century. Many *maskilim*, proponents of the *Haskalah* movement, had wanted to see the introduction of a modern Hebrew; these early rebels rejected Yiddish, with its admixture of German and Slavic words, as a mere "jargon." In exasperation, one of them had exclaimed, "Why the Judeo-German language [Yiddish] in the land of Poland? Either the holy language [Hebrew] or Polish!"[11] In fact, the choices were not that simple. Other *maskilim* had believed that High German, used by the literary writers and philosophers of the time, should be the language of choice for Galician Jews.

On the other side of the debate, the *Hasidim* had found no difficulty in making their choice; according to them, the language of the masses, Yiddish, was not to be deviated from. Although they came from a persecuted group, they themselves became stern persecutors within many Jewish communities, whenever they achieved a majority. The lines of bitter battles were drawn. To the *Hasidim*, the small group of Jews who advocated western education had been seen as a dangerous bunch of heretics, only a step removed from Jews' conversion to Christianity. At least in this respect, they agreed with Rabbi Lichtenstein. The modernists, in turn, had seen in the Hasidim either "deluded dreamers" overtaken by misguided religious mysticism or "vile frauds" with courts of *tsadikim* who misled common people. Their hesitation at participating in the affairs of the external world earned them the label "rebels against the light" from the Galician *maskilim*.[12]

There had been those among the *maskilim*, however, who seemed more grounded in the reality of Galicia; they recognized that to appeal to more than a few learned men, they had to reach the majority of Jews in Yiddish. By the mid-nineteenth century earnest translations of books written by others, and homegrown, scathing satires of local Jewish life, all in Yiddish, would be their tools to spread the message of the Enlightenment.

As if this rich debate of past decades was not enough, new voices could be heard around the time Hillel Lichtenstein arrived in Kołomyja. The full legal emancipation of Jews in the Austro-Hungarian Empire in 1867 was followed by the introduction of political autonomy for Galicia, visible a few years later. On a symbolic level, the use of German names for Galician towns like Lemberg or Kolomea fell out of favor; those were quickly replaced with Polish-sounding names: Lwów and Kołomyja. In the Jewish community, earlier appeals for immersion in German language and culture now competed with the idea that the Jewish vernacular should switch to Polish. The latter was no longer a shout of exasperation from the frustrated *maskil*. Instead, it was a pragmatic recognition of the local scene, which was dominated by Polish schools, and the opening of the ranks of a growing civil administration to native talent.

Poles also searched their consciences about ways to build unity in the newly autonomous Galicia; even their right-wing newspaper, in a rare break from its usual tone, exhorted its readers to go beyond the letter of the law and accept Jewish neighbors without prejudice or preconditions. It warned the reader that waiting for their complete linguistic assimilation before accepting Jews as members of the new society was a mistake.

Kołomyja (*Kolomea*). View of the market square. *(Postcards from the early twentieth century.)*

On the Jewish side: a few years before, Moritz Rappaport, composing his famous "*Bajazzo*," a highly acclaimed poem written in German, had captured the multidimensional dilemma of his brethren: "To be both Pole and Jew is a double crown of melancholy!" This Galician Jew—immersed in German culture—was identifying himself, through his masterful poetry, with the national aspirations of his neighbors, the ethnic Poles. In a brief break from its typical diatribes, a front-page article under the headline "Voices from the Country" tried to answer the poet's concerns.[13] Indeed, the choices facing the Jews of Galicia in the latter part of the nineteenth century could not have been more striking.

Rabbi Hillel Lichtenstein was opposed to all these recent trends. In partnership with his son-in-law, he spelled out in unambiguous terms his resistance to any changes in symbols of Jewish identity, whether expressed in name, language, or dress. The rabbi did not hesitate to unleash his wrath even on the *Hasidim* if they dared to transgress his rules. Galicia, however, was different from his native Hungary; here, the powerful Hasidic dynasties were a force to reckon with. When he openly challenged their leader over appointing a ritual slaughterer for the community, passions would run high. The controversy in doctrinal matters was clearly mixed with a power struggle. The disagreements easily triggered unrest in the synagogues and study halls, with police intervening to restore calm. On one occasion, even a small detachment from the army had to be called for help. But Kołomyja's rabbi was not only critical of the Hasidic leader. Famously, he once interrupted his sermon to chastise a young man for the "dreadful sin" of learning how to dance in his free time![14]

In spite of all this, the life of Salomon Hübner would be clear evidence that not all Jews closely followed the teachings of that inflexible rabbi. Rabbi Lichtenstein's stern warnings against Jews owning land in Galicia, or participating in secular education, were increasingly out of step with the opportunities offered in the slowly opening society. Like his father, Salomon went into business; and soon there were signs that he was successful. With his marriage to Rachel Fränkel, opportunities to grow the family land enterprise with his father-in-law in Słobódka Leśna must have seemed too good to pass up.

Business aside, Salomon and Rachel's family life was not easy at first. When in the first seven or eight years of marriage, they lost three small children to illness (two in one awful year), feelings of sadness and worries about the future must have been with them for some time. Even in those days, when losing a child was common, the misfortune that repeatedly emptied the cribs at home, one after another, was more than would have been expected. But in 1877, with the arrival of Bronisława (Bruche in Yiddish), their luck as parents finally turned around. From then on, every two years Rachel would deliver a healthy baby, five in all. Among them was Joachim (Chaim Nussin in Yiddish) Hübner, my paternal grandfather, who was born on July 25, 1881, in Słobódka Leśna. When seven days later, after the *bris* ceremony, the child's name was entered into the records in Kołomyja, Salomon Leib Hübner proudly signed as the father.

The signature of Salomon Leib Hübner (1849–1904), my great-grandfather, from the registration of the birth of his son, Joachim, born in 1881 in Słobódka Leśna.

Kołomyja continued with its strong Jewish fabric, which meant that sooner or later, Jews would enter politics. As if stepping carefully into uncharted territory, one of the first Jewish deputies representing the town was Simon Schreiber, a member of the Orthodox political party Upholders of the Faith. This elderly man had many virtues but, since he spoke only Yiddish, he was unable to engage in debates in the national parliament in Vienna. A few years later, he was replaced by Rabbi Joseph Bloch, who was quite the opposite. This new member of parliament was both erudite and thoughtful, earning respect after exposing the most egregious examples of anti-Semitism. He did not shy away from using literary polemics or courts of law to combat prejudice.

With an increasingly crowded political scene, the citizens of Kołomyja hotly debated in their homes, in the public square, and at the ballot boxes, whom to support. Now, they had many choices, including those who advocated Jewish assimilation into Polish culture, others who argued for a distinct ethnic identity linked with Austria, and a growing Jewish national movement on the opposite side of the spectrum.[15]

On other occasions, the Jewish character of Kołomyja emerged in unexpected ways. Less than a year before Joachim Hübner's birth, Emperor Franz Joseph had toured Galicia. In Lwów, there were visits by the emperor to two city synagogues, one Reform and the other Orthodox. The last stop in Galicia was Kołomyja. When the imperial train filled with the political establishment and the press arrived from Lwów, even the cantankerous Rabbi Lichtenstein turned up at the station with local officialdom. The stated purpose for the brief visit was the monarch's tour of ethnographic exhibitions on display in town, one organized by Poles and the other by the competing group, Ruthenians. However, to the disappointment of many, the festivities were marred by rain that had been falling for days. The streets and walkways of Kołomyja had turned into an unsightly sea of mud. After the emperor and his top echelon boarded a few carriages prepared to take them to the exhibits, dozens of less prominent visitors, including members of the press, found themselves walking in ankle-deep mud to the city center. To their dismay, not a single *fiacre* was available for the quarter-mile ride to bring them to the planned ceremonies. As it turned out,

Jewish carriage drivers from Kołomyja (*Kolomea*).

nobody had planned a boycott or meant any disrespect; the planners of the imperial tour had simply overlooked the fact that the visit fell on Yom Kippur, a holy day when Jewish carriage drivers, who were exclusively in charge of that form of transportation, had the day off. It was not lost on one hapless reporter trekking through the streets that although Jews could not work on this day, many of them greeted the emperor from the sidewalks nonetheless.[16]

⟁

MEANWHILE, SALOMON HÜBNER'S AFFLUENCE was growing. With the passing of Rachel's father in 1891, control of the family estate was transferred to him. Apparently the late Mordko Fränkel had viewed his son-in-law as more trustworthy in financial matters than Rachel's brother Leiser who nonetheless continued to live in Słobódka Leśna and work in the family enterprise. No longer was Salomon Hübner's occupation listed in town records as a merchant; he was now referred to as "landowner." Business must have been brisk under his watch, for over the next few years, the Hübner enterprises would expand further, to watermills in the neighboring towns of Śniatyn and Kołomyja.

The family's immediate surroundings were also changing. In 1899, the Jewish Colonization Association, a company established by philanthropist Baron de Hirsch, bought land next to Salomon and Rachel's. In a few years, a modern Jewish agricultural school opened there. Its purpose was to provide professional training to young Jewish men near home, and to assure their self-reliance in farming if they chose to leave for other countries. In addition to agricultural courses, the school established a large distillery and trained blacksmiths.

The year 1904 was full of contradictions for the Hübner family. In the span of a few months, two new lives were added to the family, but two others were extinguished. In May of that year, everything had seemed to be on the right track. Erna Erbsen, the youngest of Joachim's sisters, married just one year earlier, had her first child. Joachim became the godfather who offered blessings on that occasion; a small note on the document referred to his residence as still in Słobódka Leśna. Yet the next month, the family was shaken to its core when Salomon Hübner, Joachim's father, suddenly suffered a stroke and died at the age of fifty-five. The shock and sadness had not even had time to lessen when, a couple of months later, Chaje Badian, another sister of Joachim's, passed away after giving birth to a son. Doubtless these were anxious months, when feelings of personal loss among family members were mixed with the need for pragmatic decisions about what to do next. Ultimately, the Hübners decided to sell or lease the Słobódka Leśna estate. The next year, someone else was in charge of that enterprise.

After the death of his father, Joachim did not linger for long in Kołomyja. The next year, he became the land administrator of the estate of Felicya Fredro, one hundred miles north. The countess, as she was known, was related to a famous playwright, Alexander Fredro, whose fables and comedies had delighted audiences for years. Through marriage, the Fredro family was also connected with distinguished Ruthenian (now increasingly called Ukrainian) nobility. The Sheptytsky (Szeptycki) clan owned estates in the nearby area.[17] How twenty-five-year-old Joachim Hübner found the position there, overseeing land management on the countess's property, remains unknown. He settled in Bryńce Cerkiewne, less than a mile's walk from a small town called Wybranówka, to where the countess's estate extended. This was not an entirely remote place; the train station in Wybranówka connected Joachim with Lwów to the north, and to a number of Galician towns: Chodorów, Rohatyn, and Bursztyn, and the always-inviting Stanisławów farther south. In any case, it was a fortuitous choice; the young newcomer soon met a young woman named Regina Dub. Paradoxically, fewer details have survived about Regina's youth than about her accomplished grandfather; whether the young woman was employed in the household of the countess or met Joachim under different circumstances can only be a matter of speculation. What is known, however, is that both she and Joachim were in their mid-twenties, single and looking with confidence to the future. Romance seems to have blossomed quickly between the two.

During their courtship, the couple often visited Rohatyn, which acquainted Joachim with places that were familiar to Regina. There, they also visited her sister, Taube Katz, who had only recently returned from Stanisławów to Rohatyn, where Taube's husband had opened a successful law practice. Clearly, the Katzes seemed fond of Joachim, soon inviting the young suitor to be a witness at their newborn son's *bris*.

When my paternal grandparents decided to marry less than one year after falling in love, their decision was a clear reflection of the changing times. Theirs

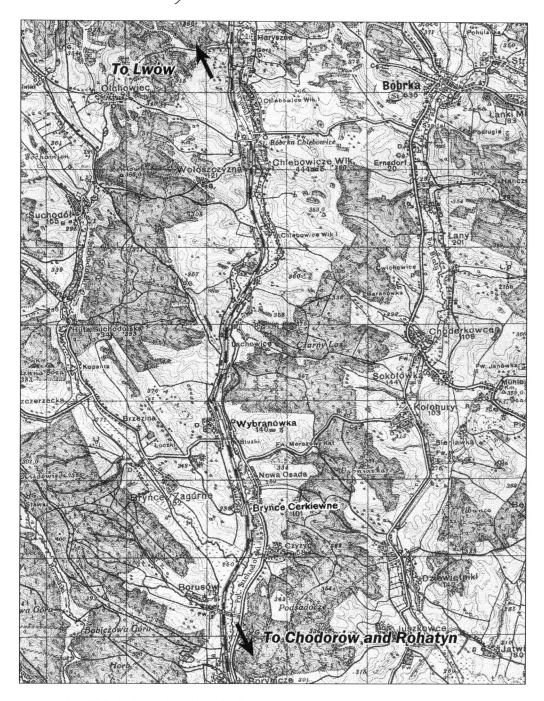

Map of Bóbrka district located south of Lwów. Joachim Hübner moved to Bryńce Cerkiewne, near the town of Wybranówka, in 1905. *(Section of a map from 1923.)*

The Chodorów Synagogue. This wooden synagogue was built in 1652. My grandparents,
Regina Dub (1879–1941) and Joachim Hübner (1881–1947), were married there on December 5, 1905.
The synagogue was destroyed by the Nazis during World War II. Photograph circa 1910.
(Courtesy of Beit Hatfutsot, the Museum of the Jewish People, Tel Aviv, Israel.)

would most likely be the first marriage of choice in their families' long histories; by then, young people were increasingly making decisions for themselves. But from what followed next, we can only surmise that Regina's parents did not necessarily approve of this union. Contrary to the tradition followed by her sisters and many young women before, Regina Dub did not marry in the place where her parents lived. Instead, the ceremony took place not far from Countess Fredro's estate.

When the young couple neared Chodorów's synagogue for the ceremony, they would have seen an unusual building. On the outside, it was an austere-looking structure; built entirely of timber in the seventeenth century, it was now darkened and frayed in a few places. Inside, they would have seen a masterfully carved pulpit (*bima*) and the ark that held the Torah scroll (*aron hakodesh*). But that was not all, for many synagogues in the area could boast these features. What distinguished this one were the vibrant scenes painted on the wooden ceiling. Passages from

The Chodorów Synagogue, interior view. Photograph circa 1916.
(Courtesy of Beit Hatfutsot, the Museum of the Jewish People, Tel Aviv, Israel.)

the scriptures in Hebrew surrounded twelve signs of the zodiac, which were, in turn, encircled by a flowering vine. Images of exotic animals never seen in Galicia: elephants, lions, and monkeys, all conveying special meaning (according to the Talmud, those seeing an elephant or a monkey were to say a special blessing, while elephants with castles on their backs represented the wisdom of the Torah), expressed the unusual artistry of the Galician painter who had created them almost two centuries before. Other scenes, with more familiar local themes, were no less beautiful; they showed turkeys, geese, sheep, and goats. In the excitement of the occasion Joachim and Regina, standing inside, might have only briefly glanced at the signature of that talented artist, who had left an inscription on the ceiling: "Behold All That Was Painted My Hand Has Wrought."[18]

In a symbolic way on that Friday in December 1905, tradition was bridged to modernity in more than one way. In a sense, the wedding was a culmination of not only Joachim and Regina's courtship, but also of the inspiring life of Regina's elderly grandfather. Nobody in the family knew exactly how old Sender Dub was; some believed that he was approaching one hundred years. During his time, he had witnessed many changes, including those affecting his own family. When Sender died one month later in his hometown, Rohatyn, he seemed almost to be sending a message that his job was done, and it was time to pass on the family baton. Its recipient was this young and modern couple who was starting their union in this history-steeped place, but who would not shy away from embracing new ways of life, whether for themselves or for their children.[19]

Chapter 8

UNMASKING FALSEHOOD:

ROHLING VERSUS

BLOCH

$\mathcal{T}$HE BEGINNINGS OF JOSEPH S. BLOCH'S life were rather inconspicuous. He was born in 1850 into a poor baker's family; as a young boy Joseph brought fresh rolls to the market in Dukla, a mainly Jewish town in Galicia. Quite early in life, he began moving from one Jewish community to another, between relatives, from one *yeshivot* (institution of Talmudic studies) to another. There were short periods of time in various Galician towns, including Sambor, Lwów, Stanisławów, and Czortków, where he encountered a few famous rabbis. In general, it was an itinerant life for a child but not uncommon for many sons born in the Orthodox families. Joseph, like other young Jewish boys engaged in religious studies, depended for his support on the generosity of the Jewish communities.

Joseph was a quick learner of the Talmud; he swiftly mastered its rich commentaries and other religious texts. And his intelligence did not go unnoticed, even at this early age. When the boy was only fifteen years old, a respected rabbinical authority from Lwów mentioned him by name in one of his writings, as one of his most gifted students. Not everything was serious to this hardworking young man; his religious studies were mixed with a few boyish pranks. But in any case, young Joseph's world remained fairly insulated from its surroundings. Until his late teens, he received almost no secular education, and had no knowledge of German or Polish, speaking only Yiddish and Hebrew.

Then in the 1860s, with a few letters of recommendation from some rabbis to others, young Joseph left Galicia for Germany. There, he moved around again, this time offering his knowledge of the Talmud to rabbis in return for lessons in non-religious subjects. On the surface, it was an unusual arrangement; a young man from Galicia was offering his recently acquired, almost encyclopedic knowledge and interpretations of the Talmud to a few German rabbis who felt they needed some help with a sermon or scholarly writings. It was more than a convenient way for a wanderer to secure room and board. As Bloch later recalled, this was also the first real chance for him to close the gaps in his nonreligious education before going to university. When he was finally well prepared, he immersed himself in secular studies in Germany and Switzerland.

In 1875, Joseph Bloch received a doctorate in philosophy from the University of Zurich. For the next few years, he continued his nomadic life, moving around Jewish communities in Germany and Bohemia, serving as a preacher or rabbi. His career seemed to reach its peak when he was appointed the Orthodox rabbi of a small working-class neighborhood, Floridsdorf, near Vienna. Over the next few years, Dr. Bloch, as he was now called, would venture only a short distance beyond his synagogue, giving a few lectures in Vienna, mostly on the Bible but including a few secular matters. That was not too bad for a poor Jewish boy who was unaccustomed to settling down. But as it turned out, life had some surprises in store for Rabbi Joseph S. Bloch.[1]

For more than a decade, Jews' full civil rights had been enshrined in the constitution of Austro-Hungary. Articles of the new constitution, signed by Emperor Franz Joseph in December of 1867, were unambiguous. They clearly stated that all citizens were equal before the law, with the right to run for any public office. In contrast to prior times, there were no loopholes or deferral to future laws about who could own what; now, "complete freedom of religion and conscience," guaranteed by the state, seemed to invite fundamental changes.[2] However, the extent to which those progressive laws were accepted by non-Jews varied greatly across the country. Nobody denied that there had been real progress made by Jews in Vienna, Prague, and Lwów—and elsewhere, but it was a precariously fragile process nonetheless. Interactions of Jews and gentiles in business and on the streets were frequent, but mixing at social events was initially rare.

Nonetheless, barriers were slowly being breached; it was heralded as a new beginning when one year Jews and gentiles celebrated together at the wedding of a Jewish couple in Lwów. Not lost on observers was the fact that the bride and groom were ordinary people, with no special wealth or connections. But this sort of event was still an exception, which was what prompted a newspaper to comment on it.[3] Flare-ups of intolerance were not uncommon; differences in language, dress code, and customs between Jews and the rest of the society were often blamed, but that was too simple an explanation.

In recent years, many Austro-Hungarian Jews had aspired to escape the isolation—imposed by the traditional lifestyle of their parents or forced upon them by less tolerant neighbors—and debated the issue of their own future in the society. Some advocated a preservation of religious distinctiveness but wished to blend their secular lives with Poles in Galicia, Czechs in Moravia, or Germans in Lower Austria, creating a hyphenated identity. Others, like Joseph Bloch, argued that Jews, always a minority in the multiethnic empire, should adopt a deeper civic bond with the pan-Austrian state, while fully embracing their Jewish ethnicity regardless of where they lived. The Galician-born rabbi, educated in Germany and serving a congregation near Vienna, wanted Jews of the Empire to identify as neither German nor Czech (nor Pole) but as Jews and also Austrians. Yet the concept of Austrian identity could easily come into conflict with the nationalistic tendencies that were on the rise in the lands of the empire, where Poles, Ruthenians, Czechs, and Hungarians all tried to establish dominance on their own. Among them, being an Austrian Jew did not always invite sympathy.[4]

"The Jewish Issue" was a frequent headline in many newspapers, with a recurring focus on the competition between Jewish and non-Jewish businesses. This was always a hot-button issue in Galicia and elsewhere. Even in areas of a common ground, such as the integration of Jews into the larger society through secular education, caveats were often raised. It seemed that the non-Jewish press was suspicious about the intent of philanthropic Jewish organizations in Vienna and abroad. The opening of new schools funded by one of these, the Alliance Israelite, was praised by some in the press, although any focus on teaching craftsmanship or modern agricultural skills was viewed with some wariness. The question was asked by a reporter: Was the only intent to uplift the impoverished Jews of Galicia, or was it to create economic advantages along ethnic lines? Suddenly, Jews were being praised for their industriousness and ability to achieve high literacy if given the right opportunity. But in the same breath, even open-minded voices pointed out that skilled Jewish craftsmen or farmers were guaranteed to overtake their uneducated gentile counterparts. Perhaps, they said, their talents should be directed somewhere else.[5]

The latter part of the nineteenth century brought a new wave of problems for Jews that had little to do with economic or cultural issues. The most sinister was the growth of a coarse debate across Austro-Hungary and Germany on the alleged nature of Judaism. Both legitimate and self-appointed authorities in Hebraic studies and theology, lumped together as "Orientalists," voiced opinions on biblical or rabbinic citations that went far beyond esoteric discussion. Their audience became the general public, through constant speeches and newspaper articles on the topic. Certainly, rabid anti-Semitism was not a new phenomenon; the laws of Austro-Hungary in fact forbade inciting overt hatred, indicating that this had happened before. What was different this time was that the claims against Jews and their faith were being advanced under the cover of scientific debate and expert analysis of ancient texts.

ॐ

WHEN DR. BLOCH WAS chosen in 1880 to lead an unassuming congregation in Floridsdorf, August Rohling was already well-known in Europe as the most vocal expert on the "Jewish issue." On many levels, he could not be easily dismissed. To begin with, he was a Catholic priest. And he certainly was not a simple country cleric who could be accused of venting his prejudices during Sunday sermons. Rohling was an accepted expert in Hebraic studies who had begun his career as a lecturer at a small theological school in Münster, Germany. It was there, in 1870, in the midst of his financial troubles, that Rohling wrote a small book. It had no more than one hundred pages and carried the soon-to-be infamous title, *The Talmud Jew* (*Talmudjuden*). In the wider world, nobody knew that shortly after it was published, his superior, the head of the Theological Academy, had made public his displeasure with Rohling's book. Despite this, the slim volume grew over the next few years, being issued in the form of ever-expanding new editions. The professor from Münster claimed to have thoroughly examined the Talmud, several rabbinical texts, and even old Christian sources, to formulate grave charges against the Jews.

Rohling's academic credentials gave his views an aura of legitimacy, making them even more pernicious. Citing "translations," mainly from ancient Hebrew and on few occasions from Latin, Rohling posited that over the centuries Jews had abandoned the purity of the biblical teachings of Moses, due to indoctrination by the Talmud and other rabbinic texts. As if this was not enough, each expanded edition of *The Talmud Jew* gave new "scientific" evidence, in the form of more detailed citations, to bolster the author's belief in the deep flaws of the Jewish religion.

The book's premise was that Judaism not only condoned, but compelled every observant Jew to act with malicious intent against non-Jews, mainly Christians. Rohling opined with certainty: "The Jews are authorized by their religion to take advantage of all non-Jews, to ruin them physically, morally, to destroy their lives, honor, and property, openly by force, as well as secretly and insidiously." The harm, according to the theologian, was being inflicted "to acquire power and domination over all the world for their nation."[6] The canons of Jewish morality were presented as grotesque and harmful to everyone else. Cheating, usury, and almost all imaginable forms of abuse of gentile neighbors were portrayed as acts sanctioned under Jewish religious law. On the pages of *The Talmud Jew*, Jewish rabbinical teachings were claimed to degrade non-Jews and equate them with animals. Reading that adultery with a gentile woman was acceptable, even sometimes encouraged by rabbis, shocked readers.

At first, the book apparently did not improve Rohling's financial situation. In 1874, he disappeared from Münster only to resurface in French Canada, and later in the United States. When his request for a leave of absence was rejected by the academy and he failed to return there, Rohling was promptly dismissed from his teaching post. His fall was made worse by the creditors pursuing the cleric, who seemed to be seeking refuge beyond the ocean. The whole affair might have been seen as yet another anti-Semitic outburst, now mercifully at an end. However, nothing could have been further from the truth.[7]

Despite his career setback, August Rohling apparently had powerful supporters. In 1876, back in Europe, he was given a prestigious professorship at Charles-Ferdinand University (*Karl-Ferdinands-Universität*) in Prague. This was not another appointment to an obscure theological institution in a provincial town. Charles-Ferdinand University was renowned for its long history and top-notch faculty. Prague itself was a major city in the heart of Austro-Hungary. By joining its faculty and becoming Chair in Bible Studies, Rohling seemed to gain a visible acknowledgement of his credentials. Yet for someone voicing strong anti-Jewish views, the academic world of Prague was a somewhat unusual place to end up. There, German and Jewish professors often gravitated toward each other, forming an informal alliance against Czech nationalists who would ultimately succeed in splitting the university in two along linguistic lines. Anyone hoping that Rohling's exposure to his academic peers—a few of whom were Jewish—would slowly moderate his stand, was in for a disappointment.[8]

Although, as a condition of receiving the academic post in Prague, the cleric was cautioned not to publish his inflammatory book again, Rohling seems never to have taken that condition seriously. By no coincidence, his arrival there was greeted with the circulation of a new edition; it was promoted as a serious treatise that unmasked nefarious Jewish secrets. Even Rohling's academic colleagues, most of whom were privately aghast at the content of the book, equivocated in public. Did they fear that more pressure on one of their number might backfire, limiting their own freedom of expression in the future? The Academic Senate declined to initiate a disciplinary investigation against the inflammatory Chair in Bible Studies. Its members acknowledged that the message of Rohling's book joined "the mountain of hostilities against Judaism" but they would act against one of their own only if Rohling was proven guilty of offenses in a court of law. In the midst of the debate, someone added, "How is one to explain dragging him to defend his writings if they had just laid the foundations of his appointment in Austria?"[9]

The Talmud Jew was now being distributed throughout the lands of Austro-Hungary and Germany with even greater vigor. Hundreds of thousands of copies in German, Czech, Hungarian, Polish, and then French, English, and other languages were distributed throughout Europe at discounted prices or even for free; in Austro-Hungary alone, its circulation reached two hundred thousand. All over the continent, many newspapers carried daily ads for local editions. In some places the book's title, though not its content, was modified to appease censors. A strange subtitle, "… for cordial consideration by Jews and Christians from all walks of life" was added, which could not have been more deceiving given the hateful message that remained.

In Prague and elsewhere, Rohling's book became a bestseller. The author's pronouncements that "people observing their religion according to the Talmud ought to be suppressed and banished to Saint Helen Island or Cayenne [French Guiana]" were seeds of hate falling on fertile soil.[10] Lingering hopes that the cleric's poisonous message would simply be ignored turned out to be utterly futile. Excerpts from the book were increasingly quoted by other publications as a reputable source of facts. Otherwise-respected figures began to use language straight from Rohling's pages. A revered Polish painter from Galicia, in reply to a minor criticism by someone who happened to be a Jew, blasted out, "The followers of the Talmud consider us today as walking corpses on whom they are free to inflict cruelty." In light of such inflamed rhetoric, "The Jewish Issue" was taking a more ominous tone than before.[11] The point seemed dangerously close when an average person would simply wave away any remaining hesitation, claiming that the priest and scholar could not be too far mistaken in his conclusions.

꒰

THE NEXT STEP FOR Professor Rohling was to eagerly insert himself into the debate whenever Jews and Christians sought resolution of grievances in a court of law. Rohling and his supporters were no longer satisfied simply with written or verbal agitation against Judaism and the Jews. Now, they wanted to obtain some validation of their arguments through the legal system, the last bastion of presumed impartiality. With seemingly unending energy and persistence, Rohling barraged the courts in Austro-Hungary and Germany, offering his "expert" testimony. Whenever anti-Semitic agitators were accused by prosecutors of a breach of public order, or when Jews were accused of preposterous capital crimes against non-Jewish women, Rohling was available. He repeatedly proclaimed that his views had already been given in other courts under oath. Rohling conveyed a steady conviction that the results of his studies were irrefutable and he was not afraid of committing perjury. For the most part, the courts prudently ignored Rohling's offers. But his demagoguery had no bounds. Even though he was never admitted into legal proceedings, he began to claim that no court had ever formally contested his expert testimony.

In 1879, the Jewish community of Dresden, Germany filed a suit for libel against a local anti-Semitic author and his publisher. The defendants promptly replied that almost all their arguments had been quoted from *The Talmud Jew* and other "scholarly" publications. One of them stated that Rohling's views had never been discredited by any of his opponents. Then, the professor from Prague personally entered the fray, writing to the court that the Talmud sanctioned Jews to rob, cheat, and even murder Christians. He stated, with what he claimed to be the highest authority, that there was no scientific dispute regarding these claims against Judaism. The court even received an affidavit from another expert siding with the professor's "unbiased" view.

Rohling's crusade did not suffer from the fact that this particular "supportive expert" had professed absolutely no knowledge of the Talmud on another occasion. Such minor details did not really seem to matter. But Rohling dropped a real bombshell when he opined, in another letter to the court, that "We must act to legally reverse the emancipation of the Jews, since Judaism contains elements that are not acceptable in a Christian political system, and which entail great dangers for the state, encourage revolution, and promote destruction of the Christian monarchy for the goal of establishing Jewish world dominance."

When the case against the anti-Jewish agitator was dismissed, the court's legal opinion was that the passages in question had come from "critical scientific debates." The impact of the proceedings reverberated beyond the Dresden courtroom; many public prosecutors in Germany, seeing the outcome, grew reluctant to bring charges against other anti-Semitic agitators. Rohling was elated and emboldened.[12] Still, not everyone agreed with him. One opposing view came from an unlikely player; Franz Delitzsch, a respected Hebraist and professor of theology at the University of Leipzig, who was a Lutheran pastor and a true scholar of the Old Testament. In 1881, he

Franz Delitzsch (1813–1890). A Lutheran theologian and expert in Hebraic studies, he became an early critic of August Rohling's anti-Semitic views.

published a scholarly treatise unmasking Rohling as a fraud. He stated unequivocally that no passages of the Talmud existed to indict Jews for any malice toward Christians. Delitzsch, with his superb expertise in Hebrew, had quickly recognized the fallacies of *The Talmud Jew*.

Not surprisingly, Rohling quickly went on the offensive, but always ignoring the actual facts of the debate. Instead, he repeatedly attacked Delitzsch on a personal level. In Rohling's eyes, it seemed, being a Lutheran was as grave a sin as being a Jew! In fact, he claimed that the sinister plot ascribed to the Jews could be uncovered among Lutherans as well. Rohling wrote about those theologians who disagreed with him, "Wünsche and Delitzsch are, as is known, Jews who usurped Protestant denominations." The Jewish conspiracy was apparently everywhere.

On another occasion, the priestly academic from Prague would add, "A Protestant living according to the precepts of Luther is a monster." Delitzsch, who was more interested in scholarly pursuits than in seeing his name dragged through the mud, retreated. Frustrated with the tone of the discourse, he said, with just a hint of exasperation, "This man, who rushes with fanatical delusion into courtrooms in order to swear that lies are truth, is indefatigable. When checkmated, he sweeps the pieces from the chessboard and denounces his opponent as a cheater." With this, Rohling seemed unstoppable.[13]

Dr. Joseph Bloch and Professor Rohling found themselves on a collision course when public debate on the issue moved—from Germany and the periphery of Austro-Hungary to the capital of the country. In 1882, the public prosecutor in Vienna initiated legal proceedings against Franz Holubek, a man who had made a speech inciting local Christian merchants against Jews. The theme was sadly familiar, with the accused making claims that the Talmud described non-Jews, "As a herd of pigs, dogs, and asses!" The affair became more relevant to the national debate when the defense read into the record a portion of *The Talmud Jew* that was rich in incriminating passages. Even the prosecutor, when faced with such "scientific" evidence, stated, "I do not object to the reading. I cannot deny that this passage is in the Talmud."

Then the defendant was allowed to testify; he simply argued that his speech had contained a quote from the work of Professor Rohling, who had offered a substantial financial award to "anyone able to prove to the body of the German Association of Orientalists that a single quotation from his book *The Talmud Jew* is false." Indignant about what he believed to be passages from the Talmud, the defendant added that no civil society based on such horrible principles should be allowed in those modern times. How, he insisted, could anyone be accused of inciting violence if their text was taken from a holy book? Proclaiming his innocence, he asked why, if the statements were untrue, no single Jew had ever tried to claim the reward. When the jury unanimously acquitted the defendant, this clear legal victory for Rohling's views brought the controversy to new heights.

The outcome of this appalling affair threatened to erase whatever Jews had gained in their integration into Austro-Hungary's civil society. Silence on the issue from the Jewish community was no longer an option. Two days after the court's verdict, two respected rabbis and historians from Vienna, Adolf Jellinek and Moritz Güdemann, published a statement in most of the Viennese papers. Their text was short, and free of any of the high-blown language that had accompanied prior discourse. Both men labeled Rohling's work false; in fact, they said, it was simply a refurbished version of an old anti-Semitic publication from about one hundred years before. In closing, they said, "we declare that the Talmud contains nothing hostile to Christianity."

For the next few weeks, Joseph Bloch watched with some relief as the case slowly disappeared from newspapers' pages. But this turned out to be only the calm before the storm. By mid-December, Rohling pounced back with fury, publishing a series of articles that would later appear as a pamphlet, "My Answers to the Rabbis (*Meine Antworten an die Rabbiner*)." To make a point about his own expertise and high moral standing, Rohling reminded readers time after time that he was serving as the Imperial and Royal Professor of Hebraic Studies at a respected university in Prague, and was a Catholic priest. Of his recitations of supposedly incriminating quotes from the Talmud, Rohling asserted that he had already provided sworn testimonies on the subject. In case this was not sufficient to erase anyone's doubt about the accuracy of his arguments, he "reassured" readers about his willingness to repeat such statements under oath. With such unshakable evidence laid out, Rohling promptly accused the two rabbis, who had had the audacity to comment on his work, of "cunning knavery."[14]

When thirty-three-year-old Bloch approached his esteemed colleagues in Vienna, asking when a stronger rebuke of Rohling was coming, one of them asked in exasperation whether any further response would really be worth the trouble. It was certain, he said, that the self-appointed expert on Judaism would always cite yet another supposedly incriminating passage from rabbinic texts; this could become an unending and undignified battle. Although his colleagues seemed to feel they had fulfilled their duty, for Bloch the issue became a call to action.

The young rabbi returned home, and over the next twenty-four hours mustered his expertise on the Talmud and other Jewish religious books. Suddenly, all he had memorized during his early studies in Galicia became a tremendous asset. The result was a point-by-point response to Rohling's statements and quotes. Within days the essay was published, with no editorial changes, as a supplement to one of the Viennese newspapers; one hundred thousand copies were sold within a few weeks. Bloch's message was clear; Rohling had not only invented and falsified citations from Jewish holy books, he was also misquoting texts of the Catholic Church! Bloch concluded that this "expert" lacked scientific credentials and moral virtues.

Bloch's large readership made it apparent: interest in the controversy was not confined to a few scholars of Hebraic texts. Predictably Rohling, being Rohling, soon replied with another anti-Semitic rant. This time Bloch was ready to strike back. He taunted the professor by writing that Rohling's work showed he had been unable to understand even a single page of the Talmud. Mockingly, Bloch offered a financial award to the professor if he would undertake a translation from Hebrew of any randomly selected page from the Talmud, the book that the author of *The Talmud Jew* claimed to know so well. Not surprisingly, a reply to this offer would never come.

A few months later, two unrelated crimes, in different parts of Austro-Hungary, resulted in the violent deaths of female victims and gripped the public throughout the empire. For some, these tragedies were not just random criminal cases. Both involved Jews accused of the murder of young non-Jewish women; this in itself was enough for Rohling to point to them as examples of ritual murder! One of the cases, in Galicia, involved a Jewish innkeeper accused of an illicit sexual relationship with a gentile woman and, along with his wife, of the subsequent murder and dismemberment of his pregnant lover. The newspapers reported on gruesome details of the barbaric crime, which only added to a public sense of the bestiality of the perpetrators. Although the victim was not a young Christian virgin, as ritual murder victims were said to be, the gory details of the case were used to imply some form of the practice. In the trial, which dragged on for years, both defendants were sentenced to death by hanging, with the verdict upheld during initial appeals. Only after the reexamination of the case, by the Supreme Court in Vienna, was the verdict found to be tainted by serious judicial malpractice; the defendants, acquitted of all charges, were set free.

The second tragedy, in Hungary, involved a young Christian girl who had been killed, and whipped up even more of a storm. Her sad fate captured the public's imagination. The accused was Jewish; daily reports of his trial were published far beyond Hungary. The defendant's underage son testified, accusing his father of the murder, and claiming that he had seen the "ritual killing" through a keyhole in the synagogue on Passover night. Some cracks in the case started to appear when it came out that several gentile girls had been beaten by their parents after testifying in favor of the Jewish defendants.

As might have been expected, Rohling inserted himself into those explosive affairs. First, he wrote to the court in Lwów offering to testify under oath. When his offer was ignored by the justice system in Galicia, he shifted his attention to Hungary. In an open letter to a Hungarian politician, Rohling claimed to have found new evidence: "Wherever such a case is brought in front of a court, I feel it is my duty to inform ... I came into the possession of a work published in 1868..., which states on page 156a that the shedding of blood from a non-Jewish virgin is a holy act for Jews, and that such blood is very pleasing in heaven and makes God merciful.... I am willing to take an oath in a court of law in order to verify the truth of this passage."[15]

The gravity of this was obvious. Even if the Hungarian court ignored Rohling's offer, he could claim again with his twisted logic that no court had ever invalidated his charges. Pressing on with his anti-Semitic crusade, he could opine that he had finally unearthed recent written references to Jewish ritual murder, as opposed to some difficult-to-prove oral traditions that were allegedly followed by Jews. How could anyone doubt such a mountain of evidence?[16]

By then, Bloch had realized that another round of articles debunking Rohling's statements would not be sufficient. He sensed that different tactics were needed. In his next published answer to the expert from Prague, Bloch structured his arguments in a new way; he was setting a trap. Scholarly citations from rabbinical texts and details of Rohling's mistakes were no longer present. Instead, Bloch simply branded his adversary a liar who had committed perjury many times. Alluding to the recent cases in Galicia and Hungary, Bloch said, "We [Jews] have to defend ourselves against the threat of perjury on demand."

In less-than-subtle ways, Bloch shifted the debate from a discussion of religious texts, repeatedly provoking the professor to sue the young rabbi for libel. Many Jews in Vienna and Galicia expressed misgivings about how vocal and personal Bloch became in these exchanges. Perhaps, they worried, the tone of this public discourse had gone too far and only played into the hands of the never-ending stream of anti-Semites. Privately, many of them feared that any failure to unmask Rohling's forgeries in court could irreparably set back their cause.

After a few weeks' effort, Bloch succeeded; Rohling took the bait. On August 10, 1883, he sued the rabbi, and the newspaper that had published his work, for libel in Vienna. The famous case of Rohling versus Bloch had officially begun.[17]

ॐ

FROM THE OUTSET OF the legal proceedings, the spotlight was on Bloch. In the spring of 1883, he had taken part in a special election for deputies to the parliament (*Reichsrat*) in Vienna, aiming to represent three towns in the eastern part of Galicia. The campaign had been an example of bare-knuckle politics, with the local press warning ultra-Orthodox Jews of the district that the rabbi might be a secret supporter of Reform Judaism. Derisively, Bloch's knowledge of Galician affairs had been described as being even less than what Rohling knew about the Talmud. Nonetheless, Bloch won by a comfortable margin.

Under different circumstances, this would have been a great occasion for the rabbi to shift his full energy to the political arena. Getting along with the Polish parliamentary deputies was clearly a priority for him, since they were already watching him with suspicion. He soon published a statement promising to vote with that group, and to foster a good relationship between the Jewish and Christian populations. Back in Galicia, even an innocent congratulatory telegram from Viennese Jews was sufficient to spark comments by a newspaper reporter that the new deputy might promote policies of Jewish cultural separatism.[18]

But at that moment, another complication became a matter of utmost importance to Bloch. Under rules of parliamentary immunity, the new deputy could not be sued. Dismissal of Rohling's case based on this rule would not only have defeated the rabbi's plan to challenge the professor in open court; even worse, it would have given the false expert the opportunity to claim yet another "victory." So, taking a highly unusual step, Bloch appealed to the parliamentary rules commission to waive his newly acquired immunity. The system worked slowly, but finally in February 1884 after months of delays, a resolution was passed allowing the court proceedings to continue.

Another important issue for Joseph S. Bloch was the selection of his defense attorney. From the first day, Rohling had been represented by an erudite member of parliament. Not surprisingly, the man was known for his anti-Jewish views, but he was a formidable opponent nonetheless. On his side, Bloch rejected offers of legal representation by many Jewish attorneys. Instead, he chose Joseph Kopp, a fellow deputy who was widely respected but had no knowledge of the Talmud or rabbinic literature, which were sure to be dissected in excruciating detail during the courtroom proceedings.

Joseph (Josef) Kopp (1827–1907). A member of the national parliament (*Reichsrat*), who represented the district of Vienna from 1873 to 1907. An accomplished lawyer, he acted as the defense counsel for Dr. Joseph S. Bloch in the libel suit brought by August Rohling. *(Courtesy of the Austrian National Library, Vienna.)*

What followed were days that stretched to weeks and then to two years of almost daily conferences between the defendant and his attorney. Bloch explained, translated, interpreted, and summarized texts that Rohling had misused in his attacks against the Jews. At first, Kopp was skeptical. He was cautious in accepting the arguments of his client; perhaps, he pointed out, there was an earlier edition of this or another book, containing passages similar to those used by Rohling. Kopp knew well that in the libel trial, it was Bloch, and not the other party, who would carry the burden of proof with every contested citation. If books full of incriminating evidence against Judaism had never existed, it was up to the defense team to prove that Rohling had knowingly falsified the record. Leaving nothing to chance, Kopp ordered a number of old books, Hebrew and Christian, in not just one but all the editions available throughout Europe. Otherwise, he reasoned, it would always be easy for the professor to claim that he had used a different version. Not being a linguistic expert, Kopp traveled to different universities in Austro-Hungary and Germany to validate Bloch's translations with various experts. He also assembled a collection of sworn testimonies or affidavits in which Rohling had made outrageous charges.[19]

Their confidence on the rise, the defense took the next crucial step, locating impartial experts. Kopp was adamant that no single expert could be of the Jewish faith, and that no one with even remote Jewish heritage speak on behalf of his client. Otherwise, Rohling could easily claim bias or another Jewish conspiracy. Then, Bloch convincingly argued to his counsel that calling on separate experts for the defendant and plaintiff would only muddy the waters; regardless of the outcome, each side would then be able to claim moral victory. The public, he insisted, would meet such a skirmish between experts with a yawn. Instead, he raised the game by proposing that the court appoint a group of experts agreed upon by both sides, and empowered to determine, once and for all, what had led Bloch to label Rohling a liar. But where to find trusted authorities who would be agreeable to both sides? The candidates would need to have detailed knowledge, and not only of the tenets of Judaism and Christianity; they also had to demonstrate an expert understanding of Hebrew.

In a somewhat perverse way, Rohling's venomous writings guided the defense in the right direction. For years, the professor had been taunting his opponents by offering a financial reward: "if Juda can get a verdict from the Association of German Orientalists that my quotations are invented, untrue, or forged." Even recently, in his angry exchanges with the rabbi, Rohling had said with confidence, "Let Bloch produce a judgment from our well-known jury [of my peers] that my passages are false, invented, forged." Kopp did exactly that by convincing the court to approach the Association of German Orientalists for experts. Rohling raised some meek objections, but was overruled by court officials.

A list of eleven professors of theology from universities in Germany and Austria was offered by the court. Some were disqualified because they were considered biased by one side or the other, or because of their Jewish heritage, on the insistence of Kopp. Others refused to take part in lengthy judicial proceedings. Yet one of them could not resist writing to the court that, despite having been Rohling's friend for the past twenty years, he strongly disavowed his anti-Semitic tirades. In the end, two of the professors were selected and agreed to offer their time and expertise during the trial; they were August Wünsche of Dresden and Theodor Nöldecke of Strasbourg.

The work in front of the defense team was daunting. There were three hundred citations from various rabbinic books quoted by Rohling that supposedly incriminated Jews, and had to be checked. Then, there were various old Christian texts that allegedly spoke about ritual murder. And at the core of the libel suit was Bloch's accusation of perjury; that required careful analysis of arguments that had been raised by Rohling in sworn testimonies. More than one hundred questions were submitted in the pretrial discovery phase. Kopp soon enlisted the help of other experts and translators; slowly, a picture of deception on a massive scale unfolded in front of their eyes.

It was eventually shown that Rohling's citations from the Talmud and the rabbinic texts did not match the originals. In many cases, it was not even a matter of questionable translation; some passages could simply not be found at all. In one case, an incriminating book written by an allegedly bloodthirsty rabbi from Galicia presented a mystery. In the recent past, Rohling had opined, with the aura of an expert who knew his sources, "Even in recent times rabbis dared to publish texts encouraging and defending ritual murder, either publishing new books or new editions of previously secret old [rabbinical] writings." As he claimed that one such book had been written just twenty years before and published in many places, its impact on the case was potentially important. Rohling himself wrote about the book's author, "Although the numbers of fanatics, who commit ritual murder beyond Hungary [and] Galicia … are not large among the observant [Jews], he is fighting for spilling blood in other countries…." But Kopp and his investigators could not find a single copy of this book in any bookstore in Vienna. Then, the Imperial and Royal Ministry of Internal Affairs, which tracked all publications issued in the empire, could not find it either. An international hunt ensued through major European libraries, including the collections of Oxford and Cambridge universities, to no avail. The incriminating book had simply never existed.[20]

Old non-Jewish texts going back many centuries were also examined. This was an important way of checking Rohling's veracity, since he frequently claimed that the writings of important figures in the Catholic Church had provided eyewitness accounts of ritual murder committed by Jews. Here the task of proving that Rohling was deceitful seemed risky at first, more so than with Hebraic writings. As a Catholic priest and a professor of theology, he was fluent in Latin and an expert in the Church's history. When Rohling confidently wrote, "Accusations of Jews committing ritual murder have been known through all centuries," he cited in detail the work of a bishop of Lyon who had lived centuries before the first anti-Jewish denunciations began to surface in Europe. Few dared to consider that such a learned man could be wrong regarding the history of his church. And yet when the defense team looked at Latin texts, written by Bishop Agobard of Lyon who was well known for his hostility toward Jews, another surprise awaited them. Contrary to earlier statements by Rohling, not even one reference to the spilling of Christian blood by Jews was found, not even in texts that were not exactly friendly to the Israelites. Hence another piece of "unshakable" evidence that had been used for years by Rohling turned out to be false. This story was to repeat itself several times when Kopp's team examined other non-Jewish sources referenced by the cleric.[21]

When everything had been checked and rechecked, Bloch's team sent a massive amount of translated text to the experts. More than one hundred questions and answers were prepared as the trial date neared. But surprisingly, Rohling asked not a single question of the experts; it seemed that either he was supremely confident or something else was in the offing. In late October of 1885, all the newspapers in Austro-Hungary dryly noted that the proceedings of Rohling versus Bloch were to commence on November 18 and were expected to last approximately two weeks. It seemed that, at least in the opinion of most journalists, this was a trial to watch.

Then, unexpectedly, stories began to surface that Rohling was "worried" about the case's impact on the public; it was said that he feared the possibility of unrest if emotions ran too high among the Viennese. Supposedly out of this concern someone, on behalf of the suddenly troubled professor, floated the idea of an out-of-court agreement to prevent "public disorder." When this overture to

Bloch went unanswered, Rohling applied to the Ministry of Education, requesting a one-year sabbatical to complete some unspecified studies. But shortly before the trial was to begin, he was told his request could be granted only after the pending case was resolved.

Then, like a bombshell, news came just days before the scheduled examination of evidence. In Galicia, a newspaper announced it under the headline: "Professor Rohling's Last Chicanery." The plaintiff, August Rohling, had abruptly withdrawn his suit against Joseph Bloch from the Viennese court.[22]

Rohling's Flight. A caricature of disgraced August Rohling running away from "the light" of evidence brought by Joseph S. Bloch. It appeared in the Viennese satirical magazine (*Kikeriki*) soon after Rohling withdrew his suit against Bloch.

Within days of this retreat, another newspaper headline in bold letters read, "The butt of the jokes," referring by name to the now-infamous professor from Prague. In no uncertain terms, he was finally being labeled as a fake. Now, it became clear from the pretrial investigation that Rohling lacked even rudimentary knowledge of Hebrew or Aramaic. Suddenly it was plain for all to see that, through arrogance and blind hate, he had spread virulent lies for years, lies based on nothing more than discredited or nonexistent texts.

Rohling's fall from grace was swift. The court ordered him to pay all the costs of the pretrial discovery, and with his reputation irrevocably tarnished, he would no longer write open letters taunting the legal system to use his anti-Semitic services. Then the Ministry of Education re-launched disciplinary proceedings against Rohling, examining his almost two-year absence from academic responsibilities. Yet, somehow, he managed to retain his professorship, and it would take more than ten years for his academic career to come to a final halt.

In 1897, the Vatican found one of Rohling's recent books in violation of Church doctrine and placed it in their index of forbidden books. This time, however, the event was not a cause célèbre; the book and its author were largely being ignored by the wider public. In 1899, because of his disagreement with the ecclesiastical authorities, the Charles-Ferdinand University of Prague urged Rohling to take a temporary leave of absence from the theology department. This he did, and three years later, his state of limbo became a permanent retirement. No longer with even a shred of credibility, Rohling drifted into obscurity; yet he was allowed to collect a pension for the next thirty years. Although unrepentant allies of the cleric would argue from time to time that the court had never ruled on his contested statements, Bloch's moral victory was indisputable.[23]

As to Joseph Bloch, he continued to be an outspoken crusader against anti-Semitism through other legal actions and written polemics. His approach was always to face accusers head-on rather than avoid confrontation; it was an attitude that, at times, put him at odds with his own community in Vienna. While in the legislature, Bloch was unafraid to speak with conviction about difficult subjects; he forcefully rejected the pervasive notion that the white slavery trade and prostitution itself were somehow caused or aided by Jewish vices. When the debate in parliament veered toward impugning Jewish morality, Bloch unrelentingly confronted his interlocutors who showed anti-Semitic bias. After listing known houses of ill repute found in almost every province of the country, he informed the deputy who was making the charges that most, if not all of them were controlled by the non-Jewish owners. Was the harm being done to the Aryan trade, he asked mockingly, "because you are so indignant that a Jew encroached upon it...?"[24]

Block remained in parliament until 1895. When the next year he failed in his bid for reelection, Bloch devoted himself entirely to journalism. He owned a weekly newspaper, published in Vienna for the past ten years, and he soon renamed it *Dr. Bloch's Österreichische Wochenschrift.* It would continue to provide a platform for his editorial opinions. Over the years,

Joseph Samuel Bloch (1850–1923). A member of the national parliament (*Reichsrat*), representing a district in the eastern part of Galicia between 1883 and 1895. He was credited with a vigorous public stand against anti-Semitism in Austro-Hungary.
(Photograph from 1922.)

he would make a few trips to the United States, where his time was divided between visits with his family there and public engagements. Shortly before he died in 1923, Bloch published his memoirs, which contained personal recollections of the life journey that had taken him from the *shetl* in Galicia, to the halls of parliament, and to an unwavering search for truth and a fight against bias—in the courts of justice and the eyes of his fellow citizens.

———— ❧ ————

Chapter 9

AFTER GALICIA:

HOPES AND SETBACKS

$\mathcal{M}$Y GRANDPARENTS, JOACHIM AND REGINA Hübner, had two children. The boys were born on the rural estate of Bryńce Cerkiewne, about one hour by train from Lwów. Zygmunt came first, in 1906, and Alfred followed five years later. My father, the younger of the two, would not retain any particular memories of the conflict that soon swept through Europe. Nevertheless, the Great War (as World War I was then called) clearly interrupted the boys' childhood. Beginning in August 1914, when the advancing Tsar's army was moving from town to town in Galicia and seemed unstoppable, uncertainty became a fact of life for the Hübner family and countless others in the region. In fact, Joachim and Regina did not have to wait long to experience firsthand the consequences of the conflict; for them and their children, the war came perilously close. In the opening weeks of the fighting, the neighboring town of Bóbrka suffered an unrelenting attack by Russian artillery stationed on the hills above, soon leveling the houses around the market square. Local archives, which held the register books with both Hübner boys' birth certificates, went up in flames.[1]

Many Galicians, fearing reprisals and possible deportations by the advancing Russians, escaped with the retreating Austro-Hungarian troops. For Jews in particular, the prospect of ending up under Russian military rule was unsettling; stories about recurring pogroms and residence restrictions under the tsars were well known in neighboring Galicia. At first, many war evacuees from the eastern part of the region ended up in Kraków, which seemed beyond the reach of the enemy in the fall of 1914. Then, when that city became vulnerable to attack, tens of thousands of Galicians would seek refuge in Vienna and beyond.

The Hübners and their family were not among these, however. Instead, they decided to weather the storm at home. Joachim and Regina witnessed warily the Russian takeover of the eastern part of Galicia. The enemy's frontline troops also passed through tiny Bryńce Cerkiewne, where the couple had lived since their marriage nine years earlier. The railroad tracks and small train station nearby—signs of convenience in times of peace—could easily become a liability in time of war. Whichever side controlled the railroad had the advantage in getting troops and supplies on the move. After the defeat of Austro-Hungarian forces on a nearby battlefield, the undefended Lwów was captured by the Tsar's army on September 3, 1914. That the Jews were viewed with suspicion by the Russian military administration was not a surprise; under the Russian occupation, they were soon forbidden to travel or even to send letters written with Hebrew characters, and were often accused of subversive actions.

In June of 1915, a counteroffensive of the Central Powers, as Austro-Hungary, Germany and their allies were called, succeeded in retaking Lwów, and then recaptured most of the territory lost one year before. This time, however, it was Rohatyn that suffered serious destruction, when German units fought a relentless battle with retreating Russians. The price for regaining its control was wreckage done to nearly four hundred houses, just one more punishing episode among so many in the path of the battling adversaries.[2] But the military successes of the Central Powers that year were far from signaling peace; the war would continue in the eastern part of Galicia, with other Russian offensives to follow.

My grandparents Joachim and Regina Hübner must have had their children's future in mind when they moved the family to Lwów during the war. Perhaps the big city offered some promise of safety. With each passing year of that protracted conflict, another capture of Lwów by the enemy seemed less likely; but there

Chodorów. World War I picture from 1916. *(Courtesy of the Austrian National Library, Vienna.)*

Rohatyn. World War I picture from 1916. *(Courtesy of the Austrian National Library, Vienna.)*

could have been other considerations as well. Their older son, Zygmunt, was already of school age and Alfred was not too far behind. It was clear that Joachim and Regina wanted more for their boys than a basic education, and even that was not possible in the war-ravaged countryside. The move opened at least some opportunities for the boys, since the schools of the city were functioning off and on, as best they could.

The Hübners were not the first in their family to gravitate toward the vibrant city of Lwów, which was sometimes called the "Vienna of the East" because of its urbane character. On Regina's side, an aunt, with her husband, Rabbi Meschulem Salat, already resided there. Early during the war, the rabbi was interned by the Russian military commander of the city to assure cooperation from the restless Jewish community, upset by a string of new restrictions. Doubtless Meschulem Salat and his family breathed a big sigh of relief when was he was able to return home; in those perilous times so many were less fortunate, being deported to Russia and not heard from sometimes for months, if not years. The rabbi would later be remembered for his efforts on behalf of Lwów's Jewish community, acting as a member of the Jewish Relief Committee during the harsh Russian occupation of 1914–1915.[3]

Joachim also had family in Lwów; Erna Erbsen, his youngest sister, had lived there for a number of years. It must have been more by design than by chance that, when the Hübners went looking for suitable accommodations in Lwów, they found an apartment just a few houses up from the Erbsens on a pleasant stretch of Kochanowski Street.

30

LWÓW HAD A COMPLICATED history but a lot of charm; it was a place where the past had always blended easily with the present. By the time my grandparents and their boys moved there, its old defensive walls were long gone—they had been demolished almost a century before to create space for the city to expand. But Lwów was a changed city not only in a physical sense; its cultural character had moved with the times as well. Since 1867, the town had been transformed from Habsburg Lemberg into Polish Lwów, with monuments, public buildings, and street names reflecting Polish heritage.[4] The sound of the German language, along with German theater in the city center and German newspapers, were part of the town's distant history, although traces of urban development dating back to *Vormärz* (literally, pre-March, meaning before the March 1848 revolution) were still visible. Even in more recent times, when speaking fondly about the Austrian past had not been fashionable anymore, former city architects from that bygone era deserved some well-earned praise. Because of their work, ladies no longer protested to town officials about uneven streets. The improvements made by Lemberg's urban planners, such as the straightening of major avenues or a small river redirected underground, continued to benefit all its citizens even one hundred years later.

In eastern Galicia, however, it was always a complex matter to claim any place for a single ethnic group. Just such a situation had existed between Polish and Ukrainian students in the University of Lwów, in the years before World War I. One side viewed Polish as the language of the land, only grudgingly agreeing that a very few academic departments could allow teaching in Ukrainian. The other side considered these steps inadequate, demanding greater cultural equality for Ukrainians and protesting against Polish dominance in schools and the civil administration of Galicia. Not infrequently, verbal disputes turned into scuffles on the campus. Sadly, nationalistic passions and refusals to compromise led to even more violent incidents. In the decade before the breakout of the Great War, the assassination of the Polish governor of Galicia by a Ukrainian nationalist, and the fatal shooting of a Ukrainian student under suspicious circumstances on the restless campus, were only a prelude to the troubles ahead.[5]

Yet despite all this, Lwów in the decade before the war had been considered one of the most attractive places in Galicia to live. Its Grand Theatre, built in Viennese neo-Renaissance style, offered plays, opera, and operettas; just next to it in an older neoclassical building, the philharmonic orchestra of Lwów presented concerts. The city had its share of old churches, museums, and large ethnographic and industrial exhibits, which were frequently visited by dignitaries and throngs of curious spectators. In times of peace, the city offered not only the

Lwów. Lemberg.

Teatr. — Theatergebäude.

Lwów. The Grand Theater. *(Postcard from the early twentieth century.)*

best selection of schools, but also all sorts of entertainment and a rich cultural life for people of all ages. Lwów at the beginning of the twentieth century was the focus of steady acculturation for countless Jewish professionals, artists, and writers; by then, the bitter struggles within the Jewish community between tradition and modernity had largely been relegated to the past.

ᴥ

BY THE BEGINNING OF 1918, an uneasy cessation of hostilities with Russia, which was then consumed by its own internal power struggle, finally took hold. Certainly, the war was not over—hostilities continued on other fronts—but the prospect of yet another military conquest in Galicia was greatly diminished. Many familiar places not too far from Joachim and Regina's prewar home in Bryńce Cerkiewne showed the unmistakable scars of war. Rohatyn, Chodorów, and Stanisławów greeted visitors with many buildings in ruins. Outside the towns, there were also reminders of recent events; many fields had been dissected by labyrinths of trenches, and were littered with abandoned military hardware rather than being ready for spring plowing. Food shortages became a daily concern to all.[6]

In October, Austro-Hungary accepted provisions of the Fourteen Points, President Wilson's plan for cessation of hostilities between the Central Powers and the Allies. When the next day, the newspapers in Lwów printed on the front pages complete text of what was headlined as "Wilson's Points," and the Viennese journal carried a full-page picture of the U.S. President, it was clear that the end of the war was quite close. Among conditions for peace, one of the demands was the call for self-determination of the people within the multiethnic Habsburg Empire; another spoke about an independent state, "which should include the territories inhabited by indisputably Polish populations." A few days after diplomatic exchanges between Vienna and Washington through Swedish intermediaries, Emperor Charles I and his government publicly affirmed that future Austria would be a federal state. Its non-German-speaking nationalities were to chart their own destiny, with details left to their national councils to decide. However, as if not to leave any doubts about the Austrian agreement to the American conditions, the imperial manifesto "To My Faithful People of Austria" confirmed that historically Polish territories of Galicia were free to join future independent Poland.[7] By October 29, Austro-Hungarian troops received instructions from Vienna to cease all military actions, regardless of their location.

In the late fall of 1918, several countries in Europe were more concept than reality; others were only days old with their borders in flux. In Galicia, this was an extraordinary time when every day brought headlines of historical proportions. The excitement about the imminent end of the war mixed with uncertainty; for months, the region had been rocked already by the gossips repeated on the streets, newspaper speculations, and demonstrations across towns, all revolving about the question of who would be able to assert rights to its eastern part. In this contested land, what was "indisputably Polish" territory to some was vehemently objected to by their Ukrainian neighbors, who voiced their own claims to the same areas.[8]

In the waning days of the Habsburg Empire, Nathan Löwenstein, parliamentary deputy from Galicia who happened to be Jewish, was received by Emperor Charles I in Vienna. While speaking about the sentiments of his brethren, he stressed that Galician Jews identified themselves with Polish aspirations. Doubtless the situation was complex back at home—Ukrainian politicians promptly counterclaimed that they also had Jewish support for their cause.[9] All this was only a prelude to painful fractures ahead. Meantime, the old regime that had guaranteed some semblance of balance in multiethnic Galicia was vanishing fast, and the new order was uncertain. In the power vacuum left in the midst of disintegration of Austro-Hungary, the future of Galicia and of its eastern part, in particular, was at stake.

Sadly, the long-awaited end of the war did not bring the relief that had been hoped for. The lingering hopes for a peaceful transition of power were dashed on November 1, 1918; at four o'clock in the morning, Ukrainian

Going their separate ways. The woman's (Galicia's) parting words: "You think that I cannot live without you!" The man (Austria) snaps back: "Knowing how much you've cost me, I am entitled to this view." Published in the satirical journal (*Die Muskete*) in October 1918. *(Courtesy of the Austrian National Library, Vienna.)*

military battalions just released from the Austro-Hungarian army took key strategic positions in Lwów. Within hours, battles for the control of the city erupted between armed Poles and Ukrainian forces.[10] There was painful irony in this chapter of history; Lwów, which had largely escaped brutal bombardments during the Great War, was about to become scarred by erupting street combat. The imposing, elegant Galician parliament building was now ransacked and damaged by the fire; the main post office, the train station, and many city buildings would quickly bear the scars of bullets that had ricocheted from their walls. Both sides knew that whomever controlled Lwów, or L'viv as Ukrainians called it, would be able to claim the eastern region of former Galicia as part of newly founded Poland or the Western Ukrainian Republic.

Living in the midst of this unfinished conflict, Jews were not immune from the violence. Often lacking any legal protection, they were accused of either staying neutral or not supporting one side or the other in the internal conflict. In the aftermath of the Polish takeover of Lwów on November 22, even the freshly dug graves of victims of street battles over the past weeks, which were visible in many public squares, could not stop a new cycle of violence. Over the next few days, despicable attacks on Jewish neighborhoods were carried out by Poles, ultimately claiming hundreds of innocent lives. Unconfirmed reports, about shots supposedly fired from buildings housing Jewish establishments, whipped up the crowds that went on rampages through the Jewish district. Many businesses were burned and one of the Orthodox synagogues was vandalized. The Progressive (Reform) Synagogue, which had already become the place of worship in the Polish language, barely escaped destruction; during the night of the pogrom, an arsonist tried to burn it down. The next day, its religious sanctuary was violated by a rude military search, and false rumors quickly spread about a cache of arms allegedly found on its premises. That could only further fuel anti-Semitic sentiments, and did, even years after the hostilities had ended.[11]

Lwów. Orthodox synagogue vandalized in the attacks in November 1918.

As with the adversities of prior years, Lwów and its resilient Jewish community recovered more quickly than could have been anticipated. Perhaps a new threat to the entire region that appeared on the horizon helped heal the trauma of the recent past. This time, the Polish-Soviet War that had simmered since 1919 came perilously close to Lwów. When Soviets attacked north and east of the city, Lwów came under siege; other Soviet armies marched deep into newly formed Poland, threatening its capital and the very survival of the country. In July–August 1920 Lwów was full of various military units, which were temporarily quartered in schools and other public buildings. The situation was dire; trenches were dug at the city outskirts and twenty thousand volunteers, including many older students and teachers in Zygmunt's school, responded to the appeal to defend Lwów against approaching Soviet cavalry units.

In August of 1920, a newspaper article stated, "Today Lwów resembles a military camp; everywhere one sees mainly uniforms." Perhaps with a bit of humor, the correspondent from the beleaguered city added, "It looks as if the tailors serving civilians will soon have to announce bankruptcy."[12] Some battles took place no more than twenty miles away. Luckily, a military takeover never materialized, and Lwów's residents breathed a big sigh of relief when a ceasefire was announced in the fall of 1920. The bloody conflict officially ended with a peace treaty signed in March of 1921. Finally, the eastern border of Poland was accepted, by both her recent adversary and the international community.

❧

BY THE BEGINNING OF THE 1920s, Zygmunt Hübner, the older of Joachim and Regina's two boys, was attending Lwów's classical *gymnasium*. With the period of instability fading away, the Hübners' life had begun to return to normal. Now in their mid-forties, Joachim and Regina must have felt happy to have come out of the Great War, and all the upheavals that followed, unscathed. There was a sense of a cautious optimism that future conflicts would be resolved by the League of Nations rather than on the battlefield; another global war was simply unthinkable, given the state of exhaustion throughout the nations of Europe.

Few personal details have been preserved about Joachim and Regina, but their union seems to have been a modern one. Joachim handled the finances of the estate in Bryńce Cerkiewne. He had started there as the land administrator, then continued as a leaseholder and, by the 1930s, would become the owner of the property. The proceeds from this enterprise provided steady income for the family. At the same time, Regina maintained some degree of financial independence. Records indicate that she owned real estate in Lwów; it was most likely bought after the passing of her well-off grandfather, Sender Dub.

Joachim Hübner (1881–1947). The picture was taken in May 1920 in Lwów.

Zygmunt's experiences in school must have been good; my father, Alfred, followed in his older brother's footsteps. Although the younger boy started his high school education in a different institution, after a few years he would transfer to the same *gymnasium*. That school placed great emphasis on learning German, along with a hefty dose of the classics. Even decades later, my father would be able to recite some of the opening paragraphs of the *Iliad* in Homeric Greek. In jest, he would compete with one of his old friends about who could remember more of the epic.

That sense of humor must have been with Alfred from a very young age; it seems the 1920s were not spent on serious studies alone. Years later, my father would recall with great relish a few school pranks with which he had been involved. Alfred and his classmates had found it hard to control their glee while they watched a teacher try in vain to lift a large registration book that the boys had glued to his desk. Then there was an old biology professor, as the story was told, who kept cleaning his eyeglasses in disbelief when a human skeleton in a glass case suddenly started to wave its hand at the puzzled teacher.

My father also mentioned some snippets about long hot days spent in the country. Generally, the family stayed in Lwów for most of the school year, but summer holidays were spent at the Bryńce Cerkiewne estate. I recall my father mentioning large family gatherings around a long table, with all the fresh food one could imagine. The grownups, he said, would talk about their children, schools, and marriages. Bronia (Bronisława), Joachim's older sister, often mentioned the progress made by one of her sons who was blind and attended a special vocational school in Lwów. On one occasion, she shared an anecdote about her other son, a good athlete who, swimming with his class across the Prut river, extracted from his teacher—struggling to get to the other side—a promise of good grades in exchange for a bit of help. A few years later, Bronia would also talk about her daughter Zofia (Sonia) who was about to be married to a promising lawyer.

If Regina's sister, Taube, was visiting with her husband, the conversation would inevitably turn to whether practicing law was still a good profession. Given the choices to be made by Hübner boys, Zygmunt and Alfred, this was a topic to listen to. Taube's husband, Ferdynand Katz, was an established attorney in Rohatyn; in time his older son would follow in the father's footsteps.[13] The older Katz was also involved in local affairs beyond the practice of law. Regina's brother-in-law became a member of the city council, sharing this responsibility with the next generation from well-known families from Rohatyn: David Horn, Samuel Goldschlag, and Julian Weidman, to mention just a few.[14] As would be expected in a small town, a few of the council members' aunts, uncles, and cousins were related to Regina's family. Doubtless Regina, especially, eagerly awaited any bit of news. Some gossip about what was going on in Rohatyn must have surely spiced those summer conversations.

The Hübners spoke Polish at home, but everyone also understood some Ukrainian. Their "second" language was German. It is safe to assume that the parents understood Yiddish, but Zygmunt and Alfred were less likely to. I do not recall my father ever dropping any of the Yiddish phrases that delight us today. The family, like a number of educated Jews of the interwar period, no longer faced the dilemma of which language or culture to adopt; their choice was clear, and deeply rooted in Polish.

Joachim Hübner was apparently stern with his younger son. It was Zygmunt, and not Alfred, who was the pride of their father. Yet their mother, Regina, and several aunts who often joined them, adored "Fredek," as the younger boy was affectionately called. My father preserved a few faint memories of joyful chases around the table and through the large house after young Ukrainian maids; Alfred also recalled listening to their songs in the evening and picking up various Ukrainian phrases.

The estate housed a distillery that Joachim had leased from the late Countess Fredro during his early years in Bryńce Cerkiewne. After the countess died, the property passed to the Sheptytsky (Szeptycki) family, but the lease was regularly renewed until Joachim purchased part of the estate. The small distillery provided alcohol to manufacturers of refined spirits in Lwów. As recalled decades later by Joachim's older sister, her brother was known to look the other way when, before every Christmas and New Year's celebration, his Ukrainian employees would "secretly" tap into the pipes carrying the alcohol to siphon free supplies for their own home celebrations. This seemed to be a well-kept secret; predictably, Joachim vehemently denied that such practices had ever existed under his watch, while the workers were claiming that they had outsmarted their boss.

✄

ZYGMUNT ENROLLED IN THE University of Lwów in 1925. Aside from Regina's brother-in-law, he was the first in the family to pursue the legal profession. This was quite a leap, in the span of few generations, from an ancestor who was a merchant on his father's side, and a cattle trader on his mother's side. The University of Lwów's Faculty of Law was considered the best in the country. Because of the political and cultural autonomy that the former Galicia had enjoyed under Austrian rule, Lwów, its university and open atmosphere, was home to some of the great minds of jurisprudence. Now, Zygmunt had the opportunity to hear lectures about civil law given by Roman Longchamps de Bérier, international law by Ludwik Ehrlich, and law enforcement by highly respected legal scholar Maurycy Allerhand, to

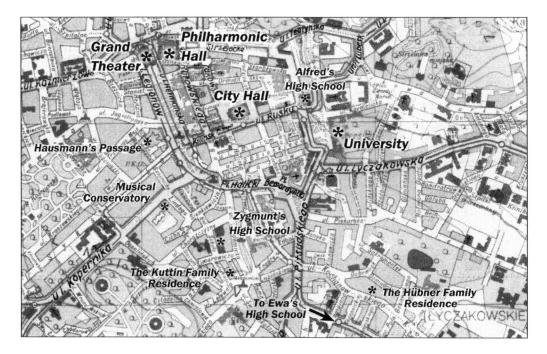

Map showing the center of Lwów. *(Section of a map from 1939.)*

mention just a few of his professors. Yet despite the esteemed faculty, Zygmunt turned out to be only an average student. During the annual examinations he received passing grades, mixed with better ones that must surely have pleased his father.[15]

In addition, there were some problems—difficult to reconstruct today—during Zygmunt's last year of university, which led to a temporary suspension followed by a transfer to another school. Yet there seems to have been no doubt in the family that he would eventually graduate and open a law practice in Lwów. Around the time of his long-awaited graduation, Zygmunt crossed paths with a young, vivacious woman, Ewa Kuttin. She was a native of Lwów; her father, Jakób Zellel Kuttin, was an engineer and a partner in Volta, a company dealing with electromechanical equipment, which had been in existence since 1908.[16]

Jakób had offices in the town's center, in a trendy shopping arcade called Hausmann's Passage. The offices were near many law firms, as well as stores that were frequented by the shopping public. For Ewa, it must have been fun to stop by her father's company occasionally, not a big deal since the Kuttins lived only a short walk away. But it is safe to assume that her main purpose would not necessarily have been to hear stories about her father's new business projects. Such a visit would have taken advantage of a wonderful opportunity for window-shopping that no young and trendy woman could easily pass up. The shops of many tailors and furriers in Hausmann's Passage displayed the newest fashions. There was also a book-renting establishment, a chance to grab the newest novel; and a famous atelier, Rembrandt, always displayed interesting photographs.

Jakób Zellel Kuttin's two daughters had musical talents that were nurtured by the family. Their interest was enhanced when the older daughter, Erna (Ernestyna), married an acclaimed classical violinist. Izydor Marek Bauer (commonly referred to as Dr. Marek Bauer) was a star in the city's artistic scene, and often gave concerts in Lwów, Vienna, and other places. As a soloist and as a member of a string quartet, Dr. Bauer also recorded for radio audiences. He became a professor of music who would teach in Lwów's Music Conservatory and other renowned institutions. It would not be long before even harsh critiques would mention Erna's husband as one among the most accomplished musicians in Lwów.[17]

Ewa, the younger of the two Kuttin daughters, attended a private all-girls high school (*gymnasium*); it was outside the immediate city center but easily reachable by tram. That institution was something of an anomaly in Lwów's cash-strapped educational scene after World War I. It had a sizeable endowment, and its modern, well-equipped building, with adjoining garden, could easily have been the envy of other schools. The *gymnasium* curriculum offered a choice between classical education and science-oriented studies. It boasted a musical ensemble, which included a large group of stringed instruments. Given her

Ewa Kuttin (1909–1943?).
The picture was taken in January 1930, most likely in Lwów.

future career, one can easily imagine today that Ewa was often seen playing among that group of students.

After graduating from the *gymnasium* in 1927, Ewa continued her musical training at the Music Conservatory in Lwów. Although she had trained as a cellist, she also played the violin quite well, and was described as having perfect pitch. It is safe to assume that the influence of her brother-in-law was felt, with good advice and perhaps some instruction. Not surprisingly, Ewa's talents were not lost on the musical world of Lwów, and the young woman was soon playing in the Philharmonic Orchestra.

When Zygmunt and Ewa started to talk about marriage, nobody could deny that they were a handsome couple. He was a tall man, standing straight by her side in photographs, with a rather reserved look on his face. But Ewa almost always radiated a big smile; picture after picture displayed her sunny disposition. Even a blurred snapshot that has survived, taken somewhere on the streets of Lwów, does not obscure her wonderful grin.

Zygmunt and Ewa were married in the Progressive (Reform) Synagogue of Lwów in September of 1931; the ceremony was presided over by Rabbi Jecheskel Lewin. This was an appropriate setting for the marriage vows taken by this couple, an aspiring lawyer and a classically trained musician, who wanted to share their joyous occasion with the Hübner and the Kuttin clans, as well as their friends. Perhaps lost in their moment of excitement, and in the natural focus of the young couple on their future, was the symbolic meaning of the building where they stood.

Ewa (née Kuttin) and Zygmunt Hübner (1906–1943) at a black-tie gala. They married in September 1931 in Lwów.

From a historical standpoint, that progressive temple was a response to the past efforts of impatient Jewish professionals, who had wanted to immerse themselves in the wider world without breaking links with their spiritual traditions. The place had also been the catalyst for many changes in Lwów's Jewish community, as it embraced a modernizing society. Zygmunt and Ewa might not have given it much thought, but they were some of the best evidence that the mission of past Jewish intellectual rebels, including the lawyers, doctors, merchants, and civil servants of Lwów, had finally succeeded. And there was another subtle and symbolic sign of change; Dr. Lewin, who offered the blessings, was a young Reform rabbi with a doctorate in philosophy from a secular university. The grandson of an Orthodox rabbi of Lwów (in his time, the grandfather had been viewed as "a pillar of Talmudic knowledge") the young man caused a stir among Orthodox Jews when he had taken the position in the Progressive (Reform) synagogue a few years before. He, too, personally reflected the long road traveled by many secular and religious Jews.[18]

My father followed in the footsteps of his older brother, receiving a law degree from the University of Lwów in 1934. However, Alfred chose quite a different career path. Never interested in traditional law practice, he went into corporate and trade law. Over the next few years, there were recurring complaints by Joachim Hübner about his younger son who, in his eyes, lacked Zygmunt's maturity. Clearly, the father-and-son relationship was strained. Even decades later, my father recalled, Regina would often come to the defense of her "baby" and smooth out disagreements.

Zygmunt and Ewa settled, immediately after their marriage, into an apartment down the street from the older Hübners. Alfred, however, was moving away, perhaps to free himself from family criticism. For a time, my father held a job in a company that was extracting oil and gas from shallow deposits in the former eastern Galicia. Then, he gladly accepted a post at the company offices in the historic city of Kraków. It was there that he met a group of artists, painters, and writers, all poor in financial resources but rich in ideas. Later in life, Alfred would recall short trips with this bohemian crowd to the nearby mountains. Those excursions were not for the purpose of walking trails and admiring vistas. Instead, they were apparently spent by the chain-smoking participants debating throughout the night over a few shared drinks. What was discussed is less clear, there were probably some passionate discussions of new literary trends and photography as an artistic medium, but above all, the young crowd vowed to be different from their parents. Perhaps there was a grain of truth in Joachim's criticism that his younger son was interested in everything but having a steady job and settling down to marriage.

In the mid-1930s, Alfred moved to Vienna for a couple of years to receive advanced legal education. Those were innocent times that left him with fond memories; when talking years later about that period, my father spoke more about the charming atmosphere of the Viennese cafés and the operettas that provided entertainment, than he did about the law courses he had taken. It was there that he became especially drawn to Stefan Zweig's novels and biographies; Zweig became my father's favorite Austrian writer. I remember him passionately describing one book, which, he said, contained a superb portrait of Napoleon.

Soon, however, happy times became a scarce commodity in Europe. There was increasing unrest and Nazi agitation for a union (*Anschluß*) of Austria with Hitler's Third Reich, and Alfred's stay in Vienna had to be cut short. For a Jew, it was better to be back home.[19]

My father returned only briefly to Lwów, where mixed news awaited him. His parents had moved out from the city center, to a new apartment in a building they owned. That part of Stryjska Street was highly desirable. Elegant buildings lined one side, and a large park was across the street; that gave a pleasant feeling of being away from the bustle of the city. Yet, it was not an entirely sedate area. Each year toward the end of summer, the "Eastern Fair" opened its doors nearby, with pavilion after pavilion mounting displays of new gadgets and inventions that the public inspected with a great deal of curiosity.

In the fall of 1937, there was also talk about a tense atmosphere at the university. Unrest provoked by the nationalist youth organization disturbed classes, caused physical violence, and led to temporary closures of the campus. In contrast to his colleagues at many other schools of higher learning in Poland, the

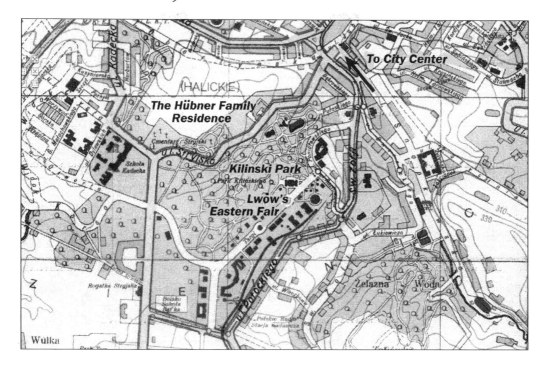

Map showing the Halicki district (south of the city center) of Lwów. *(Section of a map from 1939.)*

Lwów. Kiliński Park across from Stryjska Street, where Joachim and Regina Hübner resided
in the latter part of the 1930s. *(View from the early twentieth century.)*

university rector in Lwów refused to yield to radicals' demands. "Excesses, terror, and abuse" he warned, "cast a long shadow on university life, contributing to moral and academic decay." In the lecture halls, separate seating areas—dubbed by the press "ghetto benches"—were being imposed on Jewish students by the anti-Semitic segregationist youth group. Some undergraduates ignored these medieval-like rules and mixed in solidarity with their Jewish friends, while others shamelessly perpetuated hate or remained indifferent. When the unrest spilled outside the university—whose rector submitted his resignation in protest—the Hübner men must have been happy that their student years were behind them.[20]

But this was only the beginning of the troubles for Jews. A few radical newspapers published articles that fueled stereotypes of purported Jewish dominance in Polish trade; calls for economic boycotts were repeated by the extremists. The semiofficial newspaper in Lwów barely reported on the situation, but a wave of ugly anti-Semitism was sweeping through Poland. Sadly, this was nothing new; similar voices had been heard many times before. But the majority of Jewish professionals in Lwów and elsewhere did not express their indignation in a public manner. They felt that the agitation would simply pass.[21]

Alfred Hübner (1911–1979). The picture was dedicated to Ewa Hübner. The inscription reads: "To dear sister-in-law. Fredek." It is dated January 31, 1937.

There were also personal events to talk about. The marriage of Alfred's brother was not as good as had been hoped for. As always, it was impossible to tell objectively who was right and who was wrong. Some would later say that Zygmunt was careless with money; there were rumors that he had gambled away part of Ewa's investments in real estate. Those who sided with the husband spoke vaguely about Ewa's friendships in Lwów's artistic scene, which might have gone too far. For a time, there was talk about separation or even divorce, but eventually the couple reconciled. Then, toward the end of 1938, a renewed sense of optimism prevailed; Ewa was pregnant. When Stefan was born on May 12, 1939, the happy family event was colored by anxious talk about what might happen to the world in the coming months. That very day, however, as if not to spoil the joy in the Hübner family, one of the popular newspapers in town sounded hopeful. A large headline across its front page read, "The Chances for Peace Are Up!"

According to the paper, Hitler was gravely ill and in any case, if war was to erupt, Poland as an ally of England and France could count on the military help of others, including Soviet Russia and Romania. The reason for such optimism was the unexpected visit to Poland of an obscure commissar from Soviet Russia and a shakeup in the Foreign Ministry in Moscow. A naïve reporter took this as a sign that any future German-Soviet alliance had been unraveled. The paper's back pages carried news that a ship carrying Jewish refugees had been turned away from the waters of Palestine. Telegrams from London announced that the immigration of Jews to Palestine would soon be curtailed, though "attractive" British Guyana in South America was being designated a new "Promised Land" for Jews hastily leaving Europe. As had happened many times before, predictions on the eve of a global conflict turned out to be utterly false.[22]

Chapter 10

THE ABYSS OF DESPAIR

*T*HE FIRST DAYS OF SEPTEMBER 1939 were marked in Lwów by the recurring sound of air-raid sirens. These announced incoming German planes and, at first, they were mostly reconnaissance flights. On the ground, there were high hopes that the German attack on Poland, which had begun on September 1, would be contained; when England and France declared war on Germany three days later, small but jubilant demonstrations broke out in town. Despite the circumstances, the Eastern Fair opened across from Joachim and Regina's apartment as usual. Looking back now, it's hard to tell if that was an act of defiance on the part of its organizers, or some form of the surrealism that must have passed for everyday life in that time. In any case, there were fewer entrants from abroad than usual. Particularly notable among the missing pavilions was the customary German exhibit.

Lwów's dailies headlined the alarming news of Europe on the verge of global war; they also provided advice on securing discounted train tickets to the exhibition. Theatrical shows continued their runs each evening—special plays and operas were always staged during the fair. There was only one obvious difference: the performances would start one hour earlier than scheduled, so theatergoers could return home before nightfall. This is a sure sign that blackout regulations were already in place. By September 6, trouble had become more palpable in Lwów; in a popular Jewish daily, articles that life should be carried on as normally

230 Galician Portraits

as possible did not mesh well with short banners across the same pages: "Remain Calm in Air Shelters" and "Hasten Assistance for the Refugees."[1]

Vanguard units of the German army reached the vicinity of Lwów after twelve days' run through Poland. The city was poorly prepared for its own defense; Polish military strategists had doubted that the Nazis would get to the eastern part of the country so swiftly. And as though the breakout of war with Germany was not enough bad news, the Red Army also began a march into Poland on September 17, grabbing her eastern territory. The pretext for this, as officially stated, was the need to protect Ukrainian and Belorussian populations in the face of disintegrating Polish rule. In reality, however, another partition of Poland was in full swing. This time it was Soviet troops—rather than the imperial army of Russia—that were performing the task. Under a treaty that had been secretly signed by their foreign ministers, Molotov and Ribbentrop, just a few weeks before in Moscow, eastern Poland and the Baltic republics were being divided between Germany and the Soviets.

Now, enemy forces were approaching Lwów from both the west and the east. The defenders of the city were warned by Germany that a massive attack was imminent; nothing short of unconditional surrender would be acceptable to the *Wehrmacht* commander. But then the Germans decided the takeover of the city would best be left to their Russian allies. In any case, Lwów and the entire eastern portion of Galicia were there for the Soviets to keep.

When Russians entered the city on September 22, 1939, they were happily greeted by some, including Ukrainians and Jews, who thought this was a better outcome than falling into German hands. At first, the troops moved cautiously; but within days, parades of Soviet cavalry and military hardware—often pulled by tractors—were on full display. Massive propaganda efforts were launched to convince the entire populace about the benefits of Soviet paradise. Worthless Soviet rubles replaced Polish currency; stores in the city emptied quickly when stunned Russian soldiers discovered all kinds of goods for sale at bargain prices.

The alliance between the two aggressors continued after the cessation of military operations. Negotiators for both sides quickly agreed on outstanding border

Soviet army parade on the streets of Lwów (renamed *L'vov* in Russian) most likely in October or November 1939. A few visible store names are still in Polish.

issues. The Soviet foreign minister was unusually frank in his public statement: "Our relations with Germany underwent fundamental changes.... Agreeing on our [spheres of] interest within the territory of the former Polish state was a challenge to German-Russian friendship, but the difficulty was successfully overcome."

A political charade was also unfolding: exactly one month after the occupation of Lwów, "elections" were held in what was now called Western Ukraine. Then, within days, a "request" from the newly installed regime-sympathetic deputies, demanding to join the Soviet Union, completed the formalities. Lwów and the other conquered territories were officially incorporated into the USSR.[2]

Right: Soviet propaganda poster celebrating the "liberation" of the Ukrainian population by the Red Army.

Initially, Lwów swelled with refugees, particularly Jewish ones, who streamed in from the west escaping the Germans. The number of Jews in Lwów, estimated to have been just short of one hundred thousand before the war, now doubled. But this freedom of movement did not last long. The porous border between German-occupied Poland and the former eastern Galicia was soon sealed off for good. Some of the refugees had been attempting to join families and friends in the city, but most had hoped to move on to still-neutral Romania; however, that route was also shut down quickly.

The latest newcomers to Lwów were not the only people who were refugees. Russian plans for a rapid transformation of former Galicia were clear; several thousand Soviet citizens were moved to the city to completely take over administrative and educational posts. The commissars started to purge the university and other cultural institutions of "unfriendly" elements. As in the Russian conquest of Galicia during World War I, the new masters did not entirely trust the native Ukrainian population; they were considered too independent and of uncertain loyalty. Moderate Ukrainian activists were simply arrested and shipped somewhere east; the more radical forces in Western Ukraine either went underground or escaped to German-controlled territory. By the end of the year, all inhabitants of Lwów had Soviet passports, which were really just identity cards rather than documents that offered freedom of movement.[3]

It did not take long for the Hübners, the Kuttins, and many like them to feel the impact of the new regime. It was not just the sound of a different language or visible changes in street names, now written in the Cyrillic alphabet. Within a few months, small businesses, land, and factories were taken away from their owners and nationalized. As a result, Joachim's property in the countryside was no longer his; that important source of income for the family was gone. The same likely applied to Jakób Kuttin, who could no longer own his enterprise in Lwów; his other business ventures outside the city were also simply memories. If he was lucky, Jakób might have been allowed to work at his former factory in some low-level position. Both men would have been labeled bourgeois by the new regime.

Whether Ewa Hübner (née Kuttin) and her accomplished brother-in-law, Marek Bauer, continued their musical careers in the open under the Soviets is not known. However, on the orders of one zealous apparatchik (a certain O. L. Breskin appointed by Moscow), all archives of the prewar music conservatories of Lwów were methodically destroyed; because of this senseless order, Ewa's (and other musicians') academic records were irrevocably lost.

Soon, living spaces were intruded upon as well. The communist paradise did not allow ordinary people to own apartments or houses. A steady stream of Soviet apparatchiks needed the space, and families who had seen ownership of a flat as a measure of hard-won success were now squeezed into one or two of the rooms, from which they had to watch strangers moving in with them. But even less fortunate were those evicted when their particularly attractive apartments were taken over by the state. Luckily, nothing like that had happened to Joachim and Regina Hübner yet.

The most frightening prospect for residents of the city was deportation into the vast Russian hinterland. The People's Commissariat for Internal Affairs (NKVD) was a secret police force busily arresting all kinds of people, interrogating them, and sending all considered undesirable to prisons and penal colonies in Kazakhstan or Siberia. The fear was such that many in the city, including Jews, considered risking their lives by paying smugglers to help them illegally cross the border into German-occupied territories (some fifty miles to the west). Why would Jews be trying to escape there? The news blackout under Soviet occupation was virtually complete, for nobody could own a radio and the press was under strict censorship—so the sheer horror of the Nazis' upcoming "final solution" could not yet have even been imagined.

The first wave of deportations affected those who had occupied positions of influence in the previous administration, or were known for their political views. The Hübner family was not on that list. Then, arrests were made among refugees and naïve recipients of new passports who had applied for exit visas; the Hübners seemed to avoid that as well. But then the risk of being uprooted came dangerously close.

The Hübners were now living under an ominous black cloud. They were among those who had considered leaving, and their fear became even more acute after a close encounter with Soviet security forces. The details of the story are now murky, but what it is clear is that secret police showed up one day at Regina and Joachim's apartment. Certainly, no one in the family dared ask the officers if they had a search warrant, or inquire about the cause of the intrusion. Apparently, things did not go well, and one officer took his revolver from its holster. What the presumed offense was and what the family was threatened with we will never know; but my father recalled years later that his parents feared being deported. Apparently, only Regina's illness saved the family from a more ominous outcome that day. Joachim's wife was dying of breast cancer and there was no way the family could run anywhere.

Regina, whose out-of-focus picture I saw once or twice, died on June 26, 1941 in Lwów. Even the memory of seeing her face is now blurred in my mind. Thinking back to that hellish time and place, I realize that the tragedy of my grandmother's untimely passing must have brought some absurd feeling of consolation to her family. They knew that she would be spared the indignities and terrors that lay ahead. Four days before she died, news had reached Lwów that the Nazis were crossing into former Galicia. Germany had launched war against its former ally and partner in crime, the Soviet Union.

The Germans entered Lwów on June 30, 1941, and the inferno erupted.

ఌ

NO ONE FELT SAFE in Lwów in the first few days of July, yet those who were rounded up on the street or taken away during door-to-door searches were mostly Jews. The victims were herded to public squares, where they were forced to clean the streets on their knees, and were humiliated in various other ways. Shockingly, the anonymous crowds looking on—not just German soldiers and their willing proxies, the Ukrainian militiamen—stood by not in horror but sometimes with smiles on their faces. Jewish women were brutally attacked on the streets, often stripped of their clothes, and then chased by the barbarians wielding sticks. Prominent members of that community were hung from balconies in the

Jewish men and women are forced to clean a street near the Grand Theater, in Lwów.
The camera lens also caught a crowd of spectators, with some among them enjoying the spectacle.
(Collection of David Lee Preston.)

Jewish district; their bodies were allowed to dangle for days. With the approval of the Germans who now controlled Lwów, the Ukrainian militia went amok, accusing the Jews collectively of supporting the Soviet regime.

This latest cycle of violence had been unleashed by the discovery, in three city prisons, of thousands of mutilated bodies: political prisoners executed by the Soviet secret police. The intense stench of decomposition filled the air, even beyond the prison walls. Group after group of Jews picked up at random were taken there to bury the victims' bodies. Many of them were brutally beaten before being shot in retribution for this crime they had not committed.

Some of these victims were well known to the Hübners and Kuttins. Among them was Dr. Jecheskel Lewin, who had conducted the marriage ceremony for Zygmunt and Ewa. In the midst of the mayhem, Rabbi Lewin had sought help from the head of the Greek Catholic Church. Metropolitan Andrei Sheptytsky (*Андрей Шептицький*) promised to write a pastoral letter against the violence; he seemed the only one who had some (albeit waning) influence over the Ukrainian nationalists. Rabbi Lewin was offered a hiding place in the church residence, but declined. When he returned home, Ukrainian thugs were already waiting. That same evening, Dr. Lewin was repeatedly brutalized before being shot on the grounds of one of the infamous prisons; his son was there to witness his father's final moments. The city had fallen into total chaos, and Jews who had, for the moment, survived horrific attacks, wandered through the streets with their faces covered in blood and their limbs broken.[4]

As with other pogroms, historians would later debate the number of those murdered by the Ukrainian militia; some believed that most victims of those first two July days had perished at the hands of the SS killing machine. But for the thousands who died, it did not matter who rounded them up and who pulled the trigger.[5] And this was only the beginning of what awaited the Jews of Lwów. After three weeks of a relative lull, another cycle of violence began on July 25. This time, Ukrainian nationalists picked up Jews from prepared lists. Again, accusations of collaboration with the Soviets were their justification, and once more, thousands were executed in the span of a few days. The victims would have been neighbors, friends, and family members of the Hübners.

The Germans made the newly created District Galicia (*Distrikt Galizien*)—which included Lwów, renamed yet again to Lemberg—part of the Nazi-ruled General Governorate. Their crude propaganda, fed to newspapers in the territories back west, was silent about the killing spree. Instead, it was reported in bold letters that columns of Jews were on the streets, all wearing white armbands with the Star of David. Chillingly, the occupiers stated: "Now they will learn the meaning of work, which they have always avoided."[6] In a matter of months, mail and rail services to the city were restored, linking it with the occupied territories of central and southern Poland. But any sense of life returning to normal would have been deceptive.

The attractive area around Stryjska Street, the Hübners' prewar home, was emptied to make room for Germans. The new masters also needed furniture, so any affluent Jewish family, even if they lived elsewhere, could lose the contents of their home if the landlord or a neighbor reported them to the authorities. In mid-July, Joachim Hübner was evicted from his apartment. In the midst of all the atrocities, he was considered lucky; in this instance, he was allowed to take

Right: The southwest wing of the Golden Rose Synagogue, Lwów. It was designed by an Italian architect, Paulus Italus (also known as Paul the Fortunate), and built between 1582 and 1595 in late Renaissance style. For two centuries (until 1801), the Golden Rose was also called the Great City Synagogue. The building was declared a national architectural monument in 1938. The photograph is of the interior after it was desecrated and plundered in August 1941. *(Photograph by Janusz Witwicki; courtesy of Sergey Kravtsov.)*

some clothes and a few other belongings, but worse was yet to come. A month later, Gestapo showed up at his newly assigned room elsewhere in the city. This time, he was thrown out on the street and ordered to seek assistance from the Jewish community board.

A wave of evictions of Jewish families spread throughout the city. To make matters worse, any building associated with the Jewish community in Lwów was first looted by mobs and then burned to the ground. It did not matter if it was an Orthodox synagogue, like the "Golden Rose" built in the sixteenth century, or the Reform one that for many decades had resonated with the German language. In the end, their fate would be the same.[7]

When in the summer "The Poem About the Music" appeared in a Polish-language newspaper published by Germans in Lwów, its title was sickeningly misleading; in fact, the venomous content had nothing to do with culture or art. If only this was another diatribe, with its twisted logic once more linking Jews to the Soviet regime and alleging their unfair artistic dominance in the city, it could have been easily ignored as yet another piece of virulent Nazi propaganda. But its repugnant rhymes were more ominous than that; among several eminent musicians of the prewar period who were mocked there, the name "Bauer" was printed. At the same time, the "poem" did not hide the terrifying message of "the arrival of a new order." Now, it was obvious that Ewa's brother-in-law and his family were all singled out for worse things to come.[8]

The Golden Rose Synagogue circa
1941–1942. The building was
intentionally destroyed by the Nazis,
with its remains obliterated by
explosives in 1943.
*(Photograph by Janusz Witwicki;
courtesy of Sergey Kravtsov.)*

In November of 1941, a ghetto was established in Lwów, and Jews were ordered to move in; all others were to leave the area by January of the next year. Families streamed into the ghetto, desperate to have new roofs over their heads, carrying whatever belongings they could. But the cruelty of the oppressors knew no bounds; the Gestapo and SS forces cordoned off streets leading to the ghetto, leaving open just one road that passed under a railroad bridge. In this very spot, the old and infirm were separated from others to be taken away and murdered. When this was not enough to meet the barbaric quotas, house-to-house searches began in and outside of the ghetto.

Those were also months of suicides; almost all Jewish families somehow purchased capsules filled with cyanide. Among those who could not bear any more humiliation was Ewa's father, Jakób Zellel Kuttin, who killed himself. By the end of December 1941, approximately ten thousand Jews had perished in the city, whether through forced labor, executions under the bridge, or the taking of their own lives.[9] And the madness was only accelerating. With the arrival of the new year, the efficiency of the killing machine increased even further; now Jews were being exterminated by the tens of thousands every month. Soon, word reached Lwów that those who had not died in the ghetto but had been transported somewhere else, were being sent to a concentration camp in Bełżec—only forty-seven miles away—from where there was no return.

In the fall of 1941, the Hübner family decided it had become too difficult to remain in Lwów. Since November, placards posted on walls around town warned in no uncertain terms that aiding Jews in any way, including providing them with food, was punishable by death. At any moment, they realized, someone could recognize them on the street, or they could be denounced by a neighbor or an opportunist hoping to grab whatever material goods were being hidden. The big question for the Hübners was where to run and how; the familiar countryside of Bryńce Cerkiewne or Słobódka Leśna was no longer a friendly option.

The Ukrainian militia was always on the lookout for city folks suddenly appearing with a few suitcases in hand, a clear sign of Jews attempting to weather the storm in smaller communities. For the Hübners, the only viable option was to find a different place they could disappear into without raising the slightest suspicion. My father was the first to leave Lwów; it is not clear whether he happened to be in Warsaw at the outbreak of war or simply escaped there as soon as he could. In any case, he seems to have taken a quite realistic approach to the situation, rather than nurturing any false hopes that the persecutions back home would end soon. With his Aryan looks and papers he obtained in the name of Andrzej Zalewski, he had no difficulty blending into the big city without any traces of his past.

But the news from his relatives in Lwów grew more and more desperate. As my father told me in our only conversation on the matter, he was the one who arranged an escape for his family. There was some mention of smugglers, who for large amounts of money provided services. Several apartments were rented, awaiting those who would make the treacherous trip to Warsaw. Back in Lwów, travel documents must have been obtained, always under fear of being duped at the last moment by dishonest brokers who could disappear with large amounts of money. This time, however, the arrangements seemed to work.

Most likely, identity cards (*Kennkarte*) of people who had recently died were carefully altered; the original pictures were removed and photographs of the new owners were artificially aged and affixed by experts in this process. If the Hübners were lucky, they would have also carried forged baptismal certificates, just in case the German authorities should grow suspicious at one of the many checkpoints. The biggest risk was always for men; at any moment, they could have been ordered to lower their pants. If they were seen to be circumcised, their

Lwów outside the ghetto: street scene, with Nazi swastika visible in the background. The ghetto situated elsewhere in the city was liquidated on June 1, 1943; after just a few days, there were almost no survivors. The picture was taken in July 1943. *(Courtesy of the Austrian National Library, Vienna.)*

secret was given away, regardless of how skillfully their identity cards had been forged. A few could secure a statement signed by a trusted doctor, certifying that the circumcision had been done for medical reasons, but whether this would work in a moment of danger was anyone's guess.[10]

Those were the times of "the abyss of despair," when life-and-death questions were intertwined with moral dilemmas as never before.[11] Ewa and Zygmunt decided that their three-year-old son, Stefan, was to go with his father and the rest of the Hübners to Warsaw, while Ewa would stay behind to care for her mother. By December 1, 1941, the family started their journey into the unknown.

For those left behind, the situation became dire. The year 1942 brought one *Aktion* after another, decimating the Jews of Lwów. In March, August, and November, the Gestapo, assisted by other German units and the Ukrainian police, exterminated the sick and old, as well as those without work permits. Some victims were dragged to the nearby labor camp because they had no papers to show they were indispensable for the German war effort; others were taken for "resettlement," a code word for transport in freight cars to the concentration camp. Others were bludgeoned to death or shot for any infraction of the innumerable restrictions imposed on them. It did not matter whether the men among them were used to wearing three-piece suits or black caftans; it did not matter whether the women among them wore their hair flowing or had it piously covered; it did not matter whether they spoke Yiddish, Polish, or German; they were all condemned.[12]

By the end of 1942, the ghetto was fenced and its perimeter reduced. At first, those with badges displaying the letters W (*Wehrmacht*) or R (*Rüstungskommando*) were allowed to live; "W" stood for laborers helping to make supplies for the German army, and "R" marked those employed by the armament section. All other Jews, wearing mandatory armbands emblazoned with the Star of David, were doomed. The survivors were forced into tenements arranged according to their work assignments in the military factories.

Years later, there would be some doubt about what had happened to Ewa and her mother. Had they ended up in the ghetto, or had they desperately tried to hide somewhere else? In any case, their fate had been sealed when they were reported to the Germans by someone who had worked for Jakób Zellel Kuttin before the war. Ewa's wonderful smile was long gone, and now no one would hear from her again.

Erna, Ewa's older sister, had also remained in Lwów. In another act of desperation to save a child, she would entrust her only daughter to a Polish woman, who was to take the girl and run as far away as possible. Erna and her husband, the professor of music, managed to survive until mid-1943. Dr. Bauer was not only forced to perform manual labor, but also to display his talent in an orchestra assembled by the killers. Now, the famous musicians of Lwów were to play as an accompaniment to gruesome acts of beating and murder. In the Janowska labor camp, an orchestra played the "Radetzky March" every morning as haggard Jewish prisoners were marched out to military factories, some situated on the premises and others spread throughout the city. The sounds of Johann Strauss' uplifting music, which had once cheered on the troops and enlivened city parades, were now being grotesquely misused.[13]

While living in this hell, Erna and her husband had one lifeline. Those were a few contacts with a man addressed by them only as "Mr. Engineer." From time to time, he smuggled a few packs of cigarettes (a common medium of exchange) or brought them some money that helped to sustain them. When direct contact was no longer possible, the contacts had to be carefully staged. Letters, single sheets of paper written in pencil, were left somewhere in the factory where the men worked. Then, there were urgent pleas for money to prepare for an escape that would have to happen soon. In a few words, Dr. Bauer also wrote about longing to be reunited with his wife. But something went wrong, and Erna's husband was killed. She lived for a few months longer, grief-stricken but still asking in her last letter for some news from her friend. Perhaps in that sea of betrayal and brutality, there was a glimmer of hope for humanity; it was "Mr. Engineer" who would preserve those few scraps of paper bearing Erna and her husband's handwriting, so that no one would forget the bottom of the abyss.[14]

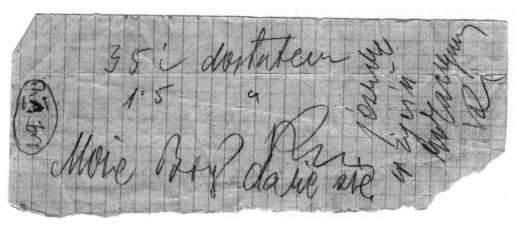

Letter from the Janowska camp in Lwów. The message confirms receipt of some unspecified items and reads: "God willing we will see each other once again during our lives." Most likely written by Marek Bauer and dated May 29, 1943. The vast majority of Jews held in the Janowska labor camp were killed the same year.

৵

JOACHIM HÜBNER TRAVELED TO Warsaw with his older son Zygmunt and grandson Stefan. His sister, Bronisława Goldenberg, followed. Perhaps they thought of themselves as lucky when the train rolled into the railway station in the big city. Indeed, their true identities had remained masked on the way there. In reality, however, this was just the first step; the hunted were not by any means free of danger. True, they were far away from the unfolding massacre in Lwów—but they could see from a distance the walls of the Warsaw ghetto; that would be a reminder that they were not safe yet. My father installed them in the two or three different apartments he had prepared, scattered throughout the city. Years later he would recall: "I warned them not to get together. But they did not listen, kept meeting in parks and elsewhere. Sadly, they would pay the price." He never told me—and I never asked—exactly to whom in the extended family he was referring.

During the war, my father met Zofia and Alexander Fedorenko. A good and honest couple with a newly born baby, they risked everything and never betrayed the trust put in them. How and when they had crossed paths with my father will unlikely ever be known. But it was obvious that Zofia and Alexander became more than fleeting acquaintances, pretending they did not know the truth. In a clear sign of closeness, my father under his new identity became the godfather of their young son, "Włodzio."

In those extraordinary times, the dynamics within the Hübner family seemed to change a bit. The younger son, the one who before the war had been considered a slacker, was now exuding confidence and, at times, guiding the entire clan. As much as I could glean from the snippets of war stories he shared, there was never a thought in my father's mind of self-pity or giving up. A few photos of my father from those years, which the Fedorenkos miraculously preserved in their family album for decades, all convey the same feeling.

Despite the tragedy all around him, or because of it, my father tried to lead as

The identity card (*Kennkarte*) issued for my father under the name of Andrzej Zalewski in December 1942 in Warsaw.

much of a normal life as possible. Yet, there were a few close calls for him; he knew that any careless gesture, any hesitation, could mean the end. Once, he said, he was suddenly stopped somewhere on the streets of Warsaw. As the German gendarmes were looking over his Aryan papers, my father, in his usual self-assured manner, struck up a conversation with their officer. In flawless German, but with his heart racing, he casually mentioned something about time spent in Vienna. A minute later he was waved away by the unsuspecting Jew-hunter, who'd turned out to be an Austrian.

After the war, my father would almost never speak about the horror of those times. Only seldom would he reminisce about the years of his youth when he outsmarted the much more powerful forces around him. Was that bravado, or a self-defense mechanism to repress painful memories? I wondered this but never had the courage to ask him.

With her new identity card, Bronisława Goldenberg—now called Maria Dynkowska—also settled down quickly in Warsaw. Money was running out. How much had they brought from Lwów? Most likely it was not much. Perhaps a few pieces of jewelry sewn somewhere in their clothes, or a few gold coins hidden in their shoes, could not carry her and the others for too long. Joachim's sister

Andrzej Zalewski as the godparent of "Włodzio" Fedorenko. On the left, Zofia Fedorenko. The woman on the right is unknown. The picture was taken in Warsaw, circa 1943.

soon began to earn money and have at least some semblance of a normal life by baking tortes and cakes to sell to Warsaw's cafes. This was not a surprising choice; those who had known her fondly remembered Bronia's culinary skills. Typically, she would deliver her wares through an establishment's back door. But sometimes, forced to come in through the patrons' entrance, she would freeze for a split second at the sight of Germans sitting at a nearby table, suddenly

Andrzej Zalewski, unknown woman, and Alexander Fedorenko.
The picture was taken on the street in Warsaw, circa 1943.

staring at her. There she was, a Jewish woman with a small body frame, carrying some fresh-baked goods in the midst of those uniformed men, trying to pass through quickly as if nothing bothered her. Despite these small bits of luck, life would be cruel to Bronisława. Three of her children would perish during the war; when and under what circumstances it is impossible to reconstruct today.

Upon arrival in Warsaw, Zygmunt and his little son Stefan took the second apartment. Like others in his family, they had been "christened" with some popular Polish surname so as not to arouse any suspicion. Despite these precautions, the family was far from being safe. When the suspicions of neighbors brought threats of blackmail and the risk of betrayal, Zygmunt and his son were forced to flee on more than one occasion. They hastily moved from the apartment in the city to the suburbs; when that place also became too dangerous, they found a room in the city center again. On June 9, 1943, Zygmunt left Stefan at home and went about his daily routine. Suddenly, on the street, he was caught up in a police roundup. German gendarmes were all over the place, street exits were cordoned off, and random people were pushed and shoved against walls. Perhaps there was something wrong with his papers, or he lacked a proper work permit, or maybe something else gave away the fact that he was Jewish. In any case, he and most of the others caught in this human hunt were loaded onto trucks and taken away.

Somehow the news that Zygmunt had not come home quickly reached his family. Soon, perhaps told by a few eyewitnesses who had watched from a distance, they learned where the Germans had picked up their victims that day. (By cruel coincidence, my father would live on the same street for decades after the war.) Meanwhile, a distraught Joachim urged his younger son to go to the German police headquarters to see if Zygmunt was among the detainees. Perhaps, he thought, something less sinister might provide an explanation for the older son's absence. What else could they do? What would have been a normal request under different circumstances now bordered on the suicidal. Some tense discussion followed; if Zygmunt's cover had been blown, any request by a family member would mean death to whomever asked the question. In this instance, no amount of self-confidence or good command of German would spare the petitioner from falling into a trap.

Decades later, on one of the rare occasions when my father spoke about those times, his emotions were still raw when remembering the insistence of his grief-stricken father. This was another moral dilemma no father or sibling should ever have to face. For the Hübner family, the days would pass and with them, any lingering hopes of Zygmunt's reappearance gave way to a slow, sad realization of the inevitable.

But what about the child who was left behind? During the first few days of bewilderment, Stefan, by then about four years old, was taken in by a stranger who looked after him in his father's absence. Then when it was obvious that Zygmunt would never return home, somewhere on a street corner, as my father recalled, the boy was hurriedly passed to him. There must have been a moment of intense anxiety for both Stefan and his uncle, the child asking where his dad was and the adult searching for answers. Another chapter in their fight for survival had begun.

———— ✦ ————

LIKE A PHOENIX

A STANDOFF BETWEEN GERMAN FORCES HOLDING the center of Warsaw, with surrounding districts, and the Soviet army, in control of the eastern part of town on the opposite side of the river, continued for months. The war finally ended there once the Red Army appeared on the other side of the river on a cold January 17, 1945. Within days, news of a German retreat westward brought a few curious people outside. With all the bridges destroyed, they trekked carefully west across the frozen river to reach the city center. They ventured through many ghostly streets to see the devastation of recent months, hoping to find family or friends.

Joachim Hübner would have been nowhere to be found. Four months earlier, he and his grandson, Stefan, along with thousands of other civilians, had been ordered by the German occupiers to leave Warsaw. In September of 1944 everyone had been sent to a processing camp (*Durchgangslager 121*) twelve miles west of the city. After more than a month of fighting, the uprising of Polish underground forces against the Germans was on the verge of collapse, failing to achieve its goal of liberating Warsaw. The brave, but outgunned and outnumbered insurgents were no match for hardened units of the SS and Wehrmacht. Warsaw was being emptied of its population for the purpose of methodical house-to-house destruction by the German units.

Before reaching *Durchgangslager 121*—where many refugees perished, others were sent to Germany as forced labor, or worse, to the concentration camps—Joachim and Stefan somehow managed to escape. They wandered for about six days until they found refuge in a small town. They emerged from hiding only in March 1945 when the Soviet army arrived there, and the grandfather and grandson could safely return to Warsaw.[1]

In July, Joachim Hübner and Bronisława Goldenberg went to a local office of the Jewish Council and registered their names, along with that of six-year-old Stefan. They were responding to a call for Jewish survivors to make their whereabouts known. At first, this was more or less a spontaneous reaction; only a few months later did the effort became more coordinated. Yet even then, the registration was simple and improvised; those who came provided no more than their first and last names, along with the place where they found themselves at the end of the war. Many did so hoping to trace family members who had managed to stay alive. But for the Hübners, there would be no sudden discovery, and for the most part, what they already suspected turned out to be true. There was one bright spot, however; one of Stefan's mother's cousins, who had left Lwów before the war, had survived; her name was luckily registered in Warsaw too.[2]

Other Jews ignored the call to register; my father was among them. Certainly he and many like him were busy putting their lives back together. Perhaps he had no illusions about who had survived in his own family. But some survivors hesitated for other reasons. They remembered too well what it had meant to be on a list not so long ago. For them, the refusal to register was the first step toward an almost complete break with the past.

When all the names collected throughout Poland were counted, there were 57,702 self-identified Jewish survivors. Each and every one of them had a tale to tell, but often they just wanted to forget. The exact number of Jews who survived the war there has always been difficult to ascertain. In 1945, the borders of the country shifted westward, and the Jewish population remained in flux for some time. There were those returning to Poland from camps in Germany and

Bronisława Goldenberg (née Hübner)
(1877–1965). A postwar picture of my
grandfather's sister.

Joachim Hübner. The picture was
taken at the end of the war or shortly
thereafter, in Warsaw, Poland.

Austria (about 40,000 through the end of 1945) or repatriated from Soviet territory (about 180,000 through the middle of 1945). At the same time, others were emigrating, mainly to Palestine (up to 150,000 through the middle of 1946). But the challenge of reconciling fluid statistics ought not to overshadow the fact that survivors represented just a little more than ten percent of Poland's prewar Jewish population of 3,500,000.

For older people like Joachim and his sister, rebuilding their lives was not easy. Coming out of hiding, they found themselves in unfamiliar places. Since 1944, the Soviets had been firmly in control of Lwów, which was now a permanent part of the Soviet Union, so they could not have even considered going "home." In fact, a large migration in the opposite direction was soon set in motion. Poles remaining in the former eastern Galicia were expelled by the Soviets. From Lwów alone, approximately one hundred thousand were swiftly repatriated westward, with no more than a couple of hundred surviving Jews among them. Their destination was communist Poland.

The vibrant Jewish presence in former Galicia, with the cherished memories of its respected scholars, pious *mitnagdim* and mystic *Hasidim*, its rebellious counterculture of *maskilim* and their more recent assimilated successors, was no more. The synagogues, whether austere or grandiose, were gone. The heated debates about big and small issues had fallen silent. What was left there were overgrown cemeteries, with row upon row of crooked or broken headstones. No longer were there new stories from Rohatyn, Kołomyja, Bryńce Cerkiewne, Lwów, and many other places that could bring smiles to Joachim's or Bronisława's faces.

My father never went back to his prewar family name; the wartime Andrzej Zalewski became the permanent one. His only subtle link with the past, which very few could recognize, was his middle name, Alfred. At the age of thirty-six he plunged into life, as if trying to restart it at full speed. There was no thought of marriage yet, but a few romances flourished. He quickly managed to get a position in the Scandinavian section of the Ministry of Foreign Affairs. Certainly, that was a safer assignment than more glamorous jobs in other departments of the foreign office of then-communist Poland. There, any whiff of sympathy toward western countries could have meant trouble during purges regularly conducted by party zealots.

Early in 1946, an opportunity came for my father to be posted to Norway in the diplomatic service. He was ecstatic, but there was one thing he had to do before reaching his goal. During an exit interview—the last hurdle before he could receive a diplomatic passport—he stated his desire to leave Poland as soon as possible. When asked why he was so interested in rushing, in February's cold, my father blurted out that it was important for him to assume his duties in Oslo in time for the Norwegian national holiday. To his surprise the interviewer— most likely the security officer—raised his eyebrows, paused, then reminded the young diplomat-to-be that the holiday was in May. For a moment, my father thought his dream job would vanish. However, everything turned out well and he soon arrived in Oslo as *chargé d'affaires* in the Polish embassy. The next three years were indisputably the best in his life; he would always remember with relish both his official duties and weekends spent far away from the ghostly ruins back home.

Andrzej Zalewski at a wreath-laying ceremony commemorating fallen Polish
soldiers in Narvik, Norway. The picture was taken May 28, 1946.

Andrzej Zalewski (seated first on the right) among the staff of the Polish diplomatic mission in Oslo, Norway. The picture was taken April 1947.

My father's stay in Norway was also an opportunity to help the Fedorenkos, who had been so good to him during the war. Most likely with my father's aid, their son, affectionately called "Włodzio," made the list of Polish children who were being sent to Norway. He became part of an international program to improve the nutritional status of children in war-ravaged countries. Apparently, some strings had to be pulled behind the scenes, since Włodzio was much younger than the other kids in his group. But despite his age, he was a brave boy who would always have fond memories of Scandinavians tossing candies into the kids' train as it passed. Perhaps so Włodzio would not get too homesick, he spent some weekends with my father in his villa in Oslo.

The good times never last forever and this was true for my father; letters from home began to report a string of bad news. Although Joachim's health had been faltering for some time, it now took a turn for the worse; Bronisława assumed the care of her ailing brother. At times, as his strength withered away, she was the one who wrote letters in Joachim's name. In this moment of another crisis for the family, someone from abroad seems to have intervened on their behalf. Starting in late 1946, telegrams and letters from officials of the American Joint Distribution Committee, a Jewish relief organization, were sent from Bucharest, Geneva, and Paris to its branch in Warsaw. Their tone conveyed a sense of urgency, with appeals to provide financial and medical help for the family. As with many elderly Jewish survivors, the end of the war's horrors did not mean that their struggle was over. Assistance notwithstanding, the situation did not improve over the next few months. In 1947, Joachim died at the age of sixty-six and was buried in the Jewish cemetery in Warsaw, where a simple headstone marks his grave.

Stefan's journey toward a normal childhood, or whatever was left of it, was never fully completed. At the end of the war or not long afterward, it became more and more difficult for the ailing grandfather to provide care for his grandson, and strangers would be called in to help. It seemed as though the ordeal of that little boy, already robbed of so many innocent years, had no end in sight. It was only when his late mother's cousin brought Stefan to her caring home that his life took a turn for the better. And yet even then, hazy flashbacks of abusive caregivers would stay with Stefan for many years to come. The void he felt at the loss of his parents

Stefan Hübner-Kwiatkowski.
At the beginning of a remarkable
journey toward fulfilling life.
A postwar picture circa 1946.

would never go away. He had been too young at the time to remember them, and he never learned more than a few snippets about their lives. Yet thanks to Stefan's strength of character and inquisitive mind, his life would ultimately blossom, becoming an uplifting story of personal triumph and professional success.

A year or so after Joachim's passing, rumors started reaching Norway that a tightening of the Stalinist regime in Poland would mean greater scrutiny of the foreign office. Among those suave men (and a few women), there could always have been someone with questionable loyalties to the totalitarian state. My father understood that well; not being a communist party member meant he could be among the first to go. Before long, there were cables calling him back; the pretext was some vague need for "consultations." Then, the prospect of a new diplomatic position in Brazil was raised between the lines. He hesitated and stalled for as long as he could. At some point, he even considered staying in the west; in reality, there was little for him to return home to. But he finally did go back to Poland in 1949. There was no new post awaiting him. As my father recalled, it had just been another shakeup within the government that served an increasingly paranoid regime. Although he personally did not face any serious consequences, his nascent diplomatic career was over, and the "iron curtain" fell behind him.

ॐ

MY PARENTS WERE MARRIED in a civil ceremony in 1951. I was born a year later, but their marriage was rocky and did not survive for long. There was an acrimonious divorce and a bitter custody battle. A few years later, they reconciled for a while, but then parted for good. My childhood routine included weekdays spent with my mother and weekends with my father. Since the divorce happened when I was four, the arrangement did not bother me; in fact, it was fun. By then, my father was an executive in a trading company. He often traveled abroad; he brought me gifts and when home, took me to good restaurants. There were also unusual treats like receiving a call from him from Chicago. Then, it was a big deal, the operator ringing to announce the upcoming call one day in advance—clearly, there were not too many conversations between the United States and Poland in the late 1950s.

When I was about ten or twelve, I noticed a large envelope on my father's desk, one clearly different from others. Carefully sealed, it bore my father's signature, covered by transparent tape in such way that opening it would be quite obvious. I never asked my father what was inside; I was not supposed to be looking through his stuff anyway. But one weekend, several months after my initial discovery, I saw that the envelope had been opened. Inside were three documents. The first that I pulled out was a copy of a law school diploma in the name of Alfred Hübner, with a line below specifying the Mosaic religion of the graduate. For a moment I was puzzled, asking myself what it meant. The second document made that clear; it was an official record pertaining to his name change, registered shortly after the war. Third in the envelope was a picture of a woman; only later would I learn that it was my grandmother, Regina Hübner (née Dub).

Finding this hidden bridge to the past was an event with many repercussions in my young mind. It seems almost irrational today, but I was utterly shocked with all those discoveries. I had been baptized as a child, and we celebrated Christmas and Easter at home. I knew that "Jewish" meant another religion, but that was about all. True, I could not recall ever seeing my father in church, except on one occasion when he'd visited a small country chapel to hear a fiery sermon chastising the communist regime. His secular lifestyle did not come as a surprise; my mother was not religious either. But beyond that, about what it meant to be Jewish, I had no point of reference. There was simply no one I knew who openly identified as a Jew. I do not think I even had an idea of what a synagogue was, or if one existed in Warsaw at the time.

In fact, my anxiety was not about one religion or another; there was something else that troubled me on a much deeper level. On the street or in the schoolyard, calling someone "Jew" meant something negative. What exactly it meant was not clear to me. Flashes of memories rushed back, like overhearing a peasant woman tell her child to stop crying, or a Jew would take him away. Later, I would feel a jolt whenever I heard (on more than a few occasions) casual comments that someone who was advancing too fast, or was making too much money, or was perhaps associated with the communist regime, must have been a Jew. This was worse than hearing Jewish jokes, which by definition were in poor taste and not funny.

The envelope and all these conflicting thoughts signaled to me that having a Jewish father was a secret I must keep. The only person I talked to about my discovery was my mother. She was matter-of-fact, saying it was not a big deal and encouraging me to speak about it with my father. I did try, clumsily, to provoke him to address the issue, but never asked him directly about his past and what it meant. Then, for different reasons, the contact between us ceased and we became estranged for a number of years; my opportunity to learn the truth seemed gone.

In 1968, a wave of anti-Semitism erupted in the open in Poland; this time it was orchestrated by the regime. Rather than looking for the true roots of student protests that rocked the universities that year, the communist government tried to channel public discontent against the Jews. An internal power struggle within the regime made it possible for a not-too-subtle nationalistic campaign to unfold. Anyone with Jewish heritage was fair game, collectively blamed for the brutality of the security apparatus in early postwar Poland. Jews who had remained in Poland were now labeled Zionists, secretly supporting Israel, not loyal citizens of the country. The press, controlled by the communist regime, spread lies about Jews' subversive role, claiming they had instigated civil unrest.

The purge had been well prepared. Only later did it became evident that a special unit of the security apparatus, more than two hundred strong, had been engaged in dubious genealogical research and was ready to distribute lists of people considered to be of questionable allegiance. Rumors of purported Jewish heritage were spread, even about individuals with not a single drop of Jewish blood in their veins. The campaign easily achieved its purpose, and directives were circulated banning Jews from key jobs. As a result, many of Jewish ancestry, religious and secular alike, were forced to resign from teaching, academic, and executive positions. They were strongly encouraged to leave the country, and the pressure further increased when it was announced—as it turned out, misleadingly—that such departures would be tolerated only for the next few months. The last Jewish exodus from Poland followed. My father was among the three thousand who were graciously welcomed in Denmark; others moved elsewhere. This only reinforced my feeling that the topic of my paternal heritage was to be treated with caution.[3]

～

AFTER OUR MARRIAGE, MARGARET and I traveled to Denmark. It was time for her and me to get to know my father. A number of long conversations followed, but it was difficult to bridge the gap after so many years of living apart. We returned a few times, but I must admit it was still awkward for me to ask questions about our family heritage. By our last visit in 1978, time was running out fast; my father was seriously ill and the "next time" for me to probe more deeply never came.

After his death, when going through my father's things—this time there was no sealed envelope—I could not stop thinking, *That's it? Is that all that is left after the full, albeit complicated, life that he had?* Almost everything remaining was about the recent past. There were no family albums with those black-and-white pictures of prior generations that we have difficulty recognizing, and no letters with frayed pages addressed to "Dear Alfred." His small library was well stocked with books published in many languages—Polish, German, English, and Danish (and most likely a few in Norwegian)—yet there were none I could find with Hebrew letters, which would have unmistakably provided a faint link with the past.

Years later, when Margaret and I already lived in the United States, it became much easier to talk about my Jewish father. This really was no longer a "big deal." I had many professional friends who happened to be Jewish. For the first time in my life, I could pass almost daily not just one, but several synagogues in my neighborhood. On our street, most of the families were Jewish; some even celebrated both Hanukkah and Christmas. Then, my growing daughter Ewa started to come home with a lot of Jewish friends. She brought us details about Sabbath activities and upcoming celebrations of Rosh Hashanah or Yom Kippur. But the symbolic link with the past really started when Ewa began to talk about converting to Judaism. She first mentioned this while in high school, as if to test our reaction. Then, the conversation restarted in earnest when talk about her own marriage became serious. When the time came and Ewa stood with Jason under the wedding canopy (*chuppah*) and the seven blessings (*sheva brachot*) were recited for the bride and her groom, I had the feeling that her grandfather and all her other Jewish ancestors, from the long line of Hübners and Dubs through the more distant Fränkels, Horns, Seinfelds, Hilsenraths and so many others, finally felt at ease. The long journey of the family, with its stretches of straight road and all its complicated detours, seemed to have brought us to this happy moment. In a very real sense, the circle had been closed.

Acknowledgments

WHILE WRITING *GALICIAN PORTRAITS* I received many words of encouragement and probing questions from my wife. Margaret was the first to comment on the findings of my research, as it slowly uncovered the lives and events that are described in these pages. Often, when there were gaps in personal stories, we debated together what could have been the fate of one person or another, checking carefully to see whether the dates when they had lived fit into the broader historical context. There were many such discussions, and Margaret's patience and interest were very important to me in this undertaking.

When the story touched on more emotionally difficult subjects, Margaret read early drafts and would tear up from time to time; she became as deeply involved in this project as I was. Our two grown children, already "scarred" by the experience of having their father deeply focused on his first book, also deserve words of thanks. They took the project without a single complaint, even when

I quickly slipped out of family gatherings to continue this work. When a few precious photographs of their newly discovered ancestors, or of places where those prior generations had lived, began to surface, I noticed cautious curiosity on Ewa and Andy's faces. And now they will be able to learn about the much fuller story.

Although I cannot directly convey my deep gratitude to the brave couple who knew my father during World War II, Zofia and Alexander Fedorenko stand tall as an example of people who adhered to the highest moral principles and chose not to be indifferent. Their son, Włodzimierz ("Włodzio") Fedorenko, who was born during the war, shared with me a few of his childhood memories of Joachim Hübner and Bronisława Goldenberg, for which I am immensely appreciative. His recollections helped me to jumpstart my research and reconstruct their lives. But I was lucky beyond that; the Fedorenko family had preserved more. Several pictures of my relatives in the last few chapters of the book came from their family album. This speaks even more about the bonds that had formed in those difficult times.

There was yet another discovery that was possible through my conversations with Włodzio. I had spent years of futile search for my father's nephew, Stefan; Włodzio solved that puzzle by helping me establish contact with Stefan Kwiatkowski's family. None of us knew what to expect, but when we met our conversations flowed freely; there was no awkward feeling. The only thing I regret is that we were not able to talk earlier, before my father's nephew's memory had started to falter. Wanda, Stefan's wife, was a gracious host and gave me many details of recollections that her husband had shared with her over the years. Their daughter, Ewa Kwiatkowska, an economist with a PhD in management, is a capable and thoughtful young woman. Despite her busy professional life, she showed an admirable interest in the complex past—I wish that I had shared my cousin's traits at a younger age. Ewa was indispensable in providing details about the Kuttin family and locating in the archives the handwritten testimony of Joachim Hübner, my grandfather and her great-grandfather. There were a few paradoxes that we discovered, such as the fact that on more than one occasion

Ewa's father and I had lived not far from each other in Poland and in the United States (where Stefan spent a few years on scholarship); unfortunately we had to wait many years before our paths would cross.

ॐ

NUMEROUS DIGITAL LIBRARIES AND postings of archival information in searchable formats, which are now available at the click of the mouse, have made historical nonfiction writing much more feasible and accurate than in the past. Further, many specialized sites such as JewishGen or Gesher Galicia, with their informative websites or powerful search engines, deserve our thanks and financial support; they are often particularly helpful with initial research about people and places. The passion of many individuals behind these resources is commendable, since they continually bring newer and newer sources to light.

One of the most gratifying experiences I had during my work on *Galician Portraits* was the opportunity to meet, electronically or in person, with numerous individuals who share similar interests in genealogy and history. On the top of my list are the two leaders of the Rohatyn Shtetl Research Group (RSRG), Dr. Alex Feller from Chicago and Marla Osborn, an American who at the time was living with her husband in Paris. I am very grateful to both of them for inviting me to join the organization that they founded, a group of nearly two hundred descendants of the former inhabitants of Rohatyn. Receiving valuable information about the history of the Faust family from Alex Feller, the Horn family from Marla Osborn, and the Turner family from Dr. Steven Turner—all "Rohatyners"—is much appreciated.

Alex's passion for genealogy and collections of archival material pertaining to that Galician town were a superb resource for me. I am grateful to Alex for numerous email exchanges and personal interactions—these were always illuminating as I worked to uncover the lives of the Dub family of Rohatyn. The time he generously devotes to RSRG is much appreciated. Marla Osborn, who frequently speaks at Jewish genealogy conferences about her own discoveries, is also dedicated to the physical preservation of sites linked to Jewish history in former

Galicia. I am thankful to Marla for her leadership in preserving the headstones at the Jewish cemetery in Rohatyn, with the involvement of many former and current Rohatyners.

I am grateful to the countless archivists, librarians and museum curators across the globe who patiently answered my queries, collected old files, provided illustrative material, or shared with me long-forgotten books that provided context. The staff of the Jewish Theological Seminary in New York deserves special mention for their efforts to provide me with material pertaining to the Galician *Haskalah*. I also want to express my particular thanks to Professor Mireia Ryškova and Dr. Miroslav Kunštát from Charles University in Prague, Czech Republic, for information about August Rohling, and Diana Peltz from the State Archives in L'viv, Ukraine, for her continued assistance in my research. Tomasz Kozłowski from the History Meeting House in Warsaw, Poland must be credited for sharing with me old pictures of Galician towns. Dr. Sergey Kravtsov and Hanna Palmon, both from The Hebrew University of Jerusalem, were generous in sharing their sources and knowledge; Dr. Kravtsov is an accomplished researcher of history of Lwów's synagogues and Hanna Palmon is passionate about bringing to light stories of Jewish musical life in the interwar period. She is credited with providing many details about Marek Bauer. David Lee Preston, who is an accomplished journalist in Philadelphia, also has had very personal experiences with the topics covered by me in these pages. His mother was one of the handful of Jewish survivors of Lwów's ghetto. I am grateful to David for sharing without hesitation an archival photograph from this tragic time, and his prior articles based on the recollections of his late mother.

In my research, I tackled several documents written in old German Gothic script, particularly some pertaining to the early period of Austrian Galicia. Whenever I reached an impasse in making sense of these texts, I could always count on the expert translation of Anne Schmidt-Lange. Her superb understanding of historical German and her sensitivity about various subjects at hand were of great help. Anne labored for weeks translating Maria Theresa's *Judenordnung* of 1776, which to my knowledge has never been translated into English in its entirety, and is included in this book.

After all my research efforts to collect information from various sources and to decipher the meaning of archival documents, then to write and rewrite this story, one more person deserves particular thanks. My editor, Penelope Franklin, has been inquisitive, probing me for the meaning of historical events or social context of many parts of the unfolding story. Her thoughtful and sensitive approach to the topics covered has been invaluable in my making of *Galician Portraits*.

Finally, in the process of learning about the Jewish history of Galicia I have been struck by the richness of its human characters and their life pursuits. The great diversity of Galician Jewry before the breakout of World War II is not only underappreciated today, but was mostly overlooked by its non-Jewish contemporaries. Then the long shadow of the tragedy that followed made it even more challenging to remember Galician fortunes and failures. Let us hope that the tales of bold aspirations and careful steps touched upon in *Galician Portraits*—and many others not covered in these pages—will be celebrated not only as an example of a vibrant Jewish heritage but also, in the broadest sense, a part of our collective human story.

Family Registers

THE DUB FAMILY REGISTER

1st Generation

1-1. Samuel Dub* date and place of birth unknown; died presumably before 1846 in Rohatyn, Galicia. Name of Samuel Dub's wife unknown. Children of Samuel and his wife:

    i.   **Sender Dub** born circa 1806 (?).

    ii.   Wolf Dub date unknown.

    iii.   Leiser Dub date unknown.

2nd Generation

2-1-i. Sender Dub (son of Samuel) born circa 1806, place unknown; died January 5, 1906, in Rohatyn, Galicia. Sender Dub married twice:

a. **Rifke** (a.k.a. Rywka or Rebeka) **Seinfeld** date and place of birth unknown, date of marriage before 1858. Rifke died between 1862 and 1864. Children of Sender and Rifke (all born in Rohatyn, Galicia):

    i.   Rachel Dub date unknown.

    ii.   **Samuel Dub** born before 1858.

    iii.   Mindel Dub date unknown.

    iv.   Rikel Dub date unknown.

    v.   Israel Dub born 1858.

    vi.   Chaje Dub born June 30, 1862.

*Highlighted entries denote author's ancestors in the direct line of ascent (or direct descendants), whereas other names in the register refer to collateral relatives.

b. Hinde Ginsbe[u]rg date and place of birth unknown, Hinde and Sender married before 1866, with their state-sanctioned marriage recorded in 1878 in Rohatyn, Galicia. Hinde died in 1892 in Rohatyn, Galicia. Child of Sender and Hinde born in Rohatyn, Galicia:

vii.   Hersch Dub born January 17, 1866.

2-1-ii. Wolf Dub (son of Samuel) was a leaseholder in Babińce in the suburbs of Rohatyn, Galicia. Wolf married Chane Rosenzweig (daughter of David and Rifke Rosenzweig) before 1861, with their state-sanctioned marriage recorded January 23, 1908, in Rohatyn, Galicia. Wolf Dub died after 1908, place unknown. Children of Wolf and Chane (all born in Rohatyn, Galicia):

i.   Malka Dub born March 16, 1861.

ii.   Nusin Dub born April 13, 1863; died May 13, 1863.

iii. Rifke Dub born October 3, 1864.

iv.   Pesil Dub born in November 1866.

v.   Samuel Dub born February 12, 1868.

vi.   Jacob Nathan Dub and Leib Dub (twins) born in May 1870. Jacob Nathan died May 3, 1871 and Leib died June 9, 1871.

vii. Marcus Dub born September 3, 1872.

viii. Blime (Dub) Rosenzweig born August 25, 1875.

ix.   Szulim Dub born June 13, 1877.

2-1-iii. Leiser Dub (son of Samuel) was a merchant in Rohatyn, Galicia. Leiser married Etel (*sic*) before 1860; Etel (*sic*) was born in 1831, place unknown, and died March 28, 1881, in Rohatyn, Galicia. Children of Leiser and Etel (*sic*) (all born in Rohatyn, Galicia):

i.   Feige Dub born April 15, 1860.

ii.   Pessel Dub born date unknown.

iii. Jente Dub born June 1862.

iv.   Abrahm (*sic*) Dub born March 23, 1865; died May 12, 1869.

v.   Marcus Sussie Dub born February 12, 1868.

3ʳᵈ Generation

3-1-i. Rachel Dub (daughter of Sender Dub and Rifke) born before 1858. Rachel married Jakob Nehmlich from Bolechów, Galicia. Children of Rachel and Jakob:

    i.   Pesie Nahmlich (*sic*) born April 1863, in Rohatyn, Galicia.

    ii.   Herz Nehmlich born December 10, 1875, in Potok, Galicia.

    iii.   Nuchim Nehmlich born June 28, 1878, in Rohatyn, Galicia.

3-1-ii. Samuel Dub (son of Sender Dub and Rifka) was born before 1858, and died date and place unknown. Samuel married **Cypre Rosa Horn** before 1874, place unknown. Cypre Rosa was a daughter of Samuel and Hinde Horn from Buczacz, Galicia. Children of Samuel Dub and Cypre Rosa (all born in Rohatyn-Załuże, Galicia):

    i.   Freide (Freude) Dub born December 11, 1874.

    ii.   Taube Dub born August 5, 1877.

    iii.   **Regina (Rifke) Dub** born July 1, 1879.

3-1-iii. Mindel Dub (daughter of Sender Dub and Rifke) born before 1858 in Rohatyn, Galicia. Mindel married Hersch Goldschlag, a merchant from Rohatyn, before 1870. Children of Mindel and Hersch Goldschlag (all born in Rohatyn, Galicia):

    i.   Sure Süssel Goldschlag born December 18, 1870.

    ii.   Rifka Goldschlag born May 1, 1873.

    iii.   Taube Goldschlag born November 15, 1877.

3-1-iv. Rikel Dub (daughter of Sender Dub and Rifke) born before 1859 in Rohatyn, Galicia. Rikel married Markus Kontes before 1874, with their state-sanctioned marriage recorded December 17, 1912, in Lwów, Galicia. Children of Rikel and Markus Kontes:

    i.   Chane Dub (Kontes) born May 29, 1878, and died August 6, 1880, in Stanisławów, Galicia.

ii. Chaim Kontes born June 11, 1879, in Stanisławów, Galicia.

iii. Osias Kontes born August 27, 1881, in Rohatyn-Załuże, Galicia.

iv. Isaak Kontes born December 28, 1885, in Stanisławów, Galicia.

3-1-v. Israel Dub (son of Sender Dub and Rifke) born in 1858 in Rohatyn. He married Fradel Seinfeld (daughter of Abraham and Rifke Seinfeld) before 1880, with their state-sanctioned marriage recorded March 28, 1897, in Chodorów, Galicia. Israel's residence at the time of civil marriage was Wierzbica in the district of Bóbrka, Galicia. Children of Israel and Fradel:

i. Moses Dub born in 1880 in Stanisławów, Galicia and died May 12, 1884, in Rohatyn-Załuże, Galicia.

ii. Mindel Dub born March 29, 1884, in Rohatyn-Załuże, Galicia. Mindel married Jacob Leib Zlatkes June 1, 1902, in Tarnopol, Galicia.

3-1-vi. Chaje Dub (daughter of Sender Dub and Rifke) born in 1862. Chaje married Meschulem Salat, candidate for the rabbi in Lwów, with their state-sanctioned marriage recorded April 23, 1899, in Lwów. Children of Chaje and Meschulem Salat:

i. Joseph Saul Salat born January 10, 1879, in Rohatyn-Załuże, Galicia.

ii. Jetty Rosa Salat born November 15, 1891, in Lwów, Galicia and died September 5, 1894, in Lwów, Galicia.

4th Generation

4-1-i. Freide (Freude) Dub (daughter of Samuel Dub and Cypre Rosa) born December 11, 1874, in Rohatyn-Załuże, Galicia. She married Jacob Hefler December 26, 1893, in Probużna, Galicia. Child of Freide and Jacob:

i. Dawid Hefler born May 17, 1902, in Kuropatniki, near Bursztyn, Galicia.

4-1-ii. Taube Dub (daughter of Samuel Dub and Cypre Rosa) born August 5, 1877, in Rohatyn-Załuże, Galicia and died place and date unknown. She married Ferdynand (Fischel) Katz (1868–1938), a candidate lawyer in Bursztyn, Galicia February 14, 1899, in Podszumlance, near Bursztyn, Galicia. Children of Taube and Ferdynand Katz:

    i.   Henryk Katz born January 1, 1900, in Stanisławów, Galicia.

    ii.   Ludwik Wilhelm Katz born October 17, 1905, in Rohatyn, Galicia.

4-1-iii. Regina (Rifke) Dub (daughter of Samuel Dub and Cypre Rosa) born July 1, 1879, in Rohatyn-Załuże, Galicia and died June 26, 1941, in Lwów under Soviet occupation. Regina Dub married **Joachim Hübner** (Hübner register 4-1-vii) December 15, 1905, in Chodorów, Galicia. The line **continues under the Hübner family register.**

THE HÜBNER FAMILY REGISTER

1st Generation

1-1. Abraham Hübner* date and place of birth unknown; died presumably before 1865. Abraham married **Sura (Sarah)** before 1827. Abraham and Sura lived in Kołomyja, Galicia. Children of Abraham and Sura:

    i.   **Samson Hübner** born in 1827.

    ii.   Mendel Hübner date unknown.

    iii.   Jona Hübner date unknown.

    iv.   Bruche Hübner born in 1844 and died January 12, 1872.

2nd Generation

2-1-i. Samson (a.k.a. Szymszon or Simson) **Hübner** (son of Abraham and Sura) born presumably in 1827 in Kołomyja and died January 2, 1885, in Kołomyja, Galicia. He married **Sossie Hilsenrath** (a.k.a. Hilsenrad) before 1849. Sossie (daughter of Froim Hilsenrath and Ester from Kołomyja) was born in 1829 and died January 14, 1899, in Kołomyja, Galicia. Children of Samson and Sossie (all born in Kołomyja, Galicia):

    i.   **Salomon Leib Hübner** born in 1849.

    ii.   Dwora Hübner born in 1853.

    iii.   Froim Hibner (*sic*) born in 1859.

    iv.   Jankil Hübner born in 1861, died December 30, 1866.

    v.   Feiwel Hübner born July 10, 1867.

    vi.   Sime Hübner born June 20, 1870, died September 19, 1871.

---

*Highlighted entries denote author's ancestors in the direct line of ascent (or direct descendants), whereas other names in the register refer to collateral relatives.

3ʳᵈ Generation

3-1-i. Salomon Leib Hübner (son of Samson and Sossie) born in 1849 in Kołomyja, Galicia and died July 19, 1904, in Słobódka Leśna, Galicia. Salomon Leib married **Rachel (Ruchel) Fränkel** before 1869, with their state-sanctioned marriage recorded May 12, 1891, in Kołomyja. Rachel (Ruchel) Fränkel was born in 1851 in Piadyki, next to Kołomyja, Galicia. She was a daughter of Mordko Fränkel (1824–1891) and Sura (Sarah) Rath (1830–1893). Children of Salomon Leib and Rachel (Ruchel) (all born in Słobódka Leśna, Galicia):

    i.   Israel Hübner born in 1869.

    ii.   Reisel Hübner born in 1872 (?), died February 14, 1874.

    iii.   Itzig Hübner born March 16, 1874, died September 18, 1876.

    iv.   Feiwel Hübner born November 14, 1875, died October 7, 1876.

    v.   Bronisława (Bruche) Hübner born August 11, 1877.

    vi.   Chaje Leia Hübner born September 5, 1879.

    vii.   **Joachim (Chaim Nussin) Hübner** born July 25, 1881.

    viii.   Erna (Ester) Hübner born March 2, 1883.

    ix.   Jakob Hübner born in 1884 and died June 11, 1885, in Kołomyja, Galicia.

4ᵗʰ Generation

4-1-v. Bronisława (Bruche) Hübner (daughter of Salomon Leib and Ruchel) born August 11, 1877, in Słobódka Leśna, Galicia and died October 7, 1965, in Warsaw, Poland. Bronisława married Abe Goldenberg (son of Nathan Goldenberg and Rebeka Liebman, leaseholders from Kisseleu, Bukovina) in June 1895 in Kołomyja, Galicia. Children of Bronisława and Abe:

    i.   Maksymilian Goldenberg born April 19, 1896, in Słobódka Leśna, Galicia. Died before 1939.

ii.   Szymon (Samson) Goldenberg born January 13, 1898, in Słobódka Leśna, Galicia. Perished in Holocaust.

iii.   Zofia (Sonia) Goldenberg born July 18, 1900, in Słobódka Leśna, Galicia. Zofia married Juliusz Merz before 1939. They presumably lived in Tarnów, Poland. Both perished in Holocaust.

iv.   Róża Goldenberg born date and place unknown. Died before 1939.

v.   Ludwik Goldenberg born date and place unknown. Perished in Holocaust.

4-1-vi. Chaje Leia Hübner (daughter of Salomon Leib and Ruchel) born September 5, 1879, in Słobódka Leśna, Galicia and died September 10, 1904, in Słobódka Leśna, Galicia. She married Munish Badian, a merchant from Grzymałów, on June 24, 1899, in Kołomyja, Galicia. Children of Chaje and Munisch (all born in Słobódka Leśna, Galicia):

i.   Arnold Badian born April 18, 1900.

ii.   Karol Ludwik Badian born September 4, 1904.

4-1-vii. Joachim (Chaim Nussin) Hübner (son of Salomon Leib and Rachel) born July 25, 1881, in Kołomyja, Galicia and died August 20, 1947, in Warsaw, Poland. Joachim married **Regina (Rifke) Dub** (Dub register 4-1-iii) December 15, 1905, Chodorów, Galicia. Regina (daughter of Samuel Dub and Cypre Rosa) was born July 1, 1879, in Rohatyn-Załuże, Galicia and died June 26, 1941, in Lwów under the Soviet occupation. Children of Joachim and Regina (all born in Bryńce Cerkiewne, Galicia):

i.   Zygmunt Hübner born November 24, 1906.

ii.   **Alfred Hübner** born October 13, 1911.

4-1-viii. Erna (Ester) Hübner (daughter of Solomon Leib and Rachel) born March 2, 1883, in Słobódka Leśna, Galicia and died date and place unknown. She married Moritz (Moses) Erbsen, a leaseholder of the estate in Dżurków, Galicia, in 1903. Children of Erna and Moritz:

i.   Henryk Erbsen born May 13, 1904, in Słobódka Leśna, Galicia.

ii.   Ludwik Zygmunt Erbsen born March 28, 1911, in Dżurków, Galicia.

5ᵗʰ Generation

5-1-i. Zygmunt Hübner (son of Joachim and Regina) born November 24, 1906, in Bryńce Cerkiewne, Galicia. He perished during Holocaust in 1943, in Warsaw. Zygmunt married Ewa Julia Kuttin, daughter of Jakób Kuttin and Aurelia (née Hüttner) September 6, 1931, in Lwów, Poland. Ewa was born May 21, 1909, in Lwów and perished during Holocaust circa 1943, in Lwów. Child of Zygmunt and Ewa:

    i.   Stefan Hübner born May 12, 1939, in Lwów, Poland.

5-1-ii. Alfred Hübner (son of Joachim and Regina) born October 13, 1911, in Bryńce Cerkiewne, Galicia and died October 19, 1979, in Copenhagen, Denmark. Alfred changed his name to Andrzej Alfred Zalewski during World War II. He married **Irena Maria Sobolewska** (daughter of Helena and Franciszek Sobolewski) May 7, 1951, in Warsaw, Poland. Irena was born October 5, 1913, in Bohorodczany, Galicia and died November 2, 1998, in Warsaw, Poland. Child of Andrzej (Alfred) and Irena:

    i.   **Andrew Zalewski** born January 14, 1952, in Warsaw, Poland.

6ᵗʰ Generation

6-1-i. Stefan Hübner (son of Zygmunt and Ewa) was born May 12, 1939, in Lwów, Poland. Stefan's name was changed to Stefan Kwiatkowski after World War II. He married Wanda Teresa Adamowicz (daughter of Adam and Anna Adamowicz) June 28, 1968, in Hoddesdon, UK. Wanda was born January 2, 1943, in Porudomino, Lithuania. Children of Stefan and Wanda (all born in Warsaw, Poland):

    i.   Tomasz Kwiatkowski born December 1, 1969, and died December 2, 1969.

    ii.   Adam Kwiatkowski born December 7, 1972.

    iii.   Ewa Maria Kwiatkowska born July 24, 1980.

6-2-i. Andrew Zalewski (son of Andrzej and Irena) was born January 14, 1952, in Warsaw, Poland. He married Margaret Kominek February 14, 1976, in Warsaw, Poland. Margaret (daughter of Józef Kominek and Maria Morasicka) was born October 17, 1951, in Wiciejów, Poland. Children of Andrew and Margaret:

- **i.** **Ewa Margaret Zalewska** born December 19, 1978, in Warsaw, Poland.

- **ii.** **Andrew James Zalewski** born April 10, 1987, in Philadelphia, Pennsylvania, USA.

7-1-i. Adam Kwiatkowski (son of Stefan and Wanda) was born December 7, 1972, in Warsaw, Poland. He married Urszula Kwiatek September 22, 2007, in Warsaw, Poland. Urszula (daughter of Michał Kwiatek and Marianna Kwiatek) was born August 2, 1978, in Puławy, Poland. Children of Adam and Urszula (all born in Warsaw, Poland):

- **i.** Szymon Kwiatkowski born May 19, 2009.

- **ii.** Stefan Kwiatkowski born August 7, 2011.

- **iii.** Kinga Kwiatkowska born June 19, 2013.

7-2-i. Ewa Margaret Zalewska (daughter of Andrew and Margaret) born December 19, 1978, in Warsaw, Poland. She married Jason Todd Abrams September 6, 2008, in Philadelphia, Pennsylvania, USA. Jason was born September 8, 1975, in Manhasset, New York, USA. He is a son of Franklin S. Abrams and Leslie Aura Goldstein. Children of Ewa and Jason are the 8th generation in the line of Dub and Hübner descendants:

- **i.** **Eli Charles Abrams** born April 26, 2010, in New York City, New York, USA.

- **ii.** **Theo Reid Abrams** born December 16, 2011, in Manhasset, New York, USA.

- **iii.** **Zoe Leila Abrams** born December 16, 2011, in Manhasset, New York, USA.

- **iv.** **Dexter Grant Abrams** born May 29, 2013, in Manhasset, New York, USA.

JEWISH LAWS IN GALICIA

Jews are again strictly forbidden to marry without permission*

WE MARIA THERESA BY THE GRACE OF GOD,

ROMAN EMPRESS etc.

Hereby announce to all who ought to know

 ITH GREAT CONCERN, WE HAVE received news that some Jews, without the knowledge of the Rabbis and Our permission, dared to circumvent Our Manifesto from March 8th of the current year, issued on the subject of [Jewish] marriages, and have thereby brought upon themselves the harshest penalties for insolent violation of Our orders.

As the cause for committing the crime of violating Our orders could originate because the Jews did not notify their hereditary lords before the weddings, or because, as they are saying, it was not their custom, it is Our duty to see that the mentioned Manifesto is implemented to its full extent, and the path to the insolent crime is obstructed.

Accordingly, we sternly order all hereditary lords, the authorities of the towns, the stewards in the Kingdom of Galicia and Lodomeria, wherever Jews settle and live, to remember to be vigilant and to make all efforts to implement Our order. In particular, [We intend] to harshly force all Jews to notify their hereditary lord of their intent to marry, and to obtain from him a certificate, and, finally, with the certificate of the Rabbi, humbly apply with his request to obtain permission.

Proclaimed in Lemberg on 28th day of June 1773.

Count S. P. R von PERGEN.

L.S. [official seal]

---

*Continuatio Edictorum et Mandatorum Universalium in Regnis Galiciæ et Lodomeriæ. A Die 28. Mensis Junii Anno 1773 Emanatorum. Leopoli 1774; p. 4.

Patent Regarding Procedures Concerning Baptisms of Jewish Children[*]

WE etc.

$\mathcal{T}$O ALL LOYAL AND OBEDIENT subjects regardless of [their] Honor, Status, and Essence in Our Imperial — Royal Kingdom of Galicia and Lodomeria, as well as in the Duchy of Oświęcim and Zator, to Our citizens by Our Imperial, Royal Grace for the benefit of all, we announce: until now, various events were taking place in these Kingdoms following bad old practices [in which] Jewish infants were taken from their parents by Christians who were overzealous, or had other reasons, and performed baptism themselves or brought [the babies] to the clergy. However, local Jewry that remains under the Monarch's Protection brought several justified complaints, asking for a solution in this matter. In our sound judgment, We considered the matter after taking into consideration the Papal Laws; the following regulations under the general law were decided for strict implementation in the future, and are herewith ordered, as well as commanded.

1) All Christians in general, the citizens of the country, and especially midwives, are strictly forbidden under the threat of penalty to secretly take Jewish infants, who do not yet have the ability to decide for themselves, and against the will of their parents and guardians, to baptize them. However, there are two exceptions as follows: if such Jewish infant is in mortal danger, and the signs of imminent death are visible, or it is abandoned by its parents and guardians; in such instances, the powers of the mother and guardians cannot be exercised over the infant. Then, based on the Act of the Pious Congregation from the year 1678, the Christian midwife can perform baptism. In the case of an abandoned [child] or if the Jewish child is being rejected by the family and it is given to the Clergy and baptized by them, the child should be later raised according to Christian canons.

If despite Our ban, someone dares to baptize a Jewish infant, and if it is proven that the [correct] form of Sacrament was used, such baptism is valid according to all Catholic teachings. Although this [act] was forbidden, Jewish children baptized in such way are immediately to be taken from their parents and it is the responsibility of the person who performed the forbidden baptism to raise them among good and religious Christians; if this is not possible, then the baptized Jewish child should be given to the House of Widows or to the Hospital of Education and Science until it is able to learn a profession. The Jewish

[*]*Continuatio Edictorum et Mandatorum Universalium in Regnis Galiciæ et Lodomeriæ. A Die 1. Mensis Januar. Anno 1775 Emanatorum.* Leopoli 1775; pp. 165–167.

parents that are the guardians are obligated to insure that these Children receive some [financial] support.

If the Jewish Child reaches the age of decision, able to recognize the difference between good and bad, and it demands baptism, then such child can join the Church without any difficulty through the Sacred baptism, regardless of permission by the parents. For everyone to know what is the age sufficient to make such a decision, the following is ordered the most graciously.

2) The mind begins to develop a good sense after seven years and the Jewish child of this age, who demands baptism on its own volition, can be baptized against the will of its parents and guardians. If the Jewish children desire to be baptized before reaching age of seven years, first, an investigation by the clergy and then by a secular authority should decide if they have a sufficiently enlightened mind to undertake this great act, and then they are initially given up to the Hospital or to the House of Widows, or taken in by religious Christians. And if subsequently educated in Christian teaching, they are brought to the Sacred Sacrament of baptism, their Jewish Parents, that is the Guardians, are liable according to their means to provide not only food to the Child, but also to insure its part of any inheritance.

3) By Our Grace, we wish to permit that if one of the Jewish parents, either the man or the woman, adopts the Catholic faith, the children can be baptized against the will of the spouse that remains in the Jewish faith; those Children that reach the age of the enlightened mind according to the above age have the right to decide whether they take the Christian Side or remain Jewish, and in the other instance the newly born ought to be baptized.

Lastly, we want to make it clear and widely known that a grandfather who accepts the Christian faith ought to have the freedom to decide on behalf of his underage grandsons, who do not yet have enlightened minds, to follow in his footsteps to baptism regardless of whether his son is dead or alive. And if, despite the clear announcement in Paragraph 1, Jewish children are baptized in the face of a mortal danger but later recover, by the Grace of the Monarch's Protection such act should remain legally valid, and the person who conducted the baptism is absolved from the penalty stipulated by the law for committing such act.

4) In the above law, it is most graciously contained and understood as far as the baptism of a Jewish newborn is concerned, that legal evidence that the Christian dared to perform baptism against the will of the parents and guardians (except for two circumstances noted in paragraph 1: a mortal danger or abandonment by the parents and guardians) or that a witness did not interfere with such conduct, makes [the Christian] liable for the prescribed punishment for this Act. They can only be absolved from it if

they submit testimony from a doctor, a surgeon, or a midwife, but in its absence, [the statement] from another reputable witness that the Jewish infant was in danger of imminent death is appropriate. If unable to present it, [the accused] is to provide support for the infant by paying a financial penalty of ten thousand ducats to the treasury; however, if such payment is not fulfilled based on the situation of the person and circumstances, a punishment of two years in prison is applied.

To implement Our highest decree, Our Imperial—Royal Governments will not only steadily intervene when the mentioned events occur, but in order to assure its strict application, the subordinate district offices will announce [the law] in the entire country, as well as separately notify the bishops of both rites [Latin and Greek-Catholic], so they will inform their subordinate lay and ordained clergy. In case of violations or obstructions, [they are to] immediately apply the penalty of one thousand ducats, or if this is not possible due to financial insolvency [of the violator], mete out exemplary punishments. As such, this is the fulfillment of Our most kind Will and Mind.

Proclaimed in Lemberg, Our Imperial—Royal Capital City, on 11th day November 1775.

L.S. [official seal]

Count HEINRICH des S. P. R. von AUERSPERG.

Joh. Mar. Riegler, Secretary.

PATENT*

Concerning the Introduction of the New Regulations Concerning Jews

We etc.

*O*FFER EACH AND EVERY ONE of our most loyally obedient vassals and subjects in our Kingdom of Galicia and Lodomeria, of whatever class, rank, or condition, our imperial and royal grace, also all good wishes, and make known herewith:

The tolerance of the Jews requires above all that they be brought into a non-damaging relationship with the Christian population [as a class]; but the more necessary the growing number of Jews makes the establishment of this relationship, the more it has been neglected in our countries up to now; and finally to the extent that we, in the course of reclaiming possession of our Hereditary Kingdom of Galicia and Lodomeria, have found the Jewish population in a state of extreme disarray, to the detriment of our general welfare as well as to their own ruin.

The basic cause of this poor condition is primarily to be attributed to the fact that the Jews have no [organizational] connection to each other, but rather each *Kahal* [Jewish community council] has been a separate body and independent of all other Jewish communities. The proliferation of these separate Jewish communities, whose fate is left in their own hands, has made it absolutely impossible to supervise them, to take responsibility for the necessary supervision over the way the congregational treasuries are managed, and especially, to bring forth the necessary funds to pay back the debts of the Jewish congregations, which have been growing larger and larger due to exactly this situation, and to deal efficiently with the disorders (and failures) which have become common.

Since Our motherly concern as ruler of our countries is always directed toward maintaining in the best possible prosperity, not only our Christian subjects—but also to allow all of those benefits which are compatible with the common good to flow to the Jewish population as well. So that, through this, the Jewish population should also be put in a position to contribute their part to the general welfare, we have therefore most graciously decided to issue the following Regulations for the Jewish population in our reclaimed

Continuatio Edictorum et Mandatorum Universalium in Regnis Galiciæ et Lodomeriæ. A Die 1. Januar. Ad Ultimam Decembr. Anno 1776 Emanatorum. Leopoli 1776; pp. 76–121.

Hereditary Kingdom of Galicia and Lodomeria, which they must follow themselves in future in the greatest detail in all of their common as well as private matters.

We decree and order upon this herewith that all of our upper and lower state officers, courts, state treasurers, noble landowners with local authority, and city magistrates, and all those who are otherwise concerned with the exact implementation of our highest orders, make this our salutary law known in an appropriate way and to, under threat of our severe displeasure and punishment, at all times oversee its implementation in the most dutiful way, for this is our earnest desire, command, and opinion.

Given in Our imperial and royal capital Lemberg, the 16th of July 1776.

(L.S.) [official seal]

Heinrich des H. K. K. Graf von Auersperg

Mathias Ertl, Secretary.

General Regulations for All of the Jewish Population of the Kingdoms of Galicia and Lodomeria

Part One.

Concerning the Administration and Supervision of the Galician Jewish Population in General.

Article One.
Concerning the Establishment and Composition of a Jewish Body.

§. I.

*A*BOVE ALL IT HAS BEEN taken to be the basis of the present Regulations for the Jews that the Jewish population should be gathered together into one general *corpus* [body], since solely by this means their supervision and instruction for the general welfare can be achieved.

§. II.

But this general body which is to be established is to be understood such that the entire Jewish population must be subject to the authority of one General Administration, which under the overall supervision of the *Landes-Gubernium* [governing body for the country] shall take care of all matters concerning the Jewish population in general, as well as in particular those [matters concerning] the Jewish community councils.

§. III.

But the Jewish community councils will not be dissolved by this body which is to be established, but only be brought into a structured relationship and be made subject to the General Administration.

§. IV.

However, the general supervision, also in respect to the separate Jewish communities, requires that those Jewish communities which are much too small and have become a burden to themselves through their administrative expenses which surpass many times over their capacity [to pay] should be reduced and combined into larger ones.

Article Two.

Concerning the Individuals Who Should Make Up the Jewish General Administration.

§. I.

*I*N ORDER, HOWEVER, THAT THE governing of this general body be made more practical, it has been decided to divide *Direction* [the Jewish General Administration] into two parts, namely, into one which [is in charge of] the introduction of the decrees which proceed from the governing body for the country [Galicia] and in general the ordering of all measures necessary to the maintenance of the Jewish communities, and then the other which is in charge of the function and the supervision of the Jewish communities in the government districts.

§. II.

The directing part shall consist of a *Landesrabiner* [chief rabbi for the country] and 6 *Landesältesten* [elders at national level], and the executive part also of 6 elders to be distributed among the government districts, therefore the whole General Administration [should consist of] one chief rabbi for the country and 12 elders at the national level.

Article Three.

Concerning the Election of This General Administration.

§. I.

*S*O THAT ON THE ONE hand Jewish communities are led to have more trust in the national leaders, and on the other hand, since the Jewish population must be best acquainted with the abilities of the leaders, it has been determined to be useful for these national leaders to be chosen by a free election, and to leave this election to the Jewish population of this country itself and in the following manner, so that according to the current division of this kingdom into 6 government districts, in each district 2 elders at national level, and separately in the residence city of the governing body [i.e., in Lemberg] a chief rabbi [for Galicia], shall be elected.

§. II.

But since it is considered advisable to determine the procedure for electing these different functionaries by an orderly gradation from lower to higher, it is first necessary to establish the modality by which the elders of the Jewish communities are elected, since they shall elect the elders at national level and the chief rabbi for the country shall be elected by the elders at national level together with several chosen representatives from each district.

§. III.

Although the method of electing the Jewish community or *Kahal* elders should be uniform for all of the Jewish communities, nevertheless the number of community elders must be determined by the financial strength of each Jewish community.

§. IV.

Now in order to avoid confusion in this case, it has been determined to be necessary to divide all of the Jewish communities into 4 classes, and before to set that as a prerequisite and to decree that following the reminder previously given in Art[icle] I., §. 4 concerning the reduction of the [number of] small Jewish communities, so in future no Jewish community can exist that has not had to pay at least 4000 *fl. pohl.* to the treasury according to the usual individual per capita tax.

§. V.

These 4 classes are the following: The first class includes all the Jewish communities which pay from 4000 to 8000 *fl. pohl.*,* the 2nd 8000 to 12000 *fl. pohl.*, the 3rd 12000 to 14000 *fl. pohl.*, the 4th 14000 *fl. pohl.*, and more.

§. VI.

The number of community elders and treasurers is also to be determined according to the differences between these 4 first named classes, and in the following manner: the communities belonging to the first class shall be entitled to elect not more than 6 elders, those belonging to the second [class] 8 elders, those belonging to the 3rd [class] 10 elders, those belonging to the 4th [class] 12 elders, and [to elect] the same number of treasurers.

§. VII.

The act of election itself must take place in each community according to the following Order.

a) The *Kahal* elections shall take place each time in the presence of an imperial and royal official [for the government district] as a commissioner.

b) Before the election is held, the [election] committee for the community must first be selected by the aforementioned imperial and royal commissioner, along with the official in charge of the treasury, in the following manner, that

---

*Currency: *fl.*=*Gulden, florin*, a gold coin. There were two kinds of *Gulden* in use there at the time: the *fl. pohl.* and the *fl. Rheinisch*, which in 1776 was worth about four times as much as the *fl. pohl.* according to the calculations for marriage contracts in Part Five, Article Eight.

c) For the Jewish communities belonging to the first class the [election] committee should consist only of those individuals in the community who contribute at least 80 *fl. pohl.* annually.

For the communities of the second class, of those community members who [contribute] at least 120 *fl. pohl.*

For those of the third class, of individuals who [contribute] at least 160 *fl. pohl.*

For the fourth class, of Jewish community members who pay at least 200 *fl. pohl.* into the treasury of the Jewish community.

In determining the [members of] this [election] committee, the central assessment book for [required] contributions to Jewish communities is to be taken as a basis, since each individual's [required] contribution payment can be found there.

d) The names of those individual community members who are chosen [to be members of] the [election] committee shall be written on separate pieces of paper; and inserted into the same number of balls, as was already introduced in the Lemberg Jewish community, and all of these balls placed in a sack so that out of [this sack] the electors, or the so-called electors can be drawn by lot.

e) Then out of these sacks, the commissioner present at the election shall draw out balls, for communities belonging to the first two classes 4, for those in the last 2 classes 6 individuals, who should not be blood relatives in the first 3 degrees or relatives by marriage in the first 2 degrees, and the individuals drawn in this way must carry out the election by unanimous vote.

f) These electors who have been chosen by the first-mentioned of these required procedures are to be separated immediately from the rest of the members of the Jewish community, in order to prevent any secret agreements and dependency, and must then

g) Swear by a physical oath that they are honest, upright, and financially well-off, of whom none are related among themselves in the first 3 degrees of blood relationship or the first 2 degrees of relationship by marriage, and that they will elect the number of elders for the community prescribed above and the same number of treasurers, with the same exclusions of relatives by blood and by marriage. Then

h) The electors and the commissioner must then go into a separate room and there conduct the election of the prescribed number of elders and treasurers within the amount of time determined by the commissioner; but in this process

i) It is specifically determined that the electors may not elect one of their own number; in consequence, because of their capacity as electors, they shall remain excluded from [election to] the position of elder each time one or another of them is an elector for a future election. The same is understood

k) With respect to treasurers who are to be elected, whereby the electors may neither elect one of themselves nor such subjects who have the degrees of blood relationship or of relationship by marriage mentioned above either among themselves or with the previously elected elders. On the other hand the electors can

l) Also elect a Jew who is not a member of the [election] committee to be an elder or treasurer if he possesses the aforementioned characteristics for the position of elder or treasurer. However

m) Any individual who leases income-producing property belonging to the Jewish community or is in partnership with such leaseholders, or has a company doing business under their own ownership shall be excluded from the offices of elder or treasurer; in the same manner

n) Anyone who in the past year has refused to pay the required contributions to the government of the land or to the Jewish community, or who is without financial means, shall be excluded from the position of elector and from all public offices.

o) The elders who have been elected by this process and in a legal way are to be sworn in immediately in the synagogue.

p) The elected community elders and the treasurers will stay in office for 3 years, although only on the condition that at the annual election review the community does not bring up anything against them that can be proven.

q) Of the elected elders and treasurers each month a different one has the chairmanship and directs the business of the community, or is a so-called "monthly [office] holder."

r) The lower offices, including that of treasurer for the Jews, are to be filled by the elders and each time this should be reported to the imperial and royal government office for the district.

§. VIII.

Following the order for elections decreed in this manner for the [election of the] community elders, the gradation according to Art. 3 §. 2 leads to the establishment of the order for the election of the elders at national level, which, according to §. I. of this article is to take place in the government districts, and in the same way as for the elections for community elders an [election] committee will be chosen, from this the electors will be taken, and by the latter then the elders at the national level shall be elected.

§. IX.

The [election] committee in each government district shall consist of those community elders in each Jewish community to be sent as representatives to the main city of the district, the number of which is determined by the relative numbers as set out in the classification of the Jewish communities above, so that from the communities of the first class 2; from those of the second class 3; from those of the third class 4; from those of the fourth class 5 community elders, shall be sent to the election of the elders at national level of their districts as representatives of their local communities.

§. X.

Each of these community representatives or individual members of the [election] committee gathered in this manner in the main city of the district in the presence of the head [officer] of the district shall vote for 3 subjects from this [election] committee, write their names on a piece of paper, and hand it sealed to the head [officer] of the district, who, after all of these papers have been opened and the votes tallied, shall name the 6 individuals for which the majority of votes were cast as electors, keeping in mind the exclusions of blood relatives and relatives by marriage in the degrees or relationship which were set out previously in the case of the *Kahal* [Jewish community] elections.

§. XI.

These electors, who were selected in the prescribed manner, confirm with an oath sworn in person in the synagogue in the presence of the head [officer] of the district that they will elect unanimously 6 wealthy, wise men, who have a reputation as leading good lives, and who are not related to them or to each other in the forbidden degrees of blood relationship or relationship by marriage, and also not related to the current chief rabbi for the country in the first or second degree of blood relationship or in the first degree of relationship by marriage, of whom each one has served at least once as an elder in a community to the satisfaction of his community, whose names, after this election is completed, will be sent by the government office for the district to the governing body for the country [Galicia] and from these 2 individuals will be appointed as elders at the national level by the aforementioned national government office.

§. XII.

These two elders at national level who were appointed by the governing body for the country [Galicia] must immediately take the usual oath of office in the synagogue in the presence of the head [officer] of the district after which their appointment will be announced appropriately in all Jewish communities and schools of the respective government district.

§. XIII.

Finally, the election of the *Ober-Landsrabiner* [chief rabbi for the country], which, as mentioned in §. [II] of this article, must be carried out by the elders at national level, together with several representatives of each government district.

§. XIV.

If at a later time the office of chief rabbi should become vacant, first of all this vacancy should be immediately reported in all districts, and a date chosen for an election for the next chief rabbi, on which [date] the Jewish [chosen] representatives of every district shall come in the appropriate manner to the capital city Lemberg [Lwów] and with the elders at national level who are there, in the presence of the imperial and royal commissioners who have been appointed by the national government office, must carry out said election in an orderly fashion.

§. XV.

The Jewish [chosen] representatives from each district who must concur with the election of the chief rabbi are to be selected in the following way:

a) Each Jewish community shall send 2 elders of the community to the main city of the district, who then, on a day designated by the government office, shall come there in an appropriate manner and meet there.

b) They must, in the presence of the head [officer] of the district, each separately choose 4 men, namely: 2 rabbis or learned lawyers, and 2 wealthy Jews of good reputation, whose names they shall write on a separate piece of paper and give, sealed, to the head [officer] of the district:

c) After the opening of these papers and the tallying of the votes, the head [officer] of the district will name 6 representatives for the district: on the one hand the 3 rabbis or learned lawyers for which there were a majority of votes; on the other hand in the same way the 3 men who have the most votes.

d) On the election day set by the governing body for the country [Galicia] these [chosen] representatives from the district must then go to the residence city of the governing body [Lemberg] and present themselves to the elders at national level residing there to prove that they are legitimately sent, and then the elders at national level, when all of the representatives from the districts have arrived, will report this appropriately to the governing body for the country.

e) On the day of the election itself the 12 elders at national level shall meet with the 6 representatives who have arrived from each district; 48 in all, in the synagogue, where they must, in the presence of two members of the imperial and royal governing body who will be appointed by the high government office for the country, take an oath that they will elect, as candidates for the office of chief rabbi for the country, 3 of the most learned, most humble men, who have a reputation for good behavior in their personal lives, selfless-ness, and having thorough knowledge both of their Jewish religious regulations and their internal constitution, and also are not blood relatives in the first two degrees nor relatives by marriage in the first degree of the current 12 elders at national level.

f) After the oath has been taken, the election itself should take place in the following way, that each of the 48 electors shall write 3 names on a separate piece of paper with his signature and all of these papers shall be sealed and given over to the imperial and royal commissioners who are present, after these sealed papers are opened the 3 subjects who have received the majority of votes will be named in a report by the commissioners to the *Landes-Gubernio* [governing body of the country], from whom a further report on the selection of the chief rabbi for the country, which is to be most graciously made, will be sent to the very highest level [to make a selection].

g) When the report of the will of the most high [official] has been received, then the most graciously appointed chief rabbi for the country will be given the appropriate oath of office in the presence of two *Gubernial-Commissarien* [commissioners from the govern-ing body for the country] and will be presented to the elders at national level present and his appointment will be announced by the government offices in the districts in all of the Jewish communities.

Article Four.

Concerning the Internal Composition and the Reciprocal Relationships of This General Administration

§. I.

In Art[icle]2 §. 2 above it has been established that the directing part should consist of a chief rabbi for the country and 6 elders at national level; and the executing part in the same way, 6 elders who are to be distributed among the government districts. According to the nature of its work the *Direction* [General Administration] must remain in the city of residence of the governing body [i.e., in Lemberg], where the business of the whole country is concentrated, and on the other hand the implementation must take place in the government districts. In consequence of this, the chief rabbi for the country as well as the 6 directing elders at national level must stay in the *Residenzstadt*, and the 6 elders at district level must stay in the cities where the government offices for the district are located during the whole duration of their period of office.

§. II.

The chief rabbi for the country shall carry out his office for the rest of his life, unless it should be that he had become unfit to serve in this office due to his incompetence or the commission of a crime.

§. III.

On the other hand, the 6 elders at national level living in Lemberg [Lwów] must alternate every 3 years with the rest of the elders distributed among the government districts in the following way. The first, at the end of a 3 year period of service, must resign completely, and the latter, who have also served for 3 years in the district, will move up to fill the positions of the 6 elders at national level who have resigned from the General Administration, and immediately the positions of the elders at district level which have become vacant in this way must be replaced with new individuals by the prescribed election [process].

§. IV.

From the above, the obvious conclusion is: although in Art. 3. §. 10. it was established that in the election, to be held in each government district for the elders at national level, 6 candidates will be presented by the electors, this number of candidates can only be presented if the current elder at national level for the district has been found to be negligent or dishonest in his service in this office, thereby making himself unfit to move up into the General Administration. Also, in the case of 2 elders at national level, 6 candidates must be elected for these two positions. On the other hand, when these conditions do not exist, only 3 candidates are to be elected [in the process of] filling the vacant position of elder at district level.

§. V.

Now as reported already in §. I of this Article, the establishment of good order dictates: the chief rabbi for the country, with the elders at national level who carry out the General Administration, shall have their continuous place of residence in the city of the governing body [in Lemberg]. The elders at national level for the districts, [shall live] in their respective main cities of the district; but on the other hand sometimes cases might arise when the chief rabbi for the country or a elder at national level for a district must be away from the place of his official duties for some time, either on business concerning all of the Jewish population of the country or on private business. Also, in the case of illness, he might be unable to carry out his office; [so] it will be necessary to provide the chief rabbi for the country, as well as each of the elders at national level for the districts, with a substitute who has taken the oath of office, because each of these 7 individuals must carry out business specific to his individual office, which would have to come to a standstill in the case of absence, illness, or even death. This observation does not apply, however, to the 6 elders at national level who live in the city of residence [of the governing body of Galicia] because if one or even two of them should be missing, the rest of them can easily fill in for them.

§. VI.

None of the 12 elders at national level nor the chief rabbi for the country may absent themselves from the place of their official duties without beforehand having appropriately requested and received permission to do so from the national government office here [in Lemberg]; neither shall the aforementioned chief rabbi for the country or the 6 elders at national level for the districts, as long as they are present at the place of their official duties, be allowed to entrust the business of their office to their substitutes, unless they have appropriately reported the special reasons in advance and received permission for this.

§. VII.

Neither by the chief rabbi for the country nor by the 6 elders at national level for the districts can these substitutes be appointed at will, but rather within 3 months of their appointment, each of these persons holding office shall suggest to the national government office for this purpose the names of 3 individuals [who are] well known to them, wise, and having the reputation of leading a good life; [the national government office] shall then choose among them and appoint each substitute separately.

§. VIII.

Concerning the responsibilities of the chief rabbi for the country as well as the 12 elders at national level, and this entire Administration in general, the chief rabbi for the country shall:

a) Exercise the highest level supervision over all community rabbis, synagogues, and schools, and in general over all matters which concern the Jewish religion and *Sitten* [traditional practices].

b) Arbitrate and decide on all Jewish legal disputes currently in process which are brought to him by the community rabbis, according to the regulations which follow in Part Five.

c) Together with the 6 elders at national level present in Lemberg, take care of all matters concerning the Jewish population in this country.

§. IX.

The 6 elders at national level carrying out the work of the General Administration must take the decrees which they receive from the imperial and royal governing body and make these known appropriately to the 6 elders at national level for the districts, and depending on the nature of the matters either to be announced or to be obeyed, keep a strong hand on such matters and under the chairmanship of the chief rabbi for the country, direct all matters which concern the Jewish population of this country, also in more important cases make their most dutiful reports to the national government office.

§. X.

The elders at national level for the districts shall accept most obediently all orders they receive from the Jewish General Administration in Lemberg [Lwów], and without delay have them followed exactly in their respective government districts, and report back to the General Administration placed over them, the necessary information concerning all important occurrences which take place in the district entrusted to their care.

§. XI.

In order for both the Jewish General Administration located in Lemberg [Lwów] and the elders at national level for the districts, who must be in a position to fulfill the duties of the offices entrusted to them in a timely manner and to an appropriate degree, and in order to take care of the exchange of official correspondence, their accounts, minutes of meetings, reports, and so on, under threat of most severe punishment must at all times be written in the German language. Further, for the written work, both in the Jewish [Hebrew] and German languages, for the aforementioned Jewish General Administration, a Christian accountant and scribe, and a Jewish treasurer; as well as two Jewish scribes, and for each of the elders at national level for the districts one Jewish and one Christian scribe, have been approved.

§. XII.

From which it becomes clear that all matters pertaining to the Jewish population of this country, and especially the implementation of these Regulations Concerning the Jews, and then all orders issuing from the government office, both in direction and in execution, shall be under the supervision of this general body.

Part Two.

Concerning the Policy of the Galician Jewish Population with Regards to Their Internal Religious and Traditional Practices, as far as These are Connected with the General National Policy.

Article One.

Concerning the Instruction of the Youth.

1) IT IS ESTABLISHED that each *Kahal* [Jewish community] must be provided with one rabbi and 3 public schools, including the teachers necessary for this.

2) The chief rabbi [for the country] shall in future have supervision of the schools, as well as the teachers and the progress of the youth.

3) According to the usual practice in this country, the schools will be divided into 3 classes, namely:

   a) The first school, where the children are instructed in reading and writing, and the first foundations of the religion, and in the Bible.

   b) The second in which the Talmud, or the so-called interpretation of the Bible, will be read aloud.

   c) In the third or higher school, where the law and the civil and religious principles of the Jews are presented, which latter school actually is intended for the education of rabbis, lawyers, and scribes or authorities on the scriptures; however, it is open to anyone to attend, since in it, in addition to civil laws and religious principles, that which each person should follow in living his own private life is discussed.

4) Each of these schools must be provided with a public teacher, whom the rabbi must hire, in consultation with the *Schriftgelehrten* [authorities on the scriptures] of the town, and following a detailed examination.

5) These public schools are actually intended for the instruction of poor youth; however, anyone, even though having more means, may send his children to have them instructed in these schools.

6) However, anyone who intends not to send his child to these public schools but to give them private instruction must show appropriately to the rabbi in what manner he has provided for the instruction of his child, and the rabbi will be allowed to call such a child for examination at any time, and just as:

7) No one can serve as a private teacher who has not been first examined by the Rabbi and the authority on the scriptures and given a written statement showing that he is qualified for this.

8) Also, the false practice which has existed in this country up to now (whereby no public schools were held among the Jews and any scholar could allow himself to be used as a teacher, according to the will of the parents, without the rabbi or the community being given any particular supervision in the case) is herewith completely ended.

9) Since here in our country, especially in larger cities, the praiseworthy practice exists that, for the instruction of indigent children, special guilds or brotherhoods are established, made up of wealthier individuals in the community, who go together and in the form of voluntary alms, make an annual contribution, which is used to pay for the instruction of the poor children. This very good practice is herewith confirmed with the additional stipulation that these contributions be directed to a fund, from which in future the [cost of the] schools and the public teachers will be paid; that this sum of money in future no longer shall remain in the hands of the collectors and brotherhood chairmen to be used freely at their discretion, but each time a collection takes place the alms boxes shall be opened in the presence of the community treasurer, his auditor, and one or two sworn witnesses, the money counted, and given to the community treasury in exchange for a receipt. But in order to encourage public confidence and the generous contributions of the wealthier Jewish community members even more, the expenses of the school, namely the repairs, *Beleichtung* [lighting], and in general the upkeep of the same, as well as the payment of the salaries of the teachers, shall be left up to the aforementioned brotherhood chairmen or school fathers alone. But they, however, as mentioned before, will not have discretion over the sums of money collected, but rather must turn these in to the community treasury in the prescribed manner, then according to need take money from the aforementioned community treasury and report the expenditures there.

10) No objection will be made if foreign students also request to be accepted in the public schools in this country, but this will only be approved if they are supported by their wealthy parents at their own expense and receive instruction in the same manner.

11) The community rabbis and community elders must keep a careful watch so that parents and guardians send their children and orphans to school promptly, as soon as they are able to be instructed, and to require that they attend school regularly at least into their 13th year, and when this age is reached then each father and guardian will be allowed to direct his child either to further studies, or to business, or to make it possible for him to learn a trade.

12) Each week on a certain day the teachers must examine the children on the things they have learned during the week; in the same way, the rabbis themselves are not to forget to set aside time on certain days in the year on which the children, in the presence of the parents, are publicly examined either by them, the rabbis, or by learned men but in their presence.

13) Those communities which are not provided with their own rabbi shall be required to employ their own schoolmaster, who has been certified and examined by the rabbi of the Jewish community and who must instruct the children in reading, writing, and the Law of Moses. On the other hand, in the villages where there is only one or another *Bestandsjude* or *Arendator* [holder of a type of lease] living, these Jews, if they do not want to or are not able to keep their own teacher for their children, must send their children to the school in the next community to which they belong. And since:

14) The highest level supervision over all Jewish schools in this country lies with the chief rabbi for the country, it is understood that, considering this responsibility, in case any dysfunction should arise he either should go in person to the place where a disorder in the studies and the manner of teaching has appeared to investigate and alleviate the dysfunction, or by sending a capable substitute there, achieve a remedy in this case. Whereby, in addition:

15) The practice up to now (whereby each rabbi in his city twice a year, namely after Easter and after the Sukkoth dictates that a disputation be held, called in Hebrew *Chiluk*, that is, certain controversial verses drawn from the Talmud, upon which the authorities on scripture from the town prepare [to debate]; and then on a day to be determined in advance by the rabbi, meet together and dispute with him *pro* and *contra* is to be encouraged even more, since this practice on the one hand allows the rabbi to attain a greater reputation because of his erudition; and on the other hand the authorities on scripture of the town may become better known, in order to aid their rise on a national level.

Article Two.

Concerning the Election of Community Rabbis, their Duties, Compensation, Legal Jurisdiction, and Responsibilities.

1) E A C H A N D E V E R Y *Kahal* shall freely retain the right to elect a rabbi for themselves, according to the old tradition as it is written in the book for community, by the [election] committee of the community and by community members, who must attend a large general meeting of the community, according to the prescribed election modalities. And so that:

2) Functioning offices such as these are always filled by god-fearing and wise subjects, the right the community has had up to now to act in this regard is herewith specifically limited in the manner that vacant positions for rabbis shall be filled only [by choosing] from subjects who have previously been examined by the chief rabbi for the country concerning their learnedness and have been provided with convincing recommendations on this both from the chief rabbi for the country and, concerning their good moral behavior, from the congregational elders of their place of residence.

3) However, should someone who is currently substituting in the office of rabbi in one community or another, (or has already substituted there without having been moved there) he will also be sufficiently qualified without first having submitted to a new examination by the chief rabbi for the country.

4) If, however, the chief rabbi [for Galicia] is unable to carry out such examinations due to the mass of work entailed in his official duties, or should the place of residence of the newly elected rabbi be located too far from the location of the chief rabbi and he is not able to make the trip there due to poverty, the latter will, in the first instance, have the right; in the second [instance] however, after submission of a request by the rabbi candidate, should economy require it, the chief rabbi [for Galicia] may substitute for himself another rabbi located nearby, who, in the presence of at least two learned men of his town, after receiving the assignment, shall immediately undertake the examination and upon determining his capability shall be responsible for giving to the examined candidate the appropriate statement of qualification and also for reporting upon this to the chief rabbi [for Galicia].

5) However, this examination, either by the chief rabbi or by the rabbi who substitutes for him *pro hoc actu* [for this act], will be held without charge; in the same way the statement of qualification in this case will be prepared free of charge for the examined candidate who was found to be competent.

6) If a community [wishes] to make a complaint against their rabbi either because of his incompetence or because of [incorrect] service in his office, or immorality in leading his life, and wish to have him removed [from their community], a complaint of this kind should be brought directly to the chief rabbi [for Galicia], who will immediately call together, at the expense of the party who loses the case, a commission of several neighboring rabbis and learned men; they will then go to the place and well and thoroughly investigate the complaints which have been brought against the rabbi there, record the results of this process in writing, and then send this along with their recommendation in the matter to the chief rabbi [for Galicia] for further study and a decision to be undertaken by him. And although:

7) The chief rabbi [for Galicia] has dealt with this case according to Jewish law and traditions and punished any local rabbi found to be guilty with an appropriate punishment, it is understood that in a case where the local rabbi who was found guilty is also found to have transgressed against the policy of the country and the generally published decrees, such a judgment by the chief rabbi cannot stand in the way of his being sentenced to punishment by the respective official department depending on the degree of transgression against the laws of the land.

8) The prerogatives and titles of honor used by the rabbis in this country, according to which they are held in respect by all the members of the community; their official decrees which must be obeyed; and [the practice that] in the synagogue their names are called out first at the reading of the Torah are herewith further confirmed.

On the other hand, concerning the exemption from all required contributions to the community generally allowed them in this country: this, too, can remain in place if they are satisfied to cover their living expenses solely from the salary they receive and other payments for services as a rabbi. However, should one or another rabbi have business dealings not in his own person (which is against the Jewish tradition) but run a business through his wife and children or through especially appointed persons, or in this case be part of a company with other Jews allowed to do business, in this case because of his role as a businessman, he should, the same as other businesspeople, be charged the usual [required] contributions for the business and for the additional income.

9) The salaries received by the rabbis here in this country, as they are determined by the *Vocationsbrief* [letter of call] and [if applicable] the agreement made between the community and the rabbi, and the other emoluments, which consist of certain fees and perquisites which are fixed once and for all for each community and recorded in an orderly manner in their community books, are herewith also confirmed according to the old tradition, but with the stipulation that the *K.K. Landesgubernio* [imperial and royal governing body for the country] may, in cases where one or another community should complain because of the overly high level of the rabbi's fees and perquisites, after examining the situation, undertake a price reduction for the same.

10) Each newly-elected rabbi will be required to submit to the *Landesstelle* [national government office] a request for his confirmation, and for this purpose present appropriately the letter of call issued by the community, as well as the aforementioned statements of qualification, and to wait to receive from national government office the confirmation for [a period of] 3 years; however it is understood that [the newly elected rabbi] is in no way authorized to take up his office before confirmation has been received and, in connection with this, payment of the fees set for this matter. If, however:

11) A community rabbi wishes to resign from the office of rabbi before the end of his period of call, due to expectation of a better position elsewhere, this will be allowed without objection if he has submitted a request in the matter to the national government office and first made appropriate [financial] arrangements with his community; however, in such a case no partial refund will be allowed for the confirmation fee paid for the whole period of the call.

12) The duties of office and responsibilities of a local rabbi concern everything related to religion and justice. The word justice, however, does not include damages or injuries, business dealings, quarrels, and in general simple police matters, which are reserved for the decision of the community elders.

13) Good order and the ranking previously established, whereby the community rabbis in future without exception are subordinate to the chief rabbi [for Galicia], require that with regard to all matters which are part of the business of their office, they must most dutifully accept the decrees sent them by the chief rabbi, follow them, and recognize them in cases where they have supervisory authority; for which reason the independence of the rabbis in this country up to now and the titles carried by some of them of *Landes-*, *Groß-*, or *Oberrabiner* [national, great, or chief rabbi] as well as the jurisdiction some have had over so-called minor rabbis, will be ended completely.

Article Three.

Concerning the Jewish Titles of Honor.

1) THERE ARE TWO kinds of titles of honor which are awarded, some by the community rabbis, but some by the chief rabbi [for Galicia]; they are: *Reb-Rain* or *Chaber*, and *Reb-Reb* or *Morain*.

Since according to the practice up to now, the community rabbis were given the right to award the title of a simple *Rebs* or *Chaber*, this authority is also confirmed for the future so that they, the community rabbis, can award the title of a simple *Rebs* to those Jews requesting this solely due to their learnedness, in exchange for a fee, which is set herewith, of 2 *Gulden Rheinisch*; to wealthy Jews, however, those who request the title of *Rebs*, aside from learnedness, because of other achievements or intentions, [are subject to] a set fee of 1 *Dukat*. On the other hand:

2) The right to award the second title, of a *Reb-Reb* or *Morain*, remains a private right reserved for the chief rabbi [for Galicia] and herewith the fee is set for a learned man at 1 *Dukat*; for those, on the other hand, who request this for other achievements or intentions, in addition to the fee of 1 *Dukat*, a special fee is set herewith, based on their annual

contributions to the community treasury, namely for each 100 *fl. pohln.* paid, 1 *Dukat* to be paid to the chief rabbi [for Galicia] as a fee for the title.

3) Since according to the existing practice up to now, no Jew can receive the position of a lawyer or associate on the court without first having been given the title of honor of *Reb* or *Chaber*, and *Reb-Reb* or *Morain*, in a case where aspirants who are of an upright way of life and, in addition to their learnedness, have an excellent reputation, but lack the financial means so are unable to pay the set fee for a *Reb-Reb*, their respective Jewish communities are given authority and permission to pay the aforementioned fees from the funds in the community treasury. Which then:

4) In itself leads to the conclusion that the practice of these titles being awarded by the community elders will be completely ended.

5) Considering the age to receive titles of honor of this kind, and in order to prevent all misunderstandings, it is herewith decreed that the title of a *Reb* cannot be received until after the second year of marriage (since an unmarried man is not qualified for such titles nor in general to serve in any office).

Article Four.
Concerning the Jewish Synagogues, Worship Services, and Prayers in General.

1) ALTHOUGH IN ACCORDANCE with the law previously established, the smaller Jewish communities will be closed and with this, in the places where no community exists any more, the rabbis will also be removed, the Jewish population will still be allowed to hold their prayers in the synagogues which already exist, and in addition to this all to hold Jewish ceremonies such as circumcisions, weddings, blessings, and in general all usual religious practices in [the synagogue]. However, in future they are strictly forbidden to choose a private house as a meeting place for prayer, and to use the Torah and in general to hold weddings, blessings, and religious practices of whatever name, anywhere else but in the synagogues of the town or the Jewish community to which they belong; exact compliance with this the community rabbis must supervise most closely on their own responsibility.

2) So that prayer in their houses of prayer may take place with order and dignity, those communities which in the future will not be provided with a rabbi shall be required to keep a cantor at the expense of the community; [he] will also instruct the youth and with that also act as schoolmaster. However, at all times this cantor must be hired with the previous knowledge and approval of the community rabbi, and in each and every way

he must share with the community rabbi what is owed to him, and follow the rules sent by him exactly; the community rabbi is also required to keep a close eye on his service in office according to his duties.

3) No Jewish community shall, under threat of the most serious punishment, undertake to replace the roof of their synagogue, school, or house of prayer, to repair [the synagogue], to expand it, or even to build it again from the ground up, without first having received permission for this from the national government office.

4) The praiseworthy practice in the other imperial and royal kingdoms and hereditary lands, whereby in the synagogues at the reading from the Torah the cantor announces with a raised voice which can be heard well by all those present, a public prayer for the wellbeing of Their Majesties, after which the entire Jewish community of both sexes calls out Amen, is also herewith legally ordered to be followed here in this country in all places.

Article Five.

Concerning the Employment of a Kosher Butcher, Cantor, and *Gemeingeschwornen* or *Beglaubigten* [notaries].

1) CONCERNING THE HIRING of a *Schächer* [kosher butcher], it is the wish to allow the practice to continue as usual currently in each town; however in every town he should be examined by the rabbi and provided with a statement concerning his competence.

2) It is understood that whether the rabbi alone or the rabbi together with the elders hire the kosher butcher according to the existing practice in the town, in employing him the primary concern should be with his good behavior and learnedness.

Should it happen that the rabbi or the elders in the course of the examination or in the employment of such a subject have allowed themselves to be influenced by money, gifts, promises, or in whatever way and under whatever pretenses, such a rabbi or such elder, and even an individual member of the community who has had a part in this, shall after careful investigation of the matter be immediately removed from his office and declared unfit for his lifetime for any Jewish offices, and this will be published in the whole country by the chief rabbi for the country and the *Ober-Landes-Collegium* [the 6 Jewish elders at national level] in Lemberg [Lwów], and one who has given a bribe shall also receive this punishment.

3) This punishment is herewith extended to include all cases of bribery which take place in the awarding of any Jewish offices, whatever names they may have.

4) The kosher butcher, according to the practice here in this country, as the holder of an office which is solely connected with the religion, is dependent solely on the rabbi, by whom he must be examined according to the Jewish law several times a year.

5) As far as the payment for the kosher butcher is concerned, it shall be left as is according to the current practice in each town, until in one or another town, in the case of a difficulty, it becomes necessary to make a change.

6) In the same manner, concerning the cantor and notaries, their salaries shall stay as they are regulated in the community books in each *Kahal* [Jewish community], with the stipulation as above.

Article Six.

Concerning Jewish Engagements and Marriages.

1) IT SHALL NOT be allowed, under threat of the prescribed penalties listed below, for any Jew to marry before he has reliably proven the true amount of his financial assets, according to the previously approved regulations (or assessment table), received permission from the imperial and royal governing body [for Galicia], and properly paid the appropriate fee.

2) Foreign Jews, however, who intend to marry in this country and to establish themselves here must, prior to [taking] their residence here, submit a request to the national government office, showing in a convincing and provable way the financial assets they own.

3) If Jews in this country, who from a lack of their own financial assets or a profession [or trade], dedicate their themselves to service [in an official position in] the community, and are recognized by their respective communities as competent for this both in their ability and in their behavior, should in the future apply for *Heiratsconsens* [permission to marry], this permission can be given to them without objection if their congregation applies to the national government office on their behalf; however, the marriage fee is not to be reduced, but rather the payment due for this, in the case that the applicant should be unable to pay, should be paid by the community itself.

4) In order to avoid costs for meals and travel, it is herewith determined that in future it will not be necessary to apply to the national government office in person, but rather marriage candidates will submit their written requests addressed to the national government office to the *Kreislandesältesten* [elders at national level for the district], who then every two weeks will send these collected marriage permission requests, together with their added signatures, to the district office, which must see to it that this is forwarded to the aforementioned national government office.

5) In this matter it is most important that the marriage candidates prove, by means of a sufficient deposit provided by the whole community, that in at least the first 3 years [the marriage candidates] will be able to pay properly both the contributions [or taxes] owed by the marriage candidates to the prince of the country and to the community, according to the contribution rate of the town.

6) The punishment of expulsion from the country for Jews who marry without consent, and the synagogue leaders who take part, which has already been introduced in this country by imperial manifesto shall remain unchanged in the future, and strict enforcement is to be practiced against the transgressors. Concerning the other Jewish accomplices, from case to case the severity of the punishment will remain up to the judgment of the aforementioned court.

7) Against those magistrates and local rulers participating in such a transgression a strictly enforced monetary fine of 100 *Dukaten* is herewith decreed.

Article Seven.

Concerning the Immigration of Foreign and the Emigration of Native Jews.

1) SINCE IN THIS country the entire Jewish population is in no way under the legal authority accorded to landowning nobles, but rather are solely subject to the *landesfürstliche Obristen-Herrschaft* [highest level authority of the ruling prince of the country], and from him alone must enjoy the highest level of protection, it is understood that:

2) If a Jew intends to emigrate out of the country, he must first settle his debts properly with his community leadership and with all of his creditors, and provide himself with credible statements showing that he has paid all of his outstanding obligations and passive debts; and have a statement prepared by his community showing all the assets he owns, consisting of cash as well as wares and other equipment, and then enclose all of these statements together with his letter of request addressed to the national government office, which is to be handed in to the government office of the district. The latter will, after first consulting with the elder at national level for the district, forward this request to the national government office along with a recommendation on the matter, and will await a decision concerning whether this emigration request should be approved, and if it is approved, for how many years' payments the applicant will be required to leave money for both the contributions due to the princely ruler of the land and the [required] contributions to the community.

3) If, however, a Jew wishes to move from one community to another within this country, in this case he will be required to report in the appropriate manner to his elder at the district level, and to present convincing proofs both that he has settled all of his outstanding obligations and passive debts and that the community which he wishes to join has no objection to his residing there, after which then the elder at the district level shall give him permission [to move] providing that he leave behind in his Jewish community both the contribution due to the princely ruler of the land and the contribution to the community which are required of him. And the elder at the district level shall report this to the Jewish administrative body above him.

4) As a rule, foreign Jews are not to be allowed to settle in this country; the exception to this is if a foreign Jew who wishes to settle in this country should own considerable assets, of at least 5000 *fl. Rheinisch*, and was in a position to prove this, upon which the national government office would decide from case to case and after coming to a decision give their consent in the matter in exchange for payment of the fee for a foreign resident of 10 percent of the assets he owns.

5) Any Jew who is emigrating must, before he moves away, take the emigration consent document received from the national government office and the receipt for payment of the emigration fee both to the government office of the district and to the community he is leaving in order to prove that he has permission, and the latter shall immediately notify the elder at national level for the district responsible for them. Should one or another Jew wish to leave without having first fulfilled these prescribed conditions, or already have secretly moved away, the leaders of the community must, under penalty of the most severe monetary fine and physical punishment if they do not do so, report this immediately both to the elder at the district level responsible for them as well as to the district governmental office itself, who shall then have the responsibility of recommending further action in the matter.

6) So that the country, in accordance with the intention of the most high [the Empress], may be cleansed of the swarm of *Betteljuden* [poor Jews, literally: "begging Jews"], the leaders of each community, under threat of severe physical punishment, must take the greatest care that wandering foreign, lazy, and begging Jews, and in general the disorderly rabble, is not allowed to stay anywhere, but rather that any such foreign poor Jews who let themselves be seen are to be immediately held, and turned over to the appropriate [larger] government district or government office of a [smaller] government district for further action. In accordance with this, it is:

7) decreed as a law in order to achieve this intention, that all Jews who are not able to pay in cash a total of 4 *fl. Rheinisch* in contributions for the *Toleranz* [tolerance

contribution] and the levied personal property tax, and for the [required] contribution to the community, shall immediately be considered to be *Betteljuden* [poor Jews], and shall not be tolerated in the country. In addition, all Jewish community leaders are most strictly required, under threat of punishment by monetary fines and physical punishment, must, each time after the assessment of each person is made by the assessors in regards to the individual payments to be made as [a required] contribution to the community, make an orderly list of those individual community members who are assessed under 4 *fl. Rheinisch* for the whole year; as well as, every quarter of a year, make an exact list of those community members who are unable to contribute 1 *fl. Rheinisch* each quarter for all contributions together, and to send these lists without delay to the elder at national level for the district. He shall, under threat of the most severe punishment, bring to the government office for the district all of the lists sent to him by the communities for which he is responsible. The latter must, according to the regulations prescribed for every government office for each district, see to it that such *Betteljuden* [poor Jews] who are reported to him are taken out of the country.

Article Eight.

Concerning the Care of both Native and Foreign Poor and Sick Jews.

1) ALTHOUGH IT IS mentioned above and established that on the one hand tramps and vagabonds, namely those who have no fixed abode and source of nourishment, and on the other hand those Jewish community members who are not able to contribute 4 *fl. Rheinisch* in cash for both the contributions to the princely ruler and to the community, shall immediately be considered to be *Betteljuden* [poor Jews] and be removed from the country, human charity requires that individual community members be excluded from this class who either, due to their age or physical frailty, are not able to secure the necessary support for their lives and are, through no fault of their own, in a condition of poverty and hunger. Indigent and weak Jews can, with good reason, hope for the help and mercy of their brethren.

2) Abandoned minor orphan children deserve the same consideration, and also widows in poor circumstances left behind by office holders serving in the community or those Jews who have served the welfare of the community or previously made considerable contributions to the same community.

3) For all of these types of needy Jews listed here and not belonging to the class of *Betteljuden* [poor Jews] or wandering rabble, necessary help is usually provided by their respective communities in a twofold way, namely either through insurance for certain

persons from the community treasury or by distribution of alms from the poor fund, which praiseworthy practice should remain in place in the future.

4) The pensions should be determined in the Jewish community meetings and so-called large general meetings of the community, and cannot be paid out to the parties without specific instructions having been given by the elders to the community treasury. Accordingly, the pensions are to be treated in the same way as all other expenditures and accounts.

5) Concerning the cash collections for, and administration of, the poor fund, various abuses have occurred, which in future must be prevented by a special regulation.

6) The funds which exist for feeding of the poor and healing of sick Jews in the communities in this country are in general of three kinds:

a) Twice a week in the schools, alms are collected by the so-called school fathers or hospital administrators and an alms box carried around for this purpose; afterwards a permanent alms box is attached near the entrance of the school, in which Jews who are entering and leaving place alms.

b) Wealthier Jews have the practice of committing themselves voluntarily to a monthly payment for the care of the poor and sick, and wealthier Jews, when they become ill, out of piety give a certain sum of money into the hands of the hospital administrators, and in this case wealthier Jews can also make legacies or charitable trusts.

c) Here and there, especially in larger cities, a designated payment is made annually from the community treasury.

7) Since all of these charitable cash contributions, under improper practice up to now, have come directly into the hands of the so-called hospital fathers and brotherhood chairmen, without being provided with any supervision concerning the amounts of money collected and used for this purpose, and sufficient security,

8) As a means to end this improper practice and introduce good order in these matters, it is established for the future that:

1) The special brotherhood which exists in communities in this country for the feeding of the poor and care for the sick shall remain as it is and also in the future will be given without interference the supervision they have had up to now in this regard. However:

2) In future the chairmen of these brotherhoods will no longer administer the funds, nor should they receive the charitable contributions of wealthier Jews in their own hands, but rather all money which is collected as alms contributions for the care of the poor and sick, or is contributed by wealthier Jews or given into the hands of the hospital

administrators, and spent from these funds which are specially dedicated for this purpose, in future must be deposited directly in the alms boxes designated for this purpose and the keys be given each time to the elder doing business for the community for the month, who must keep them in a safe place.

3) The money which has come into these boxes during the whole week is to be counted at the end of each week by the community treasurer in the presence of the elder doing business for the community for the month (who must unlock the box) and a sworn witness for the community [official religious office], and then handed over by the hospital administrators to the community treasurer in exchange for a receipt, to be given by the latter as received for the care of the poor and sick.

4) Just as now, all funds designated for the care of the poor or sick should flow directly into the community treasury; it follows from this that all expenditures necessary to fulfill this twofold final purpose must be taken from these funds by the community treasury. For which reason, then:

5) The hospital administrators and brotherhood chairmen should make known each time to the community elder, the amount of the expenditure that will be necessary when alms are to be distributed, as well as when any other kind of expenditure is necessary for the care of the poor and sick and the maintenance of the hospitals. He will then send the request for funds appropriately to the community treasury; they should withdraw the funds and submit an accounting [to the community treasury] showing how they were used.

6) Just as the administrators of the hospitals and the brotherhoods are most emphatically ordered to see to the correct collection and appropriate use of these kinds of charitable funds, it is also understood that they, according to their important responsibilities, will take the most exact care that the poor are given the necessary food, and the hospitals are kept clean; and provide for good care, service, and feeding for the sick, and for their healing, by means of the employment of talented and hardworking doctors and medical assistants, and that the necessary medications are obtained; will exercise appropriate supervision, and in general see to it that this twofold charitable intention may be achieved in the most efficient manner.

7) The auditing of the accounting to be submitted by the school fathers and brotherhood chairmen is to be under the supervision of the head community treasurers, as is the auditing of the accounting of the community.

8) Concerning the selection of the officeholders of this kind, most of them would be appointed in the future according to the practice now existing in most of the towns; that is, they will be appointed by the electors when the election for community elders is held.

9) Poor Jews who are traveling, who do not count among the number of vagabonds, shall, according to the custom in this country, be tolerated for no longer than 3 days in a community that is not their own, and then be given a small sum of money for travel or, in cases of physical disability when they are unable to journey on foot, be taken in a wagon to the next community.

10) The same is ordered, even more importantly, with respect to traveling preachers and foreign cantors, who already, according to the practice which exists in this country, must report appropriately to the rabbi and the elders of the community to which they have come, and may not be tolerated at all without such permission, since people of this sort can cause many expenses for the community.

11) If a traveling foreign poor Jew should suddenly become ill, he is to be taken in immediately by the hospital and appropriate care be taken for his healing the same as for sick local residents, but after his recovery, consideration should be given to his further transportation, as stated above.

12) Which leads to the conclusion that it is in no way allowed for foreign sick Jews to be pushed off onto another community and left helpless, nor, as it has often happened in this country as a bad practice, that the mentally retarded and mentally ill be sent to other communities. However, if a mentally incompetent person should break away from his own community and become a burden to another community, he should be taken back to his own community, which did not take close enough care of him, at their expense.

13) Since it is a religious requirement for the Jews that before the beginning of Passover the necessary quantity of flour for the whole community for the whole period of the holidays should be brought in, each community should make a most exact list of all wealthy and poor Jewish community members, determine the supply requirements for each, and deliver this at the proper time, provide the poor with this without cost to them, but provide the wealthier ones on the other hand with their required supply for a price which is to be determined, in which the cost of the supply distributed to the poor is included.

Article Nine.

Concerning Burials and Cemeteries.

1) EACH COMMUNITY WISHING to establish a new cemetery or to enlarge the old one must make a request to the national government office for permission for this, for which [the national office] will determine a fee commensurate with the community's ability to pay.

2) Those congregations or *Paraphien* which are provided with no cemetery of their own must, under threat of severe punishment, transport their dead immediately to the next cemetery of their *Kahal* [Jewish community].

3) The brotherhoods for burial of the dead and care for the cemeteries which exist in most towns will in the future continue as they are; however the usual contributions and fees paid for burials and gravestones will not be collected by the individual brotherhood chairmen but must rather, following instructions of the elders but in the presence each time of the brotherhood chairmen, be paid directly into the community fund, from which the amounts required to pay the salaries of personnel required for burial of the dead and keeping watch over the gravesite, acquiring the necessary equipment, fencing the gravesite, etc., shall be made available in exchange for a receipt and future accounting for the expenditures.

4) Poor Jews who have died shall be buried without charge; foreign wealthy Jews on the other hand will be required to pay higher fees than local residents.

Article Ten.

Aid for Victims of Misfortune, both Private Jews and Whole Jewish Communities.

1) WHEN A WHOLE Jewish community is struck by misfortune due to fire damage or other accidents, the elder at national level for the district will go immediately to the place in person, or send his representative there, and in consultation with the rabbi, the elders, and the most respected Jews of the place which suffered the damage, determine and assess the value of each individual damage separately, have a reliable list of all of the damages prepared by those present, preferably the elders and notaries, and then forward the list with a report to the Jewish *Direction* [General Administration] here [in Lemberg], which will send their most obedient recommendation on the matter to the national government office and await the decision as to whether and in what measure the community which suffered the damage may be allowed to have a collection taken for alms for their aid, either in the district to which they belong or possibly in the whole country.

2) Following approval on the part of the national government office, then, in order to avoid any worrisome abuses and negative consequences, the alms are not to be collected as they have been up to now by several deputies of the community traveling from place to place, but rather the alms collection approved by the governing body for the country shall be publicized by the Jewish General Administration in the district to which the community belongs or possibly in the whole country.

3) After the collection has been taken up, each generous community shall send the contribution they have raised to the elder at national level for the district in exchange for his receipt, which latter will then, as soon as all the alms have come to him, be responsible for distributing this money according to the proportion of the damage suffered by each Jewish family, and for reporting this obediently to the Jewish General Administration which supervises him, and for proving by means of receipts for money received and receipts for expenditures, that he received all of the alms which were collected and how he made use of them.

4) If, however, a respected individual merchant or tradesman should suffer misfortune through no fault of his own, he will receive temporary aid from generous contributions of sympathetic relatives and other Jews of the place. In addition, in the case that such an unfortunate Jew who, due to the large size of his business and his good personal characteristics, has earned special consideration and support, his community will not be prevented from giving him a hand and in doing this making him able to pay contributions again; however, [the community] must first, by going through the elder at national level, obtain permission from the Jewish General Administration [in Lemberg].

Article Eleven.
Concerning the Storage of the Written Records and of the Jewish Community Seal.

1) ALL COMMUNITY BOOKS, papers of the community, and documents of each Jewish community, must remain under the care and storage of the notaries and sworn witnesses of the community council, who, upon taking these into their care, must be given a list of all of the community books and documents, for their own protection, of which a copy must always remain with the elders; also, any community documents or written records which arrive later are to be added to the aforementioned list in the same manner.

2) Furthermore, each community must provide itself with a community seal for its use and give this, as well, to the sworn witnesses of the community for storage.

Article Twelve.

Concerning the Meetings or So-called *Seßionen* of Each Community.

1) ALL OF THOSE Jews who, according to the current practice of each community, have the right to attend the *große Seßion* [large general meeting of the community] and to have an active vote in it, represent, whenever they are called together by the community elders, their local community in the manner that their decisions must in all respects be regarded as decisions of the community.

2) And since the qualifications for the Jews who may attend such community meetings is already determined and prescribed in the community books of each *Kahal*, it shall remain in future as the traditional practice of each Jewish community council.

3) Further, although in general the elders of the community are primarily responsible for the administration of the community, the welfare and preservation of the community requires that all important matters that may relate to any advantage for or damage to the community should be arbitrated and decided in the so-called large general meetings of the community. For this reason, in all situations of this kind that arise, the community elders must, under threat of the most severe punishment, hold a large general meeting of the community.

Article Thirteen.

Concerning the Jewish Bans.

1) THE *GROSSER BANN* [great ban] shall in future only be used by the chief rabbi for the country, and only in extraordinary cases; however, the chief rabbi for the country shall not have the right to proclaim it on his own but must, from case to case, obtain the approval and decision of the national government office.

2) Concerning the smaller Jewish bans, however, the practice of this, insofar as it is proclaimed after a statement of a witness is obtained or in general in order to discern the truth, shall also in future be permitted for community rabbis and community elders.

3) Whenever one or another Jew is to be placed under the ban as punishment for a crime committed, each time before the person is placed under the ban the decision and approval of, respectively, the chief rabbi for the country or the Jewish General Administration [in Lemberg], according to the circumstances, is to be obtained by the rabbi or community elder concerned.

Article Fourteen.
Concerning the Internal Jewish Police Offices in General.

1) EACH JEWISH COMMUNITY must elect at least 2 well-behaved and humble men who must be responsible for enforcing exact standards for *Maas* [volume measure for grain], *Elle* [measure of length], and weight, and reporting any transgressors they find immediately to the community elders for the punishment they deserve; and in addition to seeing that police regulations are followed exactly, they shall most energetically and carefully see to the cleanliness of the streets, squares (or marketplaces), and houses of the Jews, as well as to prevention of the wasteful use of fire and lighting, harmful gambling, immorality and other disorderly behavior, and also see that not, contrary to the wishes of the honored rulers, several Jewish families live together in one room; and to this end twice or at least once a week undertake surprise visits, and the community elders on their own responsibility and under threat of severe punishment shall ensure that this requirement is fulfilled most exactly by the Jewish police supervisors under them.

Part Three.

Concerning the Jewish Contributions and *Domestico* [local community finances].

Article One.
Concerning the Taxes Due to the Princely Ruler of the Country, Their Assessment and Collection.

1) THE *JUDENKOPFSTEUER* [head tax for Jews] which was the previous practice, is herewith ended and changed into a *Schutzgeld* [protection fee] and a *Toleranzgebühr* [tolerance fee] in the following manner: so that all of the Jewish communities according to the previous measure shall now be required to send the previous per capita tax as a tolerance fee annually to the imperial treasury according to the modalities which are determined below; since it is appropriate that those who enjoy the protection of the *Landesfürst* [ruling prince of the country] also contribute to the general expenses.

2) Since the required payment is only made for protection and tolerance, but in respect to the whole Jewish population of this country this [fee] comes to a negligible

amount which is not at all appropriate [in proportion to] their business dealings, life style, and other income; and as such it would not establish them in any way on an equal footing with the Christian residents of the country, other citizens, business people, and professional people, since almost all business and income is up to now in their hands, it is herewith most graciously declared as law:

3) A new general tax [shall be levied] on the entire Jewish population *in Corpore* [as a body], on all of their business, trade, and assets, in an amount equal to the aforementioned tolerance fee; which, pending a further decision of the most high [the Empress] will remain together with the aforementioned tolerance tax at currently determined levels.

4) The tolerance fee, as can be understood from the above, will remain at the same assessment and with the same amounts and should be paid, in the same way as the head tax, through the Jewish community.

5) The assessment for the tax on trade and assets, however, will be left completely up to the whole Jewish population itself, and in the following manner: that the Jewish General Administration described in the First Section, namely the chief rabbi for the country and the 12 elders at national level will, when they are called together following the procedure mentioned at the beginning [of these Regulations], immediately and conscientiously divide up the existing Jewish communities according to the proportion of assets located there and present this assessment to the national government office for approval.

6) After receiving the approval, this is to be immediately announced to the Jewish General Administration [in Lemberg], the elders at national level for the districts, and by them to the Jewish communities in each district.

7) The individual assessment of both taxes due must take place in the following manner in each Jewish community in a large general meeting of the community; the portion of tax will then be assessed directly to each individual and collected from them, but in no way, however, paid out of the community treasury, as has happened up to now improperly. This *Subrepartition* [subassessment] will be left up to the Jewish community councils because the assets, the trade, and the earnings of each individual must be best known to them.

8) This individual subassessment, signed and confirmed by all of the elders of the Jewish community, must be submitted immediately to the respective elder at national level for the district, submitted by him to the Jewish General Administration [in Lemberg], and submitted by them to the governing body for [Galicia] for approval, along with a note of any serious objections, if applicable.

9) After approval has taken place, the subassessments are to be sent back to the respective Jewish congregations by the same route and herewith:

10) The individual collection of the tax on trade and assets, as well as the tolerance fee, as has been the practice up to now, is also in future left up to the respective Jewish communities, in exchange for the following: that the amount due from each Jewish congregation be paid into the district treasury in quarterly installments, properly and in cash with no arrears allowed, under threat of the most severe penalty.

11) In the same way, the Jewish community councils will receive unfailing assistance and enforcement against individuals who are late in paying [the taxes], if they request this from the respective government office of the district.

12) If a community has suffered misfortune through fire damage or other accidents, the elder at national level for the district, after a thorough and orderly investigation of the matter, should make the suggestion that payment of the whole amount of [required] taxes due from them insofar as their payment cannot be afforded, be waived either partially or completely until [the time of] a possible recovery, and an additional assessment for this portion of the contributions be divided among all of the remaining Jewish communities; and he should send this proposed new assessment to the Jewish General Administration to whom he is responsible, which will then submit this aforementioned suggestion with any memorandum they consider necessary, to the governing body [for Galicia], and await approval.

The same procedure is understood to be appropriate when one or another Jewish contributor suffers misfortune or accident, in which case the elders of the community shall remove the amount of [required] contribution assessed to him from the list of his debts and divide it among the other contributors in the community and report this change to the elder at national level for the district responsible for them, and he will report this to the [Jewish] General Administration.

Second Article.

Concerning the Income of the Jewish Communities and Expenditures of the Communities in General.

1) THERE IS SUCH a multitude of classifications of income in the Jewish communities or *Kahalen* here in this country that it is impossible to attempt to begin a new description or form for them at this time; for this reason, they shall be allowed to remain in the future as they are now according to the old practice.

2) The same is established with respect to the expenditures of their communities, which [are supervised by the] elders of the community already and also by means of the

modalities prescribed in the following article are reliably supervised and checked by the community head treasurer.

3) But it is understood that, whenever the debt system of any community which will be described below requires a closer regulation of this, other measures must be taken as they are needed.

4) Although, it has been decided to leave the aforementioned existing income and expenditure classifications for each Jewish community as they are for the time being, Her Majesty wishes, as the one to whose most high grace alone the Jewish population owes its tolerance in this country, to strongly protect them against all oppression by the noble landowners or religious institutions and [against] demands for inappropriate payments, so that they always remain in a position to pay [required] contributions [or taxes]; on the other hand, it is not intended to deny the [noble] landowners the right to require of those Jews residing on their estates the payments which are legally due to them.

5) If one or another noble landowner insists on the further collection of the payments of this kind which were usual in the past, it is their responsibility to bring appropriate proofs for this, which is also understood to apply to the church institutions [as property owners].

6) However, it is particularly known from experience that one or another noble landowner, on the basis of various fictitious excuses, has attempted to wrest from the hands of the communities and illegally take into their own possession the funds received from the *Krupka* or Jewish community meat tax, which are solely dedicated to covering the expenses of the community and repayment of the community's debts, and with that are by their nature inseparable from the Jewish communities and inalienable [to them]. Doing so has caused ruinous decay for communities damaged in this way, required them to take on new capital debt, and with this caused them to have an even greater burden of debt; therefore illegal practices of this kind and payments required by the local ruler or noble [or church institutional] landowner are ended for all time and all of the Jewish communities in this country are assured the unhindered possession of their *Krupka*-income as their property.

Article Three.

Concerning the Management, Collection, Use,

and Accounting of the Jewish Community Finances.

1) THE COMMUNITY ELDERS will be allowed to retain, as up to now, the right to make decisions concerning the needs of the community and the necessary money

to cover these expenses; however, the management itself and the collection both of the fixed community expenses and income and also miscellaneous incoming monies is most strictly ended forever.

2) So it is understood that the improper practice which existed in the Jewish communities here in this country, whereby [community elders] collected certain extraordinary income, for instance fines, death fees, wedding contributions, privately, and could do with it whatever they wished, must stop completely from now on.

3) The collection of all fixed as well as unfixed fees and income, whatever names they may have, must in the future be solely under the supervision of the sworn Jewish community treasurer; in the same way, also, the payment of all expenses for the community shall be undertaken only by him, following the direction of and in consultation with the elders of the community.

4) It follows from this, therefore, that all Jewish communities must provide themselves with a sworn Jewish treasurer, whose appointment and election must take place by the whole community in a large general meeting of the Jewish community and in this the only consideration should be for the talent and honesty of the subject.

5) The treasurer must receive and disperse all monies which come under his supervision in the following manner: that he, with regard to every action which occurs concerning the treasury, must provide himself with and be covered by a proper purchase directive signed by the elder serving as head elder for the month, together with at least two other co-elders.

6) However, so that he can prove that he has complied exactly with all of the directives of the elders, he shall obtain receipts from all parties for all funds received and receipts for all expenditures, and record both money received and expenditures immediately in detail, that is with notations of the amount collected or paid out, the item (or object), and the payer or recipient in an account book kept especially for this purpose.

7) The head treasurers of the communities must exercise oversight over, and check the work of, not only the elders, but also the community treasurer and the others who collect the income.

8) This check of their work must consist of the following: at the end of the month, namely whenever the elder doing business for the community for the month hands over the office to his successor, all purchase directives, receipts for money received, and receipts for money spent which are in the hands of the community treasurer, and every item of funds received and spent recorded in his account book, shall be properly audited and any objections that are found written down.

9) These objections to the accounting must immediately be delivered to both the elder doing business for the community for the month who is leaving and to the community treasurer as their joint responsibility, and after they have explained the discrepancies in the accounting and corrected them as appropriate, then the account book of the treasurer, as corrected in this manner, is to be signed by the head treasurer and also the former elder doing business for the congregation for the month [and] is to be handed over with a letter of absolution prepared by the head treasurer, to prove to all that he fulfilled the duties of the office appropriately.

10) In addition, the elders of the community, under threat of severe punishment, must pay the most careful attention to see that: [the income of the community] is collected correctly and without payment delays by the community treasurers; required contributions of the community are paid in quarterly installments, the other income of the community at the usual times; and the lease fees, according to the payment schedule stipulated in the relevant contracts.

Article Four.

Concerning the Debts of the Jewish Communities, their Liquidation and Repayment, then Payment of the Interest, and Assumption of New Capital Loans.

1) SINCE THE REPAYMENT of the community debts of every Jewish community is a matter which deserves the utmost attention, even more so because the management of public credit depends on it, it is herewith decreed most emphatically that each Jewish community should give the greatest possible attention to the payment of its passive debts and the interest due on them, at the interest rates stipulated as standard for the country; and also that the Jewish General Administration which has been set up over the Galician Jewish population shall do its utmost to exercise the most exact supervision in this regard, and under threat of severe punishment use a firm hand in these matters.

2) However, so that the successive amortization of the passive debts of each Jewish community can be achieved with the greatest possible order, economy, and saving of time, and at the same time not interfere with the maintenance and advisable relief of the indebted Jewish communities, it is the intention [of the Empress], to prescribe for each Jewish community at the appropriate time, following the liquidation of its passive debts and payment of the interest due on them, an orderly debt repayment system; and it is understood that Jewish communities, according to their most obedient duty, will concur even more enthusiastically with this beneficial intention, since due to the ending of their responsibility to pay excessive or inappropriate fees or taxes to their local noble landowners and to

the church institutions [as landowners] and the exemption of the Jewish *Fleischkreuzer* [meat tax] or so-called *Krupka,* and responsibility to pay from the community income any taxation by local noble landowners, a sufficient fund will be accumulated for them to cover the repayment of their debts.

3) Just as it will be impossible to accomplish the aforementioned systematization of the Jewish debts in this country without first having thorough knowledge of and discussion of the state of the local finances of each Jewish community, the wellbeing of the indebted Jewish communities requires that the Jewish General Administration have the elders at national level for the districts for which they are responsible, as soon as possible reliably determine all annual local income and expenditures, both fixed and variable, for each Jewish community, prepare an orderly list of these, and present all of the proofs, along with recommendations in each case on what each indebted Jewish community, after payment of interest due, could be required to set aside annually and use for repayment of the passive debts, to the national government office for assessment and a decision, after which the Jewish General Administration must see to it in the most obedient manner that this [decision] is followed exactly and most quickly.

4) Further, the Jewish communities in this country are most explicitly forbidden, under threat of the most severe punishment, to take on new passive capital loans and in doing so further exhaust their community funds, which are already overburdened by the weight of the old debts.

5) Should, however, one community or another find itself in an emergency situation which could only be relieved by taking out a new capital loan, [that community] in this case [should] turn to the elder at national level for the district responsible for them, who will [have to] consider carefully the circumstances of urgent need or lack of urgent need, damage or benefit and report these along with their recommendation to the Jewish General Administration [in Lemberg], as well as to show within what period of time and with what funds this [new] capital loan can be repaid, including payment of the interest; [the Jewish General Administration] must then obtain the final decision on the matter from the national government office.

Article Five.

Concerning the Salaries of Both the Leading and Subordinate Officials Belonging to the General Jewish Administration, and other Financial Requirements Related to This.

1) SINCE IN THE present Jewish Regulations, the Jewish General Administration [in Lemberg] and the elders at national level distributed among the districts, are

required to carry out official duties which involve such far-reaching and extremely diffi-cult responsibilities, which require on their part tireless and uninterrupted work taking precedence over all of their private and household matters, it is also the intention to provide them with very generous salaries, for their appropriate accommodation, and so that they do not allow themselves to be tempted down criminal paths due to the lack of abundant financial means; and they must apply themselves even more diligently to the faithful fulfillment of the responsibilities entrusted to them, since in case any actions take place for their own profit, are dishonest, or are contrary to their duties, these would be punished with the utmost severity and depending on the circumstances would also be treated as criminal offences.

2) In consideration of which the following salaries are established:

a) For the *Ober-Landrabiner* (chief rabbi for the country) ....800 *fl. Rh.*

b) For each of the 6 *Ober-Landesältesten* (elders at national level in
Lemberg) ....600 *fl. Rh.*
makes a total of ....3,600 *fl. Rh.*

c) For each of the 6 *Kreis-Landesältesten* (elders at national level for
the districts) ....400 *fl. Rh.*
makes a total of ....2,400 *fl. Rh.*

d) For the Jewish treasurer to be installed to manage the administrative
treasury to be established [in Lemberg] into which the funds
dedicated to covering the necessary expenditures for these matters
must be paid ....500 *fl. Rh.*

e) For each of the 2 Jewish scribes to be employed at the Jewish
General Administration [in Lemberg] 150 *fl.*, a total of...............................300 *fl. Rh.*

f) For the Christian accountant..400 *fl. Rh.*
For the Christian scribe ....300 *fl. Rh.*

g) For the 6 Jewish scribes to be employed for the elders at national
level for the districts 100 *fl.*, a total of...600 *fl. Rh.*

h) For the 6 Christian scribes 200 *fl.*, a total of...1,200 *fl. Rh.*

i) Then the cost of writing materials, postage, and other equipment
as necessary will require ....3,000 *fl. Rh.*
Herewith the whole amount of money which must be paid into
the administrative treasury comes to the total sum of.......................... 131,000 *fl. Rh.*

3) Each year this sum of money will be apportioned among the districts and local Jewish communities by the Jewish General Administration, in consultation with the elders at national level for the districts. [Local Jewish communities] will then collect the sum apportioned to them and send it to the respective elder at national level for the district, and it will be sent by him to the Jewish administrative treasury [in Lemberg].

4) In addition, the Jewish treasurer to be employed for the administrative treasury [in Lemberg] should stand in the same relationship and degree of official subordination to the Jewish General Administration responsible for him as prescribed in the third article of this section for the Jewish community treasurer and the elders of the community; only he will have to submit his accounts, written in an orderly manner and accompanied by the appropriate purchase directives, receipts for money received, and receipts for money spent, directly to the accounting office of the governing body for the country [Galicia] for auditing of the same.

Part Four.

Concerning the Business and Trades of the Jews.

Article One.

Concerning Jewish Letters of Obligation And Debts Owed on Letters of Obligation.

1) SINCE THE IMPORTANT characteristic of the Jewish letters of obligation or *Mamera* (*sic*) usually used in this country, which distinguishes them from ordinary handwritten promissory notes or letters of obligation, is that the name of the creditor is not printed, but that they are usually issued only in the name of the holder or presenter of the letter of obligation, without naming the actual creditor, with added signature(s) of one or more debtors: this old tradition, which is in conformity with Jewish laws, shall remain in the future as it is.

2) No less [importantly], the Jewish letters of obligation or *Marmaren* (*sic*) will be allowed to retain completely the function that they have had up to now, whereby, if the validity of a letter of obligation which is due for payment is denied and legally disputed, in no way is the presenter of the letter of obligation obliged to prove the validity of the debt, but rather the debtor must present [in court] the grounds for his objections to it, and if

he is unable to present sufficient evidence, in no way will the debtor denying the debt be required to swear under oath [concerning the validity of his statement], but rather, much more, the presenter of the letter of obligation [must be required to swear under oath] in showing his justification for it.

3) Nevertheless, in order for the letter of obligation to be considered and dealt with in the courts as a true debt based on a letter of obligation, it is necessary that, in conformity with the Jewish laws, the owner of the letter of obligation shall obtain from the rabbi or his lawyers, together with two community notaries of the town to which the debtor belongs and in exchange for payment of the fee which is usual in every Jewish community, in these cases, a signed statement that the signature which appears in the letter of obligation, really is the signature of the debtor.

4) Now as soon as the signature of the debtor has been confirmed to be valid in this manner, the debtor is to be required by the court to deposit immediately the sum of the debt, which shall be kept in the possession of the community notaries temporarily until a legal decision has been issued in the matter, or to present a sufficient security deposit or guarantee of a third party for it.

5) However, should the debtor be unwilling to do either of these, the court will send the appropriate report immediately to the elder of the community for the purpose that the latter should immediately take the utmost care to begin a stricter enforcement against the accused by means of confiscation of property or arrest.

6) Now if one of the two parties should not be willing to accept the decisions made by the rabbinical courts, [that party] shall still retain the right to submit an appeal within 8 days to the elder at national level for the district, who must consult a rabbi concerning legal knowledge in this case, after whose decision the deposit which has remained with the community notaries will immediately and without further delay be handed over to the winning party.

7) A completely different procedure takes place if the letter of obligation or *Mamera* (*sic*) has expired due to the inactivity of the owner; in this case a distinction is made between those letters of obligation with and without agreement to receive a percentage of the profits; in the case of the former 6 years, in the case of the second 3 years are required before a letter of obligation whose owner has neglected to apply to the courts within this time will be considered to have expired. The effect of this expiration is that the owner of such [a letter of obligation] which has remained unpaid for such a long time, in case he is unable to show a written letter of protest or [to show] that he has sent a sworn witness [an officer of the community] [to attempt to collect the debt]), in the first instance must

present to the Jewish courts sufficient proof on his behalf that throughout this whole time he has not been able to send a sworn witness to the debtor and confront him [with the debt]; now if he [the owner] can bring proof of this and can justify his inactivity, his *Mamaren* [letter of obligation] should be dealt with in the courts as a debt owed on a Jewish letter of obligation; if sufficient proof is lacking, however, [his letter of obligation should be dealt with in the courts] as a simple debt on the basis of a handwritten promissory note, and the debtor who has remained constantly with a negative credit balance [be] legally ordered to pay the debt which the owner of the letter of obligation was not able to collect, and after his making of a statement under oath the letter of obligation shall immediately be collected and declared null and void.

8) However, all of these decrees concerning the debts owed on letters of obligation are restricted exclusively to such legal complaints as are brought by Jews against Jews in the Jewish courts; in contrast to this, Christian creditors shall not be prevented at any time from having letters of obligation, issued by Jewish debtors and which are due for payment, dealt with in the courts according to the general regulations for legal treatment of letters of obligation which have been introduced in this country, and to bring cases of this kind in the Christian courts.

Article Two.

Concerning the Jewish Business Practices and Laws.

1) IT HAPPENS FREQUENTLY that a wealthy Jew provides a Jewish businessman with money in the following manner, that in exchange for the issuance of a letter of obligation or *Mameram*, he takes a portion of the [proceeds of] the business dealings that the businessman uses it for; in which case the money lender either reserves for himself half of the profit; and if instead of the anticipated profit a loss should be incurred, he takes half of the latter upon himself, or, in order to avoid the complications of the accounting on both sides, stipulates by contract that he shall receive a certain percentage of the capital he has loaned and allow all of the rest of the proceeds, even though they may amount to 50 and more percent, to go to the party carrying out the business dealing.

2) So that all disputes and unfair aggressive practices which may arise from this may be prevented as well as possible, in conformity with their Jewish regulations it is decreed as law that anyone has the right to require by contract, as high a percentage for his capital which is to be loaned for business purposes as the businessman who is to be provided with the money is willing to agree to give the money lender; however, payment of such a contractually required percentage without any restriction or moderation can be only

demanded from the businessman who has been provided with the money if the latter states that on the business dealing for which he was provided with money, he has made a profit of at least as much as the amount of the contracted percentage.

3) Now should the party carrying out the business dealings claim not to have made a profit of a higher amount than the agreed percentage, he must confirm this statement under oath within 6 months, counted from the day the contract was made; and after his being required to make a sworn statement immediately, the money lender, without regard to the percent agreed upon, in proportion to the profit made, will have to be content to receive one half of [the profit] or similarly, if the party carrying out the business dealing has sworn to have made no profit, [be content to receive] only his capital.

4) After a period of 6 months, on the other hand, it is not enough for the party who has carried out the business dealing to confirm the stated low profit with a sworn statement, but rather he must prove with credible witness statements (or documentation) that throughout the whole time the business dealings for which he was provided with money were going on, he did not make a profit of a higher amount than the percentage agreed upon with the money lender, or if applicable, that he made no profit at all.

5) If, finally, the businessman who was provided with money should even wish to claim that he not only had not made a profit on this business dealing but had suffered a real loss, it will be required in any case, whether he reports this within 6 months or after 6 months have elapsed (and if so be liable to prosecution), that he not only swear under oath to have incurred this loss but also show by the statements of competent and credible witnesses that this loss was incurred only from and through the business dealings for which the money lender had given his approval, and not through other causes or affairs, in which case fairness also requires that the lender should carry half of a loss of this kind.

6) It is a completely different situation for those moneylenders who have provided money for business dealings without taking a portion of the profit or loss, and should immediately be considered to be simply creditors but in no way business partners, since the moneylender on the one hand does not have the right to require a higher rate of interest than is customary in this country for his loaned capital, on the other hand, in case the business dealings should result in a loss, [he is] not obliged to carry a portion of the [loss] nor to suffer immediately a *pro rata* reduction of his loaned capital.

7) When a purchase has been agreed upon and [the deal] has been closed and a handshake has been given in confirmation of this, both the buyer and the seller are most strongly bound to keep to the business deal that has been made, and the party who on his own refuses to carry out this sale is obliged to compensate the other for all damages and

expenses; in addition the courts are required to keep the strictest supervision over a sale agreed upon in good faith in this manner.

8) However, if a cash deposit had been made for the goods that were to be purchased in this business dealing, it is only fair that the purchaser should forfeit this [deposit] if he refuses to complete the sale; on the other hand, if the seller refuses on his part to complete a sale that has been agreed upon in good faith, the [seller] shall be required not only to pay back to the purchaser the deposit received but also to give him the equivalent value of the goods they agreed upon, either *in natura* or in cash.

9) If, with respect to a sale that has been agreed upon, a fraudulent dealing on the part of the seller should be discovered, in conformity with the Jewish laws the goods sold shall be appraised at the request of the accuser, and if it should be proven that the seller profited [from his fraudulent activity] by more than one sixth of the value, and that the buyer suffered a loss of more than one sixth of the value through this, the sale shall be annulled by the courts and the seller who perpetrated the fraud given an appropriate punishment.

10) Jewish businesspeople should use true *Maas* (measure of volume, i.e. for grain), *Ellen* (measure of length), and weight measure as they have been introduced at the time in this country, or may be introduced in the future, in order to avoid the severe punishment which is dictated for these cases by the generally published decrees or [those] which may otherwise apply.

11) With respect to foreign Jewish merchants, the practice shall remain in the future as it has been in this country in each Jewish community, according to which [practice], at the times of fairs or special market days a foreign Jewish merchant is allowed to sell the goods he is bringing into the community both in bulk lots and as by the *Elle* [lit: by the yard as in cloth measure, as piece goods, i.e. individual retail sale], not only to the members of the Jewish community and local residents but also to foreigners; outside the dates of the fairs and special market days, however, foreign Jewish merchants are only allowed to sell goods in bulk lots to the residents and merchants of the town, and sales by the retail sales are most strictly forbidden.

Article Three.

Concerning Ending Various Bad Practices Which Occur in Jewish Business and Life.

1) IT HAPPENS NOT seldom that at the special market days some bad people buy various goods on credit, both from Christian and from Jewish merchants, and in order to gain the trust of these merchants who are allowing them to purchase on credit, show

some money which has been loaned to them by other accomplices, but have no intention to pay for the goods they have been given nor to see to it that payment is made.

In case this happens, swindlers of this kind, as well as their accomplices, should be punished most severely by the elders of the community and local judges and, as much as possible, the honest merchants [should be] seriously warned about these swindles.

2) However, insofar as someone, for reasons of jealousy or revenge, should attempt to destroy the credit of a merchant who has honestly taken goods on credit by spreading a groundless rumor of this kind to the detriment of his good name, the local elders should exert the utmost effort to punish this person [who spread the rumor] most severely, not only for the protection of the reputation of the one who has been insulted in this way, but also for his maliciousness in doing this.

3) It sometimes happens that one buyer comes before another buyer and buys goods that the latter had already negotiated for, contracted to buy, and for which he had paid a deposit, or that the seller offers to sell for a lower price to the second buyer, at a loss to himself, a certain type of goods which this buyer had already negotiated for with another [seller], only in order to push out the first buyer; now since these kinds of undertakings go against all honesty and usual business practices, they shall be forbidden, both in private business dealings and at weekly markets and public special market days, with the warning that the transgressors will, after a complaint in the court in the matter, with the utmost strictness be required to provide compensation for any damages and costs arising from these corrupt selling and buying practices.

4) All business dealings and leases which are exclusionary and result in a monopoly are [herewith] ended and forbidden, all the more emphatically since through them business competition is not only restricted and the public treated unfairly; but also other Jewish individuals who earn their living in the same business are placed in a position of extreme poverty and as a consequence are unable to pay [the required] contributions.

5) And although the right of Jews to lease individual *Bestandhäuser* [houses for lease, often long-term leases of properties owned by local nobility] will in future not be denied to them, they will, however, not be authorized to take whole villages by a lease, and this practice will be most seriously ended for them for all time.

6) If a Jewish businessman has taken a cellar, stalls, and cottages into his possession by a proper rental agreement and pays his rent and deposit for them, it is fair that he should not be pushed out by either local residents or by non-local residents, but rather be allowed to keep his stalls or barns in peace.

7) Also, no one shall be allowed, under punishment of compensation for all damages and costs, to push out someone who already has leased [or rented] a cellar for several years, by attempting for reasons of jealousy or revenge to rent it himself by offering the owner a higher rent (or lease fee) which is impossible for the [current leaseholder] to pay, since through this not only the local noble landowner who owns and rents out the property is fraudulently circumvented, but also the Jewish leaseholder who has been honestly paying his rent [or lease fee], who often has moved his place of residence to that location, left his own business at home, spent a great deal of money for materials and expenses, has had his own [business at home] run in his place temporarily by the neighbors, will lose his means of making a living and his chances to better himself in the future, which is contrary to all the rules of fairness and love of neighbor.

8) No Jewish businessman shall attempt to hire away and employ another's business employee without the prior approval of and orderly release from service by his employer; in addition, also, the Christians working as servants for the Jews shall not be required to do any other work on Sundays and holidays than those tasks which are allowed to be done by servants working for Christians on these days.

Article Four.

Concerning the Jewish Professions and Trades.

1) ALL JEWISH PROFESSIONAL people are not prevented from practicing their profession in their own local communities, not only among Jews but also among the Christians, however, this is only to be done in cases where there is no Christian tradesman/craftsman practicing that trade or craft located in the town. In other cases, however, Jews are only allowed to make their living by means of the professions they have learned within their Jewish community but in no way, to provide their services to the Christians.

2) Further, the Galician Jewish population must see to it that whatever Her Imperial and Royal Majesty may in future most kindly decide to prescribe, both in business matters and in matters of trades, is followed most exactly and most obediently.

Part Five.

Concerning Jewish Legal Matters and How They Are to Be Dealt With in the Courts.

Article One.

Concerning the Legal Jurisdiction of the Jewish Courts and Their Activity.

1) THE COMMUNITY RABBIS are to give legal rulings only on matters concerning religion and money; and in general when it concerns the property of the parties in a dispute, damage claims and other business matters fall solely under the jurisdiction of the elders of the community of each town.

2) However for the latter, when more important events occur, the community rabbi can also be brought in to decide on the dispute, either at the request of the parties or upon recommendation of the elders.

3) If the party against whom the judgment is made in the rabbinical court believes that he has been treated unjustly by it, that party has a right to submit an appeal to the royal court of appeals within 14 days, and also to apply to the imperial and royal supreme court for review, for which everything which is prescribed by law concerning appeals or reviews must be followed.

4) A similar procedure is to be observed with respect to the legal decisions made by the Jewish community elders in cases of damages, where the path can be taken to the elder at national level for the district, and from there a further appeal sent to the Jewish General Administration [in Lemberg] within 14 days, however without payment of a fee in this instance.

5) Should, however, the party against whom the judgment is made also not be satisfied with the decision of the aforementioned Jewish General Administration, in that case that party will have the right to submit a letter of complaint to the district government office responsible for them, which, after reviewing the matter, will either deal with the matter or in more important cases send the matter, with their recommendation, to the national government office for a decision.

6) The procedures prescribed above concern only those legal matters in which a Jew is seeking a legal decision against a Jew, in which case the matter must always first and

foremost be brought to the Jewish courts according to the first legal path prescribed and continue from there.

7) On the other hand, if a Christian should have a demand or other complaint to bring legally against a Jew, he shall have the right either to call the other party before the Jewish court which has jurisdiction or to bypass the latter and take his legal matter directly to the Christian judge who has jurisdiction, reserving a right to the usual further legal path; also, those Jews who reside alone in towns where there is no Jewish community belong under the jurisdiction of the *Obrigkeit* [local noble ruler or landowner] of the place where they are staying or have their residence. In the same way also, any disputes concerning real estate shall be dealt with not by the Jewish but by the Christian court in the jurisdiction in which the property is located.

8) If, however, a Jew should have to call a Christian before the court, the matter must always be brought before the appropriate [legal] forum for the matter.

9) Finally, in criminal cases the Jewish courts have no jurisdiction at all, since that jurisdiction belongs only with the Christian courts which exercise the law of the sword; in which, whether it is a matter of Jew against Jew or Christian against Jew, strict attention must be paid to what is prescribed by the *allerhöchste* [Empress's] laws.

Article Two.

Concerning the Internal Composition of the Jewish Courts.

1) WHEN MAKING LEGAL decisions on the disputes which come before him, the chief rabbi for [Galicia], shall be required to do so in consultation with 5 lawyers at national level, or so-called *Tuchoven.*

2) These 5 lawyers at national level shall be elected each time by the 12 elders at national level [in Lemberg] and elders at national level in the district and 36 representatives from the districts, and from the city of Lemberg, where a chief rabbi for the country currently in office will have his permanent residence, who have gathered for the election of the chief rabbi for the country and in doing so, care is to be taken that these lawyers at national level are not related to each other or to the chief rabbi for the country by blood or by marriage up to the 3rd degree.

3) Should, however, one of these lawyers at national level elected in the manner described above, die before the end of the life of the chief rabbi for the country [Galicia] or the resignation from his office because he can find a better opportunity elsewhere, the chief rabbi for [Galicia] in consultation with the 6 elders at national level [in Lemberg] and the remaining lawyers at national level, must fill the vacant position of *Tuchoven* [lawyer

at national level] by appointing a qualified individual who is to be taken from the Lemberg Jewish community and is not related to him nor to the other lawyers at national level within the forbidden degrees of relationship by blood or by marriage.

4) The community rabbis, on the other hand, should sit in judgment with at least two lawyers, which also in the future are to be appointed according to the practice which is usual in each community.

5) Twice a week, that is on Monday and Thursday, the chief rabbi for [Galicia] shall call the lawyers at national level to him and hold court, where the parties to disputes, one after another and following a previous court summons, can be heard with careful consideration, the written documents they have brought along and other legal aids carefully considered, and then following a summary court discussion with participation by both sides, the judgment issued, and without delay handed to the parties in written form with the signatures of the chief rabbi for [Galicia] and of the lawyers in their own hand.

6) Both the legal decisions which will be handed down by the court of the chief rabbi for [Galicia], and everything which was brought forward against each other by the parties to the dispute in the summary court hearing, shall be accurately recorded in a book especially dedicated to this purpose, and written down and entered therein not only in the Hebrew but also in the German language.

7) A similar process is prescribed for and must be followed most closely by community rabbis, who are referred to the usual practice introduced in their respective communities for everything else regarding the holding of court.

8) If, however, in the case of the court of the chief rabbi for [Galicia] the parties to a dispute were to request that an extraordinary court session be held at another time than the 2 usual court days, this will be allowed them, but only in exchange for a fee of 1 *fl.* 30 *kr.*

Article Three.

Concerning the Jewish Arbitrated Settlements.

Although as mentioned above, there are different levels of courts which have been established to settle the various disputes which may arise among Jews, the parties to the disputes still retain the right at any time to circumvent the courts and select one or more persons, give them the right to make a decision in their dispute, and to make a settlement based on the decision they make, or also for both parties to appoint equal numbers of arbitrators and to give the rabbi the role of head arbitrator over them.

Article Four.

Concerning the Various Legal Matters Which Do Not Fall Under the Jurisdiction of the Various Levels of Official Courts.

1) IF A JEWISH congregation has a claim to make of another community or a particular Jew of another local community, or of another community than its own, the matter should be either dealt with by arbitrators to be selected by each side or directly by the chief rabbi for [Galicia], either by means of an out of court settlement or in the courts.

On the other hand, cases which may arise among the parties mentioned above and involve damages should be decided by the appropriate elder at national level for the district.

2) Any claims which one Jew or another may have against the community rabbi or against the chief rabbi for [Galicia] himself are to be legally decided either by the lawyers of the town or, respectively, by the lawyers at national level, or if the party bringing the claim should find reason to refuse to be bound by their decision, both parties should appoint arbitrators to settle such a dispute.

3) If a Jew has a claim against one or more of the community elders placed above him, the matter will be decided either by the community rabbi or, at the request of the party bringing the complaint, by arbitrators appointed by both sides.

4) If the chief rabbi for [Galicia] or a community rabbi, and in the same way an elder at national level [in Lemberg] or elder at national level for the district, or the community elder is related to the parties in the dispute by blood or marriage up to the 3rd degree, he is to [recuse himself] from the court when such a legal matter is being decided, and give his position to a substitute or to the first associate judge; the same is understood to be the case concerning lawyers at national level and community lawyers who find themselves in a similar position, and who also shall not be authorized to take part in court proceedings in matters concerning one of their relatives by blood or by marriage.

Article Five.

Concerning Taking The Statements of Witnesses.

1) IF WITNESSES ARE presented, whether the matter concerns a financial claim or a claim for damages, they must be questioned *unter den Bann* [literally: "under the ban," under threat of being placed under the ban if they lie] by the community rabbi or the [lawyers'] court, after it has been determined whether they are qualified to give testimony in the legal matter in question, their testimony has been written on paper and in the final written form signed by the rabbi and lawyers.

2) If the witness testimony is given outside the location of the dispute, the witness statement or the notation of the testimony given, whether concerning financial matters or matters of damage, shall be sent signed and sealed to the courts in the towns in which it belongs.

3) In claims for damage, it will remain in the future that witnesses must be named and their testimony heard within a year to the day, counted from the time of the insult, and the person bringing the witnesses shall have no right to expect legal consideration of his claim if he misses this set date by his own negligence.

Article Six.

Concerning the Oaths Required by the Courts.

If one party is required by the Jewish courts to the swearing under oath, he has the right nevertheless to submit an appeal against this to the next higher court, as also in the opposite case, if he feels that he has been treated unjustly through this, he retains the right to submit an appeal against it.

Article Seven.

Concerning the Enforcement of Court Judgments, Punishment of Those who Refuse to Cooperate With Their Punishment and Removal from Office.

1) THE ENFORCEMENT OF the judgments made by the rabbinical courts and court of the [chief rabbi for Galicia] is solely the responsibility of the local elders, who, after fruitless attempts in using means to force cooperation against the party judged guilty, if these are of no avail, shall with the approval of the community rabbi, report this to the Jewish General Administration [in Lemberg] and bring it before them for further decision as to whether in this case, further steps should be taken against the obstinate person, by placing him under the ban.

2) Should the condemned person, however, despite his having been placed under the ban with the approval of the Jewish General Administration, disregarding this punishment, continue in his obstinacy, the community elders must immediately arrest him and keep him in custody until he has paid the amount of payment he owes according to the court decree. Should, however, the elders be guilty of any connivance in favor of the banned person and not deal with him according to the strict letter of the law, the accuser who brought the case for which the person was placed under the ban will have the right to bring, to the appropriate place, a complaint in court against them for refusal of their obligatory legal duties.

3) If a member of a Jewish community, who is serving in office as the result of a proper election, is guilty of a crime which absolutely requires dismissal from office, after determining the gravity of his transgression or the danger which may be presented by retaining him further in office, the community elders can suspend him from his official duties and salary and if necessary secure his person, however they shall in no way be authorized to remove him from the office he holds, but rather must report the matter by way of the elder at national level for the district to the Jewish General Administration, and await their further decision in the matter.

Article Eight.

Concerning Jewish Marriage Contracts.

1) THE OLD, TRADITIONAL practices which are currently followed in this country concerning Jewish marriage contracts shall remain unchanged in the future.

2) According to these, a distinction is to be made in the writing of these contracts between cases where the bride has brought some money with her and those who lack any dowry. In the case of the former, the bridegroom must always set aside for the bride by written contract the entire sum she has brought with her plus half [of this sum]; so that if, for instance, the dowry brought [with the bride] should consist of 1,000 *fl.*, the bridegroom must set aside for the bride by written contract 1,500 *fl.* If, on the other hand, the bride brings no money at all with her, the bridegroom is not obligated to set aside for [the bride] by written contract more than 320 *fl. pohl.* or 80 *fl. Rheinisch*, and if she is a widow only the half of the aforementioned sum, namely 160 *fl. pohl.* or 40 *fl. Rheinisch.*

3) In accordance with the practice up to now, these marriage contracts written in the manner described shall be signed each time by 2 community notaries.

4) After the death of the husband, the surviving widow must immediately take the usual oath and swear that during the lifetime of her husband and also after his death she has not taken or put aside anything to the disadvantage of the children or heirs.

5) After the swearing of this oath she must go to the rabbi and lawyers of the town and ask to be given the money set aside for her in the marriage contract and to be given back the clothing, jewelry, and other items that she brought with her.

6) On the other hand, the widow must immediately give up to the heirs the jewelry and clothing she received from her husband and in exchange for this, be content to receive for herself the percentage of the value of the same which is set according to the usual practice of each community.

Article Nine.

Concerning the Legal Provisions for Orphans of Minor Age.

1) When a Jew dies and leaves behind orphans of minor age, a distinction is to be made according to whether or not the deceased left behind a will and appointed a guardian.

2) If there is a will and in it the deceased has not made his last wishes known concerning the guardian to be appointed for his children, it is the duty of the rabbi and his lawyers immediately to make an exact and fair inventory of his assets left behind, declare them to be frozen, and in this, in the case that there should be Christian creditors, to consult with the noble rulers with jurisdiction there to determine the amount of money owed to [the deceased] and debts and, if the mother is either no longer living or sufficient trust cannot be placed in her, appoint a guardian for the minor children; then to bring in the money which is determined to be owed to the deceased, to pay any debts that are found to be owed, to satisfy the claims of the widow who is left behind, and to hand the remainder of the assets to the guardian who has now been appointed, which latter must exercise the most exact care for the wards entrusted to him, use the money handed over to him and any other assets belonging to them without benefit to himself for the greatest benefit to the wards, and from time to time, whenever the community elders request it, show that he is doing this and give an accounting for his activity, especially since the nature of the office they hold obliges them [the elders] to exercise careful supervision over widows and orphans.

3) If, however, in the will left behind by the father a guardian has been appointed and he commits himself to satisfying the creditors and it is determined that he has the means to do so, in this case the assets shall not be frozen by the rabbi and lawyers but rather this be completely avoided.

Article Ten.

Concerning Matters of Debts and Bankruptcies.

1) IF A JEW has contracted debts to one or more creditors and neither makes payment at the date it is due nor is able to pay these debts in response to a lawsuit brought on the part of the creditors, he is to be dealt with by the courts as a bankrupt person, but immediately all of his assets both movable and immovable are to be described exactly, to be appraised by neutral experts, and then, in accordance with the legal procedures which have been introduced and the practice which is usual in each community, if the creditors are not willing to agree on a later date for payment, to be sold for the highest offer, but the money received for this be deposited temporarily with the courts or

community notaries until the creditors are satisfied, after which the bankrupt person must be required by the court to swear under oath whether and where he might still own hidden assets, and he must swear this oath in the presence of his wife.

2) Following this the courts shall promptly begin with the liquidation of all of the debts, and examine most carefully whether there is any dishonesty on the part of the creditors, for which purpose the courts, after prior careful research, shall also require of the latter that they swear under oath that they are not appearing with evil intentions.

3) The aforementioned liquidated debts are to be paid out of the total collected assets, to which any outstanding debts owed to the deceased which have been found are added, to each creditor in proportion to the debt owed to him, whereby the wife of the bankrupt person must come together [with other debtors] in the following manner with regard to her marriage contract.

4) She is to be given back, according to the usual practice here in this country, the clothing, jewelry, and other items she brought with her, which is understood to include any house or seat in the synagogue brought into the marriage and still owned. On the other hand, with regard to her dowry which she brought with her and has already given into the custody of her husband and other marriage contract obligations, she is to be regarded in the exactly the same way as all of the other creditors and paid *pro rata* according to the amount of the claims.

5) However, should the money brought with her not yet have been handed to the husband, this will not be part of the total of debts, nor will an inheritance belonging to the wife and not yet signed over to her husband.

6) A different procedure will be followed if the bankruptcy takes place after the death of her husband, in which case she, according to the practice in this country, in addition to the return of clothing, jewelry, and other items she brought with her, as well as any house or seat in the synagogue which is still owned, will be entitled to receive in cash 320 *fl. pohl.* if this was her first marriage, and 160 *fl. pohl.* if she had already been married before; with respect to the rest of the sum by which all of her money set aside for her by marriage contract exceeds the sum of money listed above which is to be handed out to her, this will be added along with the sums owed to the other creditors and paid *pro rata* with the other creditors in the manner determined above.

7) If, on the other hand, some promissory notes or letters of obligation are found which are co-signed by the wife, she will be responsible for these from her own assets in equal parts with her husband.

8) If one or more Christian creditors should appear in bankruptcy cases which occur [suddenly] in this way, the matter should be dealt with by the Christian noble landowner with jurisdiction for the place and all of the relevant information, with consideration to the laws regarding matters of debt, be brought forward.

9) If in the course of dealing with the bankruptcy it should come out that the bankrupt person had taken advantage of his creditors deliberately and with malice aforethought, he should have the ban proclaimed against him for 8 days and then be sentenced by the elders of the local community or also by the noble landowner with jurisdiction for the place to 4 weeks of imprisonment; and if in the course of this a considerable fraud and deception should be discovered, he shall not only be declared unfit to hold any Jewish offices for the rest of his life, but also, depending on the type and extent of the crime, after the report of his guilt is made by the elders of the community to the government office, be punished with the utmost severity through public work.

10) If, in the course of procedures of this kind dealing with bankruptcy, some wares or goods *in natura* are found which were not given to the debtor on purchase but entrusted to him for safekeeping or loaned to him, the owner, after appropriate proofs are given in the matter, is authorized to take back the things which belong to him as his property.

11) It happens often that one or another Jew who is not wealthy, in order to marry off their daughters to someone rich and respectable, will promise and confirm that they will give [their daughters] large dowries, but not from their own but from borrowed money and assets; now in order to avoid all deceitful consequences, if such a situation occurs within 3 months after the marriage of the daughter, except in cases of misfortune where it became apparent that the father had suffered a great [loss] by fire or theft, her husband should be required to put aside any dowry that was received in order to repay the creditors who had been deliberately misled.

12) If one or another debtor who does not own enough assets to pay all of his debts wants to show favoritism by treating one or another creditor more advantageously than the other creditors, because they are relatives or with other reasons in mind, or shortly before his insolvency becomes known, by deceptive means satisfies the claims of only a few of his creditors to the disadvantage of the rest, if this has taken place 3 months before the date the bankruptcy was declared, those creditors who were paid and are proven to have engaged in a fraudulent collusion with the debtor will in all cases be required to pay back the money they received *ad Massam* (into the general fund) so that each [creditor] can be paid back *pro rata*.

13) If, after the bankruptcy has been completely dealt with, a debtor whose money and possessions have been sold by the court in the prescribed manner and the proceeds used to satisfy the creditors, should still find a good friend who would give him a hand by giving him a loan toward restarting his business in order to help him back up, in this case the new creditor as well as the debtor must report the matter appropriately to the court and request a written statement concerning this, so that the previously unpaid creditors may not require payment of their outstanding demands through funds from this new loan; should the debtor, however, make a demonstrable profit from this, at the request of his previous creditors he can be called before the court every half year and required under oath to give an accounting for the income he has made and also what part of it he can use for the payment of his previous debts, and after swearing an oath, he will be bound in all cases to pay the sum decided upon correctly.

14) If young people incur debts, and especially single people, both during the lifetime of their parents as well as when they are orphaned, and issue written promissory notes or letters of obligation for this, often at a higher amount [rate of interest] simply in order to get money, these promissory notes or letters of obligation which were issued without the previous knowledge of their parents or guardians shall be declared null and void unless such a young person runs his own business or practices a trade for himself, and if it is found that a usurious deal has taken place, even if between Jews only, legal action shall be undertaken against them.

Article Eleven.

Concerning Loans and Collateral.

1) IF ONE JEW borrows money from another and gives collateral for this, and does not repay [the loan] within the time agreed upon, the creditor cannot just assume ownership of this collateral, but he must have a message about this sent to the debtor through a sworn witness of the community.

2) However, if the debtor regardless of this does not want to keep to the payment, the Jewish court, at the request of the creditor, can allow the debtor 3 days to redeem the collateral, and after 3 days have passed without results, to have the collateral appraised by an expert and then allow the debtor 4 weeks to reclaim, redeem it, and if, as well,

3) This date passes without results, the creditor will then be allowed to offer the collateral for sale publicly, by calling in two community notaries, and sell it to the highest bidder, from the proceeds repay himself with respect to the debt as well as interest and provable expenses, but to hand the remainder of the proceeds to the debtor.

4) All of this, however, is understood to apply to Jewish debtors; if the collateral has been given by a Christian, the creditor must turn to the Christian judicial level responsible for [the debtor], and await further action according to the prescribed legal process.

Article Twelve.

Concerning the Recording in Writing of Court Appraisals, and Sale of Jewish Houses and *Schulsessel* (seats in the synagogue).

1) EACH COMMUNITY SHALL keep a main real estate register book for all Jewish houses of their town, and then keep records in a separate book for all of the seats in the synagogue, and these are to be stored safely in a locked trunk which must remain permanently with the community notaries, and the keys are to be kept in the possession of the elders of the community, and this book, which should be considered conclusive, shall only be taken out of the trunk and opened in the presence of two elders of the community and one community notary.

2) The appraisal of the houses and seats in the synagogue must be carried out by the rabbi and lawyers in consultation with an expert, by whom then, in exchange for the usual fee, the appraisal document must be prepared.

3) In case this appraisal should be made for purposes of debts and there should be Christian creditors involved, this cannot be done without prior knowledge of and consultation with the noble landowner with jurisdiction for the place.

4) If someone wishes to sell his house or seat in the synagogue, he retains the right to make a contract with the buyer in this regard, however, this contract will not be entered into the real estate register book until the seller has reported this appropriately to the rabbi and requested to have the usual announcement made concerning the pending sale, which, according to the Jewish traditional practice must take place publicly in the school three times, namely the first time on a Monday, the second time on the following Thursday, and the last time on the next following Monday, at morning prayers, because on these days several Jews come together, and in this it is to be announced for the knowledge of everyone that all who have a legal claim to this house or seat in the synagogue should report this to the rabbi and lawyers, so that before the sale is concluded any objections can be dealt with honestly and cleared out of the way. After this formal requirement has been fulfilled, the rabbi and the lawyers must then prepare for the seller, in exchange for payment of the usual fee, a document for transfer of ownership, and must enter this word for word in the real estate register book.

Article Thirteen.

Concerning Accusations of Damage Brought to the Courts.

When disputes occur between Jewish neighbors, the party having suffered damage must bring their accusation concerning damage to the rabbi and the lawyers, one of whom, along with the community notaries, shall form a commission together with the litigants to view the scene, inform the legal advisors of each party in writing of this, and after a viewing of the scene, inform them of the decision of the court.

Article Fourteen.

Concerning the Court Fees.

All of the court fees which have usually been charged up to now by the rabbis, lawyers, and community notaries according to the old traditional practice in this country and according to the rate prescribed and recorded in the community record books of each Jewish community, shall remain in place unchanged unless the circumstances of one town or another require that a change in these be made.

PATENT*

About the Highest Privileges Accorded to the Neophytes

We etc.

*T*O ALL AND EVERY VASSAL and Citizen irrespective of the status, privilege and condition who find themselves in all Our Hereditary Kingdoms and Possessions is announced by Our Imperial—Royal, and also the Archduke's, Grace, that considering most charitably that in the Kingdom of Galicia and Lodomeria, among a large number of Jewry, more than a few of them take the Sacred Baptism, as such converting to a true and only Christian Catholic Faith that can offer salvation, We see it necessary to decree and order the privileges and the Rights of the Jewry that adopt the Christian Faith in regard to their future income and living conditions, so they themselves and their children who take the Sacred Baptism or are born in the Christian Faith can consider their future happiness. Accordingly, We order and charitably establish that

First. The Neophytes have immediate rights to settle in various Cities and Towns of Our Kingdoms and Principalities and We want them to enjoy the same freedoms as all other Citizens without any payments as herewith is declared in the most charitable manner. In addition,

Repeated for those Neophytes who want to settle on the Land, they are free to own Land, Fields, and Meadows; after paying to local Authority necessary Fees and other agricultural taxes, they can assume their ownership.

Third. We allow by Our Grace that the Neophytes can continue without the interference [to work] in the same Trade, in the way of making living or practice Profession, which they learned and practiced as Jews, and finally

Fourth. We charitably order that the Neophytes, in the places where they settle, are not to be prohibited from displaying symbols of their trade in front of the Houses or the places of living in the same way as [such practices] are customary among the Christian Craftsmen and Artisans, and in this manner:

Continuatio Edictorum et Mandatorum Universalium in Regnis Galiciæ et Lodomeriæ. A Die 1. Januarii Ad Ultimam Decembris 1780 Emanatorum. Leopoli 1780; pp: 46–47.

Fifth. We order that Neophytes, as other Foremen, are allowed [to keep] Christian apprentices; their Children who are conceived from the Christian marriage or brought together to the Sacred Baptism are to be admitted to the Crafts and Arts after paying the same tax as the children of the Christian Foremen.

Our highest Decree, as we herewith order, [should be] the most effectively implemented by Our Imperial—Royal Governments and their subordinate District Offices and, in special circumstances, they are to support the Neophytes according to these Regulations, and in such way they will not forget Our most kind Grace.

As such, Our most charitable Will and Intention will be fulfilled.

Proclaimed in Our Royal Capital the City of Lemberg on 30th day of September in the year of 1780.

Count Joseph des S. P. R. von Brigido.

L.S. [official seal]

Johann Maria Riegler, Secretary

PATENT*

On Abolition of the Jewish Administration and the
District Rabbis and On the Privileges Given to Jews

*T*HE CURRENT JEWISH REGULATION IN Galicia has provided little of the intended benefit, which led us to consider drafting an entirely new one. Because such comprehensive change will require some time to prepare, we consider it useful to send some decrees, which ought to be immediately and precisely implemented as the beginning of the new law.

Thus, we order:

1. The Jewish Administration, District Superiors, the so-called *Kahal* superiors, along with their clerks, as well as the rabbinic courts, which are not currently functioning, are to be abolished by the end of July. They are allowed to close their accounts over the next three months, which is until the last day of October; by that time they are expected to transfer their expenses or they could expect the most severe investigation.

2. The entire Jewish community and the individual Jews, along with other inhabitants of [Galicia], are under the jurisdiction of the proper authorities; in civil affairs, [they remain] under a local authority, a district office, and the national [Galician] government; in judicial matters, [they are under] local courts and the General Appellate Court, which are to judge Jewish interests and court cases according to general decrees and rules.

3. To serve Jewish communal (*Kahal*) affairs, whereby attention is paid to the *Kahal* order to take care of the poor and sick, to oversee everything related to religious customs or God's worship, to collect contributions for communal affairs and so on: each Jewish community should select six fit, good, and trusted people in the next fourteen days for submission to the District Authority [for approval]. The District Authority will select and confirm three out of the six proposed men, and in due time reward them for their honest work, which will be determined during the planning of domestic [communal] expenses.

Two populous Jewish communities in Lwów and Brody are allowed to select fourteen people to manage their many interests, and [their] District Authorities will choose and

Continuatio Edictorum et Mandatorum Universalium in Regnis Galicae et Lodomeriae. A Die 1. Januarii Ad Ultimam Decembris Anno 1785. Emanatorum. Leopoli 1785; pp. 91–93.

confirm seven communal elders. To avoid any misunderstandings and unrest in these two communities, these selections will take place in the presence of the district commissioner. Finally, the selection of communal elders will be renewed every three years in all Jewish communities. The communal elders will receive in due course more detailed official instructions. In the meantime, under this heavy responsibility, they are obligated to fulfill their office without any prejudice or exploitation of others.

To encourage Galician Jewry toward farming and other useful crafts and [means of] earning wages, Jews are given freedom to buy land and to learn crafts, as well as to use them. Those of them who will buy land or take leases on it are allowed to employ Christian laborers for the first three years, so they can sufficiently learn from them how to till the fields.

Those Jews who will take to useful crafts should not be prevented from carrying on their work or even [establishing] guilds for their own professions, as they will have the right to form them similarly to the Christians, and they are allowed to work their crafts among Christians and Jews as they wish, and they can sell their labor both at homes and in the public fairs. Not less, leasing of open spaces to the Jews ought to be allowed.

4. Jewish merchants and stall owners are required to maintain books regarding their trades in order and in a straightforward manner, and to keep these accountings in German or the local language; and their letters of obligation are to be written and issued in the customary format but not in the peculiar Jewish trading manner which has been prevalent to date. Those who refuse to follow this order will not only be forbidden to trade, but as arrogant bankrupts, they will be denied without warning [the right to] residence in the country.

5. Jews are broadly forbidden from peddling goods from house to house. However, they are allowed to buy local products from the peasants in the countryside. The land authorities and the district offices are to remain vigilant, to prevent Jews from acquiring these products in exchange for alcohol or bad [quality] goods. From those who are caught for the first time, their money, spirits, or goods are to be taken away, with one third given to the informant and the rest to the police; if caught for a second time, in addition, they should pay a substantial monetary fine; and finally, on the third occasion, in addition to confiscation [of their goods], they ought to be penalized with the loss of their residence permit and be thrown out of the country.

6. Jews wishing to marry are to pay the marriage tax according to the promulgated new Jewish regulation; however, a Jew who is not involved in anything other than farming will be entirely exempted from such tax. Finally, those who are subject to the tax according to their income and lifestyle are equitably organized according to the following three classes:

In the first class, to which belong those who earn a living with their own hands or service and have an annual income of only 100 *fl.*, the permitted [marriage] tax is 3 Ducats for the first son, 6 for the second son, 12 for the third son and so on for each subsequent son: for each next son the amount is double that of the previous [son]. Jews who belong to this class but earn more than 100 fl. will pay double the amount.

In the second class, Jews in public service will pay 12 Ducats for the first son, 24 for the second, 48 for the third and in the same manner, with each son the amount is doubled as compared with the previous [son].

In the third class, to which all Jews engaged in proper trade belong, if the father's annual income does not exceed 400 fl., they will pay 20 Ducats for the first son, 40 for the second son, 80 for the third son, and so on with the amount doubled for each successive son; however, if the father's annual income is [at least] 400 fl., then the payments are 30 Ducats for the first son, 60 for the second, and 120 for the third son. These [marriage] agreement taxes are paid now in money; after 3 years, they ought to be satisfied with goods produced by Jewish hands.

As to the tributes and obligations owed to the manorial estates, a Jew who owns the land like a Christian landowner, or one who owns no land like a tenant farmer but engages in a trade similar to a Christian merchant, should be treated by the [manorial] authority in the same manner, and except for routine obligations, additional money for protection or other [privileges] could not be demanded.

from Vienna May 27, 1785.

JOSEPH.

(L. S.)

Count Leopold von Kollowrat.

Johann Wenzel von Margelik

PATENT*

That every Jew adopts a permanent surname from January 1, 1788

WE JOSEPH etc.

*T*O AVOID ALL DISTURBANCES, WHICH must happen among certain groups of people in political and judicial affairs, as well as in their private lives, when their Families do not have fixed surnames, particularly when the individuals have no established names, the following is decided for all Hereditary Lands.

§. I. Herewith *the Jewry* is urged in all Provinces that each house owner for his own family — each guardian of the orphans under his care, all single men neither under Paternal powers nor under their care, or those men not remaining under a tutelage adopt *permanent surnames* from January 1, 1788, and so females of *unmarried status* adopt the name of their *Fathers* — *married* women to take *their husbands'* surnames — every person in particular and without exceptions is to take a *German name* and such is not to be changed ever during their lives.

§. 2. All surnames used until now in the *Jewish language* that are derived from a permanent or a temporary residence, e.g., *Schaulem Töpliz* — *Jochem Kollin* etc., based on a customary adoption [of the name], will entirely cease to be in use.

§. 3. Until *the end of November 1787*, every Father on behalf of his Family [and] every [other] person will provide in writing, in German, the adopted name and the surname to a local magistrate or a local Authority, where [the petitioners] have been allowed to live or to take a residence; after such declaration, the certificate — without stamps — signed by the district clerks and by the district [rabbi] or the highest rabbi should read: *that they now and forever have taken the Family name of X. together with the German given names for each individual — that they are from the same generation and before used the name of X.X.*

§. 4. From January 1, 1788, in the books of *the circumcisions* and *births* kept in the German language without exception — all *born, married or dead* ought not to be recorded in any other way than using the German given name and *permanently adopted* surname as well.

Continuatio Edictorum et Mandatorum Universalium in Regnis Galiciæ et Lodomeriæ. A Die 1. Januar. Ad Ultimam Decembr. Anno 1787 Emanatorum. Leopoli 1787; pp. 169–171.

§. 5. The certificate from local Authorities or their clerks ordered in §. 3. is to be carefully safeguarded; [it ought to be] shown to the Officer during the first house search on the occasion of conscription; for the first time in the year 1788, *two sets of names*— that is: the name used up to now, then the name and the surname, which are adopted forever and are recorded in German. In the conscription books for the next year *only newly adopted names* will be found.

§. 6. Hereby, it is generally announced that these requirements are waived for Jews who until the end of December 1787 can produce signed documents procured in the past, which will remain in power.

§. 7. To prevent the circumventing [of this law] in various ways and to implement this law, the following penalties are in force.

a) Any Rabbi who from January 1, 1788 will not maintain the [records of] births, marriages, and deaths in the German language in accordance with the permanent surnames; or if such books will not be kept in the German language; [he] will pay a penalty of 50. Zł. Ryń. for the first offense; for the next offense, he will be relieved of his duties and declared unfit to serve in this capacity.

b) Anyone, regardless of gender, who will not use the given name and the surname permanently chosen, adopting something else — if financially well-off — will be also punished with the penalty of 50. Zł. Ryń. If the offender is poor, he will be removed together with his Family from all Our Lands; however, the obligations on the account of his debts will always remain valid.

c) Anyone who will not present his own documents according to the above procedures until the end of November 1787 will be punished with the penalty of 10. Zł. Ryń.; or, in case of poverty, should be punished with 8 days of public works.

d) A half of all financial penalties will be given to the Jewish domestic fund in each province — another half will be appropriated to those reporting violations.

Proclaimed in Our Capital and Residence City of Vienna on 28th day of August, 1787. In 24th year of our [Holy] Roman reign, and in 7th year of [the reign in] the hereditary lands [of the Monarchy].

JOSEPH.

L.S. [official seal]

COUNT LEOPOLDUS von KOLLOWRAT.

Anton Friedrich von Mayern.

PATENT*

Jews are accorded equal rights and freedoms to those of Christians

WE etc.

*A*FTER RENDERING PRIOR DECREES CONCERNING Jewry, it was judged based on and according to the undertaken laws of Toleration, as well as for the general benefit, that all existing differences between Christian and Jewish subjects that have been sanctioned by the law until now be abolished, and to provide the safeguards for the Jews living in *Galicia* to benefit from all rights and freedoms enjoyed by our other subjects.

In general, from now on, Galician Jewry has the same rights and duties as other subjects. In particular, the decree stipulates the implementation of changes in regard to *the practice of Religion, Education, Community Regulations, Population, Life Style, Political and Judicial Affairs* in the following manner.

Religion

§. 1. All Jews are to be free to practice the Religion of their ancestors, the faith learned since childhood, without the slightest impediment for as long as it is in accordance with the current [civil] laws and regulations of the country.

§. 2. Instead of *local Rabbis* who are present among many communities, there will be only one *official Rabbi* [seated] in every district to serve the Jewish Community in the district town, or if the district town does not have the Jewish community, the rabbi will be placed in another town of the same district where a larger Jewish community is found. All other Jewish communities are allowed to have only *the teachers of Religion*.

§. 3. The district Rabbi has the oversight over the teachers of Religion *in the entire* district; he issues the certificates after administering exams to those applying for the job.

§. 4. Similar to the responsibilities for the teacher of Religion, it is the duty of the district Rabbi 1. to keep the register of births, marriages, and deaths in his Jewish Community, and 2. to oversee kosher butchers (*schächter*).

---

*Continuatio Edictorum et Mandatorum Universalium in Regnis Galiciæ et Lodomeriæ. A Die 1. Januar. Ad Ultimam Decembr. Anno 1789 Emanatorum. Leopoli 1789; pp. 101–111.

§. 5. The election of district Rabbis is to take place on the day, in the manner of, and for duration of the term described in §. 18, which details the election of the Authorities in the community, with the difference that only one Rabbi is elected and it is not required that he is from the Community of electors. To make sure that the selected individual accepts the offered seat, it is required to notify the district [governmental] office about the election after the passage of four weeks.

Six years after the first election, carried out according to this Manifesto, the candidates for the Office of the Rabbi will be required to demonstrate knowledge of the German educational system in schools.

§. 6. In case of the district Rabbi's death while in office and with the election more than four months away, a temporary [rabbi] is needed to be placed; [the Jewish community] is required to notify the district [governmental] office within six weeks.

§. 7. The teachers of Religion also known as *Szams,* and other community servants, can be installed according to the will of the community. However, they are required to be from the community, proportionally to [the community's] size and its wealth. They ought to receive decent salaries or be rewarded for their services on an annual basis; this reward ought to be precisely defined and confirmed by the district [governmental] office. All [Jewish] communities should contribute to such salaries according to their wealth.

§. 8. The alien preachers and the teachers of religion are forbidden to join the community, and considered vagrants liable to punishment.

§. 9. Those communities, which for the practice of their Religion have a *Synagogue* or selected private home for public services, are allowed to continue with those, to improve them or to build new; the district [governmental] office will issue permission irrespective of the wealth of the community.

If any Jew wishes to receive permission for himself to have religious services in his own home with Torah, he will pay tax of 50 Zł. Ryń. per year, which will be directed to secular Jewish schools.

§. 10. Each [Jewish] community is permitted to have their own cemetery, called *okopisko,* with the land purchased from the government. For the permits to build a *new* Synagogue or to establish a cemetery, the appropriate local taxes have to be paid.

Education

§. 11. For the betterment of Jewry through the enlightenment of mind and [for the purpose of] learning useful customs, so salutary efforts of the Government could succeed,

German schools that are styled on secular schools will be established for the Jewish youth in each community as much as possible. The teachers in these schools, *the Community Translators*, ought to be sworn.

§. 12. Because of the current system, the Jewry benefits in more than one way from the knowledge of the German language and having the ability to write, as such, in those localities where the German school is established, no youngster will be admitted to receive lessons from the Talmud without the certificate from the teacher of the German School that he appropriately attended the German School and succeeded in learning.

To maintain this regulation, the above School workers and Teachers appointed in the German Schools in the Jewish communities should remain vigilant and immediately report any violations to the district office; the head of the family whose children receive [religious] education without the certificate from the teacher of the German school will be punished with three days in jail for each child, and the efforts are to be made to send the pupils to the German school.

§. 13. No Jew can get married without showing the certificate as stipulated in §. 12, which [states] that he was trained in the German language either in a public School or at home. A waiver is issued for those who are 13 years of age in 1786.

Those who will violate this regulation and get married will be punished; those who administer the marriage vows will be removed from office and declared unfit to serve in any official capacity.

§. 14. To allow those Jews who want to commit themselves to a career in the profession of teacher, to receive appropriate training, the Jewish School Teacher Seminary is established by the Main Normal School in Lemberg, under the oversight of the School Directorate. It will be financed from the mandatory protection tax in the amount of 5 Zł. Ryń. paid by every head of the family irrespective of wealth and profession.

Community Regulations

§. 15. Galician Jewry has been divided into 141 [administrative] communities and with the addition of Bukovina into 143 [communities]; as such, these divisions should remain.

§. 16. Joining [administrative] communities by the Jews is designed to benefit *especially the Jews*; these communities ought to be considered [community] associations and there will be no differences between their members and any other subject living elsewhere. Hence, every Jewish dweller belongs to a [local] community where both the Christian and the Jewish dwellers belong; and [the Jew] can be elected as the superior of a local community and it is forbidden to prevent him from representing all, despite the fact that he as a Jew was assigned to one of the 143 communities.

§. 17. To direct the interests [of the local population], *its superiors* should be elected in every community. Their number is decided to be three in all Communities, except the cities of Lemberg and Brody, where because of their size it is determined that seven are needed.

§. 18. The election of the community superiors should be carried out under following principles.

1. Every three years on the 15th day of September, or the next day in case of the Jewish holiday; the first election is to take place in 1789.

2. *All house owners* in the community have the right to participate in the election. If there are many owners of a house, only *one* who has the largest portion of it ought to vote.

3. *Superiors* are to be chosen from the members of the Community.

4. Those who do not own a house are not eligible [to participate] in the election. After the time, as indicated in the §. 5 in respect to a Rabbi, they should also demonstrate knowledge from German education in schools.

5. Each Community elects *six*, whereas Lemberg and Brody elect [a total of] *fourteen* superiors.

6. During elections, a deputy nominated by local authorities, whereas in Lemberg and Brody, a *District Commissioner,* will oversee votes together with the current community superior.

7. The latter will compile voting ballots from those who are deemed qualified; he has the right to add his *own* name [to the ballot].

   Every voter will be given a voting ballot; then he will *tear away* the name [of the candidate] and will give it to a person collecting votes. The majority vote decides [the election].

8. Six or fourteen candidates selected by the majority vote will be submitted no later than fourteen days to the district office; the list is to be *signed* by the Deputy of the Authorities or the District Commissioner in Lemberg and Brody.

9. From the submitted list of the candidates, the district office will appoint without any delay *three*, whereas for Lemberg and Brody *seven* actual

community superiors will be appointed. [Their names] will be reported to the Provincial Government and announced as the superiors to [each] gathered Jewish community.

10. If there are disagreements during an election, the district office will appoint the community superiors on its own.

11. The community superiors appointed by the district office will take up their duties on the 1st of November.

12. The election and the submission of the candidates will always take place, even if the community wishes to reconfirm the current superiors occupying the office. In such a case, the community will inform the district office about its wish or provide in writing the *signed* list with the results of the majority vote; if there are no important objections such demand will always be considered.

13. If during the *first* two years, any of the superiors die or leave the office in any other way, then the community will select and submit *two* candidates as replacement *in the same manner* as above. In the *third* year, the position will be left vacant until a popular vote.

§. 19. *Superiors have the following duties*: when needed, they represent their community in name, they defend its rights, they take care of feeding poor Jews, they administer payments for community affairs; in unusual circumstances, they appeal to the district office and negotiate or maintain whatever is needed for the benefit of the community.

In this and all community affairs and accounting, only the *German language will be used*.

As to detailed information regarding official duties, [the community] superiors will receive separate instructions.

In their official duties on behalf of the community, an individual superior will answer for all and all will answer for everyone; hence, they ought to divide the responsibilities among themselves according to the agreement, or rotate official duties among themselves.

§. 20. Communities will honor their superiors, obey and follow them in their official capacity. The magistrates and district offices will also treat them with deference.

According to its size and resources, each community will establish *annual* monetary compensation or will determine other *benefits*, which will be confirmed by the district office. Their election tax will be entirely waived.

§. 21. In reciprocity, the community superiors will fulfill their duties precisely, faithfully, and eagerly; they will avoid [making] any demands for money in open or in secret, as well as desist from any illegal actions. Otherwise, in case of violations, they will be punished with double severity and commensurate with the felony, they will receive *corporal punishment*, they will be punished with removal from the office, and [they will receive] banishment from the country.

§. 22. To cover expenses in the community and [to address] its needs, each house owner should contribute money according to his *earning Groups*.

There are three Groups.

First Group consists of those who sow [seeds] on their own or the leased fields, those who make living from working with their hands or providing service to others, as well as craftsmen, agents, peddlers, wagon drivers, and innkeepers.

Second Group consists of persons in public or community service, such as physicians, surgeons, rabbis, Jewish teachers, as well as those who are trained in the free arts [possibly medicine or law].

Third Group consists of those who make a living from proper homestead or commerce, as well as leaseholders, manufacturers, moneychangers, merchants, and capitalists.

Population Status

§. 23. Information regarding the *Jewish population and the variations* [in regard to their residence], which are also needed for the country will be gathered; *conscription of the souls* by the military will be carried out and continued among the Jews, as it is customarily done among the Christian subjects.

§. 24. Any [prior] *restrictions* as to their numbers or the place [of residence] of the Jewish families come to an end entirely. Thus the Jews have the same freedoms as those guaranteed by the decrees for the Christian subjects, and further, this Manifesto for the Jews does not contain any hindrance, so they can marry without paying any taxes for the permission to marry according to the general laws for the citizens and they ought to follow the general *Regulations* [for all citizens] that cover marriage contracts issued for Galicia.

§. 25. After the year 1790, *only* Jews who are farmers or craftsmen will be allowed to live in the villages. After this deadline, Jews who are caught in the villages while making a living in any other way, as well as lords who are hosting them or tolerating them, will be severely punished.

§. 26. Foreign Jews are allowed to immigrate to and settle in Galicia according to the current decree only if they declare that they want to devote themselves to toiling in agricultural fields and will cover the cost of their homestead.

In case of a useful merchant or an artisan who wants to settle in Galicia, such a person is to apply for permission to the appropriate country government [office].

§. 27. [Jews are] allowed to relocate from one place to another in the same way as other subjects are free to move from one [feudal] possession to another to improve their own living conditions.

§. 28. *Emigration* of individual Jews or entire families is allowed after the exit tax prescribed by the law is paid. Those considering emigration [from Galicia] ought to settle financial matters with their land authority, their community, or if applicable, their creditors, and submit trustworthy statements to the district offices, as well as to indicate how much of their possessions they intend to take; [the district offices] will forward their request to the Provincial Government. Those caught emigrating without permission from the Provincial Government will be treated according to the Manifesto Regulating Emigration.

§. 29. To maintain order both in the conscription registers and in other current affairs, it has been already announced that each Head of the family adopt a fixed *surname.*

He will be addressed using such surname, and his children and descendants ought to carry the same name for as long as they live in the Hereditary Lands [of the Monarchy]. Anyone who signs a public statement without the adopted surname, or submits it to the civil administration regardless of the level, will be punished with a 14 day jail term.

§. 30. In order to maintain precise and timely information regarding the Jewish population, each Head of the family is obligated to inform the community superiors about the changes in his own family; in conjunction with the rabbi, or if the rabbi is not present with the Head Teacher [of the Jewish School], a reliable register of births, marriages, and deaths is to be kept in the German language similar to the registers required from the clergy in the Christian communities.

Lifestyle

§. 31. The Jewry is allowed to take any *craftsmanship* [of their choice] and all other means of succeeding in life, which have been available for other citizens of the country and permitted by the law; accordingly, all existing limitations that exclusively concerned Jews cease in entirety.

§. 32. The exception is made only regarding [the right to] the *leases* that lead to more laziness than beneficial diligence among the Jews; those ought to be forbidden as long as they demonstrate participation and diligence in other ways of earning a living. For these reasons, the limitation where Jews have been excluded from the *leases on the taverns*, both in the villages and in towns, should remain in effect.

The district offices will diligently uphold [the law]; in case of violations, a Jew holding a *tavern lease* will receive sufficient corporal punishment and will be removed from the lease. The owners who permit such leases [to occur] will be subjected to financial penalties related to the anticipated income; in the *first instance*, a half year's income, in the *second instance*, the sum of the full profit from the lease for the entire year, in the *third instance*, they will be separated from the management of their own estates.

§. 33. Alcohol distribution by the Jews is now only permitted in towns where it is carried out in their own houses on their own behalf.

The regulation dated 5th of November 1784, which had permitted Jews who carried this profession until then to continue to earn a living in such way, is hereby renewed. This right is terminated in case of death of the tavern owner or when the house is sold and it cannot be transferred onto the successors of the owner.

§. 34. For the same reasons that require removal of Jews from tavern leases, they are excluded for the benefit of Galician Subjects from [taking leases on]:

1. Single fields that belong to the subject paying contributions [to the owner]

2. Mills

3. Tithe collection on behalf of lords or the clergy

4. Market fair, stable, animal fat, road or pavement as the objects [of the lease]; the hereditary or term-based lease of the entire estate is not subject to these restrictions; as such, neither the lease of the real estate or the collection of a lord's revenues [are forbidden] for as long they are not divided.

A Jew who will engage in the lease, which is forbidden by law, as well as those who create such opportunities, will be liable to the penalties stated in §. 32.

§. 35. Besides craftsmanship, professions, and permitted leases, Galician Jews are allowed to engage in a variety of commerce, with all types of merchandise, if they follow general Merchant Regulations and maintain bookkeeping in the customary language of the country. The same permission covers foreign Jews and the Jewish citizens of Brody, which is analogous to trade permits received by alien Christian merchants in Galicia.

§. 36. Jews are permitted to carry merchandise from one house to another, similarly in the cities and towns, as well as villages, in accordance with general regulations.

§. 37. To introduce Jews into agriculture and to assist poor Jewish families in making livings while cultivating fields, each Jewish Community will settle a certain number of Jewish families on the land at its own expense and support them according to the category of income.

§. 38. In light of opening a variety of honest ways to the Jewry, it is appropriate to strictly maintain regulations in regard to idlers, vagabonds, and aggressive beggars, as well as to legitimately poor [Jews].

§. 39. Hence, each Jewish community ought to make efforts to feed their poor in the same manner as is customary among Christians; in those communities where Jews and Christians are [living] together, both the Jews and the Christians should undertake the support of the local poor and equally contribute to [them].

§. 40. In case of disaster, when one or more Jewish households is burned without their fault, the district office may allow those victims to collect donations as [is allowed] to the Christian subjects.

Political and Judicial Regulations

§. 41. In political [civil] affairs, the Jewry remains under a general national authority according to the mandated law.

To this end, in the same manner as other citizens, a Jew will first submit a complaint or request to his [local] land authority, then to the district office, and finally to the Country Government; the complaints are to be submitted always in German when applying at the last two levels [of the administration] and to demonstrate that this regulation is being followed, the resolutions undertaken by lower levels are to be appended, with the exception of a complaint concerning a delay by the lower level [of the administration] when such appendix cannot be produced.

§. 42. Internal community disagreements will be addressed by local authorities and it is not necessary to burden the district offices with these affairs.

§. 43. If the Jews, in their capacity as land authorities, become part of disputes between *the serfs against the authority*, then they should be treated as other subjects according to the Decree from the 1ˢᵗ of September, 1781 concerning serfdom.

§. 44. As the Galician Jewry is subordinated in their civil affairs to the Country Government, they ought to depend on secular courts [concerning] *Judicial Affairs* accordingly.

As their Judicial Powers are *suspended*, rabbis are forbidden from announcing small and big bans under penalty of 50 guldens, [also from] meting out penalties in public, and performing any duties that belong to the Judicial Powers.

§. 45. To avoid submission of numerous demands or requests in the name of the Jewish community to the district offices and the Country Government, the papers on behalf of an *individual* person or *a single* group will not be accepted from any Jewish community, unless they are signed by the superiors of the community, as appropriate deputies of the community, and stamped with the seal of the community.

§. 46. All legal disputes between Jews and Christians, regardless of the subject, or among themselves, ought to be processed and ruled by the judge of the first instance who is a *local authority, magistrate*, or the one to whom the case is assigned, according to the country general legal code. Further appeals are then to proceed to the *appellate court*.

§. 47. As the Jewry is considered in all aspects the same as other subjects, in consequence, all formerly ordered or implemented superficial signs according to the customs that distinguish [Jews] in carrying themselves or in dress are *ordered to cease entirely* beginning in 1791; in use until now, the special garment of rabbis is left [without change] and *allowed*.

Civic Duties

§. 48. Equal benefits for Jews and the Christians that stem from the public defense [law], call for the common civic duties for [the benefit of the country], which are shared by them and the Christians. These responsibilities consist of public service and contributions.

Accordingly, they are obligated to provide *messengers*, to make *road improvements*, those who permanently have cattle to provide supplies to the military, as other local citizens do; Jewish house owners in places where there is work done on local roads, should conduct work around the roads themselves, or using their Jewish household members, or [hire] Jewish laborers.

In places where the Jews receive land from lords, they ought to behave according to what is established in this respect by a new *Urbarium* Manifesto [i.e., taxation regulations].

§. 49 The Jews can be drafted into *Militia* as are Christian subjects; as such, all current regulations governing conscription apply to the Jews.

To prevent their dispersion among different Regiments, they ought to be conscripted mainly to military transportation support units, where they can follow together the dietary laws of their religion and customs.

It further is ordered that Jews are not to be forced to do any work on their Sabbath other than what is necessary and similar to the work ordered to be done by Christians on Sundays and Holy Days.

To those Jews who wish to be under arms rather than in the transportation units, such requests should be granted.

§. 50. Jewish contributions are: *Protection tax and Consumption of the Kosher Meat tax.*

§. 51. Every Jewish household head ought to pay annually 4 Zł as the Protection tax; with the exception of those who till the soil or are exempted for other reasons.

The contribution will be [collected] in the same manner as among Christian subjects.

§. 52. *The Tax on Consumption of Kosher Meat is paid:*

1. Per Polish pound of Beef, Veal, Lamb or Goat Meat 1¾ Kr.

2. Per hen or pigeon 1 Kr.

3. Per goose 7 Kr.

4. Per turkey 10 Kr.

§. 53. *Payments* are to be submitted in the following way:

All Beef meats have to be taxed, except for the *head, legs, and the internal* organs that can be left for the butcher for sale in compensation for the slaughter [of the animal].

§. 54. Any portion of kosher beef that is cleaned and can be sold to the Jews should be taxed.

The so-called *impure* [tainted] *meat* that is not kosher can be sold by Jewish butchers.

§. 55. Butchers should never be forced to sell kosher meat at regular prices to the military or to other Christian citizens of the country, while higher prices are set only for the Jews.

§. 56. On the other hand, Jewish butchers are sternly forbidden to sell kosher meat under any pretext at the extraordinary prices, with the surcharge calculated excessively, so the defenseless Jewry could not be burdened while exercising their customs.

§. 57. The [Jewish] butcher should not engage in the service without *permission* in writing from the directorate of treasury; the first time violator will be fined 50 Zł. Ryń, but the second time, he will be deemed unfit to [continue in] the profession.

Local rabbis [and] teachers of religion are to compel kosher butchers not to dare to operate without permission.

Where local rabbis and teachers of religion will forfeit this duty, resulting in a violation of the ban, they will be removed from office and fined with a financial penalty of 100 Zł. Ryń., from which one half will belong to the income account and the second half to the police account.

§. 58. To prevent stealing, kosher butchers will always live in towns. When a Jew, who wants to have his cattle slaughtered in a proper way, lives at a distance, he ought to bring the cattle to the closest kosher butcher or call for the butcher to come to him.

§. 59. It is equally forbidden to transport meat from one place to another. If meat in violation of this rule is found anywhere, it will be subject to confiscation; the criminal will be forced to pay not only tax, but also an additional 1 Zł. Ryń. per each pound. From this amount one half will be remitted to the income account and the second half to the police account in the district.

§. 60. No Galician Jew is allowed to work beyond the country borders or transport foreign meat from abroad, nor bring alien kosher butcher into the country.

Further, foreign Jews coming to the country are forbidden to bring the type of the meat that is subject to taxation. All such products ought to be taken from their owners and divided among the local poor. In addition, the owners will be ordered to pay the penalties stated in §. 59.

§. 61. Whomever will report [to the authorities] about illegal income will be awarded a financial prize for as long as the proceeds will be deposited in the income account [for the purpose of taxation].

§. 62. If Jewish butchers and those dealing with kosher meat cannot provide sufficient meat to the Jews, then the directorate of the treasury is allowed to appoint their own butchers.

§. 63. Finally, each community should furnish necessary scales from the income generated by the leases [given] to the butchers.

§. 64. All above regulations concerning Jewish contributions do not apply to Jews living in the district of Bukovina. In this regard, current taxes remain in force until further notice.

Thus given our attention to all aspects of law concerning Galician Jewry, having our interest in providing true and permanent benefit of the Monarch's Protection for them, which is assured by this decree, we expect the Galician Jewry to become worthy of it through strict compliance with the duties imposed on them.

In Vienna, 7th Day of May 1789.

JOSEPH.

L.S. [official seal]

Franz Karl von Kressel.   Joseph von Alten Sumerau.

CIRCULAR*

In regard to Jewish marriage rights

*B*ASED ON THE COURT DECREE from February 18 regarding various complaints of Jews against the marriage regulations, and request for removal from the marriage regulations, specifically from chapter 3 of the first part of the Civil code, two points concerning the forbidden degree of kinship [between the two] and concerning divorce Letters, His Grace [the Emperor] most kindly rendered an opinion. Accordingly:

First: The marriage should not be forbidden based on blood relationships except for a marriage between Brother and Sister, and between Sister and the Son or Grandson of her Brother or Sister. The kinship between them will make them ineligible for marriage only for the closest relationships; that is, the husband is not allowed to marry a relative of the wife up and down the line, nor he is allowed to marry the wife's sister, and the wife is not permitted to marry a relative of her husband up and down the line, neither is she allowed to marry the brother of her husband, nor the son or the grandson of her husband's brother or sister.

Only under special circumstances, the request for the Waiver can be applied to the [civil] Authority when the husband wants to marry the sister of his deceased wife.

Two: Legally bound marriage contracts can be dissolved only by a Letter of divorce presented from the husband to his wife. Although such letters can be written on the request of both sides by their co-religionists, they are neither legally bound nor is the marriage dissolved, unless both sides are present in person in front of the [civil] Authority and thereby the husband presents the wife with the divorce Letter.

If the wife committed adultery, then the husband has right to send her away by the divorce Letter, even against her will; however, her action has to be first proven in court.

Except for the above instance, no Letter of divorce is valid, unless the husband freely and without duress agrees to give such a letter, and the wife freely and without duress agrees to receive such. At the same time, the Authority over the couple wishing to divorce should not hear their case before they present a written statement from their Rabbi or Teacher.

To this end, such married couple should present themselves to their Rabbi or Teacher, and those should use all arguments and similar convincing steps to reunite them, and only

---

Continuatio Edictorum et Mandatorum Universalium in Regnis Galiciæ et Lodomeriæ. A Die 1. Januarii Ad Ultimam Decembris 1791 Emanatorum. Leopoli 1791; pp. 29–30.

in cases when such persuasions are futile, they will issue a statement in writing that they fulfilled their duty, but despite all efforts failed to dissuade the couple from divorcing.

If the Authority determines that there is a hope of reconciliation for the married couple, then divorce should not be immediately declared, but the couple be sent away for one to two months to reconsider [the decision]; however, if that the step is futile, or from the beginning the reconciliation is not given any hope, the Authority should permit giving the Letter of divorce, but only in the case that both spouses once again attest that they are freely committed to agree to give and to take the resolution.

In Lwów, the 21st day of March 1791.

Sigmund Count de Gallenberg.

Jozef Theodor de Thoren.

GUBERNIUM REGULATION*

Illegal Jewish Marriages Should Not Be Allowed

*A*CCORDING TO DATA PROVIDED IN the military year of 1825 by the county offices to the provincial government of the crownland, in the entirety of Galicia and Bukovina taken together there were not more than 137 Jewish couples legally married. Such a discrepancy between the number of the known [legal] ceremonies and the size of the Jewish population leaves the vast majority of Jewish marriages that are not registered in the district offices therefore invalid.

It will not escape the district offices, how necessary it is to put the end to this situation that results in confusion due to illegal marriages, where so many Jews in such civil relations produce illegitimate children facing barriers [in the society]. Therefore, the district offices should urge the subordinate magistrate clerk, the director of the Jewish community board, the rabbi, and the teacher of religion to exercise all available means to them to prevent those illegal marriages, and especially act on marriages where [the couple] did not attend the German school necessary to fulfill existing requirements for obtaining permission [issued] by the district office. [In such cases, they are] to determine whether [the couple] can apply for the waiver according to the regulations of the provincial diet.

Also, both the magistrates and local authorities in the district ought to pay special attention to the law on the discovery and punishment of Jews living in unlawful marriages. The efforts of the district offices should double, and this will be assessed in the next administrative year, based on statements from the provincial government of the crownland on Jewish wedding ceremonies.

Gubernium Regulation from June 28, 1826. Gub. number 38788.

*Provinzial Gesetzsammmlung des Königreiche Galizien und Lodomerien für das Jahr 1826. Lemberg 1826; pp. 101–102.

CHAPTER 1

1.   Simon M. Dubnow. *History of the Jews in Russia and Poland from the Earliest Times until the Present Day*. Philadelphia 1916; vol. 1, pp. 39–42. Described the earliest alleged sightings of Jews in the Slavic lands. Stories of Jewish merchants from the German provinces of Charlemagne's Empire of the ninth century were mentioned. The legend was also told about a certain Abraham who was offered (and declined) a princely honor by some assembly of Slavs in the future Polish lands. The first documented migration from Bohemia was in 1098.

2.   Simon M. Dubnow. *History of the Jews in Russia and Poland from the Earliest Times until the Present Day*. Philadelphia 1916; vol. 1, pp. 50–54.

3.   Simon M. Dubnow. *History of the Jews in Russia and Poland from the Earliest Times until the Present Day*. Philadelphia 1916; vol. 1, pp. 123–124 and 127–129. Moses Isserles (1520–1572) was one of the greatest Jewish scholars of the period; he wrote a commentary for the Code of the Jewish Laws (*Shulchan Aruch*), highlighting the differences between Sephardic and Ashkenazim traditions. Others, however, often resorted to investigations and issuing *"responsa"* to seemingly minute issues (for example, providing detailed arguments on whether a woman was guilty of adultery, if the act was committed with a devil presenting himself in the guise of her husband or a Polish nobleman).

4.   Nathan Hannover. *Abyss of Despair*. Transaction Publishers New Brunswick (USA) and London (UK) 2005; p. 115. The fairs were held in the summer in Zasław and Jarosław; they took place in the winter in Lwów and Lublin. The author lived in the seventeenth century and referred to times prior to 1648.

5.   *The Memoirs of Ber of Bolechów (1723–1805)*. Humphrey Milford Oxford University Press 1922; p. 29. Cited economic policies of the municipal councils and the national assembly, directed against Jewish merchants. The law of 1643 stipulated that the profit on imported goods was to be capped at three percent for Jewish traders, at five percent for foreign merchants, and at seven percent for Poles selling the merchandise. Further, customs dues were applied differentially; Jews and Protestants (Lutherans) paid ten percent and twelve percent of the value of the imported goods, whereas Catholic traders were obligated to pay only eight percent.

6.   *Słownik Geograficzny Królestwa Polskiego i Innych Krajów Słowiańskich.* Editors B. Chlebowski, W. Walewski, F. Sulimerski; Warszawa 1888; vol. IX, pp. 692–695; and J. S. Zubrzycki. *Rohatyn Miasto Królewskie.* Kraków 1914; pp. 2–10. Provides details of Rohatyn's early history. There is some discrepancy regarding the exact time when the village of Filipowice became a town. Besides "*Rohagyn* in the Halicz diocese" mentioned in 1390, another document referred to Rohatyn becoming a town only in 1415.

7.   Roxolana (circa 1500–1558) was a historical figure, the daughter of a local Orthodox priest from Rohatyn. She was captured by the Tatars circa 1520, and brought as a slave to the city of Kaffa. From there, Roxolana was transported to Istanbul and sold to the harem of the sultan. She was mentioned in the mid-1500s in a report from Istanbul; her original name was reported to be Alexandra Anastasia Lisowska or Barbara Glinska. Roxolana is buried in the Süleymaniye Mosque in Istanbul.

8.   Based on the royal privileges issued by Polish king Władysław IV (1633) and reaffirmed by King John II Casimir (1663) (The Czartoryski Archives, Kraków, Poland).

9.   Israel Zinberg. *A History of Jewish Literature. The German-Polish Cultural Center.* The Ktav Publishing House, Inc. 1975, vol. VI; pp. 121–126. Described the life of Nathan (Natan Note) Hannover (?–1683) who witnessed the massacres of the Cossack rebellion in 1648 in the town of Zasław, approximately one hundred and forty miles east of Rohatyn. He escaped first to Germany and then to Italy. Hannover published *Abyss of Despair* (*Yeven Metzulah*) in Venice in 1653, which was translated from Hebrew to Yiddish in Amsterdam in 1655. The book was also published in several European languages.

10.   Simon M. Dubnow. *History of the Jews in Russia and Poland from the Earliest Times until the Present Day.* Philadelphia 1916; vol;. 1, pp. 150–151. The siege of Lwów took place in September 1648.

11.   Based on the royal privilege issued by King Michael Korybut (1669) in response to "the infidel Jews from Rohatyn [regarding] the trading fair that was traditionally held on Tuesdays" (The Czartoryski Archives, Kraków, Poland).

12.   Based on annual inventory records of Rohatyn for the years 1686–1725 (The Czartoryski Archives, Kraków, Poland).

13.   Israel Zinberg. *A History of Jewish Literature. The German-Polish Cultural Center.* The Ktav Publishing House, Inc. 1975, vol. VI; pp. 135–145. Provides a critical picture of the teaching methods (*pilpul* and *hillukim*) that dominated the period of decline in the late seventeenth and early eighteenth centuries. The quote is from Berechiah Berach Spira, a preacher from Kraków, who published his sermons in *Zera Berach* (Amsterdam edition 1730).

14.   Tobias Cohn (1652–1729) was educated at the University of Padua in Italy. The quote is from his book *Lost in the Doorway* (*Maaseh Tuviyyah*), first published in Venice in 1707. Contradicting his belief in rational thought, Cohn made reference in the same book to Copernicus's theory of the earth moving around the sun; but he ultimately rejected it because of Biblical verses to the contrary (Israel Zinberg. *A History of Jewish Literature. The German-Polish Cultural Center.* The Ktav Publishing House, Inc. 1975, vol. VI; p. 144).

15.   Israel Zinberg. *A History of Jewish Literature. The German-Polish Cultural Center.* The Ktav Publishing House, Inc. 1975, vol. VI; pp. 169–171 and 191–213. Described a climate of bitter disputes about the movement that erupted in the Jewish world, involving Ashkenazic, Sephardic, and Italian rabbis. On the fringes of the Polish-Lithuanian Commonwealth, covert sympathies with messianic beliefs were particularly strong. In 1722, a council of rabbis who gathered in Lwów condemned these in the strongest possible terms.

16.   Israel Zinberg. *A History of Jewish Literature. Hasidism and Enlightenment.* The Ktav Publishing House, Inc. 1976, vol. IX; pp. 3–26. Captured superbly the historical context of the messianic sectarian movement of Sabbatai Zevi (*Shabbetai Tzevi*) (1626–1676), which was followed by that of Jacob Frank (1726–1791). The quote is from Israel Zinberg, who explained well some aspects of Frank's teachings.

17.   Israel Zinberg. *A History of Jewish Literature. The German-Polish Cultural Center.* The Ktav Publishing House, Inc. 1975, vol. VI; pp. 204–213. A few years before Frank's emergence, controversy had erupted between Jonathan Eybeschütz (1690–1764) and Jacob Emden (1697–1776), who competed for rabbinical seats in Germany. Eybeschütz, an authority in rabbinic circles, was accused of hidden sympathies with Sabbateans, based on the arrangement of Hebrew letters on an amulet he had given to a woman in childbirth. The controversy engulfed numerous Jewish communities in Europe, each favoring one side or another and issuing excommunications against each other, over the next six years. Eybeschütz ultimately prevailed; he had denied all accusations in "the war of amulets" and struck back, recruiting his former students throughout the Jewish world to defend their former teacher.

18.　Paweł Maciejko. *The Mixed Multitude: Jacob Frank and the Frankist Movement, 1755–1816.* University of Pennsylvania Press 2011; pp. 1–3, 18, 31–39. Jacob Frank intermittently stayed in Rohatyn in 1756 and in 1757. In 1756, the rabbinical courts in Satanów and in Brody heard confessions of the members of the sect and rendered the ban (*herem*).

19.　Alexander Kraushar. *Frank i Frankiści Polscy.* Kraków 1895; pp. 78–93. Described preparations and the ecclesiastical court proceedings in Kamieniec Podolski. At least four members of Rohatyn's Jewish community traveled there in 1756 and 1757, siding with Jacob Frank and his movement. The disputation took place on June 20–28, 1757.

20.　Jecheskiel Caro. *Geschichte der Juden in Lemberg von den ältesten Zeiten bis zur Theilung Polens im Jahre 1792.* Krakau 1894; p. 108.

21.　Jecheskiel Caro. *Geschichte der Juden in Lemberg von den ältesten Zeiten bis zur Theilung Polens im Jahre 1792.* Krakau 1894; pp. 131–133. Chaim Cohen Rapoport (sometimes cited as *Rappoport* or *Rapaport*) (circa 1700–1771) had become the chief rabbi of Lwów in 1741. Caro alluded to his difficulties in attempting "to play a brilliant role during the Frankist turmoil," due to his limited understanding of languages other than Hebrew (this account is disputed by other historians). His chief translator was Ber of Bolechów, who was fluent in literary Polish, Latin, and other European languages.

22.　Alexander Kraushar. *Frank i Frankiści Polscy.* Kraków 1895; pp. 144–154. Referred to Salomon Shorr presenting the manifesto of the movement and Frank's arrival in Lwów to observe the debate. It described the proceedings, which took place from July 17 to September 10, 1759; pp. 341–377. Listed 508 names of Jewish converts. A number of them were identified as coming from Rohatyn.

23.　*The Memoirs of Ber of Bolechów (1723–1805).* Humphrey Milford Oxford University Press 1922; pp. 5–9, 79–80, 91–95, 170–174. In the 1740s, the Jewish community became suspicious of young Ber's secular studies. He also wrote about renting wine cellars and the apartment that he held for twenty-five years in a building owned by the Carmelite Order in Lwów.

CHAPTER 2

1.   *The Memoirs of Ber of Bolechów (1723–1805).* Humphrey Milford Oxford University Press 1922; p. 150. This record is likely more precise and accurate than others, since the author lived in eastern Galicia.

2.   The order of the emperor to Hadik was dated August 26, 1772. The lack of correct cartographic information about Galicia was also described in Johann Pergen's voluminous report to Joseph II in July 1773 referred to later in this chapter.

3.   Franz Kratter. *Dreyßig Briefe über Galizien oder Beobachtungen eines unpartheyischen Mannen.* Wien 1787; vol. 3: pp. 33–34. Kratter makes reference to lawlessness under Polish rule. It is difficult to confirm the veracity of his report, as he tended to exaggerate facts in his book. He described executions and gruesome violence outside the Austrian zone of control: "To kill a Jew to pass the time or to beat him to death was nothing. They threw on the dead body 12 Polish Guilders (3 Rheinisch) as compensation for the widow and her children, and quietly continued on their way."

4.   *Leopolis* in Latin, *Lemberg* in German, Львів *L'viv* in Ruthenian, and Львов *L'vov* in Russian.

5.   *Wienerisches Diarium*, October 14, 1772. "Lemberg, September 16. Yesterday, the Russians pulled out through the Halicz Gate and the Austrians entered the city through the Kraków Gate. The remaining company from the [Russian] regiment protecting the castle and the archives left the city once General Hadik ordered them to march immediately out. Now, the castle is also under Austrian command." The Russian garrison had been positioned in the city since 1764.

Russians had occupied the main part of Kraków (*Krakau* in German) since the end of August 1772. Only a few months later, Austrian forces moved from the right bank of the Vistula River and claimed the historical capital of Poland for themselves. *Wienerisches Diarium* March 10, 1773: "According to reliable reports, the Austrians occupied the Castle in *Krakau* on the 13th [of February]. After Russians evacuated their [supply] magazines, they left the city on the 15th [of February]; it is [now] an Austrian possession."

6.   *Wienerisches Diarium* November 4, 1772. Printed the communiqué from Lemberg (former Lwów) dated October 3, which announced the installation of a new governor of the province, Count Johann Anton Pergen, under the military occupation.

Stanisław Schnür-Pepłowski. *Z Przeszłości Galicyi (1772–1862).* Lwów 1895; pp. 1–10. Described the military campaign that led to the conquest of Galicia and the ceremony in which the new governor was installed. Pergen was an experienced diplomat, a former deputy foreign minister, and a proponent of secular modern education. He served as the governor of Galicia from October 1772 to January 1774.

7.   *Wienerisches Diarium* December 23, 1772 and February 16, 1773. The statement from December 1772, which referred to "the accurate record of the people," might have signaled completion of the first census in Austrian Galicia.

The Hereditary Lands (*Erblande*) referred to approximately the present-day Austria and Carniola (today's Slovenia), which from the Middle Ages had formed the original Habsburg territories. Later, the lands of the Bohemian Crown (today's Czech Republic) had joined the core of the Austrian Monarchy's territory.

8.   *Wienerisches Diarium* April 7–28, 1773. Printed Prussian claims to the partitioned section of Poland.

9.   Johann Polek. *Joseph's II. Reisen nach Galizien und der Bukowina und Ihre Bedeutung für Letztere Provinz.* Czernowitz 1895; pp. 2–10 provided the texts of Joseph II's and Maria Theresa's letters and his detailed itinerary.

10.   Stanisław Schnür-Pepłowski. *Z Przeszłości Galicyi (1772–1862).* Lwów 1895; pp. 16–21 described the first visit of Joseph II to Galicia and provided the source of the emperor's statements.

11.   The title of the memorandum was *Beschreibung der Königreichen Galizien und Lodomerien nach dem Zustand, in welchen sie sich zur Zeit der Revindicirung durch Ihre Keiserl. Konigl. Apostolische Majestät und besonders im Monat Julius 1773 befunden haben.* It had six parts: (a) on geography, inhabitants, and commerce; (b) on nobility; (c) on religion and clergy; (d) on towns and municipal industries; (e) on the status of peasantry; (f) on Jews. Despite imperial criticism the document was considered meritorious, and certainly provided unique views of Galicia at the outset of Austrian rule there.

12.   Alfred Ritter von Arneth. *Geschichte Maria Theresa's.* Wien 1877; vol. VIII: pp. 413 and 418–419. Cited letters of Joseph II from Lemberg (Lwów) to his mother in Vienna. Despite the emperor's initial objections about his domestic situation and age, Hadik would receive the governorship of Galicia the next year. He served briefly in this post, between January and June 1774.

13.   Franz Kratter. *Briefe über den itzigen Zustand von Galizien.* Leipzig 1786; vol. 2: pp. 154–156 and 175–176. The author visited Lemberg (Lwów) a few years after Joseph II. He left an unflattering description of the city: "For the pedestrians stones were laid, but they were set so far from each other that it is difficult to walk on them.... New pavement is not appreciated by anyone; it is for the extra delicate ladies—who made a habit of conspiring to visit the governor together, and making to him very urgent pleas [about the conditions in the city]—that the primitive pavement be covered with straw because it would be impossible for their bodies to endure the rough bumps."

14.   Markian Prokopovych. *Habsburg Lemberg. Architecture, Public Space, and Politics in the Galician Capital, 1772–1914.* Purdue University Press, West Lafayette, Indiana 2009; pp. 66–69. Gave a perspective on Austrian Lemberg through the eyes of the bureaucrats employed there.

Franz Kratter authored the first quote in 1786 and Joseph Rohrer the second in 1804. They wrote their accounts while retracing the emperor's visit (cited with minor modifications). In the hills outside the city, there was a small memorial plaque for Joseph II, whose policies both authors admired.

15.   The emperor entered Galicia from Homonna in Hungary (*Humenné* in today's eastern Slovakia) on July 27, 1773 and left the crownland through Biała (*Bialitz*) on September 8, 1773. Progressing through Austrian Silesia and Moravia, he reached Vienna on September 13, 1773.

16.   For the first two years, the civil administrative body (*Galizisches Landegubernium*) and the military authorities were in charge, under the overall control of Prince Wenzel Anton Kaunitz, powerful Chancellor of State and Minister of Foreign Affairs. Shortly after returning from his trip, however, Joseph II convinced his mother that Kaunitz should step aside from his role in policymaking for the crownland. The separate Galician Court Chancellery, established on May 21, 1774, was under much greater control of the emperor. In 1776, on his initiative, the affairs of Galicia were transferred to the Bohemian-Austrian Court Chancellery, supported by the provincial government (*Landegubernium* or *Gubernium*) based in Lemberg (Lwów), which sealed the administrative oversight of Galicia within the Monarchy.

17.   Majer Bałaban. *Dzieje Żydów w Galicyi i Rzeczpospolitej Krakowskiej 1772–1868.* Lwów 1914; pp. 6 and 32. Referred to towns such as Wadowice and Wieliczka that had local ordinances of "non-tolerance" of Jews as late as 1754. Recently discovered survey data from 1775 and 1787 showed that in the neighboring town of Andrychów not a single Jew was recorded.

18.   Majer Bałaban. *Dzieje Żydów w Galicyi i Rzeczpospolitej Krakowskiej 1772–1868.* Lwów 1914; pp. 8–9 and 21. Cited statistics regarding the Jewish population in Galicia. Jews reportedly constituted 224,981 (9.6 percent) of the 2,307,973 inhabitants. For comparison, Hungary had only eighty thousand Jews. This first census was reportedly conducted as early as December 1772.

19.   Derek Beales. *Joseph II. Vol. 2; Against the World, 1780–1790.* Cambridge University Press 2010; pp. 196–200. Provided a superb description of Maria Theresa and Joseph II's attitude toward Jews during their co-regency and during Joseph's solo rule. The expulsion of Jews from Prague was in effect between 1744 and 1748.

20.   Alfred Ritter von Arneth. *Geschichte Maria Theresa's.* Wien 1877; vol. VIII: p. 420. Gave a full text of Joseph II's letter. Despite his progressive message regarding freedom of religion for all faiths, he was not free from the then-typical social biases against Jews, which are apparent throughout that missive.

21.   *The Memoirs of Ber of Bolechów (1723–1805).* Humphrey Milford Oxford University Press 1922; pp. 26–28, 36–40, 126–127 and 143–145. In 1764, desire to collect higher revenues from Jews was the government's main reason for the dissolution of the Council of Four Lands, in existence since 1579. Nevertheless, unsubstantiated rumors of alleged Jewish involvement in legislative chaos were printed in pseudohistorical essays as late as 1906 (see L. Glatman. *Szkice Historyczne.* Kraków 1906; pp. 103–117).

22.   Joseph Rohrer. *Bemerkungen auf einer Reise von den türkischen Gränze über die Bukowina durch Ost- Westgalizien, Schlesien und Mähren nach Wien.* Wien 1804; pp. 101–102, 105, 125–126. Rohrer (an ethnic German, native of Bohemia) offered a unique picture of Galicia. His commentaries about the Jewish communities are written with a then-typical paternalistic bias, but they give important glimpses of life there nonetheless.

23.   Ludwik Finkle. "Memoryał Antoniego hr. Pergena, pierwszego gubernatora Galicyi, o stanie kraju." In *Kwartalnik Historyczny*. Lwów 1900; vol. XIV; p. 36. Cited the statement of Johann Pergen from his 1773 *Beschreibung der Königreichen Galizien und Lodomerien nach dem Zustand, in welchen sie sich zur Zeit der Revindicirung durch Ihre Keiserl. Konigl. Apostolische Majestät und besonders im Monat Julius 1773 befunden haben.*

24.   *Continuatio Edictorum et Mandatorum Universalium in Regnis Galiciæ et Lodomeriæ. A Die 28. Mensis Junii Anno 1773. Emanatorum.* Leopoli 1774; p. 4. Quote from the marriage edict (full text in the Appendix).

25.   *Continuatio Edictorum et Mandatorum Universalium in Regnis Galiciæ et Lodomeriæ. A Die 1. Januar. Ad Ultimam Decembr. Anno 1776. Emanatorum.* Leopoli 1776; p. 93. Quote from the Jewish Regulations of 1776. Article Six described laws regulating Jewish engagements and marriages (full text in the Appendix).

26.   Carl Hock, Hermann I. Bidermann. *Der Österreichische Staatsrath (1760–1848).* Wien 1879; p. 382. Summarized the report of the Bohemian-Austrian Court Chancellery from October 20, 1785. Twelve years after Maria Theresa's first attempt to restrict the size of the Jewish population, only 464 marriages were recorded during the entire year in Galicia, despite the fact that the Jewish population had grown to 225,067.

27.   This is a reference to a huge loan of a million gulden from Count Joseph Potocki, reportedly given to Brody's citizens after the fire of 1742. The quote is from the memoirs of Ber of Bolechów (based on Israel Zinberg. *A History of Jewish Literature. Hasidism and Enlightenment.* The Ktav Publishing House, Inc. 1976, vol. IX; p. 214).

28.   *Continuatio Edictorum et Mandatorum Universalium in Regnis Galiciæ et Lodomeriæ. A Die 1. Mensis Januar. Anno 1779. Emanatorum.* Leopoli 1779; pp. 52–55. Declared the town of Brody as the Free Mercantile City outside the commercial tariffs of Galicia. The privilege was effective as of October 1, 1779; the special status was revoked in 1879.

Brody was visited by Emperor Joseph II in 1773 and once again in 1780. During the reign of Emperor Francis, the imperial party toured the town in July 1817. Francis met delegation of local civilian and military officials as well as the merchants. Part of the visit also included stop at famous synagogue *(Gazeta Lwowska July 26, 1817).*

Franz Kratter. *Briefe über den itzigen Zustand von Galizien.* Leipzig 1786; vol. 2: pp. 102–106. Left in his writings an enthusiastic picture of Brody, with the details of commercial activities there.

29.   *Continuatio Edictorum et Mandatorum Universalium in Regnis Galiciæ et Lodomeriæ. A Die 1. Mensis Januar. Anno 1775. Emanatorum.* Leopoli 1775; pp. 165–167. "Manifesto regarding procedures concerning Baptisms of Jewish Children" was issued on November 11, 1775 (full text in the Appendix). Maria Theresa's law was drafted according to a papal bulla of Benedict XIV. The problem of unlawful baptisms of Jewish children seemed to be widespread, since a similar reminder to the clergy and general population had to be issued by a Catholic archbishop in 1785 in neighboring Poland.

30.   *Continuatio Edictorum et Mandatorum Universalium in Regnis Galiciæ et Lodomeriæ. A Die 1. Januar. Ad Ultimam Decembr. Anno 1776. Emanatorum.* Leopoli 1776; pp. 76–121. The subsequent quotations are derived from *Judenordnung* issued on July 16, 1776 (full text in the Appendix).

31.   Wacław Tokarz. *Galicya w Początkach Ery Józefińskiej w Świetle Ankiety Urzędowej z Roku 1783.* Kraków 1909; p. 176.

32.   Franz Kratter. *Briefe über den itzigen Zustand von Galizien.* Leipzig 1786; vol. 2: pp. 47–48. Kratter's comment about the brutality of forced deportations of poor Jews from Galicia is in stark contrast to his other passages, in which he revealed biased views of Jews, accusing them of various vices.

33.   Wacław Tokarz. *Galicya w Początkach Ery Józefińskiej w Świetle Ankiety Urzędowej z Roku 1783.* Kraków 1909; pp. 363 and 365. Referred to the views of certain Kohlmanhuber, Austrian head of the Zamość district.

34.   Carl Hock, Hermann I. Bidermann. *Der Österreichische Staatsrath (1760–1848).* Wien 1879; p. 392. As late as 1782, the State Council was divided in the debate concerning forced expulsions of impoverished Jews from Galicia.

35.   Derek Beales. *Joseph II. Vol. 2; Against the World, 1780–1790.* Cambridge University Press 2010; pp. 176 and 198. Provided the content of both letters from June 1777. Ultimately, the order of Maria Theresa to the Bohemian-Austrian Court Chancellery was never implemented. Whether Joseph's letter to his mother was in a direct response to her proposal is unclear. It does reflect, however, fundamental differences between them. Their subsequent correspondence on the topic of religious tolerance focused on the Protestants (July 1777). Four years later, the emperor would unleash the first in a long series of the imperial Toleration edicts affecting both Protestants and Jews.

CHAPTER 3

1.   Johann Polek. *Joseph's II. Reisen nach Galizien und der Bukowina und Ihre Bedeutung für Letztere Provinz*. Czernowitz 1895; pp. 17, 21–22, and 27–28. The two letters were written to Maria Theresa's ambassador to France and to the Archduke Ferdinand, her younger son and duke of one of her Italian possessions, respectively.

2.   Alfred Arneth. *Maria Theresa und Joseph II. August 1778–1880*. Wien 1868; vol. 3, pp. 242–243. In a letter from the emperor to his mother dated May 19, 1780 written in Lemberg (Lwów).

3.   Joseph Brigido (1732–1817) and his family had moved to Trieste when he was a young man; his brother Pompeo Brigido later became its governor (1783–1803). Before arriving in Galicia, Joseph Brigido had been an advisor to the governor of Carniola (in today's Slovenia). Then, he proved to be an effective administrator of Banat (in today's Serbia, Romania, and Hungary), successfully incorporating the military frontier district into the Habsburg Kingdom of Hungary. He became vice president of the Austrian administration of Galicia in 1777, and served as the fourth governor of Galicia between 1780 and 1794.

4.   Michael Streeter. *Catherine the Great*. Haus Publishing Ltd. 2007; p. 108. Provided the quote from a letter of Catherine the Great to Friedrich Melchior Grimm. The visit solidified Austria's support for Russia in case of any conflict with the Ottomans, and as such spelled the end of Joseph's worries that Russia and Prussia might align their interests against the Habsburg territories.

5.   Alfred Arneth. *Maria Theresa und Joseph II. August 1778–1880*. Wien 1868; vol. 3, p. 301. The letter of the emperor to his mother dated August 6, 1780 was written in Zamość (the town was within Austrian Galicia until 1809). Joseph returned to Vienna on August 20, 1780.

In the same letter, Joseph chastised Maria Theresa for new appointments in Galicia. He wrote: "In just over two months [after my return] … six or seven new [officials] have arrived, all [from] Bohemia or Austria. I testified to you that they were too numerous, and useless, and this is what happens. If we go on like this, the result will always be that these gentlemen, in order to do nothing, or worse than nothing, while making it appear that they are doing something, will cream the revenues of the Estates" (cited in Derek Beales. *Joseph II. Vol. 1; In the Shadow of Maria Theresa, 1741–1780*. Cambridge University Press 1987; p. 366).

6.   Derek Beales. *Joseph II. Vol. 2; Against the World, 1780–1790*. Cambridge University Press 2010; pp. 13–19, 25–41. Described Joseph II's reactions to his mother's death. The quotes are from Frederick the Great of Prussia and Henry Swinburne of England (who visited Vienna weeks after the emperor's return from Galicia).

7.   Derek Beales. *Joseph II. Vol. 2; Against the World, 1780–1790*. Cambridge University Press 2010; pp. 203–204. The preamble to the Patent for Lower Austria was written on the order of Joseph II by Freiherr Joseph von Sonnenfels, a baptized Jew. Restrictive laws for Jews, which were rescinded toward the end of the Patent, dated back to Maria Theresa's laws of 1764, which had limited Jews to their own communities in many ways.

8.   Derek Beales. *Joseph II. Vol. 2; Against the World, 1780–1790*. Cambridge University Press 2010; pp. 201–208. The first Jewish decree, issued on October 19, 1781, referred to the Jews of Bohemia. Austrian Silesia, with its tiny Jewish population, received an imperial *Toleranzpatent* on December 15, 1781; the law stipulated for the first time that Jewish children be admitted to Christian schools. On January 2, 1782, the Jews of Lower Austria (including Vienna) received their imperial *Toleranzpatent*. The Jews of Moravia received one on February 27, 1782. The Jewish *Toleranzpatent* for Hungary was announced on March 31, 1783. It emphasized secular education of Jewish children; after ten years no Jew was to obtain employment without a certificate of school attendance. Christian and Jewish schools were to use the same textbooks, with religious passages removed. The Jews in the Italian provinces did not receive an imperial Edict of Toleration. There, Jews already spoke the native language and attended public schools.

9.   Naphtali Herz Wessely (1725–1805) published four pamphlets between 1782 and 1784. The first offered the most radical support for major reform of Jewish education.

10.   Moshe Pelli. *The Age of Haskalah: Studies in Hebrew Literature of the Enlightenment on in Germany*. Brill 1979; pp. 113–130. Offered discussion on the evolution of Wessely's thoughts that led to the publication of "Words of Peace and Truth," and its conclusion that Judaism in modern times (i.e., in the age of Enlightenment at the end of the eighteenth century) could not exist as an entity in itself.

The Jew in the Modern World: A Documentary History. Edited by Paul R. Mendes-Flohr, Jehufa Reinharz. Oxford University Press, Inc. 1995; pp. 70–74. Provided the source of an English translation of Wessely's work.

11.   *The Jew in the Modern World: A Documentary History*. Edited by Paul R. Mendes-Flohr, Jehufa Reinharz. Oxford University Press, Inc. 1995; pp. 74–78. Provided the text of the sermons by David (Tevele) Ben Nathan of Lissa in Poland and Ezekiel Landau of Prague against Wessely's "Words of Peace and Truth." The burning of the pamphlet occurred in Kraków despite the fact that Galicia did not receive the Jewish Patent until 1789 (Majer Bałaban. *Dzieje Żydów w Galicyi i Rzeczpospolitej Krakowskiej 1772–1868*. Lwów 1914; p. 57).

12.   Israel Zinberg. *A History of Jewish Literature. The Berlin Haskalah*. Ktav Publishing House, Inc. New York 1976, vol. VIII; pp. 59, 65, 70–74. Described the attitudes of Moses Mendelssohn (1729–1786) about the pamphlet. He was a highly accomplished German-Jewish philosopher who translated the Bible into High German. Mendelssohn supported the founding of a modern Jewish school for boys that opened in 1778, in Berlin, where teaching of secular subjects was combined with more typical religious education.

13.   *Continuatio Edictorum et Mandatorum Universalium in Regnis Galiciæ et Lodomeriæ. A Die 1. Januarii Ad Ultimam Decembris Anno 1781. Emanatorum*. Leopoli 1781; p. 54. This supplement to judicial practices confirmed the legality of Jewish testimony in the courts. Neither religion nor gender could be used to invalidate a witness's veracity.

Continuatio Edictorum et Mandatorum Universalium in Regnis Galicae et Lodomeriae. A Die 1. Januarii Ad Ultimam Decembris Anno 1785. Emanatorum. Leopoli 1785; pp. 91–93. In anticipation of a major Toleration Patent for Galicia, this imperial edict abolished the Jewish Administration and rabbinic courts, and explicitly stated that Jews should be governed by the same political and judicial institutions as other inhabitants of Galicia (full text in the Appendix).

14.   Johann Polek. *Joseph's II. Reisen nach Galizien und der Bukowina und Ihre Bedeutung für Letztere Provinz*. Czernowitz 1895; p. 38. In a letter written to General Hadik by Joseph II during his inspection tour of Hungary, Bukovina and Galicia in 1783.

15.   Franz Kratter. *Briefe über den itzigen Zustand von Galizien*. Leipzig 1786; vol. 2: pp. 52–54.

16.   Carl Hock, Hermann I. Bidermann. *Der Österreichische Staatsrath (1760–1848)*. Wien 1879; p. 379–380 (footnote). It refers to a discussion in the *Staatsrath* in 1786 when its members rejected a proposal for the forced relocation of Galician Jews who were not employed in agriculture or industry to certain communities where they would have been forced to perform mandatory farm labor (*roboten*).

17.   Carl Hock, Hermann I. Bidermann. *Der Österreichische Staatsrath (1760–1848)*. Wien 1879; p. 379–380 (footnote). The Council of State (*Staatsrath*) provided advice to the emperor on almost all aspects of policy. During Joseph II's reign its members provided written opinions (*Vota*) that were collated and submitted to the emperor. The policy reviews on Galicia were held in March and May 1786. In May, Lemberg's (Lwów) urban planning was the subject.

18.   Michael K. Silber. "From Tolerated Aliens to Citizens-Soldiers. Jewish Military Service in the Era of Joseph II." In *Constructing Nationalities in East Central Europe (Austrian and Habsburg Studies 6)*. Edited by P.M. Judson and M. L. Rozenblit. Berghahn 2004; pp. 24–25. Excellent overview of the topic and the source of quotes by Moses Mendelssohn. Early debate (1781–1782) on the issue of the military service for Jews was conducted through the polemical writings of Christian Wilhelm Dohm (a bureaucrat from Prussia), Johann David Michaelis (a Prussian theologian and expert on Jewish biblical history), and Moses Mendelssohn. Of the three, only Michaelis felt that Jews would not be able to serve in the army due to their religious beliefs.

19.   *Continuatio Edictorum et Mandatorum Universalium in Regnis Galiciæ et Lodomeriæ. A Die 1. Januar. Ad Ultimam Decembr. Anno 1787. Emanatorum*. Leopoli 1787; pp. 169–171. The imperial edict regarding surnames (full text in the Appendix).

20.   Derek Beales. *Joseph II. Vol. 2; Against the World, 1780–1790*. Cambridge University Press 2010; p. 578. In 1787, Count Brigido, the governor of Galicia, submitted his proposal concerning the draft of Jewish recruits in Galicia, who would be the first Jews to serve in the entire Monarchy. The imperial order regarding Jewish conscription in Galicia was issued on February 18, 1788. In a few months, it was extended to the rest of the country.

Michael K. Silber. "From Tolerated Aliens to Citizens-Soldiers. Jewish Military Service in the Era of Joseph II." In *Constructing Nationalities in East Central Europe (Austrian and Habsburg Studies 6)*. Edited by P.M. Judson and M. L. Rozenblit. Berghahn 2004; p. 25. Hadik's protests were lodged throughout the year. He even argued that there was no shortage of young recruits and that the decision about Jews in the military could be safely postponed until a later time. The War Council was rebuked again by Joseph II in September 1788, when he rejected its recommendation to accept a Jewish petition from Galicia that the draft be replaced with hired mercenaries.

21. Carl Hock, Hermann I. Bidermann. *Der Österreichische Staatsrath (1760–1848)*. Wien 1879; p. 379. States that discussions on the Galician Patent continued for a long time, until 1789. A draft dated May 19, 1788 bore the comments of the emperor and those of Johann Wenzel Margelik, who was one of his trusted experts on Galicia, and Franz Anton Sonnenfels. Sonnenfels was the Court Councilor (*Hofrath*) appointed by Joseph II, and the brother of a famous jurist, Joseph Sonnenfels. Their Jewish father had converted to Catholicism and became a professor of Semitic languages in the University of Vienna, while their mother had remained in the Jewish faith. All three Sonnenfels, the father and his two sons, were eventually knighted.

22. *Continuatio Edictorum et Mandatorum Universalium in Regnis Galiciæ et Lodomeriæ. A Die 1. Januar. Ad Ultimam Decembr. Anno 1789. Emanatorum.* Leopoli 1789; pp. 101–111 (full text in the Appendix).

23. The statement was attributed to Count Stanislaus Clermont-Tonnere, speaking on December 23, 1789 (based on research by Michael K. Silber, Senior Lecturer in Jewish History, Department of the History of the Jewish People, Hebrew University of Jerusalem).

24. Derek Beales. *Joseph II. Vol. 2; Against the World, 1780–1790.* Cambridge University Press 2010; pp. 605–622, 639, 689–690. Provided superb analysis of Joseph's legacy. The laconic quote is from Prince Wenzel Anton Kaunitz, who had served as state chancellor since 1754. The last quote is from a letter of Princess Eleonore Liechtenstein to her sister of June 4, 1791. Both are included in Beales' magisterial work.

Israel Zinberg. *A History of Jewish literature. The Berlin Haskalah.* The Ktav Publishing House, Inc. 1976, vol. VIII; p. 83. Quoted from the Jewish literary periodical *Ha-Meassef* published in 1790 in Berlin (pp. 88–89). Such fond memories of Joseph II—all expressed in an exaggerated style—were found in those pages even four years later.

CHAPTER 4

1. *Continuatio Edictorum et Mandatorum Universalium in Regnis Galiciæ et Lodomeriæ. A Die 1. Januar. Ad Ultimam Decembr. Anno 1789. Emanatorum.* Leopoli 1789; pp. 49–54. The land reform stipulated an average income tax of 8.2 percent in Galicia, which compared favorably to 12.1 percent imposed in the central provinces.

2. Michael K. Silber. "From Tolerated Aliens to Citizens-Soldiers. Jewish Military Service in the Era of Joseph II." In *Constructing Nationalities in East Central Europe (Austrian and Habsburg Studies 6).* Edited by P.M. Judson and M. L. Rozenblit. Berghahn 2004; pp. 26, 28 and 32–33. Cited excerpts from a letter sent by Hirsh Bernstein of Brody and Chaim Margolis of Lemberg (Lwów) to the Jewish community in Mantua. The letter predated the Galician Toleration Patent, which reaffirmed the military draft for the Jews ordered in 1788. Issues with the military draft also occurred in Bohemia and Hungary.

3. Shmuel Feiner. *The Jewish Enlightenment.* University of Pennsylvania Press 2004; pp. 269–270. Described open letters to the traditional rabbis of Galicia.

Majer Balaban. *Dzieje Żydów w Galicyi i Rzeczpospolitej Krakowskiej 1772–1868.* Lwów 1914; pp. 37–45. Provided a rare Jewish perspective on early reforms. Soon after the death of Joseph II, Jews were exempted from military service in exchange for certain fees (in year 1790). The draft of Jewish recruits was reinstated in 1804.

4. Franz Kratter. *Briefe über den itzigen Zustand von Galizien.* Leipzig 1786; vol. 1: pp. 121 and 128–129. The author visited Galicia a few years before the arrival of Herz Homberg. It is apparent that by then the first German-Jewish schools were already operating in Lemberg (Lwów), Zamość, Tyśmienica, Zbaraz, Złoczów, Stryj, and Rzeszów. Overall, Galicia had only forty-six public schools similar to the secular public schools in other lands of the Austrian Monarchy, with seven of them dedicated exclusively to the education of Jewish pupils.

5. Moses Mendelssohn, the least radical of those in the *Haskalah* movement, considered Yiddish a mechanical mixture of Hebrew and German, writing: "This jargon contributed not a little to the moral barbarization of the common man...." His translation of Pentateuch (the first part of the Old Testament) into literary German was printed in Hebrew letters in an attempt to replace Old-Yiddish Bible translations and move the German Jews toward mastery of the German language.

Naphtali Herz Wessely showed open contempt for Yiddish "jargon." David Friedländer, Mendelssohn's literary collaborator and his successor as the leader of the movement, seethed with disdain toward the language spoken by the majority of German Jews and all Jews of Galicia: "The Judeo-German customary among us, a tongue that is without rules, mutilated, and incomprehensible outside our circles, must be completely eliminated."

6. Shmuel Feiner. *The Jewish Enlightenment.* University of Pennsylvania Press 2004; pp. 271–272. Homberg's letter was also published in *Ha-Measesef*, a Hebrew periodical printed in Prussia.

7. Israel Zinberg. *A History of Jewish Literature. The Berlin Haskalah.* The Ktav Publishing House, Inc. 1976, vol. VIII; pp. 108–112.

Majer Bałaban. *Dzieje Żydów w Galicyi i Rzeczpospolitej Krakowskiej 1772–1868.* Lwów 1914; pp. 59–62. Referred to confidential exchanges between Herz Homberg and the governmental commission in 1794.

8. Emperor Joseph II had been succeeded in 1790 by his brother Leopold II (1747–1792). After Leopold's sudden death two years after ascending to the throne, his oldest son, Francis II (1768–1835) became the Holy Roman Emperor. Francis dissolved the Holy Roman Empire in 1806. In 1804, he had established the Austrian Empire, taking the title of Emperor Francis I, thus serving in the unique role of dual emperor for two years. He was succeeded in 1835 by his sickly son, Emperor Ferdinand I (1793–1875) who abdicated in the midst of revolution in 1848.

9. Majer Balaban. *Herz Homberg i Szkoły Józefińskie w Galicyi (1787–1806).* Lwów 1906; pp. 15–16. Salomon Kofler proposed new taxes on the Jews in September 1795. The emperor requested expert opinion on the new law from Herz Homberg in December 1796. In June of the next year, the new tax was announced.

10. *Continuatio Edictorum et Mandatorum Universalium in Regnis Galiciæ et Lodomeriæ. A Die 1. Januarii Ad Ultimam Decembris 1797 Emanatorum.* Leopoli 1797; pp. 56–59. The candle tax was imposed in place of the tolerance tax. Families had the option of paying tax before every Sabbath (in the amount of 2 Kreuzers per every candle or oil lamp) or on an annual basis, payable in installments every two months. In later years, the government distributed a limited number of candle tax waivers to the poor (*Provinzial-Gesetzsammlung des Königreichs Galizien und Lodomerien für das Jahr 1841.* Lemberg 1844; pp. 107–109).

11.   Herz Homberg. *Bnei Zion ein religiös moralisches Lehrbuch für die Jugend israelitischer Nation, von Herz Homberg, einem Schüler Mendelsohns.* Augsburg 1812. The decrees mandating the passing of a premarital examination for Bohemia and Galicia were issued by the Court Chancellery in 1811.

The morality test based on Homberg's book was rescinded only in 1857 by order of the Galician administration. Then, in 1859, the requirement of obtaining permission to marry from local civil authorities, exclusively pertaining to the Jews in several crown lands, was made obsolete by imperial decree. In a legal sense, the decree made prior ritual Jewish marriages (i.e., those performed without permits) valid. Nonetheless, the tradition of ritual marriages not officiated over by state-approved rabbis continued until the end of the nineteenth century.

12.   *Provinzial Gesetzsammmlung des Königreiche Galizien und Lodomerien für das Jahr 1826.* Lemberg 1826; pp. 101–102 contained internal regulations for administrative offices in Galicia on Jewish marriages (full text in the Appendix).

13.   Emperor Francis II limited Jewish land ownership (*Continuatio Edictorum et Mandatorum Universalium in Regnis Galiciæ et Lodomeriæ. A Die 1. Januarii Ad Ultimam Decembris Anno 1793 Emanatorum.* Leopoli 1793, p. 16). In 1805, in a twist in the opposite direction, Galician Jews were allowed to purchase dominical land (parts of large estates cultivated, but not owned, by peasants). Only in 1819 did Francis II preserve their right to inheritance of land purchased before 1793, but he reaffirmed other prohibitions (*Nachtrags-Band zur Provinzial Gesetzsammmlung der Königreiche Galizien und Lodomerien vom Jahre 1819 bis einschlüssig 1826.* Lemberg 1834, p. 23). The restrictions were relaxed somewhat in 1835, when some Jews were allowed to buy land from Christians, with the subsequent right to pass it to their heirs (*Provinzial-Gesetzsammlung des Königreichs Galizien und Lodomerien 1836.* Lemberg 1838, p. 55).

With the threat of Napoleon and his courting the Jews of Europe, Jewish loyalty was questioned and their alleged sympathies toward French regime feared. In 1807, the governor of Galicia, Count Christian de Wurmser, issued a declaration that Jews who traveled to Vienna were permitted to enter the city only with written documents issued by the authorities, stating that their trips were for either trade or legal matters (*Continuatio Edictorum et Mandatorum Universalium in Regnis Galiciæ et Lodomeriæ. A Die 1. Januarii Ad Ultimam Decembris 1807 Emanatorum.* Leopoli 1807, p. 180).

14.   Israel Zinberg. *A History of Jewish Literature. The Science of Judaism and Galician Haskalah.* The Ktav Publishing House, Inc. 1977, vol. X; pp. 92–95. Isaac Erter (1792–1851) authored the quote based on his own upbringing as a Hasid. Only after meeting a secular teacher, Joseph Tarler, did he begin his education in other subjects and move to Lemberg (Lwów).

Joseph Chotzner. "A Modern Hebrew Humourist." *The Jewish Quarterly Review*, vol. 3 October 1890; pp. 106–119. Chotzner wrote an essay about Isaac Erter in which he referred to Galician Jewish writers of the Enlightenment as the Galician School. Erter became admired for his satirical writings that, according to Chotzner, were fine examples of modern Hebrew literature: "It would be no easy task for anyone to reproduce in English, or in any other language, the many beauties of form and style found in the original Hebrew of these essays."

15.   Israel Zinberg. *A History of Jewish Literature. The Science of Judaism and Galician Haskalah.* Ktav Publishing House, Inc., New York 1977, vol. X; pp. 44–54. Provided details on the life of Nachman Krochmal (1785–1840) and is the source of the quotes. Krochmal was born in Brody but spent most of his life in Żółkiew, near Lwów. In contrast to many of his younger followers, he never attended university but was considered a towering figure in the Jewish Enlightenment in Galicia. His greatest literary accomplishment was *A Guide for the Perplexed of the Time,* published posthumously.

16.   Franz Kratter. *Briefe über den itzigen Zustand von Galizien.* Leipzig 1786; vol. 2: p. 57. Unfortunately, Kratter did not record the name of the first Jewish graduate from the Faculty of Medicine . He mentioned the fact in support of a law that read: "The sick Jews must, as the Christians, be provided with country physicians. Also, skilled [in the profession] and duly certified Jews should not be prevented from exercising their art."

17.   Ludwik Finkel, Stanisław Starzyński. *Historya Uniwersytetu Lwowskiego.* Lwów 1894; p. 116. Dr. Benedykt Riedel volunteered to give the series of lectures in 1793.

18. Majer Bałaban. *Historia Lwowskiej Synagogi Postępowej.* Lwów 1937; pp. 15–17. Provided unique information about Jakob Rappaport (1775–1855), whose name was sometimes recorded as "Rapaport" or "Rapoport." His father was a rabbi and a practitioner of medicine who authored an addendum in Latin to his book written in Yiddish (1767 or 1768); his mother published a collection of prayers for women. Where Rappaport's father received his university training is unclear; European universities were generally closed to Jews (one exception was the University of Padua). Nevertheless, he received a medical license "to heal externally and internally in the entirety of Galicia" in 1781. It was issued to Markus Szapszowicz [Rappaport] who had passed the required exam in botany and chemistry.

Schematismus der Königreiche Galizien und Lodomerien für das Jahr 1808. Lemberg 1808; p. 253. Mentioned for the first time Jakob Rappaport among twenty-two physicians practicing in Lemberg in 1808.

Constant Wurzbach. *Biographisches Lexikon des Kaiserthums Oesterreich.* Wien 1872, vol. 24; pp. 355–356. Gave an additional biography of Jakob Rappaport. It referred to the friendship between the young physician and a professor in the university, Vienna-born Valentin Hildebrand, who introduced his student to clinical practice in Lemberg (Lwów). The glowing account of Dr. Rappaport's life gives another example of his accomplishments.

19. Joseph Perl (1773–1839) was also a satirical writer, targeting and ridiculing *Hasidim*. He handed over his school and the library to the Jewish community in 1819. The school remained in operation until World War II.

20. Israel Zinberg. *A History of Jewish Literature. The Science of Judaism and Galician Haskalah.* The Ktav Publishing House, Inc. 1977, vol. X; p. 99. The reference to the present-day Salomon, and allusion to a tax company owned by Salomon Kofler, was published in Isaac Erter's most popular satire, *Reincarnation* (*Gilgul Nefesh*).

CHAPTER 5

1.   Adam Burghaber, Joachim Camerarius. *Statistische Übersicht der Königreiche Galizien und Lodomerien im Jahre 1840.* Place of publication unknown; pp. 18–20. Indicated 24,374 Jews among 185,007 inhabitants of the Lemberg (Lwów) district (13 percent of the population).

2.   Although Jews had earned titles of JD (Juris Doctor) since the end of the eighteenth century, few were admitted to the bar at first. Leo Kolischer was the first known Jew to accomplish that in Lemberg (Lwów) in the early 1820s (*Schematismus des Königreiches Galizien und Lodomerien für das Jahr 1824.* Lemberg 1824; p. 353). He was shortly followed by Emanuel Blumenfeld, around 1828. One area that remained closed to Jews was that of the notary. Only in the early 1870s was Joseph Blumenfeld (the son of Emanuel), to became the first Jew granted the title of imperial and royal notary in Lwów (*Szematyzm królestwa Galicyi i Lodomeryi z wielkim księstwem krakowskiem Na Rok 1873.* Lwów 1873; p. 101).

3.   Joseph Rohrer. *Bemerkungen auf einer Reise von den türkischen Gränze über die Bukowina durch Ost- Westgalizien, Schlesien und Mähren nach Wien.* Wien 1804; pp. 147–148 and 155–157. Provided a description of the city and the lively "Lemberg Contracts" during the winter months. Rohrer's account is the source of the quotes.

Anonymous. "Uwagi nad kontraktami lwowskiemi." In *Pamiętnik Lwowski.* Lwów 1818, vol. III (September–December); pp. 64–71. Gave another contemporaneous account of the "Lemberg Contracts." The fair shifted from January to February starting in 1798. Later, it was held in May extending to June (1810). The author claimed that the heyday of the fair was when the gatherings occurred during the wintertime.

4.   Joseph Rohrer. *Bemerkungen auf einer Reise von den türkischen Gränze über die Bukowina durch Ost- Westgalizien, Schlesien und Mähren nach Wien.* Wien 1804; pp. 143, 172–176. Gave an eyewitness account of Jewish life in Lemberg. Although he was an enlightened man who believed in freedom of religion, his comments on Jews' lifestyle, role in the economy, and sanitary conditions were often insensitive, and at times even hostile to them. Nonetheless, Rohrer was an inquisitive observer of various customs, and collected these stories from acquaintances he made along the way and his Jewish assistant (for example, the allowance of deviation from some customs when traveling to hostile foreign lands).

5.   Israel Zinberg. *A History of Jewish Literature. The Science of Judaism and Galician Haskalah.* The Ktav Publishing House, Inc. 1977, vol. X; pp. 49–51. The source of the quotes. The rabbi of Lemberg (Lwów), Jacob Ornstein, declared a religious ban on four young members of the intellectual circle in 1815. The reports vary on who the "condemned" were; Zinberg listed two, Solomon Judah Löb Rapoport and Hirsch Natkes; whereas Bałaban also mentioned Isaac Erter and Judah Leib Pastor. There are four mentioned in the Rabbi's speech below.

6.   Michael Stanislawski. *A Murder in Lemberg. Politics, Religion, and Violence in Modern Jewish History.* Princeton University Press 2007; pp. 27–28. Quoted a contemporaneous letter describing the address by Rabbi Ornstein. The young man mocking Jacob Ornstein was seventeen-year-old Jehudah Leib Miesis.

7.   Isaac Erter was the author of the satirical pamphlets; he suspected that his former accuser, Rabbi Ornstein, was a plagiarizer. Erter's satire *The Scale. A Vision of the Night (Moznei Mishkal)* appeared in 1823. After fleeing from Lemberg (Lwów) to Brody, Erter went to Budapest to study medicine. He was supported by his earlier teacher and friend, Joseph Tarler. Upon returning to Galicia, he was active during a cholera epidemic in the 1830s.

8.   Solomon Judah Löb Rapoport was an unusual Talmudic scholar who authored six highly acclaimed monographs on medieval Jewish scholars, which made him a towering figure in the literary movement called Science of Judaism (*Wissenschaft des Judentums*). With the support of Joseph Perl, he became the district rabbi in Tarnopol in 1836. After many battles with Hasidic Jews, Rapoport left for Prague, Bohemia in 1840. (Majer Bałaban. *Dzieje Żydów w Galicyi i Rzeczpospolitej Krakowskiej 1772–1868.* Lwów 1914; p. 97).

9.   Israel Zinberg. *A History of Jewish Literature. Hasidism and Enlightenment.* The Ktav Publishing House, Inc. 1976, vol. IX; pp. 214–215. Attributed the statement to Solomon Judah Löb Rapoport, who fought the orthodoxy in Lemberg (Lwów) by writing a scathing critique after the ban of excommunication.

10.   Israel Zinberg. *A History of Jewish Literature. The Science of Judaism and Galician Haskalah.* Ktav Publishing House, Inc., New York 1977, vol. X; p. 120. The quotes are from a letter of Isaac Reggio, from the Italian-Austrian province of Gorizia, to Ignatz Blumenfeld of Brody, Galicia.

11. Majer Bałaban. *Dzieje Żydów w Galicyi i Rzeczpospolitej Krakowskiej 1772–1868.* Lwów 1914; pp. 103 and 219. Mentioned that Michael Perl, the son of Galician educator and writer Joseph Perl, had received imperial permission to open a pharmacy in Tarnopol, despite a general ban against granting such licenses to Jews. The younger Perl had studied pharmacy in Vienna.

12. Moritz Rappaport (1808–1880) received his medical degree in Vienna in 1832. By 1843, there were a number of other Jewish physicians in Lemberg (Lwów), including Adam Barach-Rapoport, Samuel Diamant, Lazarus Dubs, Isaac Epstein (then the physician-in-chief of the Jewish hospital), Isaac Goldberg, Marcus Liebstein, Abraham Natkis, Jakob Rappaport, and Isaac Ulrich (*Schematismus der Königreiche Galizien und Lodomerien für das Jahr 1843.* Lemberg 1843; pp. 440–441). Moritz Rappaport became physician-in-chief (*Primararzt*) of the Jewish hospital in Lemberg (Lwów) in 1857. In 1872, he moved to Vienna. He wrote poetry in German; his first book was published in 1842, dedicated to the Jewish philanthropist Sir Moses Montefiore.

13. The active members of the so-called "German" faction included Dr. Emanuel Blumenfeld (lawyer), Dr. Leo Kolischer (lawyer), Dr. Adam Barach-Rapoport (physician), and Marcus Dubs (industrialist).

14. Michael Stanislawski. *A Murder in Lemberg. Politics, Religion, and Violence in Modern Jewish History.* Princeton University Press 2007; pp. 45–50 and 135. Provided descriptions of Abraham Kohn's publications. It is likely that his articles published in *Wissenschaftliche Zeitschrift für jüdische Theologie* (*Scientific Journal of Jewish Theology*) attracted the attention of the reformers in Lemberg. The first articles denounced some Jewish mourning rituals. The last two, "*Ueber Musik an Feiertagen* (About Music on Holidays)" and "*Noch ein Wort über das Haartragen der Frauen* (Another Word about the Hair-Coverings of Women)" were published in 1839.

15. Michael Stanislawski. *A Murder in Lemberg. Politics, Religion, and Violence in Modern Jewish History.* Princeton University Press 2007; pp. 52–54. Provided a translation from Hebrew of the quoted announcement of July 23, 1843, regarding the sermon to be given in Lemberg (Lwów) by Abraham Kohn on August 19, 1843.

Gotthilf Kohn. *Panteon Miasta Lwowa. I. Żywot Prawego Męża.* Lwów 1906; pp. 16–30. On August 20, 1843, the board signed a contract on behalf the Jewish community in Lemberg (Lwów) with Rabbi Abraham Kohn. He and his family arrived on May 5, 1844.

16. Majer Bałaban. *Historia Lwowskiej Synagogi Postępowej.* Lwów 1937; pp. 36–38. Described the event. The reactions of the orthodox were captured in a pamphlet, "*Meifir acath rszaim*," published in Yiddish in 1848. A descriptive letter by the stepbrother of Abraham Kohn, an eyewitness, was written some forty years later.

17. Michael A. Meyer. *Response to Modernity. A History of the Reform Movement in Judaism.* Oxford University Press 1988; p. 157.

18. *Allgemeine Zeitung des Judentums* November 30, 1846, printed a "privately submitted report" from Lemberg (Lwów), which included description of educational activities of Abraham Kohn. The author criticized German and Jewish press outside Galicia for failing to write good things about the Jews living there and only reporting from Galicia when an insult or a scandal occurred.

19. Sergey R. Kravtsov. "The Progressive Synagogue in Lemberg/Lwów/Lviv: Architecture and Community." In *Jews and Slavs*, vol. 23. The Hebrew University of Jerusalem 2013; pp. 185–193. Provided an excellent description of the years leading to the opening of the Temple in Lemberg (Lwów). The quote from Jakob Rappaport's address of 1840 is from the same source.

20. Sergey R. Kravtsov. "The Progressive Synagogue in Lemberg/Lwów/Lviv: Architecture and Community." In *Jews and Slavs*, vol. 23. The Hebrew University of Jerusalem 2013; pp. 195–201. Described the design and the architectural elements of the Temple in Lwów. In an 1890s wave of polonization in Galicia, the synagogue was renamed from The German-Israelite Prayer House (*Deutsch-israelitisches Bethaus*) to the Progressive Synagogue (*Synagoga Postępowa*). It was destroyed by the Nazis during World War II.

21. *Gazeta Lwowska* September 24, 1846. Provided an interesting eyewitness report of the ceremony; Majer Bałaban. *Historia Lwowskiej Synagogi Postępowej.* Lwów 1937; pp. 5–6 and 41–45. Described the event in greater detail.

Gotthilf Kohn. *Panteon Miasta Lwowa. I. Żywot Prawego Męża.* Lwów 1906; p. 32. Interestingly, one of the major donors was a Polish magnate, Adam Zamoyski, who contributed money and donated lumber for the building's construction. After the opening of the Reform synagogue, he was given an honorary seat for life (despite being Christian).

22.   *Allgemeine Zeitung des Judentums* November 2 and 30, 1846. The journal was published in Germany, with wide circulation in Germany, Austria, and Holland. This explains reports of the alleged enthusiastic embrace of German culture among Galician Jews (copies of the journal courtesy of Sergey R. Kravtsov).

23.   The petition was presented to Emperor Ferdinand on April 6, 1848. Because of the size of the group, Kohn was not included among the final thirteen people who met with the emperor, who was quickly losing his grip on power.

The pamphlet to the Jewish community *"Ein Ruf in die Israeliten!"* was published on April 29, 1848, in Lemberg (Lwów). It was signed: "Your Friend, a Pole (*Euer Fruend ein Pole*)."

24.   Gotthilf Kohn. *Panteon Miasta Lwowa. I. Żywot Prawego Męża.* Lwów 1906; pp. 83–94. The son of the slain rabbi noted in this volume that several alleged conspirators had been promptly arrested, but were quickly released for lack of evidence. He also cited a report from *Gazeta Narodowa* published in Lemberg (Lwów). During the trial, Lieber Pilpel was sentenced to twenty years in prison, but he was ultimately acquitted on appeal. A final petition to the Supreme Court of Justice and Cassation in Vienna was filed by Magdalena Kohn. On March 19, 1851, her claims were rejected and the case was closed, with the perpetrators going unpunished.

25.   Majer Bałaban. *Dzieje Żydów w Galicyi i Rzeczpospolitej Krakowskiej 1772–1868.* Lwów 1914; pp. 168–169 and 193. Described the debate regarding Jewish taxation that took place in the national parliament on October 5, 1848. After a period of neoabsolutism that followed in the Austrian Empire (1849–1860), the national *diet* of Galicia was restored in 1861. In the first election to the Galician legislature, Marcus Dubs and Dr. Lazarus Dubs were elected to represent Jewish communities in Lemberg (Lwów) and Kolomea (Kołomyja), respectively.

CHAPTER 6

1.   In 1786, the governor of Galicia, Count Joseph Brigido, decreed that the estate owners had to present evidence of residence in the Hereditary Lands of the Monarchy. Otherwise, they were required to pay double taxes to the treasury (*Continuatio Edictorum Mandatorum et Universalium in Regnis Galiciae et Lodomeriae A Die 1. Januarii Ad Ultimam Decembris Anno 1786.* Leopoli 1786; p. 182).

2.   The widow of Count Sieniawski, Elżbieta Helena Sieniawska (née Lubomirska) (1669–1729) gave temporary rights to the administration of Rohatyn and its district to the Greek-Catholic Archbishop of Lwów Athanasiy Sheptytskyi in 1728. Her daughter, Countess Maria Zofia Czartoryska (née Sieniawska) (1698–1771) inherited the eastern estates after her mother's death, making her one of the wealthiest women in Europe. (The Czartoryski Archives, Kraków, Poland).

3.   *Słownik Geograficzny Królestwa Polskiego i Innych Krajów Słowiańskich.* Editors B. Chlebowski, W. Walewski, F. Sulimerski. Warszawa 1888; vol. IX, pp. 692–695, and M. D. Wasowicz. *Rohatyn Miasto Królewskie.* Kraków 1869; pp. 10 and 13–14. Referred to the land titles given to Countess Zofia Lubomirska (1718–1790). The county of Rohatyn was transferred to her on June 24, 1775, and the town sometime in 1780.

4.   Maria Bogucka. *Women in Early Modern Polish Society, Against the European Background.* Ashgate Publishing Ltd. 2004; p. 169. Raised the possibility that Countess Lubomirska (née Krasińska) authored *Remarks on the Noble and Burgher's Estates in Poland* and *A Proposal for Public Order* in 1770. Her relative, Count Józef Krasiński, inherited the Rohatyn district and then purchased additional properties from the Catholic Church, including Rohatyn's castle. They were already in the hands of that family in 1820 (according to the Francis land survey).

5.   The details about Rohatyn in the early years of Austrian Galicia were derived from the Josephian land survey of 1787. At that time, approximately 44 percent of the town's land belonged to the Church, 36 percent to the manorial estate, and only 20 percent was owned by the community. In addition, the Church owned the key buildings in town, both religious and secular.

6.   *Continuatio Edictorum Mandatorum et Universalium in Regnis Galiciae et Lodomeriae A Die 1. Januarii ad Ultimam Decembris Anno 1785. Emanatorum.* Leopoli 1785; pp. 59–76. The imperial edict from April 12, 1785 stipulated massive real estate and land surveys in Bohemia, Moravia, Austrian Silesia, Galicia, Lower Austria, Styria, Carinthia, Croatia, Gorizia and Gradiska. In addition to land measurements, agricultural output was to be compiled.

7.   *Continuatio Edictorum Mandatorum et Universalium in Regnis Galiciae et Lodomeriae A Die 1. Januarii ad Ultimam Decembris Anno 1785. Emanatorum.* Leopoli 1785; pp. 91–93. The imperial edict from May 27, 1785 codified for the first time the rights of Jews to buy land for the purpose of farming (full text in the Appendix).

8.   Alexander Beider, an expert on the topic, provided this potential explanation for the origin of the surname *Dub.* The names of the Jews of Rohatyn were recorded in the Francis land survey of 1820. Unfortunately, the Austrian civil administration did not maintain lists of old and new names, which would have provided an invaluable aid to genealogical research on Jewish roots.

Continuatio Edictorum et Mandatorum Universalium in Regnis Galiciæ et Lodomeriæ. A Die 1. Januar. Ad Ultimam Decembr. Anno 1787. Emanatorum. Leopoli 1787; pp. 169–171. The imperial edict regarding surnames (full text in the Appendix).

9.   *Gazeta Lwowska* July 26, 1817, and *Gazeta Krakowska* August 13, 1817. Described the events of July 17, 1817 in Rohatyn. The same issue of *Gazeta Lwowska* reported on the visit of Emperor Francis to Brody, a predominantly Jewish Galician town northeast of Rohatyn.

10.   Emperor Joseph II imposed a degree of state control over the Catholic Church. New measures included governmental approval of papal bulls before their dissemination, the closure of many monasteries and contemplative orders, and the need for administrative permission in cases of commercial transactions dealing with Church property (imperial Patents issued in 1781 and 1782). In Rohatyn, the Dominican cloister closed in 1784. Its buildings and land were initially administered by a religious fund. By 1797, Count Józef Krasiński (the then-owner of Rohatyn) had purchased large portions of those holdings.

The survey of 1820 showed that the former properties of the Dominican order (the manor house, the priest's house, and the piece of land) had been legally sold to new Jewish owners (Jona Wald, Ysrael Altman, and Leib Leisor).

11.   *Schematismus der Königreich Ostgalizien 1799.* Lemberg 1799; p. 201. Listed the city school (*Stadtschule*) in Rohatyn, which in subsequent years was called the *Trivialschule*. The elementary school, attached to one of the churches, was in existence even earlier, being mentioned in the Josephian survey of 1787. Much later, in the 1870s and 1880s, David Teichman owned a traditional Jewish elementary school (*heder*) in Rohatyn. Wolf Godel Bieber, Nachman Feundlich, Juda Rothen, Gdalie Baumrind, and Alter Gold were among the Jewish teachers (*melamed*) there.

12.   Majer Bałaban. *Dzieje Żydów w Galicyi i Rzeczpospolitej Krakowskiej 1772–1868.* Lwów 1914; pp. 92–94. Described the educational activities of Joseph Perl. His school opened in 1813, when Tarnopol was under Russian jurisdiction in the aftermath of the Napoleonic wars. Even after the town's return to the Austrian Empire (1815), Joseph Perl received a decoration from Tsar Alexander I for his efforts toward education. This volume is also the source for the number of Jewish children registered in the public schools of Galicia in the 1820s.

13.   *Gazeta Lwowska* September 29, 1836, and September 14 and 19 and October 24, 1837. Reported on Sender Dub's trades in Olmütz (*Ołomuniec*), Moravia. His name was also mentioned in reports from the fair in 1838 (*Gazeta Lwowska*, July 24, 1838).

14.   *Gazeta Lwowska* May 2 and 15, 1848. Listed members of the governor's advisory council and described its initial proceedings.

15.   Leiser Dub was the witness confirming the married status of Juda and Blime Rothen at the registration of the birth of their son, Abraham, born January 20, 1880. Leiser was the godfather during the circumcision ceremony of Salomon Wolf Wasser, born March 24, 1880.

16.   *Leuch Band 19b: Galizien u. Bukowina. 10. Ausgabe: 1907/1913.* Nürnberg; p. 275. The business of Sender Dub & Alter Weidmann was listed under the heading *Propinationspächter*, which translates as someone with a liquor license. Their names were also found in the Voters List compiled in Rohatyn in 1870.

17.   *Pinkas Hakehillot Polin: Encyclopedia of Jewish Communities, Poland.* Yad Vashem, Jerusalem 1980; vol. II; pp. 506–510.

18.   Rifke Dub (née Seinfeld) most likely died shortly after her youngest daughter Chaje was born. Wolf Dub and his wife Chane, as well as Leiser Dub and his wife Etel, still lived with Sender's family, together with their infant children. Wolf's daughter, who received the name Rifke, was born in October 1864, which narrows the date of Sender's wife's passing. According to Ashkenazi tradition, it was inappropriate to name children after living members of the family.

19.   Information regarding the activities taking place in Sender Dub's estates was extracted from the Land Register of Galicia (the State Archives in L'viv). The donations were destined for the hospital in the small town of Sidorów.

20.   *Słownik Geograficzny Królestwa Polskiego i Innych Krajów Słowiańskich.* Editors B. Chlebowski, W. Walewski, F. Sulimierski. Warszawa 1888; vol. IX, p. 692. Mentioned both Stanisław Krasiński and Sender Dub in relation to their activities in financial institutions of Rohatyn. The former presided over the advisory board for an institution that had the backing of the national bank in the county. Another member of the Krasiński family, Leopold Krasiński, was a financial backer of a school for girls and the hospital for the poor in Rohatyn.

21.   In January 1875, Sender Dub was a witness at the *bris* of Abraham Schumer, born in Załuże. In May and June of 1877, Sender Dub and Samuel Dub were invited to offer blessings for Glükel Feder and Eisek Tune, born to their neighbors in the village of Sołoniec.

The information about Hersch Turner (1822–1878) and the possible explanation of the origin of his surname, were provided by his great-grandson, Dr. Steven Turner. In Hersch's own hand when writing in Yiddish, his original surname was "Tur"; "ner" was possibly added by one of his ancestors in 1787.

22.   *Orts-Repertorium des Königreiches Galizien und Lodomerien mit dem Grossherzogthume Krakau.* Wien 1874; p. 176. Provided information on the estate before Sender Dub's family moved there (data from 1869). *Special Orts-Repertorium des Oesterreichischen Reichsrathe vertretenen Königreiche und Länder. XII Galizien.* Wien 1886; p. 319. Listed information about the population of the estate after it became the home of the Dub family.

23.   *Gazeta Narodowa* March 3, 1868. It is interesting that the idea of a Christian woman converting to Judaism was so new that the reporter from the town of Brzeżany suspected fraud.

24.   The Rohatyn members of the Horn family were listed in the Francis survey of 1820 and were repeatedly mentioned in business directories from Galicia in 1844, 1891, and 1906. In contrast, no one by the name Horn was recorded in Buczacz in 1820 (according to the Francis survey).

CHAPTER 7

1.   Ménie Muriel Norman. *A Girl in the Karpathians.* London 1892; pp. 3–4 and 193–194. Gave a colorful description of the highlanders while visiting the area in the 1880s.

2.   Andrew A. Bonar, Robert M. M'Cheyne. *Narrative of a Mission of Inquiry to the Jews from the Church of Scotland in 1839.* Philadelphia 1843; pp. 427–431.

3.   Details of Mordko Fränkel's transition from leaseholder to owner were derived from Galician land registers (the State Archives in L'viv, Ukraine). The description of his property was based on Tadeusz Pilat. *Skorowidz Dóbr Tabularnych w Galicyi z Wielkim Ks. Krakowskim.* Lwów 1890; pp. 190–191 (conversion based on 1 morgen=0.5755 ha) and *Special Orts-Repertorien der im Österreichischen Reichsrathe Vertretenen Königreiche und Länder. XII. Galizien.* Wien 1893; p. 263.

4.   *Special Orts-Repertorien der im Österreichischen Reichsrathe Vertretenen Königreiche und Länder. XII. Galizien.* Wien 1893; p. 260–261. Based on data from 1890, 6,479 Jews, 746 Greek Catholics, 525 Roman Catholics, and 131 of other faiths lived in *Stadt.*

5.   *Słownik Geograficzny Królestwa Polskiego i Innych Krajów Słowiańskich.* Editors F. Sulimerski, B. Chlebowski, and W. Walewski. Warszawa 1883; vol. IV, pp. 283–286. Provided descriptions of trade activities in Kołomyja. Exporters of local farm products were supplying Vienna and the towns of Prussia.

6.   N. M. Gelber. "History of the Jews of Kolomea"; and A. Y. Braver. "Kolomea—Capital of Pokutia." In *Memorial Book of Kolomey.* Editor S. Bickel. New York 1957; pp. 32–34 and pp. 101–104. This book was originally published in Hebrew and provided details of Jewish history in Kołomyja from the pre-Austrian period through World War II.

Ménie Muriel Norman. *A Girl in the Karpathians.* London 1892; pp. 12–15. Provided a brief description of the town in the 1880s.

7.   The Francis survey of 1820 does not contain anyone by the name Hübner. That does not exclude the possibility that the Hübner family already lived there; it only indicates that they did not own any property subjected to data collection. Later records of Samson Hübner suggest that he was born in Kołomyja in 1827. However, no actual birth certificate of anyone from the Jewish community has survived from that early period.

The information about the Hübner and Hilsenrath families was extracted from *Herrschaftliche Verzeichnisse der Gemeinde Kolomea: Sniatyner Vorstadt, 1858* (the State Archives in L'viv, Ukraine).

8.   Moshe Rat. "Synagogues and study-houses in Kolomey." In *Memorial Book of Kolomey.* Editor S. Bickel. New York 1957; p. 130. I estimate that Sossie's son, Salomon, was four years old at the time of this fateful event.

9.   Based on entries in the 1891 Galician Business Directory—*Kaufmännisches Adressbuch für Industrie, Handel und Gewerbe, XIV. Galizien*—L. Bergmann & Comp., Wien.

10.   N. M. Gelber. "History of the Jews of Kolomea." In *Memorial Book of Kolomey.* Editor S. Bickel. New York 1957; pp. 41–47.

11.   Israel Zinberg. *A History of Jewish Literature. The Science of Judaism and Galician Haskalah.* Ktav Publishing House, Inc. New York 1977, vol. X; p. 58. The quote was attributed to one of the greatest figures of Galician *Haskalah,* Solomon Judah Löb Rapoport.

12.   Israel Zinberg. *A History of Jewish Literature. Hasidism and Enlightenment.* The Ktav Publishing House, Inc. 1976, vol. IX; pp. 83–85, 90–91, 236. Described initial battles in Brody and Vilnus between the *Hasidim* and their rabbinic opponents. These battles were largely put to rest by the beginning of the nineteenth century.

Israel Zinberg. *A History of Jewish Literature. The Science of Judaism and Galician Haskalah.* Ktav Publishing House, Inc. New York 1977, vol. X; pp. 54–56 provided descriptions of the *Hasidim* through the eyes of the Galician *Haskalah.*

13.   *Gazeta Narodowa* August 13, 1868. Published an unusually open-minded article about how Poles should accept Jews into their society. There is also an allusion to the "double crown of melancholy" famously expressed by Moritz Rappaport in "*Bajazzo*" (published in Leipzig in 1863). This was written in the aftermath of the collapse of a Polish insurgency in quest of independence; the Jewish author was identifying himself with these aspirations.

14. N. M. Gelber. "History of the Jews of Kolomea"; and Moshe Rat. "Rabbis, Synagogues and Jewish Life in Kolomea." In *Memorial Book of Kolomey.* Editor S. Bickel. New York 1957; pp. 41–47 and 119–120. The Rabbi Hillel Lichtenstein (1815–1891) had held various religious positions before becoming a rabbi in Kołomyja.

15. Oskar Henigsman, the first Jewish representative, was elected in 1873, followed by Rabbi Simon Schreiber. The latter was from the traditional Orthodox party and served in the national parliament in Vienna between 1879 and 1883. After his death, Rabbi Joseph Samuel Bloch was elected to the vacated seat; he represented Kołomyja 1883–1895. He advocated a distinct Austrian identity for Jews while rejecting the notion of a separate nation. Of note, none of the three representatives ever lived in Kołomyja, as local residence was not required by the electoral law.

Izraelita May 8 and June 5, 1885. Reported on the campaign of three Jewish political factions in Kołomyja. Ultimately, Joseph Samuel Bloch prevailed in the election that year. The Jewish newspaper, which favored full Jewish assimilation, presented Bloch in a critical light as someone unable to foster a parliamentary alliance with Polish deputies in Vienna.

16. *Gazeta Narodowa* September 18, 1880 reported on the visit to Kołomyja of September 15. From a separate account, it is known that Rabbi Hillel Lichtenstein was among those who greeted Franz Joseph and offered religious blessings. The reporter described his ordeal of walking through mud from the train station to the festivities.

17. Felicya Fredro (née Stankiewicz) (1857–1908) was married to Stefan Jacek Fredro (1847–1914). Through marriage, she was a distant relative of the playwright Alexander Fredro (1793–1876), who was the maternal grandfather of the Sheptytsky (Szeptycki) brothers. They were Roman Aleksander Maria Szeptycki, better known as Andrei Sheptytsky (1865–1944), the Metropolitan Archbishop of the Greek Catholic Church; Stanisław Maria Szeptycki (1867–1950) who chose a military career in the Austro-Hungarian army and became a general in the Polish army during the interwar period; and Kazimierz Maria Szeptycki, Galician deputy to the national parliament in Vienna, who was later was known as Clement Sheptytsky (1869–1951), the archimandrite (superior) of the Order of Studite Monks in the Greek Catholic Church. Two other brothers, Aleksander Maria Dominik Szeptycki (1866–1940) and Leon Józef Maria Szeptycki (1877–1939), were the landowners.

After her death, the countess's land passed to Kazimierz Maria Szeptycki, who after 1913 largely withdrew from the secular world and, as Clement Sheptytsky, dedicated himself to monastic life. These changes quite likely provided an opportunity for Joachim Hübner to acquire parts of the estate during the interwar period.

18. The synagogue in Chodorów was built in 1652, with its interior painted by Israel ben Mordechai Lissnicki, who left his signature in 1714. The building was destroyed by the Nazis during WWII. The ceiling panels were reconstructed by the Bet Hatefutsoth Museum in Tel Aviv (additional details in the online review by Liz Elsby. *The Wooden Synagogue of Chodorow*; http://www.yadvashem.org/yv/en/education/newsletter/16/chodorow.asp).

19. Sender Dub passed away on January 5, 1906 in Rohatyn. He was referred to in the register as a landowner. Although his age was listed as one hundred years, such estimates were often imprecise, due to the lack of preserved birth certificates.

CHAPTER 8

1.   Joseph S. Bloch. *My Reminiscences.* Arno Press, New York 1973; pp. 11–26.

2.   The new constitution of the Austro-Hungarian Empire, *Fundamental Laws Concerning the General Rights of Citizens,* was agreed on by both chambers of the parliament and signed by the emperor on December 21, 1867. Articles 2 and 14 referred to the equality of all citizens, and freedom of religion, respectively.

3.   *Gazeta Narodowa* February 13, 1883. Described the event as one way to achieve Jewish integration into a society dominated by Poles.

4.   Ian Reifowitz. *Imagining an Austrian Nation. Joseph Samuel Bloch and the Search for a Multiethnic Austrian Identity, 1846–1919.* Columbia University Press, New York 2003; pp. 19–20, 95, 107–109. Referred to the concept of an emerging Jewish identity in the multiethnic Austro-Hungary.

5.   *Kurjer Lwowski* September 24, 25, and 27, 1885. Published an unusually progressive series of articles under the headline "The Jewish Question." Free of common anti-Semitic prejudices, the articles argued for full integration of Jews without their abandoning their cultural traditions. Recently, Alliance Israelite, a charitable organization, had appealed to the Jews of the world to contribute to its mission of improving Jewish lives in Galicia and other countries. In Galicia, their focus was on education, craftsmanship, and farming. The newspaper argued that philanthropic organizations should focus on training Jews as factory workers in fledgling industries.

6.   *The Sentinel* April 23, 1942. Printed an essay by Moses Landau entitled "A Father Coughlin Case Sixty Years Ago," with quotes from *The Talmud Jew* (*Talmudjuden*).

7.   Barnet P. Hartston. *Sensationalizing the Jewish Question: Anti-Semitic Trials and the Press in the Early German Empire.* Koninklijke Brill NV 2005; 190–191; and Alison Rose. *Jewish Women in Fin de Siècle Vienna.* The University of Texas Press 2008; pp. 73–74.

8.   John T. Blackbone. *Ernst Mach: His Life, Work, and Influence.* University of California Press, Berkley and Los Angeles 1972; pp. 80–83. The university was split into a German University and a Czech University, with separate faculties, in 1882. The theology department was one of the few exceptions. It was rumored that Rohling was involved in behind-the-scenes machinations that eventually placed the theology department outside the control of the rector of the German University, Ernst Mach. The circumstances are murky but Mach, a famous physicist, was a well-known atheist and promptly resigned as rector when the theology department was not placed under his oversight.

9.   *Neue Freie Presse* November 4, 1883. Reported from Prague that the Academic Senate had rejected the request of the Ministry of Education to initiate a disciplinary investigation against Rohling. The subcommittee making recommendations to the faculty governing body consisted of three professors, with only one voting to investigate Rohling. The majority report made arguments about free speech and argued that the Ministry of Education's directives to Rohling could not be viewed as binding. The other lame excuse was the fact that the first edition of *The Talmud Jew* had been published prior to his arrival in Austro-Hungary.

10.   The Czech edition of Rohling's book was *Židia Podľa Talmudu,* published in 1876. The introduction by the publisher described the popularity of the previous edition in Prague (where five thousand copies were sold in two weeks) and throughout Europe. In Galicia, the initial edition was published as *The Pernicious Basis of the Talmud* in 1875. Later editions carried a modified title. For weeks, the local newspapers (*Kurjer Lwowski, Dziennik Polski,* and *Gazeta Narodowa*) advertised the third edition in Polish, *The Basis of Talmud* (*Zasady Talmudyzmu: Do Serdecznej Rozwagi Żydom i Chrześcianom Wszelkiego Stanu*) in 1883. It was apparent that the book was being subsidized by someone; its price was ridiculously low, equal only to the cost of five daily newspapers.

Joseph Kopp. *W Kwestyi Żydowskiej (Zu Judenfrage).* Lwów 1887; p. 10. Quoted Rohling from the pages of *The Talmud Jew.*

11.   *Dziennik Polski* February 13, 1883. Cited the reply by Jan Matejko, famous Polish painter of historical themes. The artist was offended by the words of criticism by a Mr. Rosenblum, expressed in an open letter to one of the newspapers.

12.   Barnet P. Hartston. *Sensationalizing the Jewish Question: Anti-Semitic Trials and the Press in the Early German Empire.* Koninklijke Brill NV 2005; pp. 195–199. Described events surrounding the court case in Dresden and also provided the quote from Rohling's letter to judicial authorities there.

13.   Joseph Kopp. *W Kwestyi Żydowskiej (Zu Judenfrage)*. Lwów 1887; pp. 11, 30. Cited the quotes from Rohling about Franz Delitzsch and about the Protestants in general according to the cleric's publication of 1875.

Barnet P. Hartston. *Sensationalizing the Jewish Question: Anti-Semitic Trials and the Press in the Early German Empire*. Koninklijke Brill NV 2005; pp. 193–195. Describes the involvement of Franz Delitzsch, who exposed fraud in *Rohling's Talmudjude beleuchtet*, Leipzig 1881. The quote about Rohling was derived from his subsequent publication *Neueste Traumgeschichte des antisemitischen Propheten: Sendschreiben an Prof. Böckler in Greifswald* Erlangen. Deichert 1883.

14.   Joseph S. Bloch. *My Reminiscences*. Arno Press 1973; pp. 61–64. Described the events surrounding the trial, the acquittal of Franz Holubek in 1882 in Vienna, and the response of the two rabbis.

15.   Joseph Kopp. *W Kwestyi Żydowskiej (Zu Judenfrage)*. Lwów 1887; p. 17. Quoted text of the letter from August Rohling to Geza Onody dated June 19, 1883.

16.   Barnet P. Hartston. *Sensationalizing the Jewish Question: Anti-Semitic Trials and The Press in The Early German Empire*. Koninklijke Brill NV 2005; pp. 156–159 and pp. 136–150 described the cases, from Lutscha in Galicia and Tisza-Eszlar in Hungary, respectively. In the first, Moses Ritter and his wife, Gittel, were accused of killing and dismembering Franciszka Mnich. The defendants were sentenced to death by hanging during the initial trial in the provincial town of Rzeszow in 1883 (when Rohling volunteered to testify) and on appeals in 1884 and in 1885 (both in Kraków). They were exonerated in 1885.

In the second case, the disappearance of Eszter Solymosi in Tisza-Eszlar, Hungary, several Jews were accused of her murder and of conspiracy in moving her corpse, which had been found in a river. The most incriminating testimony against Joseph Scharf came from his underage sons (four and fifteen years old). The older one alleged seeing the ritual killing through a keyhole on Passover night in 1882. Several Jews from out of town were in Tisza-Eszlar on that fateful day, applying for the position of kosher slaughterer, and this only added to the anti-Jewish hysteria.

In 1883, Galician newspapers provided daily reports from the courtroom. Even if not overtly anti-Semitic, their tone was sympathetic to the prosecution. *Gazeta Narodowa* on July 1 and 7, 1883 reported on the dramatic confrontations between father and son in the courtroom, and on the abuse of witnesses who had sided with the Jewish defendants. Ultimately, the evidence showed that the key prosecution witness had been coerced to testify against his father. Not only was the young man revealed to have poor eyesight, but inspection of the synagogue door had shown that surveying the interior via the keyhole could not reveal much inside. After the accuser retracted his earlier statements, the case was dismissed.

17.   Joseph Kopp. *W Kwestyi Żydowskiej (Zu Judenfrage)*. Lwów 1887; pp. 17–19.

18.   *Gazeta Narodowa* April 17, 1883. Reported on campaigning for Bloch's election in Vienna. Although there was no residence requirement for such a candidate (the prior deputy had been a rabbi from faraway Kraków), the press kept highlighting Bloch's unfamiliarity with Galician affairs and his use of the German language. *Dziennik Polski*, May 8, 1883, appealed to the Jewish population of the district not to support his election.

Dziennik Polski, May 20, 1883. Reported on the election of Bloch to the national parliament in Vienna to represent the three Galician towns (Kołomyja, Śniatyn, and Buczacz). The same issue printed the declaration by Bloch, appealing to readers to judge him in the future based on his actions, rather than their prior opinions. *Kurjer Lwowski*, June 2, 1883, raised suspicions about what Bloch's post-election policies might be regarding the Jewish inhabitants of Galicia.

19.   Joseph Kopp. *W Kwestyi Żydowskiej (Zu Judenfrage)*. Lwów 1887; pp. 20–24 and Joseph S. Bloch. *My Reminiscences*. Arno Press 1973; pp. 90–102. Described in detail the preparations for the trial and the gathering of evidence.

20.   Joseph Kopp. *W Kwestyi Żydowskiej (Zu Judenfrage)*. Lwów 1887; pp. 28–30. The alleged author was Rabbi Mendel Hager from the town of Kosów in Galicia, who was a real person. However, his book, *The Love of Peace*, had nothing to do with Rohling's accusations.

21.   Joseph Kopp. *W Kwestyi Żydowskiej (Zu Judenfrage)*. Lwów 1887; pp. 25–28; 30–33. Cited several instances where Rohling's claims about ritual murder committed by Jews, supposedly based on reputable non-Jewish texts, were refuted; a close examination revealed that either details of allegedly incriminating evidence, or the sources themselves, had been fabricated.

22.   *Kurjer Lwowski* October 23, 1885 and *Nowa Reforma* October 24, 1885. Provided short announcements about the imminent trial. Within a few days, commentaries in *Nowa Reforma* became much more critical of Rohling (October 31, 1885).

Izraelita, in Lwów, November 6, 1885. Published the front-page article about the sudden withdrawal of the libel suit, under the headline "Professor Rohling's Last Chicanery."

23.   It is surprising to find no traces of the disciplinary proceedings that were instigated against Rohling at the university after he withdrew his suit. Over the next few years, he was frequently absent from teaching due to travels to Egypt, Palestine, and Italy. In 1894, Rohling published a book entitled, *The Future State* (*Der Zukunftsstaat*). The volume was placed on a list of forbidden books by the Catholic Church in 1897. For this reason, he temporarily retired in 1899, and this became permanent in 1902 (courtesy of Professor Mireia Ryšková and Dr. Miroslav Kunštát, Charles University, Prague, the Czech Republic).

24.   Alison Rose. *Jewish Women in Fin de Siècle Vienna.* The University of Texas Press 2008; pp. 77–79.

CHAPTER 9

1. *Kurjer Lwowski* September 15, 1914. Described the devastation in Bóbrka. Besides the consequence of the military operations, the town was also reportedly plundered by a mob in the aftermath of the Russian attack. From other sources, it is also evident that Zygmunt and Alfred Hübner had to reconstruct their papers after the war.

2. *Kurjer Lwowski* July 25, 1915. Reprinted a report from a Hungarian correspondent, describing damage in Rohatyn after a recent ferocious battle there.

Kurjer Lwowski August 14, 1916. Provided detailed statistics on damage suffered by the towns of Galicia, including Rohatyn and Chodorów, during the military campaigns of 1914–1915.

3. *Kurjer Lwowski* September 26, 1914. Referred to some unspecified events in the city that prompted the military to intern Meschulem Salat and David Goldberg as guarantors of public order in the Jewish community.

Majer Bałaban. *Historia Lwowskiej Synagogi Postępowej.* Lwów 1937; pp. 201, 204. Mentioned the activities of Meschulem (*Mechulim*) Salat. He was married to Chaje (née Dub), Regina Hübner's aunt, and served as one of two Orthodox rabbis in Lwów during the Russian occupation (September 3, 1914 to June 22, 1915).

4. Markian Prokopovych. *Habsburg Lemberg. Architecture, Public Space, and Politics in the Galician Capital, 1772–1914.* Purdue University Press, West Lafayette, Indiana 2009; pp. 22–31, 83–93. Delved into the history of Lwów, illustrating the interplay between different historical periods, as well as the changing architecture and identity of the town.

5. Andrew Zalewski. *Galician Trails. The Forgotten Story of One Family.* Thelzo Press 2012; pp. 211–227. Described tensions in Galicia in the decade before World War I. The governor of Galicia was assassinated by a radical Ukrainian student in 1908 in Lwów; the university was a frequent flashpoint of skirmishes between Polish and Ukrainian students. In 1910, during riots on the campus, a Ukrainian student was shot.

6. Andrew Zalewski. *Galician Trails. The Forgotten Story of One Family.* Thelzo Press 2012; pp. 245–289. Provided descriptions of life and military operations in Galicia during World War I, with particular emphasis on Stanisławów, Bohorodczany, and Lwów.

7. *Nowa Reforma* October 5, 1918 and *Kurjer Lwowski* October 6, 1918. Reported in their evening editions about the note that had been passed on October 4 by the Austro-Hungarian ambassador in Stockholm to the American government. Next day, The Fourteen Point Declaration of January 8, 1918 and additional conditions raised by President Wilson over the subsequent months were printed on the front page of *Kurjer Lwowski.*

Kurjer Lwowski October 19, 1918. Reprinted imperial manifesto signed by Emperor Charles I and his prime minister that was issued in Vienna on October 16.

8. *Kurjer Stanisławowski* May 24, 1914. The 1910 population census in Galicia showed the majority of self-identified Polish population (59 percent). Among 8,025,575 inhabitants, 47 percent were Roman Catholics (mainly Poles), 42 percent were Greek Catholic (mainly Ukrainians), and 11 percent were Jewish. The eastern part of Galicia, however, was 62 percent Ukrainian.

9. *Goniec Krakowski* October 15, 1918. Described the audience of Galician deputies to the national parliament in Vienna with Emperor Charles I. Nathan Löwenstein, who was aligned with the Polish block in the parliament, expressed the position of the vast majority of assimilated Jews of Galicia. Later in the day, the Ukrainian deputies claimed support of the orthodox Jewish segment in eastern Galicia.

10. *Gazeta Lwowska* November 3, 1918. Printed account of the takeover of the city, reporting that the last Austrian governor of Galicia, General Karl Huyn, was interned by the Ukrainian forces acting on behalf of the Ukrainian National Council.

11. Majer Bałaban. *Historia Lwowskiej Synagogi Postępowej.* Lwów 1937; pp. 157, 171 and 210–213. Dr. Samuel Wolf Guttman (1864–1935) was the first Reform rabbi born in Lwów, as opposed to his predecessors born in German-speaking lands. In 1904, he began giving at first monthly and later more frequent homilies in Polish. The pro-assimilation forces in the Jewish community were strong and at times radical. The same year, the "assimilationists" forced the Galician school administration to order that religious instructors should use a Polish translation as opposed to the Hebrew Bible. This order was rescinded in 1906.

The Lwów pogrom against Jews took place on November 22 and 23, 1918. Bałaban described the events of the attack on the Temple and the search of its premises. Even as late as 1933, utterly false reports suggesting complicity of Jews with the Ukrainian forces would surface in the press, only to be rebutted by eyewitnesses.

12. *Nowości Illustrowane* August 14, 1920. Contained a front-page report entitled "Lwów is a shining example." The article made it clear that the defense of Lwów was largely in the hands of volunteers, including older students.

13. Ferdynand Katz (1868–1938) and Taube Katz (née Dub) (1877–?) had two children. The older son, Henryk Katz, was working with his father in a law practice through the mid-1930s. After the death of Ferdynand, he most likely moved out of Rohatyn.

14. From the proceedings of the city council of Rohatyn recorded March 20, 1930 (courtesy of Alex Feller).

15. Zygmunt Hübner's records from the Faculty of Law (1925–1929) in the John Casimir University of Lwów provided insight into his academic progress. His professors included Roman Longchamps de Bérier (1883–1941), an authority on civil law who was murdered by the Germans in July 1941; Ludwik Ehrlich (1889–1968), recognized expert in international law, who also served as a judge at the International Court of Justice in the Hague; Maurycy Allerhand (1868–1942), an expert in procedural law and a legal author who would later refuse the position of chairman of the Jewish Council (*Judenrat*) in Lwów's ghetto, for which he was subsequently murdered. Other distinguished professors who taught Zygmunt (and later Alfred) were Tadeusz Bigo (administrative law), Kamil Stefko (civil law and the theory of law), and Leon Piniński (Roman law; he was also a former governor of Galicia and noted art collector).

16. *Skorowidz Adresowy Król. Stoł. Miasta Lwowa.* Lwów 1910; p. 561. Listed the address and had advertisements for Volta, a firm owned by Serefowicz, Kuttin and Company. Subsequent business directories (1913 and 1922) confirmed the ongoing presence of the company and the year of its opening in 1908.

In the 1920s, Jakób Kuttin reorganized the business, which without changing location would be known from then on as the First National Company for All Electrical Equipment of Mesrrs. Hausman and Kuttin. He had merged with a company owned by Efraim Hausman, in existence since 1898. Their combined business included both manufacturing and service (including refrigeration equipment made by Frigidaire, and other electrical machinery).

17. Alfred Plohn. "Muzyka we Lwowie a Żydzi." In *Almanach Żydowski.* Editor Herman Stachel. Lwów 1937; pp. 40–57 and 307. Marek Bauer was a graduate of the Vienna Musical Conservatory, where he completed studies with distinction in 1919. In Lwów, he was teaching in two schools: Lwów's Music Conservatory (from 1924) and the Conservatory of Polish Music Association (from 1936).

Both institutions were a short walking distance from the Kuttin family residence (on Małecki Street) where Marek and Erna lived throughout the 1930s, until the breakout of World War II.

18. Jecheskel Lewin (1897–1941) was born in Rohatyn. His maternal grandfather, Isaac Schmelkes, was an Orthodox rabbi in Lwów. Schmelkes wrote responses to many vexing questions of his generation (e.g., on the validity of civil marriages between Jews and non-Jews, the use of electric lights on Hanukkah, or whether the phonograph or the telephone could be utilized on the Sabbath). His grandson, Dr. Lewin, arrived in Lwów in 1928. He was the city's last Reform rabbi, being brutally murdered by Nazis in 1941.

19. The annexation of Austria took place on March 12, 1938. The entry of the German troops was preceded by years of political agitation by Austrian Nazis. The *Anschluß* of Austria was a critical step in a broader policy, "Back to the Reich ..." This was instigated by Hitler's Germany to increase territorial gains, by convincing ethnic Germans living outside the Third Reich to support the combining of these lands into a Greater German state (*Großdeutschland*).

20. The fights between radical student organizations and the rest of the student body wrought havoc in the universities, beginning in 1935. The anti-Semitic segregationist group All Polish Youth, however, received a governmental nod when the decision about seating arrangements for Jewish students was deferred to individual universities to resolve. In Lwów, the opening of the academic year of 1937 was marred by unrest instigated by the All Polish Youth, demanding "ghetto benches" (*Nowy Dziennik* October 23, 1937). The rector's protest resignation was rejected by the university senate. Shortly thereafter, he suspended classes and called for a referendum among the students (*Gazeta Lwowska* November 7, 1937). Its result was a strange ruling; although mandatory seating was officially rejected by the majority, Jewish students were to be seated on the left side of lecture halls, where their non-Jewish colleagues were free to sit with them. All Polish Youth were to sit on the right side, where whomever wanting to join them could do so (*Gazeta Lwowska* November 19, 1937). The headline in a Jewish newspaper announced "Ghetto officially abolished—maintained in reality" (*Nowy Dziennik* November 19, 1937).

21. *ABC: nowiny codzienne* February 1, 1938. Reported that a students' mutual aid organization called Brotherly Help (*Bratniak*), which was dominated by the nationalist All Polish Youth, had passed a statutory rule that no student of "the Mosaic religion or from a family following the Mosaic religion" could join it. When in doubt, "a prospective candidate ought to prove that he had no Jewish ancestor for three generations back."

ABC: nowiny codzienne June 30, 1938. Called for a boycott of Jewish enterprises, particularly in the eastern part of Poland. In this issue of the paper, there was also an ad for a pamphlet sponsored by this radical newspaper entitled "Liquidate Jews," which was to be available in all newsstands. Although the title referred to removal of Jewish businesses, it is particularly chilling given the events of World War II that erupted the next year.

22. The daily newspaper *Wiek Nowy,* May 12, 1939, reported warily on the international situation.

CHAPTER 10

1. *Chwila* September 1, 3 and 6, 1939. This was a popular Jewish daily newspaper published in Lwów. The last issue was sent out of the city on September 12; it contained appeals by city officials to citizens to remain in town. There was a conspicuous absence of any report on the ongoing battles in Lwów's suburbs.

2. *Goniec Krakowski* October 30, November 2 and 3, 1939. Reported on the Soviet zone. The newspaper presented German views, since it was printed in the occupied territories of Poland. The speech by the foreign minister of the Soviet Union, Vyacheslav Molotov, describing close ties between the two regimes, was printed on the front page. Other articles referred to successful agreements between German and Soviet negotiators, who had met in occupied Warsaw (for border issues) and in Moscow and Berlin (for trade issues). The November 3 issue of the paper prominently displayed a decision of the rubber-stamp legislative body, the Supreme Soviet, which unanimously agreed to the "demand" of Western Ukraine that it join the Soviet Union.

3. Jakob Weiss. *Lemberg Mosaic*. Alderbrook Press, New York 2010; pp. 129–142. Provided a detailed account of Soviet rule in Lwów (renamed L'vov) between 1939 and 1941.

4. David Kahane. *Lvov Ghetto Diary*. The University of Massachusetts Press, Amherst 1990; pp. 7–8 and 153–155. Described the first pogrom and the horrific account of two Jewish eyewitnesses, including the son of the murdered Dr. Lewin.

5. John-Paul Himka. "The Lviv Pogrom of 1941: The Germans, Ukrainian Nationalists, and the Carnival Crowd." In *Canadian Slavonic Papers* 2011; vol. 53, 209–243. In this scholarly review of events, Himka contends that the Ukrainian-led pogrom took place mainly on July 1, with a few Germans even intervening to put a stop to the bloodshed. The German atrocities, he says, began the next day when the Ukrainian nationalist militia was brought under the command of the German SS. What differed, he says, was that these subsequent murders were perpetrated without crowd participation. An internal German report from mid-July 1941 estimated that "police captured and shot some seven thousand Jews."

6. *Goniec Krakowski* August 5, 1941. Reported from Lwów the incorporation of District Galicia into the Nazi-occupied General Governorate, which covered a large portion of prewar Poland.

7. The Golden Rose (*Turei Zahav*) Synagogue of Lwów, built in 1582–1595, was designed by an Italian architect, Paulus Italus (also known as Paul the Fortunate), in late sixteenth-century Renaissance style. Initially, it was a private prayer house belonging to Yitzhak ben Nachman (Nachmanowicz), with access only through his family dwelling. It was confiscated by the Jesuit order in 1606, only to be returned three years later after the Jewish community paid a substantial ransom. Legend had it that the beautiful daughter-in-law of the synagogue's founder, known as the Golden Rose (*die guldene Rojze*) for her kindness to others, was forced to deliver the payment to a local bishop. After being detained in his house, she was said to have committed suicide. Between 1603 and 1801, the Golden Rose synagogue was also called the Great City Synagogue. In 1938, the building was declared a national architectural monument. It was obliterated by the Nazis in 1943.

8. The previously respected daily *Gazeta Lwowska* resumed its circulation in August 1941 as a Nazi propaganda tool. "The Poem About the Music" was published anonymously under the pen name Scherzo in issue number 4, most likely in August 1941. The circulation of the newspaper was approximately fifty thousand copies per day (courtesy of Hanna Palmon).

9. David Kahane. *Lvov Ghetto Diary*. The University of Massachusetts Press, Amherst 1990; pp. 18, 27–29, 32–37. Gave a chilling account of the months leading to the formation of the ghetto. It also described the neighborhoods where the Hübners and Kuttins lived. Kahane recorded the events happening in and outside of the ghetto, which provides a unique dimension to our understanding of the Jewish ordeal in Lwów.

The exact date of Jakób Zellel Kuttin's suicide is uncertain. The Yad Vashem database indicates that he was killed in the Holocaust in 1940. *Chronicle of the Lauterbach Family*. The Lauterbach Family Fund, El Paso, Texas 1992; p. 100 describes the circumstances as follows: "Under Nazi dominations (*sic*) committed suicide in protest against the regime," which more likely puts his death in the second half of 1941.

10. Jakob Weiss. *Lemberg Mosaic*. Alderbrook Press, New York 2010; pp. 194–199. Described in the chapter "Aryan Paper Mill" how a few Jews were able to secure false identity cards and other documents that allowed them to work on the Aryan side or escape from the horror of Lwów.

11.   *Abyss of Despair* was the title of a poignant book written in the mid-seventeenth century by Nathan Hannover, who described the horrors of another Jewish slaughter during the Cossack rebellion. (See chapter 1.)

12.   David Kahane. *Lvov Ghetto Diary.* The University of Massachusetts Press, Amherst 1990; pp. 48–84. Gave vivid eyewitness accounts of the repeated murderous actions against the Jewish population of Lwów.

13.   David Kahane. *Lvov Ghetto Diary.* The University of Massachusetts Press, Amherst 1990; p. 101. Described the orchestra in the Janowska camp that was comprised of well-known Jewish musicians from Lwów.

Chronicle of the Lauterbach Family. The Lauterbach Family Fund, El Paso, Texas 1992; p. 100. Mentioned Marek (Izydor M.) Bauer (1896–1943), Erna's husband, as a member of an orchestra assembled by the Germans.

14.   Based on two letters from Marek (Izydor M.) Bauer and an additional two letters from his wife, Erna Bauer (née Kuttin). The last known communication from Marek bore the date May 29, 1943. This is notable, since the ghetto was liquidated on June 1, 1943, leaving, after just a few days, practically no survivors. Erna wrote, after her husband's death, a letter dated August 4 (most likely 1943). It is not known whether Erna was in hiding somewhere in Lwów or was held in the women's section of the Janowska labor camp. The latter is more likely and it would explain how "Mr. Engineer" was able to communicate with both of them. The labor camp stayed open until its bloody liquidation by the Nazis in November 1943.

After the war, the family friend, "Mr. Engineer," turned out to be a distant cousin of Ewa and Erna. Marian (*Manio*) Hüttner also relayed to surviving relatives the story of Ewa's betrayal by a former employee of her father. The letters were provided courtesy of Ewa Kwiatkowska.

Issachar Fater. *Jewish Music in Poland between the World Wars (Hebrew).* Hakkibutz Hameuchad, Tel Aviv 1992; p. 245. Also confirmed that Marek Bauer was murdered by the Nazis in the Janowska labor camp.

EPILOGUE

1.   Details of Joachim Hübner's wartime ordeal cited in this and the previous chapter have been reconstructed based on my grandfather's handwritten testimony dated July 10, 1945. This record has been preserved in the Jewish Historical Institute in Warsaw, Poland (*Żydowski Instytut Historyczny; sygn. 301/5389*).

2.   *Register of Jewish Survivors II (Pinkas HaNitzolim II)*. List of Jews in Poland. The Jewish Agency for Palestine Search Bureau for Missing Relatives, Jerusalem 1945; pp. 93, 118 and 267. Listed Bronisława Goldenberg, Joachim and Stefan Hübner, and Eliza Unger, respectively.

3.   Josef Banas. *The Scapegoats. The Exodus of the Remnants of Polish Jewry.* London 1979; pp. 52, 90, and 158. Gave a comprehensive description of the anti-Semitic campaign in the late 1960s. The infamous index cards with names of Poles of Jewish origin had been in the works at the interior ministry since 1966. Then, at the peak of the campaign in 1969, the regime-controlled press announced a window of time for Jewish emigration to Israel, beyond which leaving Poland would be difficult. This put additional pressure on individuals who had lost, or were threatened with loss of their jobs, to make hasty decisions about leaving.

Over the next couple of years, the majority of Polish Jews left the country. By some accounts they numbered twenty-five thousand—only a small fraction of those ended up in Israel. Those Jews who remained in Poland amounted to only five to ten thousand individuals (based on David Engle in *The YIVO Encyclopedia of Jews in Eastern Europe: Poland* since 1939).

Index

Page numbers with no accompanying letters refer to main part of the book;
fr: denotes family register; n: notes

Printed in Great Britain
by Amazon

64473211R00240